BUNCOMBE BOB

The James Sprunt Studies
in History and Political Science

VOLUME 63

The James Sprunt Studies in History and Political Science are published

under the direction of the Departments of History and Political Science

of the University of North Carolina at Chapel Hill.

Buncombe Bob

[THE LIFE AND TIMES OF
ROBERT RICE REYNOLDS]

Julian M. Pleasants

The University of North Carolina Press

Chapel Hill and London

The paper in this book meets the guidelines for permanence and durability
of the Committee on Production Guidelines for Book Longevity of the Council
on Library Resources.

Material used in this book has appeared in a different
form in the following publications:

Julian M. Pleasants and Augustus M. Burns, *Frank Porter Graham and the 1950 Senate
Race in North Carolina* (Chapel Hill: University of North Carolina Press, 1990).

Julian M. Pleasants, " 'Buncombe Bob' and Red Russian Fish Eggs: The Senatorial
Election of 1932 in North Carolina," *Appalachian Journal* (Winter 1976): 51–62; "The
Beginning of Buncombe Bob," *The State*, August 1977, 20; "Our Bob and the Seniority
Fight," *The State*, June 1977, 22–24; "The Last Hurrah: Bob Reynolds and the U.S.
Senate Race in 1950," *North Carolina Historical Review* (January 1988): 52–75;
"Carolina Casanova," *The State*, August 1988, 26–31; "Robert Rice Reynolds," in
American National Biography, 18:387–88 (New York: Oxford University Press, 1999).

Library of Congress Cataloging-in-Publication Data
Pleasants, Julian M.
Buncombe Bob: the life and times of Robert Rice Reynolds / Julian M. Pleasants.
p. cm.—(The James Sprunt studies in history and political science; v. 63)
Includes bibliographical references and index.
ISBN 0-8078-5064-0 (cloth: alk. paper)
1. Reynolds, Robert Rice, 1887– 2. Legislators—United States—Biography.
3. United States. Congress. Senate—Biography. 4. United States—Politics and
government—1933–1945. 5. North Carolina—Politics and government—1865–1950.
I. Title. II. Series.
E748.R37 P58   2000   328.73'092—dc21   [B]   00-044732

04 03 02 01 00 5 4 3 2 1

FOR JAMES RODNEY PLEASANTS—

a kind and generous brother

Contents

[Illustrations]

Acknowledgments

In preparing this book, I received invaluable assistance from numerous people. Most conspicuous in their help were the curators of manuscript collections around the country; without the courtesy and professional expertise of those who staff these collections, it would be extremely difficult for historians to pursue their craft. In particular, I would like to single out Dr. Richard Shrader, John White, and Rachel Canada at the Southern Historical Collection at the University of North Carolina (UNC), Chapel Hill. Also extremely helpful were the director and staff members at the North Carolina Collection at UNC: Robert Anthony, Harry Mc-Kown, and Alice Cotten. Staff members at many other repositories, such as the North Carolina Division of Archives and History in Raleigh, the National Archives, the Library of Congress, the Perkins Library at Duke University, provided outstanding service.

At the University of North Carolina Press, I am grateful to David Perry, who saw this project through to completion. David was both encouraging and demanding. Several times I resisted some of the requested changes, but he was correct on every occasion, and his suggestions strengthened the manuscript. Pamela Upton, the assistant managing editor, and Nancy Raynor worked very hard on the book and saved me from numerous errors. I also thank Joel Williamson and the James Sprunt Fund for both financial and editorial assistance. Part of the research was done with the aid of an Archie K. Davis Fellowship from the North Caroliniana Society. Finally, thanks to Dean Will Harrison and the College of Liberal Arts and Sciences at the University of Florida for funding that enabled me to complete the project.

A special acknowledgment to my dear friend and deceased colleague Augustus M. Burns. He graciously read large portions of the manuscript, and his suggestions were always pertinent and insightful and helped sharpen the focus and conclusions. His warm support and quick wit enabled me to overcome some frustrating times.

George Brown Tindall, a master teacher and scholar, originally suggested this topic and gave generously of his time and his vast knowledge of southern history.

His continued support, ongoing friendship, and gentle good humor encouraged me to complete the project. I am grateful for all of his help.

The duties and responsibilities of a present-day United States senator are vastly different from those during the New Deal era. Bob Graham, currently a U.S. senator from Florida, is the epitome of what a senator should be. He is industrious, intelligent, compassionate, courteous, and constantly striving to do what is best for the country. In both conversation and in deed, he has demonstrated and taught me not only how the Senate operates but also how valuable a dedicated public servant can be.

Finally, my eternal gratitude to Roberta Peacock, office manager of the Proctor Oral History Program, and her staff (Danielle Vance, Alan Bliss, Ben Houston, Jenny Devine, and Jay Langdale) for the countless times they have helped me with computer glitches and research and for their good-natured, never-ending patience as I ranted and raved through the process.

BUNCOMBE BOB

[Introduction]

Robert Rice Reynolds, United States senator from 1933 to 1945, was an anomaly in the politics of both North Carolina and the South. In a bastion of Victorian morality, he married five times. In a state characterized by staid and conservative politics, Reynolds was known for his outlandish antics. Although he ran for office in a dry state deeply committed to prohibition, he was a "wet" who advocated a return to drinking. In a South characterized by conservative politics, Reynolds was an ardent New Dealer. In a region that supported a military buildup and the concept of war, Reynolds was a sincere isolationist.

As a rule, U.S. senators from the Tar Heel State in the twentieth century have been conservative, solid citizens generally representing V. O. Key Jr.'s "progressive plutocracy," providing little flash to state politics. When Bob Reynolds launched his political career in 1932, it quickly became evident that he was cut from a different cloth. In a state bored by the pedestrian presentation of political views, Bob Reynolds was a breath of fresh air. An undistinguished lawyer from Asheville, North Carolina, and a perennial failure in bids for elective office, Our Bob, as he was known to his supporters, won an astounding upset over incumbent senator Cameron Morrison in the senatorial election of 1932. Reynolds's 1932 campaign, described by one observer as "a prolonged vaudeville," captured the imagination of Tar Heel voters. A master showman, the tall, handsome Reynolds motored about the state in a ramshackle Ford while wearing tattered clothing, picturing his wealthy opponent as a glutton who made his way around Washington in a chauffeured limousine. Reynolds presented himself as a poor man of the people fighting against the corporate interests who had spawned the depression through their greed. Reynolds's huge victory over Morrison in the Democratic runoff (65.4 percent of the vote), the largest majority ever obtained in a North Carolina Democratic primary, stunned the experts. One newspaper called the win "probably without parallel for sensation in the political life of North Carolina."[1]

While in the Senate, Reynolds served as chairman of the District of Columbia Committee as well as chairman of the vitally important Military Affairs Committee during World War II. His isolationist votes during the 1930s had an important impact on debates over American neutrality. Moreover, the elevation of the isolationist Reynolds to chair of the Military Affairs Committee led to one of the most serious challenges to the Senate's system of seniority. After war was declared, however, he cooperated fully with the Roosevelt administration while working assiduously to pass the legislation necessary for winning the war.

In foreign policy, Reynolds is best described as a demagogic isolationist. He lashed out at alien criminals and increased immigration while voting against American membership in the World Court. He was the only southerner to vote against Lend Lease. Meanwhile, Reynolds began his congressional career by voting for almost all New Deal legislation and was a loyal supporter of Roosevelt until 1938. He sought reform of American society and improvement in the daily life of the average American and thought government could provide for the economic and social welfare of the masses with programs such as Social Security and the Wagner Act. Reynolds saw the inequity in society and understood the frustration and alienation of the have-nots.

In his second term, however, Reynolds abandoned New Deal idealism and concluded his career as an antilabor, anti-Communist states' righter. During the latter part of his career, Reynolds embarked on a series of ill-considered associations with such controversial individuals as Father Charles Coughlin, Gerald L. K. Smith, George Deatherage, Nazi propagandist George Sylvester Viereck, and Prescott Dennett, a paid German propaganda agent. In addition, he created two nativistic and xenophobic organizations, the American Vindicators and the Nationalist Party. Reynolds's fervent isolationism and his relationship with and praise for such radicals as Gerald L. K. Smith led to charges that he was pro-Nazi. Moreover, his lack of discretion, poor judgment, anti-Semitism, unsavory companions, and unyielding adherence to noninterventionism exposed his nativism and precipitated a rapid decline in his popularity.

In November 1943, "Buncombe Bob" Reynolds chose not to run for a third term. Reynolds withdrew, despite his love of the trappings and prestige of the U.S. Senate, because he would have been badly defeated by the popular governor, Clyde R. Hoey. His inflexible isolationist stance, his opposition to the United Nations, the pro-Nazi charges, and his dereliction of senatorial duties for world travels had destroyed his political career.

Bob Reynolds left office in January 1945, after twelve tumultuous years in the Senate during a momentous era in American history. His last hurrah was a half-hearted entry into the 1950 North Carolina Senate race, the most divisive in the state's history. The old warhorse gained just enough votes to deny Senator Frank Graham the nomination. The election of the conservative Willis Smith, whose campaign was assisted by Jesse Helms, altered the direction of the state away from the more liberal policies of Graham and Governor W. Kerr Scott toward a more conservative philosophy of government. After retiring from politics, the former senator spent his final days traveling and raising his daughter. The colorful and unique senator died on February 13, 1963, at age seventy-eight.

The purpose of this book is to flesh out Bob Reynolds's unique political career and to correct previous stereotypes and mistaken historical interpretations. V. O. Key Jr., in his 1949 book *Southern Politics*, dismissed Reynolds as "erratic and irrelevant" and a "clown," but he was more substantial than that.[2] Journalists Drew Pearson and Robert S. Allen derisively referred to him as the "Tar Heel Führer" because of his alleged praise of Hitler.[3] This opinion, while containing a modicum of truth, does not accurately depict Bob Reynolds's views or his career. Reynolds was too complex an individual to have his political life described in such simplistic terms.

Because of his campaign style, most observers of the day described "Buncombe Bob" as a demagogue. Ray Arsenault, in "The Folklore of Southern Demagoguery," identified Bob Reynolds as a fanatical demagogue who came to power during the depression while placing his trust in the politics of paranoia. He classified Reynolds as an American fascist, southern style, who offered a radical, right-wing alternative to the New Deal.[4] But as I will show, Arsenault erred in describing Reynolds as a fanatic and a fascist. Reynolds did not use race baiting in his campaigns, although he favored the status quo in civil rights. He did not rage against the Jews and Catholics in his political races, although he displayed a strong anti-Semitism in private letters and in his publications. While he appealed to the emotions of his followers, his entreaties often relied on reason. He did not promise everything to everybody but was simply a master of oratory and flamboyant campaigning. Like his contemporaries, he mainly wanted to get elected. In short, he was a unique southern demagogue in a region where demagoguery was almost always defined by race. Reynolds was certainly no statesman, but he did not follow James K. Vardaman, Theodore G. Bilbo, and "Cotton Ed" Smith on the race issue.

In political terms, perhaps Bob Reynolds could best be characterized as a "populist demagogue." Reynolds, like the Populists, recognized that the average person was vulnerable to the power of large corporations and he favored federal government intervention to regulate the banks, to provide cheap credit, and to democratize the country by returning government to "the people." But Our Bob also displayed some of the more negative aspects of Populism. He was prone to scapegoating, spouted unrealistic conspiracy theories, and exhibited the xenophobia and nativism characteristic of some Populists.

Still, Reynolds never described himself as a Populist or as a progressive despite his concurrence with many of their views. Unlike the Populists, Reynolds did not lead a political protest movement; instead, he was a lone maverick seeking office. While he railed against the rich, he failed to propose any concrete program to solve the ills of society. He merely seized on the fact that large numbers of people felt forgotten and were frightened by the severity of the Great Depression. Bob Reynolds did not concern himself primarily with interest group politics; he focused on the politics of class—a righteous war against the gluttons of privilege. Speaking out against the social and economic evils of the day, Reynolds also rebelled against the established Democratic hierarchy in North Carolina, single-handedly challenging V. O. Key's "progressive plutocrats" and the powerful O. Max Gardner machine, soundly whipping both in his senatorial campaigns.

Finally, in this book I try to explain how Bob Reynolds, a man of limited experience and abilities, was elected to two terms in the United States Senate. His rise to power says much about southern politics and the attitudes of North Carolinians in the 1930s. In studying Reynolds's unique positions as a southern New Dealer, an isolationist, and a nonracist demagogue, the reader will, I hope, understand the complexities of southern politics during this era.

I have tried, as much as possible, to write this biography from primary sources. One must refer to secondary works for background information, clarification, and transition, but I limited those references whenever possible. The secondary literature, however, was most helpful, especially relatively recent books on Charles A. Lindbergh, Huey Long, Gerald L. K. Smith, Father Charles Coughlin, Theodore Bilbo, and George Sylvester Viereck as well as a spate of books on isolationism and foreign policy during World War II. This book, however, is not about the New Deal, isolationism, or World War II. The focus is always on Bob Reynolds and his career.

In researching this book, I had to rely essentially on correspondence with colleagues, interviews, and newspapers because Senator Reynolds left no congressional papers. According to the Library of Congress and friends, Reynolds destroyed his senatorial papers when he left the Senate. No one is quite sure why he did so, but the prevailing opinion is that he had no use for them. His daughter and friends claim he did not destroy them because of derogatory or embarrassing material but because Reynolds was upset with the end of his senatorial career and simply did not want to be reminded of his years in Washington. The destruction of Reynolds's papers, while unfortunate, was not very significant. The Reynolds family, especially his daughter, Frances Reynolds Oertling, kept a scrapbook of letters and clippings. While small, this source contained some important and otherwise unavailable items. If a study of the papers of his associates in the Senate is any indication, and I think it is, then Reynolds wrote very few letters of any substance. A search through the manuscript collections of his colleagues yielded meager results. In the letters uncovered, Reynolds rarely discussed legislative issues or speeches he had made, nor did he often supply reasons for his votes. The letters he wrote to colleagues were flowery and complimentary; letters to constituents dealt with individual problems and generally contained a request for political support.

Reynolds talked constantly, honestly, and openly to the press and provided full explanations for his votes and decisions as a senator. With Bob Reynolds there was very little deceit or deception. What you saw was what you got. Thus I placed a strong emphasis on both state and national newspapers. Frequently I allowed Bob Reynolds to speak for himself, through interviews or letters, and did not always evaluate his often controversial statements. I leave that assessment to the reader.

CHAPTER ONE

The Early Years

The June 3, 1944, issue of *Time* described Robert Rice Reynolds, the two-term United States senator from North Carolina, as he performed his daily chores on the floor of the Senate, a fifty-nine-year-old who looked forty-five and had not lost his jaunty step or his confidence. As he strolled importantly through the Senate, observed *Time*, his blond hair was combed "casually over the back of his Barrymore-ish collar and his gay bow tie [was] propped at an insouciant angle." Reynolds, continued the magazine, gave "a backslap here, a glad hand there, pausing to drop a witticism at this Senator's desk, an encouraging word of counsel at another's, to confer now gravely, now casually,—dynamic, carefree, yet occasionally sober under the solemn responsibilities of statesmanship."[1]

Although Bob Reynolds reached the pinnacle of political success with his election to the United States Senate in 1932, his road to electoral prominence began in the mountain village of Asheville, North Carolina, on June 18, 1884. On this date William Taswell Reynolds and Mamie Spears Reynolds became the parents of a baby boy who early on demonstrated a great zest for life and an exuberant and independent spirit.[2]

Bob Reynolds was descended from a rather distinguished pioneering family. Colonel Daniel Smith, Reynolds's maternal great-great-grandfather, was a hero of the battle of Kings Mountain during the Revolutionary War. James M. Smith, Reynolds's great-grandfather and the son of Daniel Smith, was a pioneer builder of Asheville and the first white child in North Carolina born west of the Blue Ridge Mountains. Intensely proud of his family's accomplishments, Reynolds often boasted of their contribution to the settlement of western North Carolina.

On his father's side, Reynolds was related to the Baird family, prominent in North Carolina history, and was a cousin of Zebulon Baird Vance, the Civil War governor of North Carolina. Through the Bairds, Reynolds was second cousin to Lee S. Overman, a United States senator who represented North Carolina from November 1902 until his death in 1930.

Shortly after the end of the American Revolution, Daniel Smith and his young bride, Mary Davidson, joined a group of settlers who moved into the virgin country beyond the Blue Ridge. Smith established a home on the French Broad River and became an important figure in the political and military life of western North Carolina until his death at age sixty-seven in 1824.

Daniel Smith's eldest son, James M. Smith (born June 14, 1784), married Polly Patton and settled in Asheville, North Carolina. He eventually amassed large land-holdings and numbers of slaves and was considered a very wealthy man at his death on December 11, 1853. Fellow citizens regarded him as one of the founding fathers of the growing mountain settlement of Asheville.

James M. Smith's daughter, Jane C. Smith, married George T. Spears, a native of Charleston, South Carolina.[3] They had a daughter named Mamie Spears, the mother of Bob Reynolds. Joshua Reynolds, the paternal grandfather of Bob Rey-nolds, was an itinerant Methodist preacher who rode his horse all over western North Carolina, "with the Lord in his heart and his Bible in his saddle bag." Joshua Reynolds produced a son named William Taswell Reynolds, an Asheville business-man and later clerk of the Superior Court, who won the heart and hand of young Mamie Spears.[4]

William T. and Mamie Spears Reynolds had three children. In addition to Robert Rice Reynolds there was a daughter who died early in life and the eldest son, G. Spears Reynolds. Unfortunately, young Bob Reynolds's father died when the boy was only seven. His mother tried to raise the family alone for a few years and then married N. A. Reynolds, the brother of her deceased husband. Nathaniel Augustus Reynolds, or Uncle Gus, tried to act as a father to the young boy. But according to Frances Reynolds Oertling, Bob Reynolds's daughter, Bob and his uncle did not get along very well, and Uncle Gus had very little effect on Bob's formative years. Young Bob was raised primarily by his mother and her grandmother.[5]

Young Reynolds, bright-eyed and tough as a hickory nut, emerged as the leader of the boys in his neighborhood and organized a street gang that was both feared and admired throughout Asheville.[6] In his youth, Reynolds took great delight in organizing circuses in his neighborhood. High-spirited and reckless, Reynolds was usually the star of the circus.[7]

As a young man Reynolds attended the public schools in Asheville and then matriculated at Weaver College, a college preparatory school in Weaverville, North Carolina.[8] As Reynolds recalled in *Wanderlust,* a memoir of his early days, at age fourteen his mind began to stray from his studies to more exciting things. His extracurricular reading stirred his curiosity and quickened an already lively imagi-nation. Dime novels, such as the adventures of Jesse James, fueled his adventurous spirit and led him to think of running away from home.

In the bitterly cold month of January 1898, Bob set out on the first of many exciting travels and boarded a train for Charleston, South Carolina.[9] Reynolds quickly demonstrated that he was a resourceful and self-reliant traveler. Travel in the South in 1898, with crude and inadequate transportation and communication, proved a challenge to the most experienced traveler, let alone a fourteen-year-old boy. Traveling with extremely limited funds, Reynolds found it necessary to call on every ounce of common sense and a good bit of luck to cope with the difficulties he encountered.

After reaching Charleston, he secured a job polishing brass and washing dishes on a ship in exchange for passage to Jacksonville, Florida. After his arrival there, he hiked over much of north central Florida, begging meals from accommodating housewives along his route and sleeping wherever he could find a bed. In Sanford, Florida, he earned $1.50 for three days' work and promptly spent five cents for candy and $1.25 for a pair of snappy tan shoes that caught his eye.[10]

Reynolds next served as a cabin boy on a fruit boat plying its trade between Tampa and Key West. Returning to Jacksonville, he was spotted by a railroad detective while enjoying a free ride at the expense of the railroad. Realizing his dilemma, Reynolds quickly ducked around to the other side of the train, grabbed a piece of cotton, and began energetically shining the brass as a temporary un-salaried employee of the railroad. As was expected of a railway employee, Reynolds cooperated fully with the pursuing detective and indicated that he had seen a disreputable young tramp heading for the woods on the opposite side of the tracks. While the beleaguered official set off to capture his erstwhile prey, a relieved Reynolds quickly slipped away from the train to the other side of town.

Reynolds's wits and a substantial amount of good fortune had saved him from the grasp of the law on this occasion, but he soon tired of living on handouts and sleeping in boxcars and on benches. He made up his mind to end his travels and wired the following message to his family: "Want to return home badly. Please wire money." The following morning twenty-five dollars arrived from his mother, and he bought a train ticket for home.

"Here ended the first adventure," wrote Reynolds, "and I returned, wiser of course, and somewhat disappointed, truth to tell, in not having captured a ruffian. However, I was glad enough to have saved my skin."[11] Reynolds's travels had given him self-confidence in his ability to survive on his own and had merely whetted his appetite for future travel. Reynolds also learned much about human relationships, and his close contacts with people from all walks of life laid the foundation for his understanding of and empathy for the average American.

Back in Asheville, Reynolds managed to remain at Weaver College long enough to finish his preparatory work and in September 1902 enrolled at the University of North Carolina at Chapel Hill.[12] From 1902 until 1905, Reynolds devoted the major part of his energy to football, track, and passing math.[13] Frank Porter Graham, later president of the University of North Carolina, remembered sitting in a freshman mathematics class with Reynolds (who was then a senior) under the tutelage of the renowned professor Archibald Henderson. Reynolds, recalled Graham, finally succeeded in passing math on his fourth try and was highly elated by his achievement.[14] During his second year at the university, Reynolds was elected sports editor of the *Tar Heel*, the weekly student newspaper.[15]

In the summer of 1903, with foreign travel his number one goal, Reynolds left for Europe with several of his college chums. He organized a trip over on the cattle boat *Shenandoah* and received ten dollars per head for the eight eager companions he recruited. Reynolds and his friends spent most of their time on board watering (two hundred buckets of water per day) and feeding the cattle and cleaning the stalls. The work was hot, stifling, and marred on many occasions by seasickness.[16]

Two close friends who accompanied him to Europe were John A. Park, later publisher of the *Raleigh Times*, and O. Max Gardner, a future governor of North Carolina. Gardner, after his appointment as the United States ambassador to England in 1946, recalled the group's arrival in London in 1903, when Reynolds found them lodging for thirty cents per night.[17] In a personal letter to Reynolds in 1946, Gardner remembered their trip with great humor and affection: "If it had not been for you I would not have gone to England in the first instance, and if I had not gone in the first instance I probably would not be going now."[18]

The following summer Reynolds was once again off for Europe, working his way over on his usual conveyance, a cattle boat.[19] In the fall he returned to the University of North Carolina, concentrating on winning a varsity letter in football. After three years as a member of the scrub team, Reynolds finally made the varsity squad his senior year. He spent most of the year as a substitute halfback and played sparingly. Fred W. Morrison, a longtime friend, remembered that a cautious Reynolds had a hard time winning a varsity letter because he tried to run through the line backward without getting hurt.[20]

Fearful that he might not win his coveted letter, Reynolds pleaded with the coach for a chance to play. He got his big opportunity and started at right halfback against Virginia Polytechnic Institute but got into a fight and was expelled from the game. The *Daily Tar Heel* described the incident: "A V.P.I. player who has a reputation for being careless with his English applied an opprobrious epithet to Bob Reynolds. Reynolds gave him one straight from the shoulder and as a consequence, was requested by the umpire to retire."[21] Later in the year, Reynolds scored a touchdown against Georgetown and, by playing in the victory over Virginia, finally earned his varsity letter.[22]

According to close friends, Reynolds was, during his university days, an attractive, gregarious young man who got along with everyone and seldom offended anyone. Comrades reported that he simply had no antagonism toward any individuals or groups.[23] In addition to track and football, the popular, personable

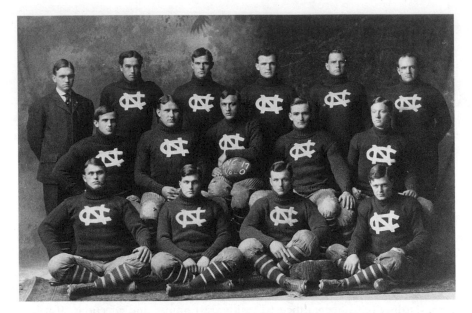

Bob Reynolds and the UNC football team, pictured in *Yackety-Yack*, 1906. Reynolds (second row, far right) played for four years before finally earning his varsity letter his senior year. (North Carolina Collection, University of North Carolina Library at Chapel Hill)

young man from Asheville participated in numerous extracurricular activities at the university. Some of his affiliations were academic, but he often neglected his studies to take part in the social clubs. Reynolds, constantly in search of new friends and fun activities, organized and served as president of the Buncombe County Club[24] and was a member of the Germans Club (social), secretary and treasurer of the Geological Club, and a member of the Beta Theta Pi social fraternity.[25]

"Cattle Boat Bob" or "Fighting Bob," as he was variously known to friends, helped found a club known as "the Boys." This group was composed of fellows "good and bad, stale and fresh who have either been to Europe . . . or who intend to go." The entrance requirements for the club were to read Stoddard's Lectures in full and to place a brand new dollar bill in Bob Reynolds's jeans. The purpose of the club, also known as the Noble Knights of the Cattle Boat, was to bring old and new navigators into contact with one another so that "the tenderfoot may learn something about the cattle boat business before he embarks on his great ride across the pond." At the meetings, papers were read on bullfights, the churches of Paris, vaudeville shows, and the cure for seasickness.[26]

Bob Reynolds's academic transcript revealed that he was, at best, an average student. In his freshman year, with 1 as the equivalent of an A grade, Reynolds

REYNOLDS, ROBERT RICE.
Asheville, N. C.

Age, 21; weight, 170; height, 6 feet; B
Θ Π; Π Σ; German Club; Secretary and
Treasurer Geological Club; President
Buncombe County Club ('04-'05); Ath-
letic Editor Tar Heel; Class Foot-ball
Team (1); Class Base-ball Team; Scrub
Foot-ball Team (2); Capt. Scrub Foot-
ball Team (3); Varsity Foot-ball Team
(4); Elected Captain Track Team (4),
resigned; Y. M. C. A.

"Cattle Boat Bob." "Fighting Bob."
Gaze upon the manly features of a
globe trotter, a foot-ballist and a newspaper man in one. For four long years
he pursued his ambition—an N. C.
sweater, and when he got it he hugged
it to his bosom and departed from our
midst. He was born with a prosperity
for yarn spinning, and this proclivity
he carefully cultivated until it is second
to none. Apparently, his experience as
a cattle puncher stood him in good stead
when it came to booting the coach—and
others.

Bob Reynolds in the UNC yearbook, 1906. The *Yackety-Yack* listed the various organizations
Reynolds joined and extolled his virtues as a storyteller.
(North Carolina Collection, University of North Carolina Library at Chapel Hill)

made all 4s and 5s (a conditional pass) in such subjects as history, English, French,
and geology. In the fall of 1905, his senior year, after getting a 4 in drawing and a 5
in English, Reynolds did not bother to take his other exams and left the university
without a degree.[27] Clearly his ardent commitment to social clubs and football left
him little time to prepare adequately for his academic responsibilities. In later
years Reynolds apparently allowed the press and friends to assume he had received
his degree from Chapel Hill. He was widely identified as a UNC graduate, an error
he did not bother to correct.

The 1906 school yearbook, the *Yackety Yack*, accurately described Reynolds's
personality: "Gaze upon the manly features of a globe trotter, a foot-ballist and a
newspaper man in one. For four long years he pursued his ambition—an N. C.
sweater, and when he got it he hugged it to his bosom and departed from our
midst. He was born with a prosperity for yarn spinning, and this proclivity he
carefully cultivated until it is second to none."[28]

At the university Bob Reynolds concentrated on having a good time, earning a
letter in football, courting the ladies, and traveling with friends. With the possible
exception of football, he was unwilling to apply himself to any arduous activity not
social in nature. He did, however, set a pattern of behavior for the rest of his life in
that he seldom prepared effectively, read little, and got by on his charm.

He left Chapel Hill feeling no need for a university degree and without any understanding of the importance of education and intellectual discipline. Reynolds did, however, develop his ability to make firm and lasting friendships. Whatever else one could say about Bob Reynolds, everyone liked him.

After leaving the university, Reynolds returned to Asheville and started a resort magazine, the *Asheville Magazine, the Magazine of the South*. The magazine's first issue was dated July 26, 1906, and the enterprise lasted for about one year.[29] A typical issue featured editorials; articles on music, drama, and the Asheville horse show; plus poems, stories, jokes, and fashion notes.[30] This undistinguished magazine consisted essentially of chatty comments on cultural events in Asheville.

In the fall of 1906, Reynolds journeyed to Washington, D.C., and landed a position as a clerk with the *Washington Times*.[31] Reynolds, quickly bored with distributing mail and accepting classified advertising, joined forces with a fellow named Bernard M. Condon, who had been recently expelled from the United States Naval Academy at Annapolis. Condon proposed a trip out west, and Reynolds promptly accepted.

The two travelers journeyed first to Chicago, where they worked to earn enough money to travel farther west. Lacking the necessary funds for travel to California, Reynolds devised a successful scheme by which they would earn more than enough to pay for their westward passage. Reynolds visited a drugstore and purchased stoppers, a basketful of second-hand bottles, two bottles of vanilla, a bottle of myrrh, and a piece of red sealing wax. He mixed the myrrh and the vanilla with alcohol and poured the concoction into several bottles, corked the bottles, and sealed them with the red wax.

Reynolds, attired in a rented full-length black coat and tall silk hat and sporting a large imitation diamond, set up a dry goods box on a street corner and offered for sale an elixir that he claimed was as potent as the Fountain of Youth. Reynolds foisted off this wonderful healing preparation on the public with an age-old gimmick. He launched into a long and persuasive spiel about the miraculous properties of his magic potion, after which his partner (Condon) desperately elbowed his way through the crowd and plunked down fifty cents on the box for the only stuff "that ever done me any good." The ploy was successful enough for the two con men to purchase train tickets to Yankton, South Dakota. Our Bob, of course, was practicing and sharpening the verbal skills that would ultimately enable him to sell himself to the people of North Carolina in 1932.

After six lonely months as ranch hands, Reynolds and Condon parted company. Condon resumed his wandering, while Reynolds decided to return to the University of North Carolina and enroll as a law student.[32] Reynolds did enroll but there was no indication that he ever took any courses.[33] If Reynolds did sit in on law courses during the summer, it was all the formal training he ever had for the practice of law.[34]

Reynolds next decided to go to California, allegedly to take law courses at Stanford University, but actually to resume his adventures with Condon. When Condon failed to show up, the itinerant Reynolds, destitute and longing to return to the mountains of North Carolina, wandered the streets of San Francisco until he noticed a life-size poster of one Jimmy Broyles, the amateur boxing champion of the Pacific Coast. Broyles offered a purse of one hundred dollars for anyone who could stay in the ring with him for six rounds. Reynolds impulsively volunteered to try his hand against Broyles.

Reynolds weighed 170 pounds compared with the 135-pound Broyles but wisely settled on a strategy of merely hanging on for six rounds and collecting his money. The challenger spent the contest clinching and retreating as Broyles chased him around the ring. Finally Broyles landed a crushing blow which sent Reynolds tumbling over the ropes and to the floor, but the punch landed after the gong ending the sixth round. A groggy Reynolds collected his money. Two days later, battered, with both eyes still swollen, he boarded a train bound for North Carolina.[35]

Back in Asheville in 1907, apparently having read for the law, Bob Reynolds was admitted to the North Carolina bar. But he was not yet ready to enter his chosen profession. Instead, he migrated to Oklahoma City, Oklahoma, where he was football coach and athletic director at a local high school. In the summer of 1908, he was off on another world journey, traveling through Central America, Australia, and back to Asheville by way of California.[36] Reynolds never lost this urge to travel and see the world. His greatest pleasure seemed to come from his travels, and this wanderlust became an integral part of his character.

Finally, in 1908, Bob Reynolds began practicing criminal law in Asheville with his brother, G. Spears Reynolds. Spears was twelve years older than Bob and an experienced, capable lawyer. Bob did not know the law well but excelled at presenting the case to the jury. Therefore, Spears studied the law and prepared the briefs, while Bob pleaded the cases.[37]

Shortly after he began practicing law, he met the first of his five wives.[38] Fannie Menge Jackson was the daughter of Judge and Mrs. William L. Jackson III of New Orleans, Louisiana. Reynolds won the blond, blue-eyed beauty's hand after a short but intense courtship. The young couple married in New Orleans on January 19, 1910, in a lavish society wedding.[39]

Mr. and Mrs. Bob Reynolds returned to Asheville to live. Fannie Reynolds brought to her marriage a considerable fortune inherited from her parents' coalfield holdings. The couple enjoyed a happy marriage, and Fannie bore two children: Frances and Robert Rice Jr. Unfortunately, Fannie Reynolds developed pneumonia and died on October 17, 1913. At her death she left an estate of some two hundred thousand dollars to her husband and two children.[40]

While pursuing his legal career in 1909, Reynolds agreed to serve as secretary of the Buncombe County Democratic Committee, his first political post. Intrigued with the game of politics, in 1910 the ambitious Reynolds decided to run for district solicitor (prosecuting attorney) in Asheville, a post traditionally held by Republicans. In 1932 Bob Reynolds reminisced about his first try for political office: "The old line politicians recognized that I had some ambitions and they thought the best way to get rid of me quick was to give me the Democratic nomination for solicitor. They thought it would be impossible to get elected. The district was overwhelmingly Republican. But I accepted the nomination. In fact I worked for it."[41]

Although Reynolds's father had been clerk of court in Asheville, young Bob was not well known at home because of his lengthy absences from there.[42] As a fledgling lawyer, Reynolds ran for solicitor primarily to improve his name recognition in the county and to build his law practice. Reynolds thought that even though he might not win the election, the twenty-dollar filing fee was a good investment in advertising. His name would be on thousands of ballots and would be mentioned in speeches to large numbers of potential clients.[43]

A genial man with an amazing memory for faces and first names, Reynolds had the grace and style of a natural politician. He treated everyone equally and flattered everyone he met.[44] Reynolds attributed his early political success to tenacity, but a more accurate appraisal emphasized his "demagogic flair for showmanship, a hearty handshake, and the ability to climb off and on the bandwagon at the right moment."[45] Author Burke Davis, writing more than thirty years later in *Harper's Magazine*, probably described Reynolds's political personality more aptly than anyone else, noting that Reynolds was "by temperament a cross between a carnival broker, a shell-game operator, and a traveling salesman."[46] As one wag put it, Reynolds "was born in Buncombe County, N.C., and had made his living—at least partly—on buncombe ever since."[47]

On the stump, Reynolds demonstrated a hearty laugh, a flamboyant personality, and an aggressive style of campaigning. His campaign equipment consisted of an old, flea-bitten, sway-backed, one-eyed nag and two saddlebags filled with red-and-white peppermint candy bearing the plea, "Ask your daddy to vote for Bob Reynolds." Reynolds rode his decrepit horse over steep mountain paths, up every creek and down every possum trail in the district, giving out candy and addressing everyone he met as "cousin."[48]

The neophyte Reynolds appealed to the average voter in a manner that made expert politicians cringe. "I don't want this job just to serve you," he told voters, "although I reckon I can do that as well as anybody. I want it for the money. I'm a young lawyer and I need experience. I want to get it at your expense."[49] The voters, tired of the hypocrisy of politicians who wanted only "to serve the people," liked Reynolds's truthful, direct approach and his ebullient personality. The voters carried Reynolds to his first political victory as Our Bob easily defeated the favored Republican candidate.[50]

His victory shocked the Republican Party but did not surprise Bob Reynolds. As he recalled in an interview forty-eight years after the election: "The people liked the truth. That job [solicitor] was paid by fees grossing about $7,500.00 per year. They knew that whatever high-falutin' talking a man might do, he really had his eyes on those fees. When I told them so right out, they knew that in Bob Reynolds they had an honest man."[51]

During his four-year term as prosecuting attorney, Reynolds tried many cases, including over one hundred murders. He failed to achieve an outstanding record, although he generally performed his duties competently. A contemporary lawyer found Reynolds forceful and effective in front of a jury but not very knowledgeable about the law and not always reliable in carrying out his duties.[52]

Despite what should have been a demanding job as solicitor, a restless Reynolds pursued other activities. He became interested in motion pictures and organized a theatrical troupe that produced a feature film which turned out to be little more than a home movie.[53] Bob Reynolds never became an effective, successful lawyer partly because his extracurricular activities simply made it impossible for him to concentrate his efforts on the study and practice of law for any extended period of time.

He could, however, focus his attention on attractive women. In 1914, at age thirty, Reynolds met his second wife, a vivacious seventeen-year-old from Augusta, Georgia, named Mary Bland. Reynolds, always charming and courtly, allegedly won Mary's affection by telling her of life on the Reynolds estate in North Carolina—neglecting at this point to distinguish his family from the wealthy R. J. Reynolds tobacco clan. Bob Reynolds, although not as wealthy as R. J. Reynolds, had inherited a substantial sum from his first wife, as well as some property from his father, and lived a very comfortable existence in Asheville. In August 1914, only a few short days after their first meeting, the couple took their vows in the rectory of the Catholic church in Aiken, South Carolina. Reynolds's daughter, Frances, said that her father married the woman who looked most like his first wife.

His second marriage was far from happy. Either Mary Bland was too young when she married Reynolds or she found it difficult to accept the responsibility of raising two children from his previous marriage. Frances Reynolds Oertling recalled that Mary Bland Reynolds mistreated her and her brother, and her cruelty was the primary cause for the divorce. At any rate, less than a year after their marriage, Bob Reynolds left his wife nursing their new baby daughter, Mary Bland.

Reynolds divorced his wife in 1917, and she took legal custody of the child. Mrs. Mary Bland Reynolds subsequently married three more times; their daughter died of Hodgkin's disease.[54]

In 1914 Reynolds finished his term as district solicitor and announced his candidacy for Congress in the Democratic primary against incumbent James Madison Gudger. Although Reynolds campaigned hard, the nomination went to Gudger partly because he was an incumbent congressman. Reynolds had difficulty overcoming his youth, inexperience, and lack of recognition outside of Asheville.[55]

Chagrined by a disappointing defeat in the race for Congress and upset by the failure of his second marriage, Reynolds decided that travel was the best cure for disappointment. He promptly set out on another trip around the world, leaving his children with their grandmother. After visits to Central and South America and to Australia, he returned to Asheville and resumed the practice of law.[56]

In 1916 Reynolds moved to Louisiana to manage property (two plantations and a sand and gravel company) left to him by his first wife. He opened up a roller skating rink in Baton Rouge to make some extra money. Reynolds later became acquainted with a fancy skater and dynamic huckster who was a fledgling attorney and salesman in the area. This new friend was none other than Huey Pierce Long, later governor of Louisiana and a United States senator.[57]

After approximately one year in Louisiana, Reynolds moved to New York City. There he joined the staff of the Cinema News Syndicate in New York, where he edited and directed a series of films about the United States Army and Navy titled *The American War News Weekly*.[58] Reynolds did not volunteer for active service in World War I, but while working in New York he registered, in September 1918, for the draft as required. The war ended, and he never served.[59]

By 1920 the nomadic Reynolds had returned to Asheville and launched a new project. He bought a Ford truck, built a "house" on the Ford chassis with room for sleeping and cooking, and set off on a tour around the country.

While driving through New York City, Reynolds struck pretty, petite, twenty-three-year-old Denise D'Arcy as she crossed the street. Although Denise did not seem seriously injured, Reynolds sensed an opportunity to display his chivalry as a southern gentleman, especially as he had fortuitously happened upon a most attractive accident victim. He gathered the young lady in his arms and carried her into the foyer of the nearby Hotel Biltmore. He engaged a room for her and took a room for himself across the hall to supervise her recovery. Reynolds sent her flowers and hovered by her bedside while her superficial wounds healed. Five days after the accident, Bob Reynolds announced that he and the young French girl had fallen in love and were to be married. Once again he apparently gave his intended the impression that he was one of the R. J. Reynolds tobacco heirs.

After their marriage, Bob and Denise Reynolds returned to Asheville and lived in a mountain cabin while Reynolds resumed the practice of law with his brother. Reynolds's third marriage dissolved in acrimony after only one year. Reynolds's family did not like Denise, and Denise had difficulty adjusting to the duties of caring for two children. She obtained a legal separation from her husband in 1922 and eventually returned to France. Reynolds filed a petition for divorce in Asheville on September 12, 1927, charging that Mrs. Denise Reynolds had abandoned her husband and children. The divorce was granted in 1929.[60]

In later years Reynolds seemed to forget about his third spouse. In an interview in 1932, he failed to list Denise D'Arcy as one of his previous wives. An alert reporter noticed the omission and asked Reynolds why he had not listed her. "Oh," said Reynolds, "I've had so many I guess I just overlooked her." On the eve of his fifth marriage in 1941, the expectant groom was again asked about his previous wives. "Oh forget about the wives," he answered. "Just say I've been married about three and one-half times." The half marriage Reynolds referred to was the brief, unsuccessful union with Denise D'Arcy.[61]

In 1923, bored with the law and distressed by his second failed marriage, Bob Reynolds constructed another travel van and planned a new worldwide tour. Again leaving his children with their grandmother, Reynolds hired an experienced movie photographer named Wheeler Jennings and set off.[62] The front door of the Ford truck was boldly lettered, "Around the World with Bob Reynolds." The two men ended up making a film about their travels titled *Gypsy Trails*, and Reynolds wrote a book with the same title.[63]

On August 18, 1923, Reynolds loaded his truck on a Belgian freighter bound for Le Havre, France. Having suffered indignities during past trips to France, Reynolds disliked the French for what he perceived to be their arrogant ways and for their failure to pay their World War I debt to the United States or even to acknowledge U.S. assistance during the war.[64] Reynolds's observations, although superficial, were of significance because they reflected his often expressed dislike and distrust of some foreign countries.

After visits to Holland, Germany, and Switzerland, Reynolds and Jennings crossed the snow-covered Alps into Aosta, Italy, a small frontier city. There they were arrested and jailed for taking photographs where prohibited.[65] Despite his love of travel, the incident in Aosta and other unpleasant encounters certainly influenced and heightened his negative attitude toward foreigners.

Always an aspirant for political office, while on his world tour Reynolds began a rather remarkable campaign for the post of lieutenant governor of North Carolina. During one of his boat excursions, Reynolds discovered that more than one hundred North Carolina soldiers were his traveling companions. He rounded up the North Carolina troops and gave them a rousing speech praising the army and the United States. Then Reynolds wrote the parents of each soldier to the effect that

"I saw Johnny today and we had a long talk. He's a splendid boy and will serve his country nobly, as befits a son of that great and lovely state of North Carolina."[66]

In addition to letters to the home folks, Reynolds purchased thousands of postcards in Europe and Asia. After consulting a North Carolina yearbook that he thoughtfully brought along, Reynolds addressed the cards to doctors, lawyers, officeholders, merchants, farmers, and other Tar Heel citizens who might help him in his campaign.[67] He asked his correspondents to mention to their friends that he was running for lieutenant governor and requested their help in the forthcoming race.[68] A number of cards arrived just before the election, bearing the message, "Having a grand time; wish you were here. May not be back in time for election but vote for me just the same."[69]

According to the *Durham Herald-Sun*, well-thumbed postcards from such faraway spots as the Taj Mahal and Suez adorned the walls of many North Carolina homes. Reynolds had sent hundreds of cards to his "God-fearing, tater-raisin', baby-havin' " constituents, and they were thrilled with picture postcards from such exotic locations.[70] Some of the cards' recipients, who had never set foot beyond the boundaries of their state, remembered that Reynolds had been thoughtful enough to write to them while he was traveling around the world and often remembered Reynolds at the polling booth.

Despite the postcards, Reynolds lost the Democratic nomination for lieutenant governor in 1924. Although he polled enough votes to call for a second primary, he refused to exercise his option, claiming that he did not want to put his friends through additional trouble on his behalf. Thus the leading vote getter in the first primary became the party nominee.[71] Reynolds chose to reserve his resources for a more favorable circumstance. Despite a loss in his first statewide race, he had his eye on a higher prize, the United States Senate.

The *Southern Tourist*, in a February 1925 article, described Bob Reynolds as a fine criminal lawyer, a marvelous public speaker, and a man who possessed enough energy, enthusiasm, and ambition to be elected to the United States Senate.[72] Reynolds, emboldened by this endorsement and the encouragement of many friends, in 1926 announced his candidacy for the United States Senate against incumbent Lee S. Overman. Reynolds knew that he had little hope of defeating Overman, his second cousin, but he wanted to set up a political organization and build up support for a later try at the same office.[73]

Until now, Reynolds could practice law whenever he chose because his brother held the practice together. But in 1924 G. Spears Reynolds died of poisoned bootleg whiskey. Reynolds then entered into a partnership with Irving C. Crawford, who agreed to run the law office so Bob could carry on with his political ambitions.

Reynolds could afford to launch a race for the U.S. Senate owing to the funds left to him by his first wife and his earnings as a lawyer. In addition, his mother owned several large buildings and valuable property in downtown Asheville, and Reynolds shared in the revenue from the rentals. Thus Reynolds, with some financial support from friends, managed to carry on a series of frugal political campaigns. He did not spend large sums of money on advertising, relying instead on personal contacts, speeches, public occasions, and letters to friends asking for votes.[74]

In July 1925 Reynolds wrote John C. Sikes of Monroe, North Carolina, as well as other friends, asking for their support in his as yet unannounced race for the United States Senate. Encouraged by the large vote he received in the contest for lieutenant governor, Reynolds urged his followers to sound out the voters in their areas and let him know how his candidacy was progressing.[75] He also composed letters to the alumni of the University of North Carolina asking for their support. Reynolds admitted that he was not "much to look at, no fit subject for M. Rodin to use as a model for his 'Thinker', but a homely, human sort of cuss, reasonably honest and loyal to the core."[76]

Unfortunately for Reynolds, John Sikes and other prominent North Carolinians, while admiring Reynolds's enthusiasm, had already pledged their support to Senator Overman. They did not believe that there was a man in the state who could defeat Overman.[77] But Reynolds, the eternal optimist, ignored reality and somehow convinced himself that he could win the nomination. P. Cleveland Gardner, of the Shelby Gardner clan, was 100 percent for Reynolds because he wanted to replace Overman with a real man of the people. Reynolds wrote Gardner that the people wanted a change—they did not believe in keeping any man in office for life.[78]

One crucial issue in the 1926 Senate campaign was Reynolds's failure to fight in World War I. Overman's advocates ran an advertisement in the *Greensboro Daily News* which indicated that many servicemen opposed Reynolds because of his failure to do his duty in the war. B. I. Moore, Reynolds's campaign aide, responded with the facts. According to the records of the War Department, Reynolds had two children, was above the age limit for the first draft order, and was not required to register. He subsequently was required to register and did so in New York City on September 12, 1918. Reynolds waived all exemptions and deferments, and the army notified him that he would be inducted into the service on November 14, 1918. The signing of the armistice on November 11, 1918, however, resulted in the canceling of Reynolds's orders. His backers explained that thousands of men honorably followed the same procedure and denounced Overman for this attack on Reynolds's character and patriotism.[79]

Despite facing a popular incumbent in the Democratic primary, Reynolds demonstrated a growing political strength by amassing 91,914 votes to Overman's total of 140,260.[80] Although he lost, Reynolds had accomplished his purpose by achieving greater statewide recognition. He believed his showing would make him a formidable candidate at some future date. P. Cleveland Gardner congratulated Reynolds on his splendid vote and agreed that his political future looked bright.[81]

Meanwhile, in 1925 Reynolds, ever the ladies' man, met the woman who was to become his fourth wife. Eva Grady of Chicago, Illinois, a Ziegfeld Follies dancer known professionally as Eva Brady, had come to Asheville in search of a cure for tuberculosis. Although they met in 1925, Reynolds and Eva Grady were not able to marry until Denise D'Arcy agreed to a divorce in 1929. Bob married Eva two years later, on February 27, 1931. His union with Eva Grady, after what amounted to a marathon courtship for Reynolds, proved to be the happiest and most successful of Reynolds's marriages.[82]

Bob Reynolds remained at home and practiced law in Asheville rather consistently from 1926 until 1932. During that six-year period he maintained close contact with politicians in the state. He was a strong supporter of Josiah W. Bailey in 1930, when Bailey challenged incumbent Furnifold M. Simmons for the United State Senate.[83]

In the Senate contest of 1930, most of the Democratic Party leaders in North Carolina and the leading newspapers in the state came out for Bailey and abandoned Simmons because of the latter's support of Republican Herbert C. Hoover in the presidential election of 1928.[84] Reynolds knew from the beginning that by siding with Bailey he had picked a winner. He expected either to share in the spoils of victory or demonstrate his party loyalty and hope for similar support from Bailey in his next bid for public office.

During the campaign, which lasted from January to June 1930, Reynolds wrote approximately twenty unsolicited letters to Josiah Bailey urging him to oppose monopolies and support reduced property taxes. Reynolds assured Bailey that he would carry that section of the state by a wide margin and made several campaign trips to rural areas on Bailey's behalf.[85] Josiah Bailey indicated his gratitude for Reynolds's interest in and assistance with the campaign. He also expressed the hope that he would have the opportunity to show his appreciation some day.[86] Reynolds interpreted Bailey's statement as an offer of future support.

Bailey won the election by a majority of 70,367 votes.[87] Although Reynolds was not rewarded for his efforts by Bailey, the Democratic Party took note of his loyalty and his contribution to Bailey's victory. Reynolds, however, was unconcerned with immediate rewards. He continued to look for the main chance and waited for the right opportunity to achieve his political dream. That opportunity came in 1932.

CHAPTER TWO

The Democratic Primary of 1932

By 1930, the Democratic Party in North Carolina had fallen into a state of internal discord and conflict caused primarily by the presidential election of 1928 and the resultant passions over prohibition, Catholicism, and political personalities. The 1928 contest between Al Smith, the Catholic, "wet" Democratic nominee, and Herbert Clark Hoover, the "dry" Republican nominee, had been bitterly contested in the South and in North Carolina. Senator Furnifold M. Simmons, a United States senator for thirty years and the dominant leader of the machine that controlled party politics in the state, led a bolt from the national Democratic Party and Al Smith. The defection of these key Democratic Party leaders helped Hoover achieve a decisive victory (349,000 to 286,000 for Smith) and swept North Carolina into the Republican column for the first time since Reconstruction.

Not all Democrats defected, of course. Loyalists included the former governor Cameron Morrison, the current governor O. Max Gardner, and Josiah W. Bailey. They all worked for Al Smith and thus emerged from the campaign as "regular" Democrats. Simmons, as a result of his support for Hoover, found himself unpopular with the rank and file of the party.[1] Bailey decisively defeated Simmons in the 1930 senatorial contest, effectively ending Simmons's political career. Bailey's victory sent the clear message that party irregularity meant political death.[2]

Despite Hoover's victory in North Carolina in the election of 1928, there was no move to two-party politics in the state. Although the Republicans retained some strength throughout the state, they fell into disfavor with the onset of the Great Depression. The new Democratic leadership of O. Max Gardner and Josiah Bailey, having achieved power by disciplining Simmons, successfully gained control of the Democratic Party organization and election machinery.[3]

The North Carolina Democratic Party in the early 1930s was ruled by what V. O. Key Jr. called the "progressive plutocracy" and what others called "business progressivism." The business progressives wanted increased spending on education and roads and expected government to be honest and efficient. While the conservative leaders of the party did not favor social welfare or labor legislation, they had a strong sense of community responsibility and were not blind to community needs. Thus the contest for power in state politics was not between Democrats and Republicans but between the moderate and the conservative wings within the Democratic Party.[4] It was in this context that the maverick Bob Reynolds prepared to challenge its leaders.

On December 3, 1930, President Herbert Hoover made a decision that was to have a profound influence on the senatorial campaign of 1932 in North Carolina. He appointed Frank R. McNinch of Charlotte to be a member of the new Federal Power Corporation for a four-year term.[5] In choosing McNinch, Hoover had tapped one of the acknowledged leaders of the anti–Al Smith campaign of 1928. The appointment was an obvious reward for his devotion to the Republican Party in 1928.

North Carolina Democrats immediately opposed McNinch's confirmation, declaring him unfit for the job because of his previously close relationships with Hoover and power companies. Congressman Lindsay Warren found the appointment shocking and an insult to Democrats in North Carolina.[6]

Governor O. Max Gardner and Josiah Bailey were likewise outspoken in their criticism of McNinch. Both men charged that McNinch had used large sums contributed by power companies in his pro-Hoover campaign of 1928. Such associations, Bailey argued, should disqualify McNinch for the Federal Power Corporation.[7] Federal law required the appointment of a Democrat to the post, but party members in North Carolina were not willing to recognize McNinch as a loyal Democrat because of his bolt from the party in 1928.[8]

McNinch promptly denied the allegations by "his political enemies" and declared that he had never received any fees from power companies or owned any stock in them. McNinch reported that his only relations with power companies came through the performance of his duties as mayor of Charlotte and as an attorney opposing an increase in electric power rates.[9]

McNinch's controversial confirmation depended on the approbation of both United States senators from North Carolina. Furnifold Simmons, the lame-duck senator, told the White House that he would be most satisfied with the selection of this devoted man of spotless character. Josiah Bailey, however, who would not take office until March 4, vehemently opposed McNinch.

The differing views of Simmons and Bailey surprised no one, and their split left Senator Lee Overman as the crucial vote. Overman, however, never had to decide. On the same day that McNinch arrived in Washington for his hearing, Overman collapsed with a fatal heart attack.[10]

Overman's death made it necessary for Governor O. Max Gardner to choose a successor. Gardner thought the best choice was his brother-in-law Clyde R. Hoey, and indicated that the position was Hoey's if he so desired. Hoey, the party leader with arguably the largest personal following in the state, quickly withdrew his name because the appointment of a brother-in-law might embarrass Governor Gardner.[11] Primarily because Democratic Party leaders all over the state insisted on it, Gardner then turned to Cameron Morrison, governor of North Carolina from 1921 to 1925 and a longtime enemy of Gardner.

The appointment of Cameron Morrison meant that Morrison would enter the senate before Josiah Bailey and, on the retirement of Simmons, would be the senior senator from the state. More significant for the election of 1932 was that the confirmation of Frank McNinch was placed squarely in Morrison's lap. Morrison had been a strong and vehement foe of party bolters and had a lingering bitterness against those who participated in the anti-Smith campaign of 1928. But he was uncertain how he would vote, and his only immediate comment was, "I like McNinch personally."[12] Morrison's decision, moreover, was complicated by the fact that McNinch was a neighbor and close friend.

Morrison's position on the confirmation would go a long way in determining the votes of a number of other senators. Morrison undoubtedly realized McNinch's unpopularity among North Carolina Democrats and had been informed that a vote for confirmation would likely be political suicide.

Morrison initially indicated that he did not wish to testify in McNinch's behalf. But after Josiah Bailey and Congressman Lindsay Warren attacked McNinch, Morrison changed his mind and came to the defense of his friend. Morrison said he honestly believed that McNinch would make an excellent appointee and praised him as a man of character, fidelity, and intelligence. Senator Morrison denied any connection between McNinch and the power interests and was quoted as saying that the Duke Power Company, to which McNinch had been linked, "was almost a religious and benevolent organization and no man connected with it would corrupt anything."[13]

The following day, Morrison issued a formal statement explaining his decision to support McNinch. "I think," argued Morrison, "it will be found that though I voted against my own political interest that I voted for justice to a fellow man who honestly disagreed with me in a great crisis in our country's history" (the election of 1928). Morrison regretted having to oppose the judgment of so many Democrats, but he believed his action was in the best interest of the Democratic Party.[14]

On December 20, 1930, Morrison, in his maiden speech as a senator, again came to the defense of McNinch. To ensure the confirmation of McNinch, Morrison decided to defend power companies in general and the Duke Power Company in particular. He declared: "The Duke Power Company in my state belongs very largely to humanity. There is not an organization on this earth, unless it is purely religious, that is doing a [sic] nobler or better work than the Duke Power Company and the Duke Foundation."[15] In a time of depression and economic dislocation, Morrison's statement supporting large business corporations, believed by the average man to be largely responsible for the depression, proved to be a serious political blunder.

Shortly after McNinch's overwhelming confirmation by the United States Senate, Democrats, newspapers, and former supporters lashed Morrison unmercifully for his stand. Frank D. Grist called Morrison "North Carolina's prize hypocrite and champion double crosser."[16] The best summation of the situation came from the editor of the *Scotland Neck Commonwealth*: "By his vote for the 'Buzzard of Democracy' [McNinch] he [Morrison] insulted every loyal Democrat in the state, alienated his former supporters by the thousands and drove the last nails in his political coffin in 1932. If this doughty demagogue possesses an iota of statesmanship, he has not revealed it. Alas! The mantle of the revered and courtly Overman has fallen upon a dunghill. Let us pray."[17]

The editor of the *Elizabeth City Independent* referred to Morrison as a "blustering, blundering, blatherskite" and noted that this view represented the sentiment of numerous Democrats with whom he had conversed.[18] One of Morrison's friends wrote that the McNinch stunt made it look "very much like he will destroy himself before 1932."[19]

Morrison, however, certain that he had made the correct decision, refused to apologize for his actions.[20] Given that Morrison knew his advocacy of McNinch would be extremely unpopular in North Carolina, why did Morrison risk his political career on this issue? First, Morrison had been thrust into the McNinch controversy and had to make a decision. He sincerely believed that his friend McNinch would make an excellent appointee and thought it was unfair to punish McNinch because he had opposed the Democratic Party in 1928. Morrison hoped that the eighteen-month period until the Democratic primary in 1932 would be long enough to cool off the anger aroused by the controversy and would give him time to repair his political fences.

Because of the McNinch dispute and because Morrison had been appointed, not elected, to the Senate, there was much interest in the 1932 Senate race. Almost a year prior to the primary date, three eager candidates had announced their intention to run.[21] Early in June 1931, Frank D. Grist, state commissioner of labor and printing, formally announced. Having taken a brief tour of the state, Grist found the people sick and tired of the government being run by the tobacco and power interests and wanted to turn the government "back to the people."[22] Although Bob Reynolds had privately informed friends as early as June 1930 that he intended to run for the Senate,[23] he did not make a formal announcement until July 26, 1931.[24] And on August 1, 1931, Judge Thomas "Tam" Bowie declared his intention to run.[25]

A key factor in the election of 1932 was Clyde Hoey's decision not to run. Many friends had urged him to make the race, but because the campaign had already begun, Hoey announced his noncandidacy.[26] Hoey preferred to wait and run for governor in 1936, an election that he did indeed win. The withdrawal of Hoey, the most effective politician in the state, turned out to be a great boon for Reynolds.

Senator Morrison, the incumbent, made it clear in July 1931 that he would seek election to the full six-year term. He announced that because there was to be a contest for his seat, "I thank heaven that I am ready for it and able to put up the best fight possible. I never felt better in my life."[27]

Morrison was a formidable, well-known candidate. He had been a successful attorney, as well as a senator in the North Carolina General Assembly, and was elected governor of the state in 1920 by defeating O. Max Gardner in a runoff. Morrison was generally a successful governor noted for his interest in schools and roads.[28]

During his last year as governor, Morrison, a widower since 1919, had married Mrs. Sarah Virginia Watts, widow of the wealthy George W. Watts of Durham.[29] Burke Davis, writing in *Harper's Magazine*, told a story about the exuberant, tobacco-chewing Morrison when he was courting the wealthy Mrs. Watts. Riding in a limousine owned by his future bride, Governor Morrison mistook one of the spotless, almost invisible windows of the car for the great outdoors and expectorated with disastrous results.[30] Morrison managed to get Mrs. Watts to marry him in spite of this unfortunate incident.

Morrison's newly acquired wealth became an issue in the campaign of 1932. Tam Bowie thought Morrison would be favored because of his incumbency, but believed that Morrison's great wealth in time of a depression and the McNinch vote would arouse resentment.[31] Frank D. Grist, considered by most observers to be a weak candidate,[32] predicted victory in a close race against Morrison, expecting Bowie and then Reynolds to bring up the rear.[33]

Although all Reynolds's opponents had loudly proclaimed their positions as drys and had denounced prohibition as a campaign issue, Reynolds quickly realized that prohibition *was* an issue of significant concern to the voters. His views against prohibition highlighted the major political difference among the candidates. At this early stage of the campaign, Reynolds seemed to have hit on a popular issue. He either understood the sentiments of the people more clearly than any other politician or he was taking a tremendous gamble on the prohibition question, hoping that the national Democratic Party would adopt a platform favoring modification of the prohibition laws.

In his campaign platform, proclaimed on July 26, 1931, Reynolds boldly stated his position on prohibition. "I believe the ends of real temperance and sobriety have been defeated by the attempt to enforce artificial restraint upon a people who were reared in liberty and tolerance." Reynolds was convinced that "the experiment has proven a failure. . . . We have . . . rendered encouragement to the nefarious trade of bootlegging, upon which gangsters and racketeers have built up impregnable empires to threaten the peace and tranquility of the nation. Only by removing from them the opportunity will we restore the country to the decent and law-abiding citizenship." Reynolds hoped his denunciation of prohibition would appeal to "straight-thinking" people who were sick of the "calamitous dose of political hypocrisy which has been fed to us for 13 years from a tarnished spoon of morality." The remainder of his platform favored a downward revision of the tariff and the elimination of all immigration into the United States in order to preserve America for Americans. Reynolds urged a vigorous enforcement of the Sherman Anti-Trust Act to benefit the people "who are suffering as the result of U.S. monopolies which are now sucking the very vitals from the American public."[34]

Reynolds adopted a realistic and politically effective platform that enabled him to pose as the champion of the little people. By attacking the trusts, prohibition, immigration, and the Republican Party, Reynolds offered convenient scapegoats for those looking for someone or something to blame for the depression.

Cameron Morrison did not find it necessary to issue a formal campaign platform but quickly defended his public record. Already under attack from his three opponents, Morrison not only had to justify his support of McNinch but also had to explain his position as a wealthy man sympathetic to big business. Bowie, Grist, and Reynolds pressured Morrison incessantly on these issues, keeping him on the defensive throughout the campaign.

Senator Morrison loved political campaigning. Journalist Carl Goerch, writing in the *Raleigh News and Observer*, assessed Morrison as a man who "likes a good scrap and gets keen enjoyment out of it. Give him a choice of two campaigns—a peaceful one and one that is filled with all sorts of belligerency—and he'll take the latter one every time." Morrison reminded Goerch of a "grey-headed cyclone," and Goerch loved to hear his booming voice, which "sounds like waves breaking around a lighthouse."[35]

Wilbur J. Cash, a keen observer of the South and less charitable in his views of Morrison, described the senator as a man who had gotten himself "into the saddle as the arch-paladin of the dry South in its crusade to save the Democratic party from the Demon Rum in 1932." Although immensely gaudy, wrote Cash, Morrison had "no more showmanship in him than that innocent minimum which naturally inheres in any true protagonist of an essentially histrionic land." Cameron Morrison, concluded Cash, had gotten along simply by being himself.[36]

Despite Cash's unflattering portrait of Morrison, the *Raleigh News and Observer*, in an early assessment of the Senate race, rated the battle-scarred old veteran as too strong for his three opponents. In fact, the newspaper believed that Morrison was in much better shape to retain his seat than at any time since "he secured the Senate confirmation of Frank McNinch and put the Duke Power Company in the same class with the benevolent Moose." Morrison would win easily, argued the *News and*

Observer, because his three opponents would split the opposition vote and because none of the three was highly regarded as a candidate. Most experts agreed that Reynolds and Grist had almost no chance to defeat Morrison, and it was doubtful that Bowie could muster enough support for victory.

The Raleigh paper observed that although Reynolds had managed to get ninety-one thousand votes on a platform of youth, personal popularity, and showmanship in his Senate race in 1926, few conceded him any chance to win. Yet the *News and Observer* admitted that he "may again surprise the state with a sizeable total." It might be hard to oust Reynolds in the first primary, deduced the Old Reliable, as the paper was known in eastern North Carolina, because Reynolds had seen a turn in the prohibition tide, which even in conservative North Carolina he saw as "a fine chance to get into the lead."[37] The *New York Times* agreed that the raising of the prohibition question in North Carolina was highly significant. The *Times*, with remarkable insight, noted that the prohibition issue, along with the issue of party regularity and the statement by Reynolds that he was running to see if a poor man could be elected to the Senate from North Carolina, presented the possibility "of as merry a campaign as the state has ever seen. If he [Morrison] can keep the campaign on a question of personality, there should be little doubt of his winning. If it becomes one of issues, he may find himself on the wrong side."[38] The senatorial campaign started slowly, overshadowed by the gubernatorial race. From the outset, Morrison was supremely confident of victory and noted that "everyone that can't get any other job or political office is announcing against me. They ought to run for President. It would do 'em about as much good and get 'em just as much publicity."[39] In October 1931 Morrison predicted that he would carry ninety-five of the state's one hundred counties and doubted if his wet opponent, Bob Reynolds, would carry a single county.[40]

A confident Morrison decided to leave the majority of the campaigning to his friends and the Gardner-Bailey machine, choosing to remain in Washington until the final weeks of the campaign, when, if needed, he would return for a whirlwind tour of the state.[41] Morrison's monumental overconfidence did not seem misplaced. The Democratic Party hierarchy preferred Morrison, and in January 1932, O. Max Gardner indicated to Morrison that he would work hard for his election.[42] Party leaders were certain that Morrison would win handily. Gardner thought that Frank Grist's attacks on Morrison were ineffective and had discredited Grist as a candidate.[43] Gardner, however, despite his promise to work diligently for Morrison, devoted much of his time and energy to the election of gubernatorial candidate J. C. B. Ehringhaus because he assumed Morrison was as good as elected.

Senator Morrison exerted considerable pressure on Senator Bailey to support him publicly and believed that Bailey should have already announced for him.[44] Bailey's close friend Judge James S. Manning advised him that there was talk in

A Word About Robert R. Reynolds

Mr. Reynolds was the first Democratic Solicitor of his district, redeeming it from the Republicans after one of his famous personal campaigns. In his race for Lieutenant-Governor of North Carolina he was runner-up and entitled to call a second primary, but he refused to do that in order to save the State the expense. One of his opponents in this Senate race ran far behind Mr. Reynolds when both of them ran for Lieutenant-Governor. In 1926 Robert R. Reynolds received 93,000 votes against the veteran Senator Overman. He was Presidential Elector for his district and spoke all over North Carolina at his own expense.

Mr. Reynolds' Platform·

"I SHALL MAKE CLEAR my position on every question that has burned its way into the consciousness of an harassed people, and I shall not paramount insignificant issues in an attempt to dodge the real ones.

"In the beginning, I favor a modification of the national prohibition laws, and if elected to the United States Senate I shall use the power and influence of that great office to effect a change in this unfortunate enactment. I believe the ends of real temperance and sobriety have been defeated by the attempt to enforce artificial restraint upon a people who were reared in liberty and tolerance.

"We have tried prohibition for 13 years, and I feel convinced that it is the true consensus of sound public thought in this State and Nation that the experiment has proven a failure. It has been the means of building up a prison population that appalls the nation, while other countries of the world, being less drastic in their experiments with social reforms, have witnessed a steady decrease in their criminal population. We have opened the road and rendered encouragement to the nefarious trade of bootlegging, upon which gangsters and racketeers have built up impregnable empires to threaten the peace and tranquility of the nation. Only by removing from them the opportunity will we restore the country to the decent and law-abiding citizenship whose glorious heritage it rightfully is.

"I am not half so strongly in favor of a revision of our prohibition laws as I am opposed to the evils that they have brought into existence. My appeal, therefore, is not to the liquor interest nor to the moral degenerates, but rather to the straight-thinking citizens who are sick and weary from our calamitous dose of political hypocrisy which has been fed to us for 13 years from a tarnished spoon of morality. I have the utmost sympathy for the moral and religious forces of our country, respecting the great leadership they have given us; but nothing is infallible save divine decree. Although the attempt has been consistently made to confuse the prohibition issue with religious fortitude, the people have become so oppressed and depressed over its sad consequences that I believe they are convinced the way to advance wholesome religious thought in the nation is to remove it from the mouths of seeking opportunists who cover up their own dissimulation with an acquired blanket of an ill-used Christianity. I am tired of forever confusing religion with an economic and social question like prohibition."

Reynolds's platform on prohibition for the 1932 Senate campaign, emphasizing the evils that resulted from prohibition. Reynolds promised to end "this unfortunate enactment" if elected to the Senate. (Josiah W. Bailey Papers, Duke University Library)

North Carolina that Bailey had not come out for Morrison because Bailey desired Morrison's defeat—which would make Bailey the senior senator from the state. Manning credited these rumors to the Reynolds's camp. Manning thought Morrison would win but feared that the senator could face a difficult race without immediate aid from Bailey and other state leaders.[45]

Bailey replied that he had decided not to come out publicly for Senator Morrison because it was a tradition in North Carolina for one senator not to name the other. Because both Tam Bowie and Bob Reynolds had assisted Bailey in his 1930 senatorial campaign, Bailey decided he owed them enough to remain neutral. He did not plan to make any public statement on the election unless forced to do so. "I am for Morrison and intend to let my friends know that I am for him, but I shall not go to the extent of doing anything that would give the other candidates just ground for criticism."[46]

Lindsay Warren, the influential congressman from Washington, North Carolina, typified the attitude of the congressional delegation from his state: "I have had nothing whatever to do with the Morrison campaign, and have written no one. I voted for Morrison and will do so again, but that is the extent of my activity."[47]

The Democratic Party leaders in the state remained certain of Morrison's victory throughout the campaign.[48] Neither Bailey nor Gardner gave his full assistance to Morrison,[49] and their limited participation provided a significant advantage to Reynolds.

Although bolstered by an intimate knowledge of the state and its people, Reynolds entered the race with several liabilities. Unlike Morrison, Reynolds had no statewide organization and no machine affiliation. He had a limited amount of money and no major bloc of support except for those opposed to prohibition. In addition, he was a wet in one of the staunch outposts of prohibition and had already been married three times—a sin according to the strict fundamentalist code of protestant North Carolina. He had not gone to war in 1918, and some considered him to have shirked his duty as a patriotic citizen.[50]

Furthermore, the great majority of newspapers were favorable to Morrison. The *Asheville Citizen*, because it could not in good conscience support the hometown Reynolds, refrained from editorial endorsement and initially gave his campaign limited coverage. The *Charlotte Observer* lent the full weight of its authority to the candidacy of Morrison, and the *Greensboro Daily News* declared that it would be a great shock to North Carolina if Reynolds were elected. "It would probably be more of a shock to Bob than to anyone else."[51]

In an attempt to overcome the bias of the daily press, Reynolds had to resort to colorful campaign oratory to ensure that the press carried his ideas to the people. Despite his campaign's shortcomings, Reynolds exuded confidence and welcomed the opportunity to joust with his opponents. His campaign received a welcome assist from Frank Grist and Tam Bowie as they rained criticism on Morrison with deadly effectiveness. Reynolds applauded while Bowie and Grist piled on. Grist wanted to know if Morrison still believed, as he had stated in 1931, that the Duke Power Company was a benevolent institution doing more than any other business

Bob Reynolds and his fourth wife, the former Eva Grady, as they
campaigned across the state in the 1932 senatorial election.
(From the *Raleigh News and Observer*, July 17, 1932;
courtesy North Carolina Division of Archives and History, Raleigh)

for the suffering and distressed of the state.[52] Grist, by constantly associating Morrison with big business, helped Reynolds chip away at Morrison's political reputation.

Morrison declined an offer by Grist to debate on the ground that as a senator he was engaged in trying to enact important legislation to restore prosperity and did not have time for debates.[53] Grist then charged that Morrison did not have the moral courage to discuss the issues, concluding that "Senator Morrison is vulnerable and he knows it."[54] Grist also accused Morrison of trying to buy the election with all his millions, but he hoped that a poor man not controlled by big business could be elected senator.[55]

Tam Bowie, considered by Morrison's supporters as his most formidable opponent, claimed that Morrison's support of McNinch could be explained only because Morrison wanted to please the power companies.[56] But while Grist and Bowie lambasted Morrison successfully, the real show was put on by Reynolds, who hoisted his traveling bag on the back of an old Ford roadster and "rattled out of Asheville to seek a seat in the United States Senate in the most remarkable campaign ever perpetrated upon the commonwealth of North Carolina."[57]

Reynolds, a born showman, captured the imagination of the people and found the correct formula for victory by appealing to fears and prejudices heightened by the economic depression.[58] One reason for his success was that he loved mingling with the people and had that personal, intimate appeal of the old-style politician which enabled him to make the average person feel important and that he or she was Reynolds's best friend.[59] Tall, handsome, and cocky, Reynolds displayed a personal magnetism and courtesy that enticed women to attend his campaign rallies. He believed that the women's vote always played a large part in his political success, and he constantly paid court to women of all ages.

Bob Reynolds's original campaign resources consisted of a paltry amount of cash, an ancient Model T Ford, a fancy menu from the exclusive Mayflower Hotel (where Morrison stayed while in Washington), and a jar of caviar.[60] On the stump, Reynolds dressed in ragged suits and worn-out shoes.[61] He would abjectly describe his own poverty-stricken status in life and chastise Morrison for his affluent station.[62] Reynolds realized that the campaign of a poor man of the people would be the most effective strategy during a time of economic dislocation. Although he did not appeal to racist sentiments, he did seek to make capital of the social discontent of the day.

The richer he could make Cam Morrison appear, the poorer Reynolds seemed to be. With biting satire, he described how Governor Max Gardner had "taken Morrison from his magnificent estate, his silken robes and his luxurious chairs to place him in Washington as representative of the common people of this state."[63] He frequently referred to his opponent as "my rich friend Mr. Morrison" and advocated reducing taxes for the little people by increasing taxes on the wealthy corporations.[64]

Reynolds often solicited contributions for gas to get to the next town. On occasion, he would borrow fifty cents for gas and repay the lender with a generous check for one dollar. Most of the checks were never cashed but were retained as souvenirs.[65] Reynolds claimed that he started the campaign with only two dollars and usually waved a couple of one dollar bills at the crowd, calling on the Almighty to witness that the sum total of his worldly goods was in his hands.[66] Brash, breezy, and charmingly effusive, Reynolds often talked his way out of his hotel bill and collected the manager's vote while doing it. Despite a lack of funds (he often had to return to Asheville to practice law for a week to raise enough money to return to the campaign trail), by the spring of 1932 Reynolds had turned a liability into an asset.[67]

The ramshackle Ford roadster driven by Reynolds invariably happened to run out of water when he was entering a small town (he stopped on the outskirts and emptied the radiator). He would ride into town with steam pouring out of his radiator and some of his supporters pushing the car. Apologizing for his tardy arrival—"sorry to keep all you wonderful people waiting"—he would then launch into his speech.[68] Between villages, however, Reynolds managed to make excellent time.[69] This act did not play well in the larger cities but was effective in the rural parts of the state.

In almost every speech, Reynolds, after elaborating on his own poverty and with exaggerated gestures, would attack and mimic the pomposity of the prosperous Morrison while the locals grabbed their sides in glee. Reynolds denied that he was related to R. J. Reynolds, the tobacco king. If he were, Bob cried, he would not be running around the state "in a rickety old Ford. I would buy me a big beautiful car like Cam Morrison's." Reynolds explained that after a day's work in the senate, Morrison's chauffeur drove him in his Rolls Royce to his suite in the fashionable Mayflower Hotel. When he got up to Washington, Reynolds announced, he was "not going to have a foreign made car and live at those swell hotels." He then played the part of Morrison's footman and rolled out a red carpet for Morrison to step on while alighting from the Rolls. Switching to the role of Morrison, he would ape the senator's voice and stride as he stepped from his long, shiny limousine.[70]

Reynolds continued his performance by telling his listeners that Morrison had rolls of money longer than toilet paper and that after Morrison reached his suite in the Mayflower, he put on full evening dress—"he can not eat in every day clothes like you and I do." Morrison, according to Reynolds's scenario, then went to the palatial dining room in the hotel. Reynolds proceeded to consult the expensive-looking menu from the restaurant and commented on the huge sums that Morrison allegedly spent on food. He pictured his opponent as a glutton who spent many hours each day devouring fancy cuisine. Knowing that many of his listeners were undernourished and hungry, Reynolds stressed the menu for all it was worth. In a sarcastic tone, Reynolds asked. "What do you think he eats? He does not eat cabbage nor turnips nor ham and eggs, nor fatback like you and I do. My friends, think of it, Senator Morrison eats caviar."

Because very few listeners had ever heard of caviar, someone would usually ask, "What the hell's caviar?" Reynolds would immediately hold up a jar of caviar and shout to his awed listeners, "This here ain't a jar of squirrel shot; it's fish eggs. Friends, it pains me to tell you that Cam Morrison eats fish eggs—and Red Russian fish eggs at that and they cost two dollars. Now let me ask you, do you want a senator who ain't too high and mighty to eat good ole North Carolina hen eggs or don't you?"[71] Reynolds, fanning the flames of religious bigotry, told the crowd that Morrison also ate "eggs Benedictine. They's regular hen eggs alright, but they's cooked up by special Benedictine monks that they keep there in the hotel just for that purpose."[72]

The crowd roared with laughter as Reynolds carried out his pantomime, and his antics assured Reynolds of large, enthusiastic crowds. The *American Mercury* saw Reynolds's onslaughts on Morrison's aloofness and the baronial splendor of his mansion as effective because the voters wanted a senator who would go among them in the flesh and help banish all their troubles.[73] In the darkest days of the depression Reynolds had found an effective formula by appealing to the common people with his satire on the luxury surrounding Morrison. In a perceptive comment, Reynolds said that Morrison "started trying to laugh me out of this campaign but it seems I'll wind up by laughing him out."[74]

Despite the semicomic nature of the campaign, Reynolds had clearly touched a nerve on the body politic. The poor people of the state were angry, bewildered, and frustrated by the economic dislocation of the day. Tobacco farmers had been especially hard hit. Tobacco exports had declined by 40 percent between 1930 and 1932, while tobacco prices had fallen from 17.3 cents a pound in 1928 to 8.4 cents in 1931. By the end of 1930 over 150,000 pieces of farm property were on sale for nonpayment of taxes, and in Nash County alone there were 3,500 foreclosures on its 5,280 tobacco farms. In addition, banks collapsed with a loss of over $103 million, and middle-class depositors lost their life savings. By 1932 over one hundred thousand industrial workers were unemployed in the state, and the furniture and textile industries were on a two- or three-day workweek; an estimated 25 percent of North Carolina's citizens were on relief rolls.[75]

The residents of the state were also acutely aware of the maldistribution of wealth in America. In 1929 the richest 20 percent of American families received 54.4 percent of the nation's personal income, with the upper five percent receiving 30 percent of the personal income. The poorest 40 percent of American families had to share only 12.5 percent of the nation's individual income. While the average citizen did not know these percentages, they understood the gross disparity of income and resented the wealth of the few. The average wages of those fortunate enough to have a job indicated the depth of the economic crisis. Average wages had dropped from $24.69 per week in 1929 to $16.65 in 1933. With bread at seven cents a loaf, milk at ten cents a quart, and eggs at twenty-nine cents a dozen, 1933 wages were woefully inadequate.[76]

Statistics alone, of course, did not reflect the harsh conditions of citizens trying to survive the depression. A letter written by a widow from Weldon, North Carolina, with three children expressed the fear and desperation of many Tar Heels. She asked President Franklin D. Roosevelt (FDR) for help because she had fallen ill and could not pay for her food and rent. "I feel I can't go on. So please help me I am desperate. . . . I am most frantic with depression." A thirty-four-year-old "colored woman" with four children wrote to President Hoover (she assumed he was still in office) asking for assistance. She wanted help in getting a job to "Get me Some Clouse an Shoes." She promised to do her best—"all I want is a Chance & I well Prove to the world that I can Come up the hill in Stead of goin Down." And from High Point yet another poor mother, this time with seven children, asked President Roosevelt for underclothes "or we will freze to Deth this cold wethr." She ended her poignant letter to FDR with a final plea: "no way to get any please help me please."[77]

Thus, by attacking Morrison and big business, Reynolds gave the poor citizens of the state a focus for their anger and discontent. By presenting himself as their savior, he gave them a symbol and some hope for a better future. Reynolds effectively combined his satire of Morrison with attacks on the centralization of government and the greed and power of Wall Street. He consistently blamed big business for the depression and constantly advocated restoration of the government to the people. "Special privileges created by the government have created monopolies, fattened big business, made millionaires of a few and reduced many to poverty. The rich are getting richer and the poor are getting poorer." Reynolds wanted the tax burden placed on those who could and should bear it.

Reynolds repeatedly asked for repeal of the Eighteenth Amendment, a guarantee of all bank deposits, a balanced budget, elimination of waste, immediate collection in full of all foreign debts, and payment of the bonus to World War I veterans. He wanted all undesirable aliens deported as there were "too many bomb-throwing racketeering foreigners in this country now, so let's clean house before it is too late." He believed that power should be sold at fair rates. Such companies as Duke Power, shouted Reynolds, were gobbling up America's natural resources, overcharging for service, and shifting the tax burden to the shoulders of the little people. Our Bob usually closed his talks by saying, "I am of the plain people, they are with me and I am with them; we are in accord."[78]

Reynolds saved some of his venom for the Republicans and blamed the Hoover administration for the depth of the depression. He ridiculed the antihoarding campaign of Hoover and told farmers that if they valued their money they should hide it in their socks. He called the Reconstruction Finance Corporation a dole to the rich and greedy.[79]

The peripatetic Reynolds often referred to the McNinch affair and called Mc-Ninch the "arch enemy of North Carolina Democracy." Morrison's support of McNinch had been ill-advised, argued Reynolds, for McNinch had done so much to knife North Carolina Democrats in the back.[80] In a delayed reaction, Morrison complained about the attacks on him and said that he had been the victim of "infamous slander." He seemed pained and surprised that anyone would attack him because of his record as a Democrat or his wife's wealth.

Promising to keep his campaign expenditures within the limits prescribed by law (twelve thousand dollars in the first primary), Morrison returned to the state in the middle of March and made three effective speeches. After recounting his contributions as governor, Morrison said he would gladly concede any county to any of his opponents if they could prove that they had done more for the Democratic Party in that county than Morrison had done. His speeches temporarily aroused his supporters and increased confidence in the Morrison camp.[81]

Reynolds responded immediately with a speech before an enthusiastic crowd of eight hundred. Reynolds opened with a reference to Morrison's claim of great service to the party: "Upon what meat does this our Caesar feed that he has grown so great?" Reynolds said the Democratic Party owed a debt to no man but that all were indebted to the party. Besides, when Morrison claimed to have done more for the party than anyone else, "he must have been talking about the Republican Party. The first thing he did after he got to Washington was to reward a man with a $10,000 job for treachery to his party." Then, continued Reynolds, Morrison got up and eulogized the Duke Power Company as a charitable and benevolent institution. Pausing for two beats, Reynolds added, "He must have thinking about what it had done for him."[82]

By mid-March 1932, Reynolds realized that he had found a hot issue in prohibition. Opposition to the Eighteenth Amendment literally swept the state, especially in the rural districts. Reynolds told everyone that taxes should be taken off land and placed on liquor.[83] He was not running on a liquor platform; rather, he was for temperance, sobriety, and the control of liquor.[84] To Reynolds, prohibition did not "prohibit, has never prohibited, and will never prohibit. It has broken down respect for law and heaped upon our shoulders taxes that are intolerable and unbearable."[85]

With a moderate approach advocating temperance, he hoped to oppose prohibition without alienating all the drys. Prohibition, noted Reynolds, with its

"The ends of real temperance and sobriety have been defeated ... "—Reynolds' Platform to the voters of North Carolina

CAMPAIGN HEADQUARTERS

For the liberal voters who are leading North Carolina out of Prohibition and into Temperance by sending

ROBERT R. REYNOLDS

To the United States Senate through the Democratic Primary in 1932.

"We are glad he stands by his convictions."—Salisbury Post.

"We will find out whether Al Smith was defeated because he was a wet or a Catholic."—Monroe Enquirer.

"Reynolds should be a candidate of consequence." —Lenoir News-Topic.

"Mr. Reynolds announces with a wet platform . . . It should be interesting."— High Point Enterprise.

"There might as well be a division of Tar Heel votes on Prohibition now as later."— Henderson Dispatch.

"His entrance in the contest will doubtless make it more interesting." — Charlotte Observer.

"Interest is bound to center upon his prohibition modification platform."—Watauga Democrat.

"Reynolds takes a plunge that no other politician has attempted."—Cleveland Star

"We applaud sincerity of belief wherever it is found." —Charlotte News.

"Reynolds rushed in where (others) feared to tread."— Greensboro News.

As late as March 1932, Reynolds's campaign stationery emphasized the importance of the prohibition issue. His "wet" stance helped him capture key votes. (Josiah W. Bailey Papers, William R. Perkins Library, Duke University)

bootlegging industry, did not promote temperance.[86] Liquor, he would assure his listeners, was "the most damnable affliction ever visited on mankind. It wrecks homes and hearts, and destroys lives. It eats away the tissues of the stomach and the cells of the brain. I hate liquor. I am fighting the same battle for sobriety that my mother fought when she stood at the gateway of her humble home with the white ribbon of temperance on her shoulder. I am not trying to bring liquor back. It is impossible to bring back something that never left."[87] Reynolds, of course, was a bon vivant of the first order and in his personal behavior paid scant attention to his stated views on temperance.

According to the *New York Times*, because Reynolds's candidacy served as a rallying point, wet sentiment in North Carolina was more aggressive in 1932 than at any time since the adoption of state prohibition in 1908. Although the *Times* expected Morrison to win, the increase in wet sentiment caused Reynolds's quest for office to be taken seriously. Nonetheless, North Carolina had been long regarded as a citadel of prohibition, and it seemed strange for a wet candidate to be a strong contender for a U.S. Senate seat.[88]

Some observers thought that the dry forces were not as well organized in 1932 as they might have been. The Anti-Saloon League's official endorsement of Hoover cost it the support of the Democratic Party in North Carolina,[89] and the resulting split reduced the influence of the league over the next four years. Daniel Whitener concluded that the demoralization of the Anti-Saloon League contributed "heavily, if not decisively" to the nomination of Bob Reynolds. Whitener claimed that Morrison, a staunch dry, received fewer votes because the drys were leaderless and confused owing to the decline of the Anti-Saloon League.[90]

Reynolds accelerated his fight against prohibition as his visits around the state convinced him that the people wanted a change. He found many individuals distressed at the lawless side of prohibition, whereas others simply wanted to take a drink of liquor and did not consider such an act a sin.

By the end of March, as Reynolds gained strength, several of Morrison's friends expressed concern. James S. Manning, for example, wrote Senator Bailey that he had encouraged Morrison to open a state headquarters with someone competent in charge. The failure to do so would cost him thousands of votes. At the very least the senator should devote more time to campaigning in the state, given that Reynolds was rapidly gaining ground. Morrison, however, refused to heed his friends' advice.[91]

Other Morrison backers believed the situation to be more critical than Manning did. Henry Moore wrote Lindsay Warren that Reynolds was forging ahead of Morrison and something had to be done and done quickly. It was absolutely necessary, concluded Moore, that Morrison pour effort and money into the battle if he expected to overtake Reynolds's lead.[92] William Bailey Jones thought Morrison was handling matters as ineptly as they could be handled,[93] Herbert G. Gulley found Morrison's campaign "badly organized,"[94] and J. C. Baskervill, in the *Asheville Citizen*, reported that the senator's campaign had been hitting plenty of bumps and ruts and he would be forced into a second primary against either Reynolds or Grist.[95]

Bob Reynolds clearly understood the shifting tide in the race. He wrote Senator Bailey on March 17 that he had Morrison on the defensive and "right at this hour he is a defeated man." Reynolds predicted that he would get twenty-five thousand votes more than his three opponents combined: "Mark my prediction."[96] On April 8, in Greensboro, he publicly predicted an overwhelming victory over Morrison,[97] and although Reynolds's views were not widely accepted by the public, those close to the political heartbeat of the state recognized that Reynolds had taken the lead in the race.

Eventually, because of the vicious assaults from his opponents, the increasingly successful campaign of Reynolds, and warnings from his backers, Morrison returned to North Carolina to defend his record. But he delayed his arrival until early May, and by then the momentum had shifted even more dramatically toward Reynolds.

In his speeches Morrison seldom attacked his opponents except to note that they had been singularly unsuccessful as political candidates.[98] He repeatedly denied that he was a defender of the trusts or that he was subservient to any special interest group. "No group has ever given me orders, and so help me God, none ever will."[99]

Speaking before twenty-five hundred people in Greensboro, Morrison denounced his opponents for impugning his decision in the McNinch case. "They say that I voted to confirm Frank McNinch because the Duke Power Company made me do it. That is a lie, unadulterated, and the man who made the statement is a liar and a coward."[100] Morrison said that if he had not voted for McNinch, Hoover would have appointed someone not half so good and from another state. Morrison did not vote for McNinch because he was a friend of the power companies but because he was a lifelong friend and neighbor.[101]

As the Democratic primary neared its climax, Morrison demonstrated a new fire and vigor and spoke with the emotion and eloquence of old.[102] He explained that his adversaries had unfairly made his praise of the Duke Endowment apply to the Duke Power Company. The Duke Endowment, according to Morrison, was a great agency to benefit mankind, and it was for the foundation and not the power company that Morrison had words of praise. Morrison hoped that this "infamous falsehood" would not be hurled at him again.[103]

Reynolds and Bowie refused to ease up on Morrison. Reynolds said that if power companies had been taxed properly while Morrison was governor, there would have been enough revenue to pay for the six-month school term and schoolbooks for every schoolchild in the state. Morrison, stated Reynolds, left a yellow streak across the state because of his unwillingness to tax power companies.[104] Bowie, in a vituperative onslaught, accused Morrison of trying to buy the election with "a dead man's money" (the estate of Mrs. Morrison's first husband).[105]

Morrison, pained by the remarks that he intended to buy the election, denied that he would ever use his money to purchase any votes. If it were not for his wife's money, Morrison complained, his opponents would never have run against him. His money was his biggest handicap, and the election had become "a question of whether I am going to lose my place because I married a noble woman who has some money. If I did not have six dollars and a quarter I could beat that bunch in 98 out of 100 counties in the state. All the harm Mrs. Morrison's and my money is to anyone is to the devil and the Republican Party."[106]

Morrison spent much of his time blaming the Republicans for the depression. The senator seemed to be running against the Republicans in November rather than against three Democrats in June. His friends, especially Senator Bailey, persuaded him that he would certainly lose to Bob Reynolds unless drastic changes were made.[107]

Morrison finally recognized Reynolds as his most serious challenger and trained his rhetoric on him. Reynolds's wet platform, noted the senator, was against the position of the Democratic Party, which had always been opposed to liquor. The aging senator then made a statement that would come back to haunt him. Any Democratic candidate should stand on the state party's dry platform: "I am a Democrat," boasted Morrison, "and a dry. But if the party decided in favor of a wet platform, I would string along with them, or give way to someone who would abide by that platform. But until they do, can we afford to nominate a man who is openly and arrogantly wet, and have him run on a dry ticket? To do so would place the party in a position so embarrassing that it would never be able to live it down."[108]

Morrison then adroitly tried to draw the voter's attention away from the liquor issue by declaring that if Reynolds were elected it would mean that all the other issues would have faded out in deference to the question of prohibition.[109] In a last-ditch effort to win, the Morrison forces pressured the Women's Christian Temperance Union for assistance but without success.[110]

Morrison, now cornered and fighting for his political life, turned on his tormentors and tried to refute the "malignant" attacks on him. In late May, in a speech in Asheville, Morrison intoned that Reynolds had "been down in my section cutting up as the showman you know him to be. He's been making sport of me, and I think I'll make a little of him."

Reynolds, continued Morrison, was born into a wealthy family. When the campaign started, declared Morrison, Reynolds dispensed with his Cadillac and his airplane, dressed himself in old clothes, and drove a Model T around the state claiming that he was poverty stricken while "making fun of an older man with whom he had never had any unpleasantness." All of Reynolds's actions, charged Morrison, were part of a conspiracy "by people outside of the state to destroy me and elect a man with their money who they hope will represent them instead of the people of North Carolina."

Morrison enthusiastically carried his counterattack across the state and spoke to large and receptive crowds. After hitting out at Reynolds, Morrison again turned to Hoover and the Republicans, charging them with ineptness and indifference to suffering. Encouraged by the positive reaction to his speeches, Morrison bravely predicted that he would win a plurality in ninety-eight of the counties in the state and would win a majority in most of them.[111]

Morrison, in his last two speeches, concentrated his invective on Reynolds. He denounced Reynolds as a consistently unsuccessful candidate who would continue to be unsuccessful. Morrison emphasized Reynolds's lack of experience by distributing around the state flyers titled "The Deadly Parallel." One side of the flyer listed Morrison's achievements as a politician and governor, whereas under Reynolds's name there was only one listing—solicitor of Buncombe County.[112]

Morrison ended his campaign before a wildly demonstrative audience of one thousand adherents in Charlotte and replied to Reynolds's charges in a manner that would have made Reynolds himself proud. Referring to the remark made by Reynolds, Morrison stated that he was an old man and sixty-three years of age, but if Reynolds ever "stands up to my face and calls me yellow [again], I'll slap him full on the nose."

Morrison vigorously denied that he had ever employed any chauffeurs or that they had spread rugs out for him to walk on when he alighted from the car. He had, Morrison admitted, hired two local boys to drive for him, but they possessed the virtues of good citizenship and right living which made them vastly superior to Bob Reynolds. In addition, some of his supporters had measured Reynolds's Cadillac and found that it was ten inches longer than Morrison's car. Finishing with a flourish, Morrison accused his opponent of hiding in Florida during World War I to avoid service, of having his campaign paid for by the DuPont family, and of having six living wives.[113]

But other than these few last-minute diatribes against Reynolds, Morrison had waited too long to fight back and defend his record, assuming that his opponents were lightweights who could not match his record of service. In late May, Morrison's supporters believed that he would still win. Reynolds had been successful with his antiprohibition campaign, and the cumulative attacks of three opponents had hit home, but they hoped that Reynolds was more froth than beer and that there was more talk about Reynolds than real votes. They believed that many Democrats would feel awkward about having a wet nominee running on a dry state platform. Morrison's adherents worked hard with several final canvasses. His staff concluded that his decision not to use his wealth to buy the nomination was paying off. The senator commanded the support of the leadership of the state party[114] and counted on this powerful group of supporters to carry him to victory. Angus McLean, however, knew it would be a close contest and forecast a second primary between Reynolds and Morrison.[115]

In contrast, Reynolds was jubilant with visions of an upset victory. He predicted that the voters were going to take Morrison by "the nape of the neck and set him back in an easy chair in his luxurious Charlotte mansion." Reynolds said that Morrison's closing speeches were helping him so much that if he kept making them there would be no need for a second primary. Reynolds claimed that he had his opponent running all over the state—a good thing because "while he is here the interests of the common people are safe in Washington." Reynolds boasted that he had broken the Gardner machine and would be elected by twenty-five to forty thousand votes.

In his final appearance, Reynolds continued to play the part of the poor man and reported that he had spent only $1,361.38 on his campaign, far short of the $12,000 maximum allowed. Concluded Reynolds, "Unless I am nominated over the field by a big majority tomorrow I am the most badly fooled man in the world."[116]

Political experts in the state disagreed with Reynolds and forecast a lead for Morrison of fifteen thousand votes. Almost everyone agreed that there would be a runoff between Morrison and Reynolds. Some observers had enjoyed Reynolds's performance and had laughed at his verbal caricatures and sarcastic sallies against Morrison, but many wondered if good looks and a pleasing personality would be enough to elect a U.S. senator.[117]

When the votes were counted on June 4, 1932, political experts, newspaper editors, and three candidates were astounded. Only Bob Reynolds had not been fooled. He received 156,548 votes to 143,176 for Morrison, a plurality of 13,372. Tam C. Bowie received 38,548 votes, and Grist garnered 31,011. While not as large a victory as Reynolds had hoped for, it was a significant political upset. Reynolds's greatest strength was in the eastern part of the state and in an eight-county area around Asheville.[118] Even without a statewide organization and on very little money, Reynolds had defeated a wealthy incumbent when few observers gave him any chance to win.

Morrison's backers were "flabbergasted" by Reynolds's vote. The *Durham Morning Herald* felt that many of the state party leaders had been overconfident and had expended most of their effort to elect Ehringhaus.[119] E. R. Preston wrote Josiah Bailey that he had warned Morrison's advisers of impending doom but that his views were treated with "scorn and discourtesy."[120] Lindsay Warren also complained that it was impossible to advise the senator on anything. "I am hoping that he will now listen."[121]

The postmortem continued. James S. Manning thought Morrison trailed because of a lack of organization in many counties, the growing sentiment against prohibition, lack of money, and Morrison's egotism.[122] Thurmond Chatham, president of Chatham Blankets, believed prohibition was the key issue.[123] William Bailey Jones saw the outcome as evidence of widespread dislike of Morrison and feared that the senator could not overcome Reynolds's large lead.[124]

Another friend of Bailey's agreed that Morrison was in danger of losing his seat primarily owing to a poorly managed race: "What Morrison needs is workers, not fine names."[125] Senator Bailey, accused of deserting Morrison, replied that he had done all he could in "a proper way" to promote Morrison but that overt activity on his part to select his new Senate colleague would have been inappropriate.[126]

Finally, a Morrison supporter, E. G. Flanagan, warned that this election was different from any other because of the depression. It was not the better class of people who deserted Morrison "but the bootlegger, the riff-raff, and largely the ignorant farmer and unemployed." The best people, continued Flanagan, who thought Morrison would win, must now take off their shirts and go to work. Flanagan believed Morrison would win the runoff but advised him, through Bailey, to modify his position on prohibition.[127]

Backers of both candidates wondered if Morrison would heed the advice of his friends and speculated about how he could overcome Reynolds's lead.

CHAPTER THREE

[Culmination of the Dream]

Reynolds's unlikely triumph in the first primary became the topic of the day in diners, filling stations, and courthouses around the state. The Reynolds forces, flushed with victory, celebrated their triumph and hoped against hope that Morrison would not call for a runoff.

Political pundits believed that Morrison would win a runoff because all the drys who had not voted for Morrison in June would rally to his support. Moreover, Gardner, Hoey, and McLean, among others, promised Morrison their best effort. McLean stated that he was certain that on sober reflection the people of the state would return Morrison to Washington.[1]

The majority of the newspapers in North Carolina continued their advocacy of Morrison while attacking Reynolds. One editor described Reynolds as a man who had "gone up and down the state with his liquor issue, plus the tongue of a demagogue." It was no time, wrote the *Raleigh Times*, to send a comedian to the Senate, and Reynolds had "the making of a splendid vaudeville artist."[2]

On June 8, Senator Morrison, after a few days' delay, formally called for a second primary and established his statewide campaign headquarters in Raleigh.[3] Simultaneously, Bob Reynolds, eager to renew the contest, announced the opening of his headquarters in Raleigh, with John Bright Hill as manager.[4] Reynolds told the *New York Times* that he had hoped to spare the voters the expense of a second primary, but even with a formidable opponent, he expected that his impregnable position in the first primary would lead to victory in the second. Reynolds's campaign got a boost when Richard L. Fountain decided to call for a second primary against J. C. B. Ehringhaus in the governor's race. Fountain's candidacy would assure a good voter turnout and was a plus for Reynolds because Fountain had run best in Reynolds's strongest counties.[5]

Reynolds reported that he had received over six hundred letters from citizens who said that they had initially voted for Morrison but would switch to Reynolds in the runoff. Similar reports from all over the state led Reynolds to conclude that he would win by a margin larger than his previous vote.[6] In addition, a smiling Reynolds divulged that he had Tam Bowie's support. Bowie explained that he would back Reynolds because the combined votes of the other three candidates against Morrison—188,000 to 136,000—made it obvious that North Carolinians did not want Morrison in the Senate.[7]

On the day that Bowie declared his loyalty, Reynolds revealed that two months earlier, before witnesses, Frank Grist had also assured Reynolds of his support if Our Bob led in the first primary.[8] Grist, however, said that he had not made up his mind.[9] On June 14 Grist surprised everyone by endorsing Morrison. Although he had made vicious attacks against Senator Morrison in the contest, upon reflection Grist had decided that Morrison was far superior to Reynolds and referred to Reynolds as a "slacker" for his failure to serve his country in World War I.[10]

On the day of Grist's announcement, former senator Furnifold Simmons, an old enemy of Morrison, put aside personal animosity and came out for the incumbent senator. Simmons believed that Morrison was best qualified for office by reason of ability, training, and experience.[11] The endorsement by Simmons, unpopular and powerless since his bolt from the Democratic ticket in 1928, turned out to be a burden rather than a boon for Morrison.

Reynolds, meanwhile, thought it expedient to answer the charges against his war record. He bitterly denied that he had in any way refused to do his duty and called Grist's charges an "out and out falsehood." Reynolds explained that he had registered as required (although as a father to two motherless children he was entitled to an exemption), passed his physical, was inducted into service and sent to camp, but the armistice was declared before he could see action. Such "slacker" charges, declaimed Reynolds, were assaults on every man who honorably awaited his call in the draft.[12]

At the Democratic Party state convention, held in Raleigh in mid-June, the issue of prohibition was paramount. The wet sentiment, fueled by Reynolds's campaign rhetoric, had become so powerful that the party was forced to work out some sort of accommodation.

After much wrangling, the convention adopted a compromise plank in which the party pledged support for the Eighteenth Amendment as long as it remained in the Constitution. The statement noted that while prohibition should be enforced, the people had the right to amend the constitution by legal methods. This vague endorsement of prohibition, which one critic called "a string of platitudes meaning nothing," was adopted by a vote of 1,758 to 511. Many of the wet delegates voted for the compromise because it would allow the party to take advantage of the wet sentiment in the state without departing from the dry position.[13]

Morrison, stubborn to the end, refused to accept the compromise, saying, "I am willing to die politically for prohibition."[14] Reynolds, on the other hand, readily accepted the agreement as he felt certain that the national party would vote for a wet platform and that Morrison, a stalwart and consistent believer in party regularity, would then be trapped. In addition, Reynolds wanted to avoid a bitter and acrimonious debate over prohibition which might split the party and endanger Reynolds's chances against the Republicans in November.[15] Reynolds understood the deep-rooted and widespread commitment to prohibition in the state and did not want to antagonize the drys more than necessary.

As campaigning resumed, O. Max Gardner observed a determined effort by the Morrison camp to convince the thinking people of the state that their candidate's experience made him the superior choice. The difficulty, believed Gardner, was that Morrison's followers were "lacking in enthusiasm, whereas the Reynolds group is filled with the wine of optimism and are very aggressive and militant."[16]

Despite his first primary defeat, some political gurus expected Morrison to win the runoff. They conjectured that thousands of votes cast in the first primary were not for Reynolds but protest votes against prohibition or to chastise Morrison for the McNinch affair. With their protests registered, these voters would switch to Morrison. While admitting that Reynolds's outgoing, enthusiastic campaign style was effective, the pundits simply could not envision a wet winning the campaign.

Morrison's campaign strategy was to characterize Reynolds as "nothing more than a good-natured and entertaining comedian" who lacked the basic qualifications to be a U.S. senator. Morrison willingly admitted some mistakes, especially voting for McNinch, but he presented himself as an honest man, a better candidate than Reynolds, and one who had been sufficiently chastised.[17]

J. C. Baskervill, writing in the *Asheville Citizen*, took exception to Morrison's scenario. He saw prohibition as the key issue and believed antiprohibition sentiment was increasing daily. He thought Reynolds would win easily because he would get most of the Bowie and Grist votes, which were anti-Morrison.[18]

Although Reynolds's followers resumed their election efforts immediately after the state convention, the candidate himself did not hit the stump hard until June 21, only eleven days before the vote. Once he began, however, he campaigned as though he expected to lose, making five speeches a day in a whirlwind tour of the state.[19]

Our Bob, who gloried in pressing the flesh and mingling with the crowds, reemphasized his platform while increasing his emphasis on prohibition. A cocky Reynolds noted that nine months ago, when he had come out in opposition to the Eighteenth Amendment, politicians in Raleigh "would cross to the other side of the street for fear of having to shake hands with me. When I go down Fayetteville Street in Raleigh today, politicians leap from the third story window to pat me on the back." Reynolds constantly reminded the voters that Cam Morrison could never be the true representative of the people, as he was the representative of Max Gardner and machine politics.[20]

Reynolds continued to poke fun at the pompous Morrison, and on one occa-

sion he had significant and surprising assistance from Nell Battle Lewis, a columnist for the *News and Observer* and a Morrison supporter. Lewis concocted a
devastating caricature of Morrison.

> Through richly furnished chambers paced a distracted figure, spitting to-
> bacco juice at random and bellowing like a wounded bull. By attentive listen-
> ing one could make out in the verbal torrent phrases such as:
>
> Ah'm ruined! Ya-a-as, mah countrymen, ah'm ruined! Ah jes can't beat it!
> Mah heart is broken! Oh, Sarah, they've broken my heart. Mah own people,
> a-trying ter ruin me, repudiatin' their Guv'nor, th' greates' Guv'nor they've
> had sence th' Civil War;—disownin' an' malignin' an' forsakin' an' humiliatin'
> their devoted public servant who never had another thought outside th'
> welfare of Grandole N'th Carolina, . . . a-votin'against me in favor of a
> dripping Wet that wants ter bring back th' vile saloon an' that ain't never done
> nothin' fer th' State a-tall. By Gawd! No, Sarah, Ah ain't blasphemin', Ah'm
> just callin' on mah Maker in a time of stress,—Ah'm goin' to show 'em! Ah'm
> a-goin' ter show 'em with th' help of th' Almighty and yo' money, yo' blessed
> funds that you're using ter fight th' Devil in th' Presbyterian Church an' that
> Ah'm a-usin' ter fight him in the Democratic Party. It does sho' look like he's
> a-gainin' on us, Sarah, for this here primary is all his work. But gimme
> another plug er tobacco an' stan' by me, an' call up th' boys an' tell 'em ter
> come on over here, that Ah want ter talk ter 'em without interruption. I tell
> yer, I love Grandole No'th Carolina, Ah sho' do, and Ah'm a-goin' ter save this
> here con-trary, hog-wild state in spite of itself. An', Sarah, one thing mo', tell
> McNinch that I ain't home.[21]

Bob Reynolds loved repeating Lewis's satirical riposte, and emboldened by rapidly
increasing support, he pressed his attack.

The beleaguered Morrison remained on the defensive. In an astonishing decision for a man who trailed in the first primary, the senator announced that he
planned to stay in Washington until the last week of the contest. His followers
eventually persuaded him to go home and fight for his seat. When Morrison finally
agreed to return to North Carolina, he admitted that he might have been a little
overconfident in the first primary, but he still expected the "sober second-thought
of the voters would nominate him."[22] To the very end, Morrison never understood
his perilous situation—he simply could not imagine losing to a nonentity such as
Bob Reynolds.

Morrison met, belatedly, with political leaders in western North Carolina to plot
campaign strategy.[23] To revive his standing, his friends decided to circulate a full-
page advertisement in newspapers around the state. The ad called Reynolds's satire
of Morrison way out of proportion. The real Morrison, according to the ad, was

not the caricature presented by Reynolds but a longtime servant and defender of the people: "He is impulsive, but his impulses are for righteousness and justice. He is wealthy, but he is one man that good fortune has not spoiled. He himself had been poor so that wealth could not diminish his long identification with and sympathy for the poor." In troubled times, the ad concluded, there was no need for playboys or grandstand artists. What was needed was a man of honesty, courage, and loyalty—Cam Morrison.[24]

Morrison continued this theme in his speeches while stepping up his attacks on Reynolds. The senator told the crowds that he did not understand how the people of North Carolina could take up with a circus traveling about the country and kick Morrison out without the courtesy of a full term. Instead of evaluating his record, his enemies resorted to lies. Then along came this showman and got "the people all excited over the prospect of getting them drunk." Morrison feared that he was going to be defeated just because he was against liquor.

Speaking of his opponent, Morrison said: "I don't know of any record of Mr. Reynolds to analyze. He hasn't got any record. I don't know of anything he ever did so I can't attack any record." Morrison ended his fight for political survival with a plea for help from his old friends. "I'm the same old Cam I always was. They are just telling more lies on me than usual."[25]

Meanwhile, the Reynolds headquarters overflowed with confidence, in sharp contrast to the desperate state of Morrison's followers, who forlornly hoped that somehow the "silent voters" would send Morrison back to Washington.[26] At least one Morrison advocate, William Bailey Jones, was very apprehensive about Morrison's chances for victory.[27]

During the last week, Reynolds campaigned especially hard in counties won by Morrison in the first primary. Reynolds, certain that he had Morrison on the ropes, predicted that he would sweep the eastern part of the state "like a prairie fire" and would win by a majority of between forty and seventy-five thousand votes.[28]

Reynolds's quest for victory received a strong assist only two days before the second primary. The national Democratic Party, with the approbation of the North Carolina delegation, overwhelmingly adopted a plank favoring the repeal of the Eighteenth Amendment. The repeal would be achieved by a constitutional amendment proposed by Congress and submitted to the states.[29]

A delighted Bob Reynolds enthusiastically commended the frankness and courage of the national party in adopting the repeal plank.[30] The *Asheville Citizen* saw the plan for repeal as reflecting the sentiment of the great majority of the party delegates. By declaring national prohibition a failure, the Democratic Party had returned the liquor problem to the states where it belonged.[31]

Morrison now faced a dilemma. He could accept the repeal plank of the national party, which meant changing his earlier views and alienating his dry support, or he could continue his commitment to prohibition and be branded a party bolter. Morrison had earlier promised to go along with whatever platform the party chose, but knowing that either decision would cost him votes, he announced that he would continue his fight against liquor. He felt, correctly as it turned out, that if the question of repeal were submitted to the people of North Carolina, they would vote it down by a large majority. Morrison concluded that he would rather be "annihilated politically before I would sell my conscience to the liquor interests."[32]

And Morrison was annihilated politically. Although Morrison believed up to the final minute that the people would carry him to victory, the final returns gave Morrison an overwhelming defeat. Reynolds received 227,864 votes (65.4 percent) to only 120,428 (34.6 percent) for Morrison, the largest majority ever attained in a Democratic primary up to that time. Reynolds even captured Mecklenburg, Morrison's home county.[33]

When conceding defeat, Morrison pledged his support to Reynolds in the November general election. Reynolds, physically exhausted and weak of voice, gloried in the happiest moment of his life. After thanking his supporters, Reynolds asked loyal Democrats to forget the strife and passion of the primary and close ranks against the Republicans in the fall. He praised Governor Franklin D. Roosevelt, the Democratic nominee for president, and believed that Roosevelt would win. Reynolds acknowledged the great responsibility he had as a servant of the people of North Carolina and promised to be an honest spokesman on the issues. The people, he opined, "are tired of hokum and promises and politics for profit. I appreciate the compliment of this day to the utmost. I shall not fail them."[34]

Reynolds's overwhelming margin shocked both politicians and prognosticators. Senator Josiah Bailey, an astute political observer, wrote Morrison that he was amazed at the result of the primary, which he, along with many others, believed Morrison would win.[35]

The state's newspapers were also stunned by the size of Reynolds's triumph. The *Asheville Citizen* called it "one of the most remarkable victories in the history of North Carolina politics." Reynolds's majority, wrote the *Citizen*, was built by the vigorous and appealing effort made by the candidate himself. The Asheville paper explained that the tide of public sentiment was with him on his antiprohibition plank, and the tide rose swiftly and irresistibly.[36] The *Raleigh Times* saw the win as "a miracle," while the *Charlotte News* perceived Reynolds's victory as "probably without a parallel for sensation in the political life of North Carolina." Reynolds, noted the *News*, without any clear political capability or experience, routed a veteran who was supposed to be unbeatable. He won because he was flashy, dramatic, and warm-hearted and had a magnetic personality.[37]

The most amazing aspect of the contest was not just that the forty-seven-year-old Asheville attorney had defeated a pillar of the Democratic Party but also that he had won with a huge majority. Reynolds compiled his large vote even though he had never won a major office, had limited campaign funds, and was the first statewide wet candidate since the adoption of state prohibition in 1908.

How did a political maverick such as Reynolds forge his lopsided triumph? One of the most important factors was Morrison's years as an active politician. Morrison had a record to criticize, whereas Reynolds had no political career to defend. Josiah Bailey thought that in 1932 anything could happen in politics and declared that "the man on the outside has an incomparable advantage over the man that is in. The latter is in a position of performance and the former is in a position of promising, and promising is much easier than performing." Reynolds also won votes, argued Bailey, with promises to support the soldiers' bonus, to redistribute the wealth, and with attacks on the wealthy: "He caught the imagination of the distressed and the enthusiasm of the younger element in the party."[38]

Some analysts concluded that poor decisions (such as the McNinch vote) and inept campaigning had hurt Morrison badly. William Bailey Jones wrote that after all was said and done, "Senator Morrison defeated himself. You can count his errors by the score, both his and those of the people who managed his campaign."[39] The *Raleigh News and Observer* was convinced that the McNinch appointment alone would have been enough to defeat Morrison even if there had been no other issues.[40]

The *New York Times* commented that the vote for Reynolds certainly included a large number of anti-Morrison voters who wanted only to punish Senator Morrison and regarded Reynolds as the candidate with the best chance to win. Reynolds got the inside track in the election because of his colorful personality and his stand on prohibition.[41] A prominent eastern North Carolina Democrat who had excoriated Morrison for the McNinch vote explained his vote for Reynolds: "Well, they tell me that Reynolds can come nearer to defeating Morrison and that is what I want."[42]

Another cause of Morrison's defeat was his association, at least in the minds of the voters, with big business. Many Tar Heels viewed the rapacious greed of big business as a major factor in the economic dislocation in America and were convinced that these powerful economic interests were avoiding their fair share of taxes. When Reynolds pointed to Morrison as a symbol of machine politics and as a member of the wealthy class responsible for the depression, thousands transferred their abstract dissatisfaction into concrete opposition.

This latter view found support from such writers as Louis Graves of the *Baltimore Sun*, who called Reynolds's victory a "revolt against bigwiggery and stuffed shirtism."[43] According to *Plain Talk* magazine, the election was a victory of the people over special privilege because the voters resented Morrison's "gratuitous endorsement of the power trust."[44]

The campaign strategy and tactics employed by each candidate strongly influenced the voters' decision. The *Raleigh Times* explained that Morrison "relied on a self-satisfied valuation of a prestige he discovered too late was chimerical." Senator Morrison refused to listen to advisers, and he did not believe the McNinch vote would actually hurt him. In addition, Morrison, wrote the *Times*, took it for granted that the people of the state would flock to the polls to express their appreciation for his many years of service and administer a rebuke to the young upstart who dared to oppose him. He stoutly maintained that "my friends ain't agonna turn their backs on me."[45]

Moreover, Morrison's campaign was loosely organized, poorly conducted, and hurt by an unexpected show of parsimony in campaign expenditures.[46] Not only was Morrison late in starting, but his supporters became quickly dispirited as well. Morrison's headquarters, according to William Bailey Jones, packed up and left three days before the primary. Jones believed that the "senator seemed to be completely demoralized and his followers soon accepted his view of the situation."[47] In addition, Reynolds had labeled Morrison as the "machine candidate," but Morrison did not receive the full benefit of the organization because Gardner and his minions were more interested in electing Ehringhaus governor than in helping Morrison.

Morrison did not react decisively or promptly to the incessant badgering and criticism by his opponents. The aging senator assumed a weak, wounded, whining defensive stance while constantly complaining of being abused. He did not mount a serious counterattack, nor did he advance a positive program to end the depression until after the momentum had shifted to Reynolds.

On the other hand, a quick-witted Bob Reynolds "conducted a brilliant and vigorous campaign even if it were one of demagoguery. He made use of his engaging personality, his companionable ways, his pungent speech, and his sense of humor. His campaign was entertaining, shrewd, and he seemed to be completely sincere. It was smart to laugh in time of economic stress and Reynolds laughed Morrison right out of the Senate."[48] An Ohio newspaper claimed that "a stalwart young comedian had hoodwinked North Carolina and the Tar Heels had succumbed to the anesthesia of audacious demagoguery that was sweeping the country."[49]

Nell Battle Lewis felt Reynolds's large margin in the runoff was due to the increase in the wet vote. Many opponents of prohibition, declared Lewis, were temperate individuals who were against the hypocrisy of prohibition and the increasing disrespect for the law. The antiprohibition forces were tired of the expensive failure of enforcement and the great success of gangsters who made millions while poor people were sent to jail for making a few pints of "white lightning." Finally, the wets took advantage of the proposal to tax liquor and use the funds to help ease the effects of the depression.[50]

The *Wilmington Star* saw prohibition as the *only* issue in the campaign,[51] while the *New York Times* considered Reynolds's victory of tremendous significance because it showed that it was no longer political suicide for a candidate in the state to advocate repeal of the Eighteenth Amendment.[52] Josephus Daniels, editor of the *Raleigh News and Observer*, disagreed that prohibition was the single issue that led to the nomination of Reynolds: "The wet and dry issue was only 33 to 40 per cent of the Reynolds's strength." Daniels insisted that Morrison's vote for McNinch and the fact that people simply wanted a change had a more important bearing.[53] The *Richmond News Leader* was also not prepared to accept either prohibition as the decisive issue or that North Carolina, one of the driest states in the union, had gone wet with such a vengeance. "Reynolds undoubtedly got the vote of all the wets because he was for repeal, but he got a great many thousand votes because he is 'agin the government.' As we see it, resentment, not repeal, accounts for the size of his victory."[54]

The adoption of the wet plank by the national Democratic Party sealed Morrison's fate. Morrison later admitted that his speech reaffirming his allegiance to the cause of prohibition had cost him many votes. But he sincerely opposed the repeal of prohibition and felt he had to keep faith with his principles: "If I had played yellow on that it would have broken my heart."[55] Charles W. Tillett, a stalwart of the Democratic Party from Charlotte, wrote Senator Bailey that surely no candidate ever went up against as many bad breaks as Morrison: "After the National Convention adopted a wet platform only God Almighty could save Cam."[56]

The significance of Reynolds's prohibition stance was partially illustrated by the fact that of the twenty-seven counties that later established liquor stores, twenty-three had voted for Reynolds in the first primary and twenty-five in the second primary.[57]

Despite Reynolds's huge plurality, prohibition was not the key issue in the campaign. Reynolds certainly rode the rising crest of popular dissatisfaction with the Eighteenth Amendment, but this movement was symptomatic of the restive, discontented condition of the people and their clamor for change. North Carolina was a dry state before the election and remained so after the election. In November 1933, North Carolina refused to ratify the Twenty-first Amendment despite a national vote in favor of eliminating prohibition.[58]

Reynolds won his party's nomination in 1932 primarily because he captured the popular imagination by transforming the people's discontent with government, big business, the depression, and prohibition into a single campaign issue. He linked this desire for change with a personal attack against his opponent. O. Max Gardner, in a letter to Franklin D. Roosevelt, perhaps best analyzed the political environment in North Carolina in 1932: "Public opinion is in a state of flux. . . . It is a mistake to say that these currents of thought are wholly the creatures of demagogues. They spring naturally from the oppressed and bewildered minds of men. . . . They are really the mass thinking of people who have either been forgotten or deceived. Demagogues do not create movements. They merely ride upon them."[59]

Did Reynolds succeed due to a demagogic campaign? V. O. Key Jr., the distinguished political scientist, thought so. Key noted that North Carolina would not normally succumb to a demagogue owing to its progressive outlook in education, race relations, and industrial development. Reynolds's maverick candidacy and demagogic rhetoric, continued Key, appealed to voters in the plantation crescent in eastern North Carolina, the heart of the Black Belt, because they had traditionally been opposed to machine politics (a form of agrarian radicalism) and resented being excluded from power and prosperity by the "economic oligarchy of manufacturing and financial interests."[60]

Gerald Johnson, of the *Baltimore Sun*, agreed with Key about the demagogic quality of Reynolds's campaign. Johnson explained the Reynolds phenomenon with the theory that every southern state, as it advanced economically, went through a period of demagoguery.[61] In the *Uncertain South*, Charles O. Lerche Jr. also noted that Reynolds took advantage of the emotional discontent of the age. Once Bob Reynolds had aroused the citizens in a crusade to rectify injustice and controlled their mass movement, political victory was inevitable.[62]

Certainly Reynolds profited from what Angus W. McLean called a "state of revolution" in North Carolina, but Key and Johnson overstated the case in regard to Reynolds's demagoguery, as he never resorted to racism or to anti-Semitism in the campaign. Reynolds, in the ancient Greek meaning of the term "demagogue," viewed himself as a leader of the common people, one who made impassioned appeals to the voters' emotions but not to their prejudices. Reynolds sincerely believed that the depression had been caused by the selfishness of greedy corporate interests and that the politicians in power, including Cam Morrison, were controlled by special interests. Reynolds could be characterized as a "populist demagogue" who thought prosperity would return only when the government was restored to the people.

Yet Reynolds, despite taking advantage of a "state of revolution," was no revolutionary. While on the hustings, he sounded no clarion call for an economic or political revolution. With the exception of the payment of the veteran's bonus and insurance for bank deposits, Reynolds did not advocate any major change in federal government. He did not propose welfare reform, unemployment relief, or a plan for agricultural recovery.[63] He did, of course, want improvement in the living conditions of America during the Great Depression and, once in the United States Senate, voted consistently for Franklin Roosevelt's New Deal legislation. Reynolds, a perennial loser in state politics, could never have won statewide office except for the extraordinary circumstances of the year 1932. Without the depression and without a wealthy, inept, and overconfident opponent such as Cam Morrison, Reynolds would have lost.

Jonathan Daniels, associate editor of the *Raleigh News and Observer* and a Democratic national committeeman, who would later change his assessment, described Reynolds shortly after his triumph over Morrison: "He will make a new sort of Senator for North Carolina. Though he shouts 'the peepul' like a demagogue, he is a long distance from being one. He is something fresh among North Carolina politicians. He is simple and folksy and enormously enthusiastic about the fact of living. He meets voters like a friend and a good fellow without a trace of pompous patriot. Far from being simple-minded he is a genuinely simple-hearted man. He really loves people. And he has the marvelous quality of making people devoted to him."[64]

In North Carolina, nomination by the Democratic Party for any office assured success in the general election. Therefore Reynolds planned to avoid politics and concentrate on his law practice in Asheville until September. He would then wage an intensive campaign against his Republican opponent, Jake F. Newell of Charlotte.[65] Reynolds expected an easy victory.[66]

State Democratic leaders dismissed the idea, raised by Republicans, that Reynolds's wet stance would hurt the party in November. Clyde R. Hoey said that Reynolds had strength throughout the state and would add many independent voters to the party. O. M. Mull, a longtime leader in the Democratic Party from Winston-Salem, predicted that the Democrats would easily vanquish the Republicans in November.[67]

Although Reynolds tried to avoid politics until September, he did pay courtesy visits to the party leaders. The morning after the runoff he went to the governor's mansion to have breakfast with his old friend O. Max Gardner, who pledged his aid in the fall.[68] Reynolds also traveled to party headquarters in Raleigh and Washington, D.C., to confer with officials about the fall campaign.[69]

Shortly after his nomination, Reynolds became embroiled in his first major political controversy, the appointment of a new chairman of the state Democratic Executive Committee. O. M. Mull's resignation set off a prolonged dispute about his successor. Reynolds believed that the large majority given him in the recent primary entitled him to a significant voice in the selection of the man who would lead the campaign against the Republicans in November. The Gardner machine, still all-powerful in party politics, knew it could not totally ignore Reynolds in matters of patronage. Gardner, however, believed that Reynolds, despite his great popular support, would have little influence among organization Democrats, and Gardner expected to control the choices without opposition.[70]

After much discussion and controversy, the question of appointment of the new party chairman languished until August 9, 1932. Conferring with Senator Bailey on the eve of the meeting of the state Democratic Executive Committee, Reynolds learned that both Ehringhaus and Max Gardner had strongly endorsed J. Wallace Winborne. Although Winborne was an old friend, Reynolds refused to accept him because he was too closely allied with the power interests and had backed Morrison. The committee, however, ignored Reynolds and, bowing to the wishes of Ehringhaus and Gardner, chose Winborne as chairman and Mrs. Thomas O'Berry as vice-chairman. As a sop to the Reynolds forces, Winborne chose John Bright Hill, Reynolds's campaign manager, for the politically insignificant post of secretary to the committee.

After the appointments, party leaders made public speeches stressing the need for unity in order to defeat the Republicans in November. Ehringhaus warmly praised Reynolds as that "brilliant, young, dashing Democrat," while Reynolds, although pledging support to all Democratic candidates, failed to mention Ehringhaus by name. Reynolds was positive that on November 8 the three R's would win: "Roosevelt, Reynolds and reform."[71]

Reynolds smarted from his failure to exert more influence on the selection of party leaders, but he was a tyro in politics and could not expect to have much power in a state where the Gardner machine still ruled. In addition, Reynolds had always been an independent campaigner who did not rely strongly on aid from the party. He was not happy with his meager influence in the party, but he needed the Gardner machine in November, and a subordinate position was clearly preferable to an open fight over political spoils.

After spending most of August attending to his law practice, on September 17 Reynolds formally opened the fall contest with an old-fashioned barbecue and political rally. Although Gardner, Bailey, and Ehringhaus were present, the irrepressible Reynolds stole the show, going through a prolonged bout of handshaking and backslapping prior to the speeches. When announced, the crowd greeted him with a huge cheer. They had come to hear Reynolds denounce the Republicans, and he did not disappoint them. "My friends," exclaimed Reynolds, "up there in the Arctic, the nights are six months long. That's natural. But down here Hoover has changed the night to four years long. Only a national Democratic victory can restore the gleaming light." Hoover, continued Reynolds, had promised a chicken in every pot and two cars in every garage, but "if you find one chicken in a garage you're lucky." At the end of his speech, Reynolds was almost mobbed as hundreds of spectators crowded about him, tugging at his coat and trying to shake his hand.

Veteran political leaders and newspapermen said it was one of the greatest demon-strations ever given a single candidate in the state's history.[72]

Reynolds's opponent, Jake Newell, a political hack who campaigned as a dry, predicted that the dry forces would rally to his banner and send him to the Senate.[73] However, an unconvincing explanation about ties with organized liquor interests and his uninspired campaigning hurt his cause.[74]

After Newell criticized another state Republican candidate for passing bad checks, the staunchly Democratic *News and Observer* lowered the boom. "As a moral leader Mr. Newell is nothing if not new. Having taken part in the fight to keep North Carolina wet, he now sets himself up as the leader of the drys. Having voted to approve the record of the Hoover administration, he now finds himself and his party disgraced by a candidate being indicted on a bad check charge. For a man who has so much trouble with gnats, Mr. Newell is adept at the swallowing of camels."[75]

By late September, an eager Bob Reynolds was on the campaign trail in full cry. In every speech he excoriated the Republican Party with righteous indignation. He constantly assured the people of his compassion for their ills, and to drive home his points, the mountain orator was alternately sarcastic, enthusiastic, angry, and humorous.

At almost every stop, the large crowds, many clad in overalls, cheered Reynolds's blows against entrenched wealth and big business.[76] To Reynolds, the Republican Party stood "for class, for destruction, for greed." He did not blame the rank-and-file Republicans but their leaders.[77] "We are sick of the deadly normalcy of Mr. Harding, disgusted with the easy pickings and wild speculation of Coolidge, dis-tressed with the bull market and suffering of Hoover."[78]

With a certain élan, the Democratic nominee accused the Grand Old Party of allowing over $3.5 million in tax credits during the fiscal years 1923 through 1931, with most of this benefit going to ultrarich corporations. If this amount of money were resting in the federal treasury in 1932, thundered Reynolds, it would be sufficient to wipe out the national debt.[79] In the campaign of 1928, he continued, twenty-four wealthy men contributed $477,000 to the Republican Party and re-ceived over $14 million in tax refunds. "This was a splendid investment for these 24 men. The favored profited, the contributors were rewarded."[80]

Candidate Reynolds further accused the Republican Party of deceiving a trust-ing people with false statements about prosperity. "We can only judge the future by the darkened fields of the past, fields strewn with broken promises." The callous Republicans were not interested in the average person in the country and had not done anything to relieve the suffering caused by the depression.[81]

Reynolds harped on excessive spending by the Republicans during a depression. "Do you know that in the Senate building they use waste baskets that cost $47 apiece? And, furthermore, they have spittoons that cost $45. Now what I want to know is what kind of tobacco a man has got to chew to be able to spit in a $45 spittoon. I invite you all to come see me when I'm elected, but when you don't find one of them in my office, don't spit out the window, for you're bound to hit a Democrat."

Reynolds also disclosed that there had been great difficulty in arriving at a name for a new bridge built across the Hudson River. The best name suggested so far, announced Reynolds, had been Hoover Bridge, because "it's wet underneath, dry on top and faces both ways."[82]

Ridiculing Hoover's claims that prosperity was just around the corner, Reynolds identified the correct corner for Hoover. "It is a point between New York City and Houston, Texas, where Roosevelt Boulevard and Garner Avenue intersect and we are going to reach it on November 8."[83] His oratory was trite and his approach to the issues negative, but Tar Heel voters loved it.

Josephus Daniels, Clyde R. Hoey, and Josiah W. Bailey all campaigned for the Democratic ticket in November, while denouncing the Republicans. Bailey wrote letters to newspapers and constituents urging them to elect Reynolds, whom he felt would represent the state faithfully and support Roosevelt.[84] Distasteful as it must have been, even Cam Morrison paid tribute to Reynolds and urged citizens of the state to vote the straight Democratic ticket.[85] The Democratic Party, explained Morrison, did not always nominate the man that Morrison preferred, but they had never nominated a candidate that he could not honorably support.[86] Reynolds thanked Morrison for his approbation and called him "one of the grandest Democrats I know."[87] These warm sentiments were a far cry from the heated exchanges of June, but political expediency mandated that Reynolds and Morrison reconcile their differences.

By late October, it had become apparent that the Democrats in North Carolina would win a smashing victory. After seeking public office for twenty years without success, Bob Reynolds was about to be admitted to the most exclusive political club in America, the United States Senate. Reynolds acknowledged that over the years he had matured as a candidate: "I'm smart because I've sense enough to appreciate my limitations (and) because I know enough to seek the advice of men smarter than I am. And I'm smart because I'll always be just Bob Reynolds. When I'm elected I ain't going to puff up like a poisoned frog."[88]

Two nights before the election, Buncombe Bob returned to Asheville for a rally where he was greeted by a crowd estimated at ten thousand persons. The torchlight parade included numerous cars, the high school band, and placards proclaiming, "Roosevelt-Reynolds: Happy Days." A friend said that Reynolds had "aroused less antagonism, fewer animosities, and has been awarded more kindly admiration than any other politician in the history of the state."[89]

In the final days of the contest Reynolds again predicted a huge victory and urged listeners to "come up and see me in Washington."[90] On election day Bob Reynolds became the junior senator from North Carolina by defeating Jake F. Newell 484,048 votes to 221,534.[91] Reynolds, however, ran behind both Franklin Roosevelt, who polled 498,006 votes in the state,[92] and Governor J. C. B. Ehringhaus, who received 497,657 votes.[93] Nonetheless, it was a sweet and gratifying victory for Reynolds.

Reynolds wired heartiest congratulations to Roosevelt on his victory. Roosevelt responded with thanks and warm personal regards and expressed his desire to discuss issues of import with Reynolds sometime in the future.[94]

Jonathan Daniels, writing in the *Raleigh News and Observer*, described the junior senator from North Carolina as he savored his victory: "At 47 Robert R. Reynolds looks 47. But he does not act it. He speaks quickly, vigorously and with a flat-handed decision. He has rushed across North Carolina making his appeal to the voters with all the physical vitality of a boy of twenty. Robert Reynolds is still an erect, vigorous man. There is no paunch. There are no jowls. His youngish clothes are in almost collegiate disarray. His whole attitude is youthful. But there is a plumpness, a healthy plumpness, the plumpness of a wanderer home from the wars, a proper plumpness for a United States Senator."[95]

While the properly plump senator basked in the limelight, he began to make plans for his new responsibilities. He had been corresponding with Senator Bailey since July 4, when Bailey had offered his new colleague assistance with committee assignments and any other matters.[96] Reynolds wrote Bailey, thanked him for all his help, and asked advice as to when he could actually take office, when he could hire his secretarial staff, and, most important, when he could expect his salary to begin.[97]

Bailey responded in detail to these inquiries and offered to present Reynolds for the oath of office. Bailey had also discussed committee assignments with Senator Joseph Robinson and reported that Reynolds would have no trouble getting on the Committee on Military Affairs and the District of Columbia Committee. Reynolds again thanked Bailey, pledged his cooperation in patronage matters, and expected that they would "get along together happily" in Washington.[98]

Reynolds took office almost immediately after the November election, as he had been elected to fill both the unexpired term of Senator Lee Overman as well as the full six-year term beginning March 4, 1933. By virtue of taking his seat at noon on December 5, the first day of the session, Reynolds gained a distinct advantage in seniority.[99]

Reynolds took the oath of office with six members of his family and a group of over 250 of his friends. Reynolds expressed pride for the friends who came to Washington to see him enter the Senate. They "came in trucks, some in fine cars, and some in my old Ford, the one I campaigned in and on which I have just spent $42 to put in senatorial condition." It pleased Reynolds that his old Ford flivver was housed in the million-dollar congressional garage along with the Packards, Cadillacs, and other luxury cars. "It is right there in the corner, high hatting the big ones because we are now in society."

In spite of his cheerfulness and levity, Reynolds had unexpectedly achieved a lifelong ambition and was awed by his new surroundings. His formal acceptance speech demonstrated his awareness of the great responsibilities of his office and the critical times in which he was serving. The new senator began his job "without being under obligation to any man or group of men." He pledged to "conscientiously apply myself to the task at hand" and was "humbly hopeful that time and application will fit me for usefulness."[100]

Unfortunately for the people who had chosen Reynolds as their representative, neither time nor application would make Reynolds a great senator. In one sense, his astonishing victory in 1932 was the apex of his political career. In his public reaction to the victory over Cam Morrison, Reynolds mentioned that voters were tired of hokum and politics for profit. He quickly forgot these sentiments and spent his Senate years in style, entertaining the people if not legislating for them. But in December 1932, although his views on many issues had not been formed, political commentators and the citizens of the state had high hopes for Senator Reynolds's career as a man of the people.

CHAPTER FOUR

Early Years in the Senate, 1933–1935

When Bob Reynolds began the first of his two terms in the U.S. Senate, there was no indication of the isolationism, ethnocentrism, and liaisons with American fascists that would ultimately destroy his career. At the outset he was a loyal New Dealer trying to get along with his new colleagues.

Somewhat awed by his surroundings, Bob Reynolds respectfully followed party leaders on matters of policy while learning the ways of the Senate. Reynolds told the press, "I am new at the game and shall learn from the older gentlemen here." Although properly circumspect, his warm and outgoing personality allowed him to make new friends easily. Even the cautious Carter Glass said that the senator from North Carolina "seems to be a fine fellow."[1]

Reynolds was appointed to the Committee on Banking and Currency and the Committee on Military Affairs and was later assigned to the District of Columbia (D.C.) Committee, an assignment few senators coveted.[2] Reynolds explained that he wanted to be the political godfather of D.C. for one reason—jobs. He figured that he could get his constituents positions as inspectors or policemen and similar work that would put him in good stead back home.[3] Reynolds probably preferred the D.C. Committee because the work was less complicated and taxing than that on other committees and because he thought that he could rise to prominence on this committee more quickly.

His early mentors in the Senate were Senator Alben W. Barkley of Kentucky and Reynolds's new administrative assistant, Wesley E. McDonald Sr. A veteran on Capitol Hill, McDonald had worked for Senators Lee Overman, Cameron Morrison, and Carter Glass, and his knowledge of the workings of Congress was invaluable to Reynolds.[4] Reynolds hired Johnston Avery, a newspaperman and aide to him during the campaign, to oversee publicity. After only one month, however, Reynolds expressed dissatisfaction with his staff. He decided to "clean house" and gave Wesley McDonald a free hand in reorganizing the office. The staff had been inept in dealing with constituent mail, and over one thousand letters had gone unanswered. Failure to answer constituent mail during a depression could

Senator Bob Reynolds, May 1934. This was Reynolds's official portrait as he began
his senatorial career. (Pack Memorial Library, Asheville)

have been a potential disaster for a politician committed to serve all the people,
and Reynolds acted swiftly to avert such problems.[5]

Reynolds had campaigned for office as a poor man of the people, but shortly
after his arrival in Washington, he moved into the fashionable Wardman Park
Hotel, in faint imitation of Cameron Morrison's lavish lifestyle. Reynolds also
attired his tall, impressive frame with elegant and stylish clothes of rather startling
color combinations. One was never quite certain where Reynolds got the money
for elegant clothes and living quarters, but he continued, at least politically, to play
the part of a poor man and refused initially to part with his Model T.

In his first year as a senator, reporters in Washington complained that while Reynolds was genteel, friendly, and extremely likable, he was a flop as a news source. The news reporters expected another Huey Long and hoped for some controversial headlines, but all Reynolds wanted to discuss was his beloved Ford.[6] Nonetheless, reporters admired his style and personality. Ray Tucker, a writer for the *New York World Telegraph*, liked Reynolds because he was more affable, agreeable, and restrained than Huey Long. Reynolds, wrote Tucker, was rapidly becoming a popular figure in the Senate, for he told a good story and greeted people with warmth and enthusiasm.[7]

The *Asheville Citizen* praised Reynolds's friendly demeanor: "He may not leave a record in the Senate as a great legislator but history will rate him as one of the best mixers ever to sit in that august body." The *Citizen* reported that Reynolds had not introduced a bill and did not plan to. He spent all his time making friends with everybody from the senate majority leader to the elevator operator. His major objective, opined the paper, appeared to be to develop as many personal contacts as possible, for that meant more jobs for his followers in North Carolina.[8]

While in pursuit of new contacts, Reynolds renewed an old acquaintance when he ran into Huey Long in a Washington hotel. Long looked at the senator from North Carolina and inquired, "Don't I know you from someplace?"

"Not to my remembrance," Reynolds replied.

"You been to Baton Rouge, ain't you?" Long insisted.

Reynolds agreed that he had.

"Why then, sure I know you," said Long. "You used to run that roller skating rink down there."

Reynolds brightened. "That's right. And now I know you. You used to come in and win all the prizes for fancy skatin'. That's when you were down there sellin' snake oil."[9]

Burton K. Wheeler, a contemporary of both Long and Reynolds, liked Bob Reynolds and enjoyed his company. Reynolds, according to Wheeler, was a great ladies' man but also confident that he could ingratiate himself with men. Wheeler believed the one man that Reynolds could not impress was Huey Long. Wheeler's account of Reynolds's meeting with Long differed significantly from that above: when Long greeted Reynolds, Long said in a dismissive tone, "I knew you when you ran an ice-skating rink in New Orleans." This sharp remark, reported Wheeler, took the wind out of Reynolds's sails.[10]

Long and Reynolds, however, became close friends after this meeting, and on at least one occasion Long came to Reynolds's assistance by lending him a rather substantial sum of money.[11] Long frequently praised Reynolds in the Senate, and in early February 1933, Long said that Reynolds and Senator Richard B. Russell of Georgia "would be outstanding progressives" after the Democrats came into power in March 1933. "You just watch these two fellows. They'll be in the senate long after we've driven that gang of eastern diplomats out of business."[12]

Huey Long, "the Kingfish," had been elected to the Senate in 1930 even though his term as governor of Louisiana did not expire until 1932. Long's brand of Populism and his Share Our Wealth program fueled his popularity in both Louisiana and on a national level.

Unlike Reynolds, Huey Long on the Senate floor was boorish and rude and flouted Senate traditions at every opportunity. His arrogance and feuds with Democratic leaders, including President Roosevelt, made him a pariah in Washington. Driven by insecurity and a lust for greater power, Long came to despise Roosevelt and planned to run against him in 1936. Long used the Senate floor to attack entrenched wealth, to urge redistribution of the wealth, and, as always, to promote himself.[13] Reynolds, however, admired Long and remained a friend until Long's death in 1935.

Despite his proclivity for socializing, Reynolds had to deal with the harsh reality of the greatest depression in the country's history. Washington in 1933 was a madhouse—overcrowded and jammed with people fighting for positions in the new administration. Reynolds was besieged by telephone calls, letters, wires, and personal visits of a rather bewildering variety by numerous office seekers. The financial distress of many was so great that the unemployed were desperate enough to borrow money to go to Washington just to beg Reynolds for a job.

Hard pressed to recommend the proper person from the myriad applicants, Reynolds claimed that he had received six thousand applications for seven jobs. He understood that there simply were not enough federal jobs to go around no matter how much he would like to find positions for all who applied.[14] Reynolds complained that "we are having a frightful time here at the Capitol now. I see personally on the average of one hundred individuals every day who are seeking federal patronage and in addition we are receiving hundreds of letters from all over North Carolina." Reynolds explained that he was spending so much time on job seekers that he could not find time to take care of his legislative responsibilities.[15]

On one occasion a huge crush of office seekers gathered in front of Reynolds's office to ask his assistance in finding work. The size of the mob was so large that the senator had to elbow his way through the crowd to enter his office. One husky fellow, not recognizing Reynolds, feared that another job seeker was getting ahead of him. The man grabbed Reynolds by the arm and jerked him back. "Hold on there, fellow, stay in line, I've been here for two days." Fortunately Reynolds managed to persuade his constituent that he was already gainfully employed and posed no threat.[16]

In dealing with state and federal patronage decisions, Reynolds learned once again that his victory in 1932 did not threaten the power of the Gardner machine.

O. Max Gardner controlled the state party machinery and, as Democratic national committeeman, exerted considerable influence over federal patronage.[17]

Reynolds and Bailey, a strong ally of Gardner, clashed on patronage matters from the beginning. Their lack of unity on recommendations for key positions caused the Tar Heel State to lose at least two jobs in the Internal Revenue Department as well as numerous chances at other positions.[18] Although both Reynolds and Bailey denied they had any sort of disagreement over patronage, it had become apparent by early December 1932 that a significant rift existed between the two men.[19]

In a November letter to Johnston Avery, Bailey registered his disgust with Reynolds's attitudes about patronage. Bailey had been willing to deal fairly with the junior senator, but he felt that Reynolds was so stubborn as to preclude any acceptable compromise: Reynolds "agreed with me that we would go along together and the first thing I knew he was running to all the departments in Washington every day recommending men whom I had not endorsed and whom I did not know. I did not consider this in any degree cooperation. I felt that he had put me to my own resources." Bailey also considered his fellow Tar Heel's suggestion that the senators collect 10 percent of the salaries of each of their appointees "deplorable and disgraceful."[20]

In late February, Reynolds, plagued by controversy and job seekers, declared a moratorium on all patronage jobs. The *Asheville Citizen* concluded that the patronage question had caused Reynolds more problems than it had any other senator. During the campaign, explained the *Citizen*, Reynolds had recklessly promised to take care of his friends, and now he was finding it extremely difficult to find enough places to go around.[21]

As the days lengthened, political supporters became bitterly disappointed when none of Reynolds's major backers had been awarded any key federal positions. Finally realizing that his public disagreement with Bailey over patronage had weakened both men's political clout, Reynolds worked out a compromise with Bailey. The impasse was broken when Reynolds gave his support to C. L. Shuping, Bailey's former campaign manager, for U.S. collector of revenues. The compromise allowed Bailey to appoint the U.S. marshal for eastern North Carolina, the U.S. district attorney for eastern and middle North Carolina, and the collector for internal revenue. Reynolds, in turn, could name the collector of customs in Wilmington, the district attorney for western North Carolina, and the marshals for western and middle North Carolina. The two senators also agreed to announce their choices jointly.[22]

The agreement between the two senators immediately unraveled when Shuping failed to get his appointment as collector of revenues. Reynolds accompanied Bailey on a "secret" visit to President Roosevelt to plead Shuping's case. When reporters asked the purpose of their visit, Reynolds responded, "Just to pay a social call." When asked if Bailey's purpose was the same, Reynolds jokingly replied, "Oh, no, I just wanted to introduce the senior senator to Franklin."[23] Bailey, offended by Reynolds's cavalier remarks and by his consistent attempts to control patronage, ended his cooperation with Reynolds and resumed their feud.

The *Durham Sun* noted the fierce battle over patronage and ventured the opinion that Bailey's candidates would get the best jobs, while Reynolds would get nothing but minor positions for his friends. The *Sun* stated that Reynolds had gotten in wrong with the powers that be in the Democratic Party and that many of his supporters who had been promised jobs returned home empty handed. Reynolds's failure to secure the promised positions for his constituents, noted the *Sun*, undoubtedly hurt his prestige in North Carolina.[24]

The *Gastonia Gazette* agreed that Reynolds had been so politically damaged that some disgusted job seekers were asking assistance from senators outside North Carolina. The *Gazette* concluded that Reynolds's loss of influence could be traced partly to his cocky and independent manner and his refusal to listen to sound advice in regard to patronage.[25]

Reynolds's stubborn stance on patronage also angered O. Max Gardner. Gardner and Bailey informed President Roosevelt and his patronage adviser, James A. Farley, that the individuals proposed by Reynolds for federal jobs were persona non grata to a large number of Democrats in the state and that they would oppose all of Reynolds's nominations.

Senator Reynolds, instead of working hard for his nominees, was gallivanting around the country to such places as Hot Springs, Arkansas, seeking a "much needed" rest. When he returned to Asheville he was besieged by irate friends who had failed to get jobs. Understanding his dilemma and aware of the potential loss of popularity, he rushed back to Washington. Never missing a beat, Reynolds appeared aghast when he learned that his appointees had not been confirmed. "I thought those appointments had already been made," he lamented. "I'll just go right up and speak to the President about them at once."[26] This last-minute attempt at bravado did not fool his supporters, nor did President Roosevelt make the appointments Reynolds desired.

The national administration convincingly demonstrated its disfavor with Reynolds when Farley visited Greensboro in July. He deliberately praised Senator Bailey, no great advocate of the New Deal, while virtually ignoring Reynolds, a loyal Roosevelt supporter. The rebuff was too obvious to be overlooked.[27] Reynolds had made a serious political mistake when he chose to buck Josiah Bailey and Max Gardner on patronage. His inexperience and an unrepentant attitude led to his comeuppance.

Following Reynolds's chastisement, Gardner tried to heal the breach. He wrote

Reynolds that any rumors that he had been hostile to Reynolds's patronage plans had "no foundation whatever." Gardner disingenuously stated that he had not aligned himself with any political faction in North Carolina or in Washington, had endorsed every recommendation Reynolds had asked of him except for two cases, and had cooperated at all times with both senators. He falsely stated that there was "no foundation in the suggestion that I have taken part in this patronage controversy."[28]

Gardner had not only failed to lend his support to Reynolds's choices for political office but also had gone directly to President Roosevelt and James Farley to oppose these choices. Nonetheless, he managed to convince Reynolds that he was guiltless. Reynolds wrote Gardner to assure him of his continuing friendship and to explain that he knew that Gardner had never been hostile to any patronage approved by Reynolds. By October, Reynolds began working more closely with both Gardner and Governor J. C. B. Ehringhaus to secure appointments.[29]

Despite the words of goodwill between Reynolds and Gardner, the conflict between Reynolds and Bailey flared up again when Reynolds endorsed two of his Asheville buddies for key appointments. Reynolds supported Marcus Erwin for U.S. district attorney for western North Carolina and McKee Cooper for U.S. marshal for the western part of the state. The regular state Democratic organization (read Gardner and Bailey) opposed these nominations because neither man had any record of being a party regular.

Reynolds was angered by the antagonism toward his friends because, by virtue of his original compromise with Bailey over patronage, he believed he was entitled to these offices. The opposition, said Reynolds, was from machine politicians who had voted against him in the election and who wanted to cause a revolt merely because he had stood by his friends in the distribution of patronage. Our Bob promised to do battle over the nominations.[30]

Reynolds soon discovered a major obstacle when Attorney General Homer Cummings informed Reynolds that Roosevelt would not appoint Erwin. At a White House session with Cummings and Reynolds to discuss the nomination, Roosevelt said that he would not appoint Erwin as district attorney because it was known that Erwin kept a "fat whore" in Charlotte. Reynolds smiled broadly and said to Roosevelt, "Well, Mr. President, she's not so fat." Roosevelt roared with laughter and understood that Reynolds did not believe Erwin's extracurricular social activities to be detrimental to his work.[31] Nonetheless, Roosevelt refused to make the appointment.

A desperate Reynolds, now faced with humiliation, refused to give up. He wrote several letters to Roosevelt about Erwin and other appointees and pleaded with the Justice Department to approve his choices.[32] The issue dragged on until October 22, when the Justice Department announced that after a thorough investigation neither Erwin nor Cooper would be appointed as neither was qualified. Reynolds immediately responded by saying that he still expected both men to be appointed. Reynolds even called Attorney General Cummings and asked him to dismiss the current U.S. attorney so Erwin could take office, noting that the investigation of Erwin "was not sufficiently detrimental to make Mr. Erwin unavailable for the position."[33]

Reynolds had chosen two cronies obviously unqualified for any law enforcement office. He picked them solely because they were old friends and mistakenly thought he was powerful enough to get their nominations approved. In November 1933, Reynolds gave up on Cooper and withdrew his name from consideration.

Senator Reynolds then proposed Charles B. Price, the house detective at the Hotel Charlotte, as marshal, a nomination that was approved.[34] Apparently, party leaders decided that Reynolds had learned his lesson, for on November 20, Roosevelt finally signed Marcus Erwin's commission as U.S. attorney. Erwin's approval probably came through the good offices of Marvin H. McIntyre, secretary to Roosevelt. McIntyre, a former editor of the *Asheville Citizen*, was an old friend of Reynolds.[35]

Despite the appointment of Erwin, Reynolds's first attempts at federal patronage proved unsuccessful, and he lost considerable prestige over his failures. In addition to bucking the Gardner machine, Reynolds had made some poor choices for appointments and had not lobbied effectively for his candidates.

Reynolds's political prestige suffered another blow in the Morris Bealle incident. Editor of *Plain Talk*, a muckraking journal in Washington, D.C., Bealle made a speech in which he was highly critical of the Democratic leadership in the United States Senate and specifically castigated Senators Joseph T. Robinson, the majority leader, and Josiah W. Bailey. On June 13, 1933, Bob Reynolds urged his Senate colleagues to read the speech and inserted it into the *Congressional Record*, "where the whole country can read it." The public and his colleagues assumed that Reynolds endorsed the contents of the speech because he inserted it into the *Congressional Record*.

The following day, there was a great outcry on the part of Democratic senators, who were incensed that Reynolds would recommend a speech attacking his colleagues. An embarrassed and contrite Reynolds, in his maiden speech in the Senate, apologized for his act and explained that he placed the speech without reading it and would not have done so had he realized that Bealle had criticized fellow senators. Reynolds withdrew the speech and apologized to Bailey, calling him a man of honor and integrity. Bailey accepted Reynolds's apology, but deep scars remained from this incident and from their patronage battles.[36]

The day after Reynolds's apology, the incident became a cause célèbre. In a letter to Reynolds, Bealle claimed that Reynolds *had* gone over Bealle's speech with him before its insertion in the *Congressional Record* and had discussed the Bailey portion of the address. Bealle stated that Reynolds's apology for putting Bealle's speech in the *Record* was in fact an attack on Bealle's veracity. Bealle lashed out at Reynolds, charging that he had a "convenient memory" and the backbone of a jellyfish. "With a kingfish from Louisiana," concluded Bealle, "and a jellyfish from North Carolina, it looks to me as though the senate will have to erect an aquarium in the capitol building."[37]

Reynolds heatedly denied Bealle's charges, and Johnston Avery claimed that the insertion of the Bealle speech was due to a misunderstanding between Avery and Reynolds. According to Avery, Reynolds had asked him if he had read the speech, and he, thinking that Reynolds was merely paying the usual courtesy to Bealle, replied that he had. Reynolds thought Avery was recommending it for placement in the *Record*, while Avery expected it to be rejected as the other Bealle offerings had been.[38] Bealle replied that Avery's explanation was untrue and charged that Reynolds planned to make one hundred thousand reprints of Bealle's speech against Bailey.[39]

Whatever Reynolds's intentions, Bealle's questioning of his truthfulness in this matter was difficult to rebut. Avery's rather lame explanation made Reynolds seem incompetent. Reynolds probably had not read the speech carefully and was unaware of the harsh comments about Senators Robinson and Bailey. Thus he had naïvely and without thought sponsored a speech attacking the majority leader of his party and his North Carolina colleague, a disastrous error for a fledgling senator.

Although he certainly loved the glamour of Washington, D.C., Senator Reynolds complained that his job was a difficult one filled with constant letter writing, handshaking, and committee meetings. He wrote C. F. Kirksey, "I am so busy that I do not have one minute." Despite his griping, the ebullient Reynolds claimed that his good health and optimistic disposition would enable him to carry out his duties without any major problems.[40]

Reynolds loved socializing with the many visitors to Washington more than anything else, as this activity was much easier than the difficult task of analyzing bills and preparing legislation. Reynolds, a naturally hospitable man, did not want to turn away his visitors, because he needed their vote in 1938. As a result, he simply did not spend enough time on the basic tasks of a legislator. Never a hard worker, Reynolds found the legislative demands on his time and mind a heavy burden. He thereupon set out on a pattern of political behavior that he followed throughout his career. He worked hard at socializing, at public relations, and at constituent demands and often, owing to lack of study and preparation, had insufficient knowledge of either the legislative process or pending legislation.

During the Seventy-third Congress, Reynolds did not make a single speech except with regard to the Bealle incident, nor did he introduce a bill.[41] He confined his activities to voting (although he missed many key votes) and an occasional insertion into the *Congressional Record*. In the first one hundred days of the Roosevelt administration, Reynolds followed the party line and voted for practically all of Roosevelt's New Deal legislation.

Although he opposed some provisions of certain bills, he did not voice any significant opposition and expressed an "abiding faith and belief in President Roosevelt's leadership." Reynolds praised "Dr." Roosevelt for the operations he had performed on the country. "Fear and panic removed without pain. Heart, pulse, and respiration normal. The patient has passed the crisis and will recover." Reynolds had complete confidence in the federal government's ability to solve the problems of the Great Depression. He denied that the government was assuming unwarranted powers and argued that its purpose in passing emergency legislation was simply to assure a sound financial structure.[42]

Reynolds supported Roosevelt's first New Deal for pragmatic political reasons as well. Deeply influenced by the great mass of voters who had placed their stamp of approval on Roosevelt in 1932, Reynolds knew that affirmation of Roosevelt's leadership was popular and the surest course to reelection.[43]

The inexperienced Reynolds, however, had difficulty dealing with conflicting constituent demands during the Seventy-third Congress. For example, Roosevelt's Economy Bill had been designed to balance the budget by reducing government expenditures, especially in federal salaries and veterans' benefits. In his 1932 campaign Reynolds had promised veterans that he would oppose such cuts and announced that he would vote against the bill. Inundated with hundreds of telegrams asking him to support the Economy Bill, Reynolds reversed his position, stating that conditions had changed since he made his promise to the veterans and he trusted that Roosevelt would eventually take care of the veterans. Reynolds said it was his solemn and patriotic duty to back the president in a time of crisis. "The house is burning down and there is no time to fuss about where we get the water."[44] Thus Reynolds ignored his earlier promises and succumbed to the pressures of the moment.

Reynolds tried to assist the unemployed in North Carolina by urging the implementation of a Civilian Conservation Corps (CCC) project in the state. When asking President Roosevelt for assistance, Reynolds estimated that twenty-five thousand men could be put to work immediately in the Great Smoky Mountains National Park near Asheville.[45]

After Congress passed the CCC bill, Reynolds met with Secretary of War George H. Derr to plan the selection of the initial group of seven hundred men for the labor camps in North Carolina. The enlistees had to be single, between the ages of seventeen and twenty-eight, out of work, and American citizens in good health.

They were selected from families in need who would use the money to get back on their feet. The enlistee would get thirty dollars a month as salary but had to assign twenty-five dollars of his wages to his family. The U.S. Army supervised the building and the organization of the camps and furnished each worker board, lodging, and a clothing allowance. Reynolds praised the program as a great boon to western North Carolina.[46]

The CCC project, conceived during the first heady days of the Roosevelt administration, was an ambitious plan to put unemployed young men to work on the conservation of natural resources. The CCC was the administration's first foray into relief work. President Roosevelt said that the greatest resource of America was its youth and he wanted the young men from one region of the country to mix with those from another so that they could see the nation and understand that they shared a common heritage. The CCC experiment was one of the most popular and most successful of all the New Deal measures.

In a 1936 poll, 82 percent of all Americans favored the CCC. During its nine-year lifespan, over 2.5 million young men served in the CCC and benefited both themselves and the nation. The CCC camps were effective in reforestation, restoring and maintaining historic sites, fighting forest fires, killing pests, and preventing soil erosion. Local communities received an economic boost from the building and provisioning of the camps, while the families of the enrollees were often spared penury by the monthly allocation checks. The participants learned a skill, received some education, improved their physical health, had pride in helping their families, and gained dramatically in maturity and self-confidence while preserving the beauty of the land.[47] The CCC was Reynolds's kind of program. Not only did it put people to work and lead to increased purchasing power, but the building of the Blue Ridge Parkway and the opening of the Great Smoky Mountains National Park also were a great boost to tourism in the state.

On September 7, 1933, while Congress grappled with critical legislation, Reynolds abruptly embarked on a trip to Russia, Norway, Sweden, Denmark, and Finland at his own expense. He claimed that the purpose of this self-imposed task was to gather data on the question of recognition of the Soviet Union by the United States. He also planned to tour the Scandinavian countries for material on the liquor control systems used in those countries.[48]

Reynolds left the country in the middle of the campaign against prohibition in North Carolina, an inexplicable move for the acknowledged leader of the antiprohibitionist forces. Moreover, he departed while many expectant North Carolinians were still hoping for federal appointments. Several newspapers, including the *Asheville Citizen*, criticized Reynolds's sudden trip to Europe, suggesting that he should stay and fight the battle for repeal, deal with patronage problems, and help the distressed tobacco farmers as he had promised. The *Citizen* claimed Reynolds left the country to get away from the pressure of supporters seeking jobs.[49] Certainly one factor in this decision was the opportunity to escape the demands of constituents. When one had been as unsuccessful as Reynolds had been in procuring jobs, a trip to Russia was perhaps the safest haven.

Reynolds, accompanied by his wife, Eva, and Senator William Gibbs McAdoo, arrived in Moscow on September 27, 1933, and the following day conferred at length with the commissar of foreign affairs Maxim Litvinov and attended a banquet in honor of the aviator Charles A. Lindbergh. Neither Reynolds nor McAdoo would comment publicly on the possibility of U.S. recognition of the Soviet Union.[50]

Two weeks later Reynolds returned to New York aboard the liner *President Roosevelt* and spoke in glowing terms of the industrial progress in Russia. Reynolds noted the new factories, improvements in Russian shipping and agriculture, and the lack of unemployment. "The people seemed content," observed Reynolds. "There was no idleness that I could see." In spite of inadequate transportation and a lack of housing, Reynolds became convinced that Russia's Second Five-Year Plan for industrial rehabilitation would be a success.

The attitude of Russians toward the United States was most favorable, continued Reynolds, and this attitude, plus the economic progress of the country, had persuaded him to support U.S. recognition of Russia. Reynolds volunteered to supply President Roosevelt with firsthand information on the subject.[51] Shortly thereafter, when President Roosevelt encouraged Russia to resume diplomatic relations, Reynolds said: "Splendid. It is what I have been urging all along."[52]

In a speech to the Durham (North Carolina) Rotary Club, Senator Reynolds explained that the recognition of Russia would be of great benefit to both nations. The American economy would benefit by trade concessions and increased export trade. Reynolds did admit he was personally opposed to the communal ownership of property but did not think this should prevent political and economic ties between the two countries.[53]

Because Franklin Roosevelt had entered the White House in 1933 on the heels of Japan's invasion of Manchuria and shortly after Adolf Hitler took command of Germany, he recognized the economic and military threat from Germany and Japan. Roosevelt favored the recognition of the Soviet Union partly because he wanted to use the Soviets to block the aggressive designs of Japan and Germany. The Soviet Union had already been threatened by Japan, and the Russians feared a growing German menace on their western border.

Roosevelt then invited Maxim Litvinov, with whom Reynolds had conferred in September, to visit the United States to negotiate an agreement establishing diplomatic relations.[54] On November 17, 1933, the United States formally recognized the Soviet Union. Although in favor of recognition, the previously outspoken Reynolds had no comment on the official announcement.[55] Reynolds probably kept silent because he realized that many isolationists opposed recognition and because he understood that his praise of a Communist country not too many years after the Red Scare might not sit well with the folks back home.

After Reynolds's florid and enthusiastic reports about the Soviet Union, a rumor surfaced that Reynolds would leave the Senate to take a ten-thousand-dollar-a-year job with Amtorg, Inc., a Russian trading company doing business in the United States. Some of Reynolds's critics were merely having a little fun with him, but Reynolds took the story seriously and responded angrily. In a speech worthy of Spiro Agnew, he called the rumors "ridiculous, absurd, pusillanimous, and malicious" and referred to the story as a "canard" and a "base falsehood." "I don't know how it started," whined Reynolds. "There were no grounds for it. They can't get me that way. They'll have me made governor of Liberia next."[56]

A crucial issue for Reynolds in 1933 was the repeal of the Eighteenth Amendment of the United States Constitution, which outlawed the sale, manufacture, and distribution of alcohol. In the campaign of 1932 he had embraced the Democratic platform, which called for repeal, and he intended to carry out his pledge.[57] On February 23, 1933, the Senate voted 63–23 to submit the Twenty-first Amendment for the repeal of prohibition to all forty-eight states (the amendment had to be ratified by three-fourths of the states). Reynolds voted in favor of rescinding the Eighteenth Amendment and predicted that North Carolina would ratify the Twenty-first Amendment.[58]

The first round of the repeal fight in North Carolina took place when the state General Assembly passed a law permitting a referendum for a convention to consider the repeal of the Eighteenth Amendment. If the majority of the votes were cast in favor of a convention, then the delegates would meet in Raleigh in December 1933 to repeal the amendment. Even if it were rescinded, the decision would merely end *federal* prohibition, and North Carolina was free to retain state prohibition if it so desired.

In late May 1933, Senator Reynolds promised to wage an active fight to repeal prohibition and agreed to make several speeches in the state, but he refused to assume leadership of the wet forces.[59] He again forecast a victory for the forces of repeal. James Farley, the Roosevelt confidant and now postmaster general of the United States, agreed with Reynolds and expected that repeal in North Carolina would carry by a margin of seventy-five thousand votes.[60]

By October 1933, the national campaign against prohibition had been singularly successful, with thirty-three states voting for repeal. Seven states voted on the same day as North Carolina, and it seemed obvious, with the power and the prestige of the Roosevelt administration behind the effort, that the Eighteenth Amendment would be repealed regardless of what North Carolina did. Although the repeal forces lacked some enthusiasm, they did mount a credible campaign, and Bob Reynolds was in the thick of the fight.[61]

From October 23 until November 6, Reynolds made twenty-two speeches and visited fifty-seven counties, concentrating his efforts in rural areas.[62] As in 1932, he denounced the Eighteenth Amendment as the greatest failure in U.S. history and continued to oppose the return of the saloon.[63] Reynolds asked everyone to end the hypocrisy of voting dry and drinking wet. The crucial issue during a depression, argued Reynolds, was whether the bootlegger would sell the liquor and earn the revenue or whether legalized agents would control liquor sales and allow the government to collect the revenue and reduce taxes.[64]

The dry forces in the state, directed by Clyde R. Hoey and Cameron Morrison, developed an excellent organization. The prohibitionists contended that liquor was not the sole cause for the rise in crime. They claimed that since prohibition, drunkenness had declined 70 percent and the only group to profit by repeal would be the distillers and liquor dealers.[65]

Reynolds replied to the drys by constantly attacking what he saw as their fuzzy thinking. Reynolds could not understand their reasoning because "they say they are for good morals, and yet they are urging you to vote for the very thing which has corrupted morals and killed respect for the law."[66] In Laurinburg, Reynolds told a large crowd that if they wanted to give Al Capone and other gangsters $700 million in revenue, vote against repeal. James Farley, dispatched by Roosevelt as his personal envoy, joined Reynolds in asking North Carolina to keep faith with the president and end this disastrous and costly experiment.[67]

Cam Morrison responded to Farley and Reynolds. Still bitter over his defeat in 1932, Morrison denounced the "poor mountain boy [who] is trying to get the masses to believe that they will save something in their taxes when the ones who will save are the selfish and greedy rich friends of Reynolds who live in other states." Reynolds's argument that taxation of liquor would produce large sums of money and reduce the taxes of citizens was, according to Morrison, "as much humbug as the poor mountain boy's campaign for the Senate in an old Ford and old clothes. . . . Does anybody believe that Our Bob and [the] whooping, howling mob which has greeted him on his triumphant return from Russia really wants to promote temperance? It would make a horse laugh."[68] Reynolds closed out his campaign with a statewide radio address in Asheville and expected the state to vote wet by a satisfactory majority.[69] On election day, however, the prohibitionists won a surprising victory by a landslide vote of 293,489 to 120,190 against a convention to consider repeal of the Eighteenth Amendment. The drys won not only Buncombe County by a wide margin but also carried Reynolds's home polling place by a 4–1 margin.[70] This vote demonstrated that North Carolina was never as wet as the election of 1932 seemed to indicate. The overconfident wets misread Reynolds's victory in 1932; his election had more to do with the depression and with his campaign strategy than with prohibition.

The drys won because they centered their campaign around states' rights, used the powerful influence of the church, and were active in all one hundred counties. The wets assumed repeal would carry easily and depended on the regular Democratic Party organization, which had limited incentive. Speeches by Reynolds and Farley were not enough to overcome a certain apathy among their supporters, since the issue had already been decided on a national level. The election indicated that North Carolina, because of its dry heritage, was committed to *state* prohibition, and the vote had little reference to national issues.[71]

Disappointed with the returns, Reynolds saw the victory of the drys as significant because the citizens of the state would lose vast sums of revenue without the sale of liquor and would thus have to bear the burden of extra taxes. In addition, he thought that the absence of liquor would hurt the state's tourist trade.[72]

During his second year in the Senate, Reynolds continued to support Roosevelt and enthusiastically praised the administration's tax and relief programs. He noted that the country was better off with FDR in office, and he credited the New Deal with bringing about a new era in the struggle for human progress and with changing the economic structure of the nation.[73]

Despite his failure to obtain jobs and his quarrels with Bailey over patronage, Reynolds had reason to feel good about his status in the Senate. The Hearst news gathering agency viewed Reynolds as one of four freshmen senators who "give especial promise of distinction."[74] Senator Hamilton Lewis, a colleague of Reynolds, praised him for making more personal friendships in the Senate in the short time that he had been there than any new senator in memory.[75]

These comments revealed much about Reynolds's senatorial activities. The praise for his ability to make friends emphasized that he spent far more time chatting with colleagues than working on Senate business. For example, he had no comment in 1934 on the violent textile strikes in the South, nor did he remark on crucial foreign policy issues. He was too busy giving pat speeches on the beauty of western North Carolina to the owners of Piggly Wiggly grocery stores and to the Sertoma Club.

For the next four years, however, Senator Reynolds worked assiduously on a pet project—a scenic highway, the Blue Ridge Parkway, which would link the Shenandoah Valley and the Great Smoky Mountains National Park. Reynolds believed the road would be of inestimable value to western North Carolina and the tourist industry. Harold L. Ickes, secretary of the interior, approved the project in December 1933, but despite this plum, Reynolds consistently complained that his state had not received its fair share of public works funds.[76]

Reynolds voted for the Revenue Act of 1934, which put higher levies on large incomes, inheritances, gifts, excess profits, and corporations. He favored an increase in taxes on large incomes because he wanted to create a more equitable distribution of wealth in America and to fulfill a campaign promise he had made in 1932.[77]

Another significant piece of legislation in 1934 was the Bankhead or Cotton Control Act. The act set up compulsory reduction of surplus cotton crops in the United States to ten million bales a year in order to increase the price of cotton. Although Reynolds planned to vote for the legislation, he made a vigorous speech in the Senate attacking the underlying principles of the act. The country, according to Reynolds, suffered from underconsumption rather than overproduction. Bob Reynolds had no formal training in economic theory. His rudimentary views on Keynesian theory had been shaped by Roosevelt's economic advisers, some members of his staff (mainly Wesley McDonald), and a reporter from a business magazine.[78] For Reynolds the solution for the depression was simple. Greater government spending led to larger incomes and inflation. The subsequent increase in purchasing power would lead America out of the depression.

Reynolds said he would vote for the Bankhead Act but could not understand why a civilized nation would indulge in willful destruction of cotton while millions were "crying for raiment with which to cover their naked bodies." The junior senator thought that perhaps the government could save money by encouraging the return of the boll weevil. "We spent millions of dollars in arresting the boll weevil which was destroying cotton. Now we are about to spend millions to do the very thing we asked the boll weevil not to do." Eventually Reynolds did vote for the Bankhead Act primarily because most of the cotton farmers in his state favored its passage. Unconvinced of the its viability, he sponsored an amendment that shortened the life of the act from two years to one year to assess its progress. His amendment failed.[79]

Reynolds broke with the administration on very few key issues during the Seventy-third Congress. As a member of the Senate Banking and Currency Committee, he bucked Roosevelt by voting against reporting the Securities Exchange Act (federal regulation of the stock exchange) out of committee to the floor of the Senate. Reynolds's colleagues were amazed at his stance and his amendment to restrict the discretionary power of the Securities and Exchange Commission. His critics, including Senator James F. Byrnes of South Carolina, accused Reynolds of opposing a bill designed to prevent American investors from having their savings wiped out by another 1929 debacle. Byrnes thought this an untenable position for a man who had campaigned as a "friend of the people" in 1932.

Reynolds denied that he had tried to gut the bill. He agreed that the legislation was necessary to control the stock market and protect investors; he merely wanted to limit the power of the commission to inquire into the private affairs of a corporation more deeply than was necessary to protect the consumer. His colleagues dismissed his lame explanation of the need to protect corporations and defeated his amendment. Reynolds managed to recoup some ground, however, by voting for the Securities Exchange Act on its final passage.[80]

Reynolds also opposed Roosevelt by voting for the Independent Offices Appropriation Act, which increased salaries of government employees by $125 million, and for the Long Amendment to the act, which set up immediate payment of the soldier's bonus of approximately $2.5 million. Roosevelt had threatened to veto the bill, but Reynolds voted for it because he wanted an increase in currency circulation that would help America spend its way out of the depression. Reynolds saw the soldier's cash bonus as the most important piece of legislation before Congress, and since relief was the goal of Congress, this was the best relief legislation yet proposed. "I don't see why," Reynolds interjected, "we should not do as much for the veterans as we have done for the banks and war profiteers."

Both houses of Congress passed the act over Roosevelt's veto, a major defeat for the president. When James Farley tried to reach Reynolds by phone just before the vote to enlist Reynolds's support for the President's position, the senator refused to come to the phone and sent word that he was busy.[81] His refusal to talk with Roosevelt's political guru was an inadvisable position for a neophyte senator, but Reynolds had promised help to the veterans and did not trust himself to resist the blandishments of the persuasive Farley.

Despite these few differences with the Roosevelt administration, Reynolds continued to commend the New Deal, its broad objectives, and his part in it. During a speech to the North Carolina State Democratic convention in 1934, he not only applauded Roosevelt's legislative program but also tried to patch up his feud with Senator Bailey. He admitted that he and Bailey disagreed on most issues in Congress but hoped the people would not censor them, because they both worked from the "early morning hours to the late midnight hours for the people of this state." Reynolds noted that he did not "hate anybody because self-preservation is the first law of nature and hate certainly will age you. I want to stay young, especially because never in my life have I seen so many beautiful women."[82]

Reynolds steadfastly defended the New Deal from a growing number of conservative critics. "We hear much of Communism, Socialism, regimentation, and loss of rugged individualism" with the New Deal, asserted Reynolds, but "I fear none of these. Congress and the Supreme Court are still alive and there is nothing in the New Deal to cause alarm." The New Deal, pronounced Reynolds, was "simply a departure from the old deal in which the cards were stacked against the masses of the people."[83]

In the general election of 1934, Reynolds energetically campaigned for New Deal candidates and Democrats in general. He defended federal expenditures of money and thanked the administration for doing a marvelous job of disbursing funds for relief of suffering, distress, and starvation. The only people complaining, declared Reynolds, were those who controlled the wealth of the country. Reynolds even praised the Bankhead Act, about which he had earlier misgivings, and other farm legislation as being responsible for the increased crop prices received by farmers. In every speech he urged an overwhelming vote of confidence for President Roosevelt and the Democratic Party. To those who would complain of the loss of liberty, "let them go to the countries of the brown, black, or silver shirt—to Russia, Italy, and Germany, there to contrast other nations fully in order to appreciate their own."[84]

On his trips around the state, Reynolds frequently stopped off on the back roads and shook hands with startled constituents, who were quite surprised to see their United States senator. Reynolds, holding out his right hand to a newsman, proclaimed that "as long as I have this pumper I don't need a state organization for my campaigns." Honing his skill as a campaigner by once again mixing with the average citizen, he noted, "I am glad that I am not highly educated lest I had lost the language of the masses or rich lest I might have missed the association with the laboring man, farmer—the little man like myself."[85] It should be noted that Reynolds was not campaigning for the Democrats in 1934 but working to insure his reelection in 1938.

At the end of the Seventy-third Congress, Reynolds concluded that he was in need of both a rest and a foreign trip. He decided to visit the ambassador to Mexico, Josephus Daniels (former editor of the *Raleigh News and Observer*) at the embassy in Mexico City. He left Washington despite pressing congressional issues, an ill wife, and an obligation to campaign for Democratic Party candidates in his state. He professed that he was going to Mexico to study the Mexican tourism business and the production of silver.[86]

While in Mexico City, Reynolds addressed a special session of the Mexican Senate and praised Ambassador Daniels and the Mexican people.[87] Josephus Daniels, in his autobiography, lambasted Reynolds. According to Daniels, Reynolds ostensibly came to Mexico to learn the truth about the country but "spent his time divided between being a play-boy, having hundreds of pictures taken in rented caballero suits [and] making a speech to the Senate, in which he was so fulsome in his praise of all things Mexican that his memorandum was used in tourist publications."[88] The National Revolutionary Bloc of the Mexican Senate sent a letter to Reynolds praising his friendly attitude toward Mexico and reported that Reynolds, in his visit to the Mexican Senate, had won the affection of its members.[89]

Meanwhile, Senator William E. Borah called on the United States to investigate alleged religious persecutions in Mexico. Reynolds opposed Borah's motion for the same reason that he later opposed America's entrance into the World Court: "I think it is no business of the United States to intervene in the internal affairs of any other country." Because Mexico had friendly relations with the United States, argued Reynolds, America should allow it to work out problems in its own way.[90] His stern protest against the Borah resolution marked the first time that Reynolds had demonstrated his isolationist sentiments in the Senate.

Reynolds suffered a personal tragedy on December 13, 1934, when his thirty-year-old wife, Eva, died of tuberculosis after a lingering illness of more than a year. Reynolds had given up their apartment to take a room near the hospital so that he could spend as much time as possible with her. He had been at his wife's bedside at Violet Sanatorium when the end came.[91] Reynolds had written Josephus Daniels only a few weeks before his wife's death to express his grave concern for her health, as her doctors reported that she was not making any progress toward recovery.[92]

Reynolds had, of course, spent two weeks on a pleasure trip to Mexico in October and had left his critically ill wife to struggle alone. Nonetheless, by all accounts, he had been truly happy with his fourth wife and grieved deeply over her death. Always very sentimental about his family, he called a close friend, T. Lamar Caudle, to sit up all night with the body of his wife so that she would not be lonely.[93]

One of the first questions to face Reynolds in 1935 was a holdover from the Seventy-third Congress, namely, senate confirmation of President Roosevelt's appointment of Frank R. McNinch as chairman of the Federal Power Commission. As early as May 1934, when FDR indicated that he planned to reappoint McNinch, Reynolds voiced strong opposition to this idea.[94] Roosevelt, however, reappointed McNinch over the objections of both North Carolina senators because he thought McNinch was eminently qualified for this job.[95]

Once Roosevelt officially appointed McNinch, Reynolds changed his tune. He had opposed the selection of McNinch but said "if the President saw fit to appoint him, I have nothing more to say." Reynolds, not wanting to cross Roosevelt,[96] realized that McNinch would be confirmed anyway and a vote against McNinch might be considered a vote against Roosevelt's policy on public power.[97]

The Senate Committee on Interstate Commerce reported favorably on Mc-Ninch's nomination and sent his name to the floor of the Senate.[98] At this point Reynolds timidly reiterated his objection to McNinch privately but refused to make a speech on the floor of the Senate. While Reynolds had not changed his views toward McNinch, he understood that McNinch had been thoroughly in accord with the liberal power policy of the Roosevelt administration and had been effective in controlling large power companies in the interest of the people. Public opinion in the state had changed toward McNinch, and the *Raleigh News and Observer* had editorially urged both Bailey and Reynolds to support his nomination, which his performance in office had earned him.[99] In late January 1935, the

Senate confirmed McNinch with a voice vote, but only after Senator Bailey show-
ered criticism on McNinch for over an hour. Bennett Champ Clark of Missouri
then insisted that the Senate was entitled to know the views of both senators from
North Carolina and urged Reynolds to take the floor. Reynolds had no intention of
taking part in the discussion, but faced with an unwanted challenge, he finally
agreed to speak "despite the fact that the galleries were not filled." The junior
senator, totally unprepared and unwilling to comment on McNinch, made a typ-
ically flowery address devoted largely to the beauty and grandeur of the North
Carolina mountains. Reynolds interjected a few references to McNinch to indicate
that he differed sharply with McNinch's support of Hoover in 1928. He explained
once again that he had to oppose McNinch's reappointment because it was a
campaign promise made in 1932.

Reynolds's rambling, obtuse speech provoked laughter from his colleagues and
a tart comment from Senator Clark: "The Constitution requires that appointments to certain offices be made with the advice and consent of the Senate. I gather
from the eloquent remarks of my friend [Reynolds] that this appointment was
made contrary to his advice but that it has his consent."[100] After the Senate adjourned, Reynolds ineffectually explained that he *had* voted against McNinch's
confirmation by shouting "no" on the voice vote. It was apparent that the confused
Reynolds was trying to uphold his campaign promise while not crossing Franklin
Roosevelt and had fouled up the entire process.[101]

The McNinch incident was not the only time during the Seventy-fourth Congress that Reynolds experienced an embarrassing moment. Reynolds was presiding over the Senate during the last days of the session when two senators tried to
secure Senate right-of-way for special bills. Reynolds, as accommodating as ever,
tried to oblige both men but having little experience in parliamentary procedures
reversed himself several times and managed to get the chamber into a monumental parliamentary tangle. There was considerable confusion on the floor until Vice
President John Nance Garner rushed into the Senate at top speed to correct the
disorder.[102]

At the beginning of the Seventy-fourth Congress President Roosevelt had outlined to Congress a program of social reform that launched the second New Deal.
This legislative program had as its goal the provision of security against old age,
unemployment, and sickness; better use of America's national resources; and the
provision of slum clearance, better housing, and more jobs for Americans. Roosevelt had decided that recovery would now be stimulated by the federal government's deficit spending, which would put purchasing power into the hands of the
least privileged Americans. Roosevelt shifted markedly away from cooperation
with business leaders and carried out an antibusiness program. Conservative businesspeople opposed the collectivism of the New Deal, excessive government

spending, the new tax programs, and labor legislation because they feared a loss of power and status. However, Democratic victories in the congressional elections of 1934 sent a more liberal group of legislators to Washington and dealt Roosevelt's right-wing opposition a severe blow. Now Roosevelt had public opinion and congressional support behind his program for social justice.[103]

Despite frequent absences from the Senate in 1935, Reynolds again voted for New Deal policies; most bills placed human rights above property rights and, according to Reynolds, were spiritually uplifting.[104] An ardent advocate of old-age pensions, Reynolds warned that supporters of the plan proposed by Francis E. Townsend of California (which would pay two hundred dollars per month to persons sixty years of age and over) and other such "fantastic schemes" were a menace to the movement for old-age assistance. These outlandish and idiotic proposals, continued Reynolds, tended to interfere with genuine pension progress. Reynolds further declared that "the nation is in no mood to brook the fanatic ravings of demagogues who flaunt false gods before a suffering army of impoverished unemployed in order that they personally might climb to the crest of fame and fortune on the backs of jobless, helpless, and hopeless, but respected citizens." This from a pol who had recently been elected with the same kind of promises. Reynolds concluded that "legislators would not be stampeded into a ludicrous law by a group of phony self-styled saviors of the aged."[105]

Reynolds's indictment of what he saw as "crackpot schemes" apparently included one by his friend Huey Long, leader of the Share-Our-Wealth Clubs, as well as Long's chief lieutenant, Gerald L. K. Smith, later a close associate of Reynolds. Long and Smith advocated a plan whereby the federal government would guarantee every American a job, a house, and a car. Reynolds voted for the Social Security Act of 1935, which provided for unemployment compensation, old-age pensions, and other social services.[106]

Our Bob sustained Roosevelt and his leftward thrust toward more government regulation and reform by voting for the Works Progress Administration, a large-scale national public works program for the jobless.[107] He also favored the Agricultural Adjustment Act of 1935[108] and voted yes on the Revenue Act of 1935, which increased inheritance taxes and raised the surtax on individual incomes over $1 million.[109] According to Reynolds, the president's tax plan was fair because "the wealthy should, by right, share a portion of their worldly goods with their less fortunate brothers."[110]

Reynolds, absent from the Senate during the discussions on the Wagner-Connery National Labor Relations Act, did not record a vote on that bill but stated that had he been in the Senate he would have voted for it. The legislation, called the Magna Carta for labor unions, outlawed company unions and enforced the right of collective bargaining through representatives chosen by the employees.[111]

Reynolds inexplicably refused to support the Wheeler-Rayburn Public Utility Holding Company Act, which required the elimination (the so-called death sentence) of powerful holding companies that were not geographically or economically integrated. Power companies in the United States mounted ferocious opposition to this bill, but the act passed by a vote of 56–32. Despite his previous denunciation of the Duke Power Company and power companies in general for their stranglehold on American energy, Reynolds voted against the act because he feared the economic disruption that would result when stocks of the dissolved companies were dumped on the market. Although a proponent of strict regulation of holding companies, Reynolds did "not believe in destroying big business."[112] Josephus Daniels wrote to his son Jonathan to express his dismay at Reynolds's vote; he thought it odd that Reynolds voted against the bill, stating that now Reynolds "is swallowed up by the utility trust."[113]

Reynolds clearly risked political damnation by not casting a vote on the Wagner Act, the most important labor legislation in the New Deal, despite his obligation to organized labor. Moreover, he voted against the dissolving of powerful public utilities after his 1932 diatribes against entrenched power companies. These decisions were seen by some critics as a violation of his campaign promises and could have hurt his chances for reelection. His votes on these bills, however, were mostly forgotten by the election of 1938.

The junior senator from North Carolina continued to fight Roosevelt over the soldier's bonus. The Patman Bonus Bill provided for the full and immediate payment of $2.2 billion to World War I veterans. Congress passed the bill but Roosevelt vetoed it because it would spur inflation and increase the national debt.[114] The House overrode Roosevelt's veto, but the Senate sustained the administration in a dramatic vote as forty senators supported the president. Reynolds voted to override the president's veto because he had promised to vote for the bill and because he consistently believed that inflation was necessary to combat the depression.[115]

The work relief bill, which would set up the Works Progress Administration (wpa), also proved to be controversial. The legislation appropriated $4.88 billion to provide work for 3.5 million unemployed workers on federal public works projects. This marked a notable shift from massive federal direct relief to work relief. Now, individuals would earn a salary rather than receive a handout and would develop pride, economic security, and gratitude toward the Democratic Party. Reynolds approved of the bill as well as the McCarran prevailing wage amendment, which ensured that all laborers on public works projects would receive the same rate as that paid for similar work in private industry. Although Roosevelt had threatened to veto the work relief bill if the McCarran amendment were included, Reynolds believed that Roosevelt was bluffing and that the amendment would in no way deter the passage of the bill.

The McCarran amendment, announced Reynolds, offered the best opportunity for guaranteeing workers a living wage and would protect wage scales in private industry. The Senate, despite Roosevelt's veto threat, passed the amendment 44–43, with Reynolds one of only three southerners to vote yes.[116]

President Roosevelt, however, saw the payment of prevailing wages as increasing the cost of relief work by millions and reducing the number of workers who could be hired. Therefore, after the adoption of the McCarran amendment, the administration diverted funds allocated for public works and placed the money into direct unemployment relief. This decision meant that the $6 million already made available for beginning the Great Smoky Mountains National Park was impounded and that there would be no funds for the highway unless the WPA bill passed. The bill, of course, would not be signed by the president with the McCarran amendment attached.

Roosevelt's hardball tactics put tremendous pressure on individual senators whose constituents wanted both the jobs and the funds for public works. North Carolinians in general, and the *Asheville Citizen* in particular, subjected Reynolds to strong criticism because of his vote for the McCarran amendment.[117] Senator Reynolds fired off a telegram to the *Citizen* explaining his vote. By voting for the McCarran amendment, Reynolds insisted that he had merely been trying to help workers who were underpaid. He opposed the dole and wanted public jobs for workers because he believed that those who worked for their money developed more character. He continued to favor the passage of the WPA bill in order that money already allocated for several projects in North Carolina could be spent.[118]

In an attempt to extricate himself from his predicament, Reynolds offered a new amendment to the WPA legislation. The amendment provided that the president begin paying the prevailing rate on government projects, but if he discovered that such a prevailing wage in any locality undermined private industry or jeopardized economic recovery, then the president was authorized to cut back wages immediately.[119]

In a Senate speech supporting his amendment, Reynolds complained that many critics believed that the McCarran amendment would lead to huge salaries for laborers and eventually kill all the public works projects in the country. Reynolds hastened to assure his colleagues and constituents that he was in favor of the president's public works program. His vote *for* the McCarran amendment did not mean he was trying to kill the WPA or that he mistrusted Roosevelt.[120]

Reynolds's primary motivation in offering his amendment was to mute the harsh criticism of his crucial vote on the McCarran amendment. This ploy failed as the *Asheville Citizen* again urged him to rally to Roosevelt's banner and restore the money for the scenic highway. One Reynolds supporter, R. L. Gwyn, praised Reynolds as a friend of the workingman who was trying to maintain a decent standard of living for the laborer. Reynolds's decision might delay the scenic highway, but better that than for Reynolds to surrender his individuality and become a rubber stamp for the administration.[121] Senator Marvel M. Logan of Kentucky questioned Reynolds's motives. He said Reynolds must accept the criticism and assume the responsibility for deterring the enactment of the Work Relief Bill.[122]

Despite repeated urging from colleagues and critics at home, Reynolds again voted for the McCarran amendment. This vote occurred even after Roosevelt and the Senate had agreed to end the deadlock by having the president pay the so-called security wage, lower than the prevailing wage.[123] This time Huey Long and Reynolds were the only southerners who voted for the McCarran amendment, which went down to defeat by a vote of 50–38.[124] On the final vote on the WPA proposal, Reynolds cast his ballot in the affirmative. The measure was the largest single legislative appropriation in U.S. history up to that time. Although vehemently opposed by conservatives who thought it would bankrupt the government, the bill passed the Senate by a 68–16 vote.[125]

Reynolds had held to his course despite a resolution adopted by the North Carolina legislature urging him to back the administration. He replied that he had continued to vote for the laborer who would never benefit financially without receiving a prevailing wage. By stubbornly supporting the McCarran amendment, he voted against the president, his hometown newspaper, the state legislature, and numerous constituents. He did so because he knew the work relief bill would eventually pass and was convinced that the worker and deficit spending would best be aided by the implementation of the prevailing wage.

While concentrating on the crucial legislation of the second New Deal, Reynolds slowly became involved with the one issue that would come to dominate his senate career—immigration. Martin Dies, a congressman from Texas and the leading spokesman for reduced immigration quotas, blamed the depression and unemployment on excess immigration. In 1934 and 1935 Dies introduced legislation in the House of Representatives to reduce immigration to America by 60 percent. Dies, however, was unsuccessful in getting any of his bills to the floor of the House and eventually tired of the issue. As Dies began to focus on the investigation of communist subversion in the United States through his House Un-American Activities Committee, Reynolds "took his place as the chief agitator on the immigration issue." From 1935 until he left the Senate, Reynolds made numerous speeches on the subject and faithfully introduced a series of bills designed to restrict immigration and deport alien criminals.[126]

Reynolds, influenced by his childhood in the mountains of western North Carolina and various unpleasant encounters while traveling in Europe, had decided that America should be for Americans. He seized on this issue as one that would be popular with the overwhelmingly Anglo-Saxon, white, Protestant, depression-ridden citizens of North Carolina. The immigration issue would appeal to the bigoted, insecure masses who were searching for a scapegoat for the depression. Reynolds expected his warning about the dangers of the alien menace would enhance his chances for reelection in 1938.

Over the radio in 1935, in his first major speech on immigration, Reynolds proposed the tightening of congressional authority over immigration because he believed that alien criminals threatened the very existence of the country. He made it clear that he did not refer to the great mass of foreign-born who came to America for religious and political freedom and had helped build up America. He referred rather to the true aliens—those who had no intention of becoming naturalized citizens or those who were criminals and could not be naturalized.[127] Reynolds then proposed a bill that would expel more than 250,000 aliens living in the United States. He held them responsible for the current crime wave and accused the aliens of putting millions of American citizens out of work.[128]

Reynolds's most vigorous efforts to fight immigration lay ahead of him, however, and he happily turned his attention to his favorite pastime, travel. As a member of the Committee on Territories and Insular Affairs, Reynolds was appointed as a subcommittee of one to conduct an investigation of conditions in the Virgin Islands. The investigation grew out of a controversy involving Governor Paul Pearson, who had been charged with a wasteful, inefficient, and corrupt administration.

Reynolds was the choice of last resort, for the other senators on the committee decided to remain in Washington to consider important legislation. Reynolds, of course, eagerly accepted the assignment. The Committee on Military Affairs also asked him to visit Puerto Rico while he was in the area and inquire as to the islands' desire for independence.[129]

When Drew Pearson, the well-known syndicated columnist, learned that Reynolds was investigating his father, he immediately got in touch with his friend O. Max Gardner. Drew Pearson provided Gardner with the Pearson version of events, which Gardner relayed to Reynolds. Reynolds privately promised Gardner that the hearings would be fair to Governor Pearson.[130] Gardner also sent his son, Ralph W. Gardner, to monitor the hearings and be alert to any unfavorable remarks or comments against Governor Pearson by Reynolds.[131]

Secretary Harold Ickes had earlier investigated Pearson and had cleared him of wrongdoing. The United States Senate, however, urged that the investigation be reopened because of charges brought by Paul Yates, a former assistant to Pearson. Yates, who had been fired by the governor, charged that Pearson was guilty of high-handed methods and corruption.[132]

On May 10, 1935, Senator Reynolds arrived in St. Thomas and declared that he would begin his investigation without prejudice.[133] Reynolds assembled and studied information on the situation, while Governor Pearson welcomed the hearing and promised to cooperate fully. The governor expected that the charges against him would be dismissed.[134]

Two days later, thousands of islanders attended a mass demonstration in St. Thomas to urge the removal of Governor Pearson. Several speakers strongly criticized the Pearson regime and accused it of inefficiency and bad government. They ridiculed the Department of Interior's inept attempt to investigate itself. Morris Davis, a local agitator violently opposed to Pearson, denounced the governor and also managed to attack Reynolds's sobriety and virtue. Davis criticized Reynolds for returning a social call to Governor Pearson (not a neutral act) and for his attempt to judge the facts individually without the benefit of the full committee. Fritz Wiener, an aide to Ickes present at the demonstration, feared violence and noted that Reynolds, "utterly disgusted" at the situation, refused to hold any more hearings.[135]

Reynolds wisely postponed the hearings until October owing to "a lack of time" and decided to return to Washington.[136] He also curtailed his investigation because of the tense situation in the islands brought on by the demonstrations, a dock workers strike, and a rumored strike by police. White residents felt that the government might not be able to handle an insurrection. Reynolds, fearing for his own safety and realizing that he was not capable of resolving the problems, got out of town.[137] At least one constituent, H. Patrick Taylor Sr., wrote Reynolds and stated that he had pursued the proper course in returning to the states.[138]

On his arrival in Puerto Rico, still upset from the rude treatment he received in St. Thomas, Reynolds angrily asserted that the purchase of the Virgin Islands from Denmark in 1917 was "one of the worst mistakes the United States ever made." The United States, announced Reynolds, should pay money to Denmark to take it back.[139]

Governor Pearson, recalled to Washington by Secretary Ickes shortly after the crisis, criticized native agitators who "libelled, shamefully mistreated, and unmercifully embarrassed" Senator Reynolds.[140] Pearson then personally apologized to Reynolds for the attacks made on him, noting that the misrepresentations were made by an antiadministration faction led by discharged employees. The "real people" in the islands were furious at the attacks, Pearson stated, adding that "Reynolds' resentment was justified."[141]

In hearings held before the full committee in Washington, senators concluded that the islands were bitterly divided over Pearson's rule, but they could not come up with a fair solution. Eventually, Roosevelt solved the problem by removing both Pearson and the opposition leader from office in an attempt to restore peace. Ever the master politician, FDR then assuaged Pearson with a position in the Public Works Administration.[142]

Contrary to his expectations, the investigation in the Virgin Islands had not increased Reynolds's prestige and visibility in the Senate. He had hoped for an easy, uncomplicated hearing while relaxing in the islands, but he stepped into a hornet's nest.

Back in Washington, Reynolds faced one of the most vital issues before the Seventy-fourth Congress: United States entrance into the World Court. While the internationalists wanted America to accept its responsibility as a world leader by joining the World Court, a strong coterie of Senate isolationists opposed this view.[143]

On January 9, 1935, the Senate Foreign Relations Committee, without hearings, favorably reported to the full Senate a resolution urging U.S. entrance into the World Court. By a 14 7 vote, the committee overcame opposition from isolation ist senators Hiram Johnson and William Borah. The resolution called for the United States to adhere to the protocols of the Permanent Court of International Justice with the understanding that the court would not rule on an American dispute if the United States filed an objection.

The full Senate began consideration of the issue on January 14. President Roosevelt sent a message urging approval of the resolution, emphasizing that the sovereignty of the United States would not be jeopardized by this action. The debate in the Senate quickly became heated and intense. Secretary of State Cordell Hull, in his memoirs, recalled that William Randolph Hearst and other extreme isolationists began a strong propaganda campaign throughout the country to defeat the measure. Their effort, noted Hull, with letters and telegrams pouring into the Capitol urging rejection of the proposal, was highly effective.[144]

In sympathy with the Hearst forces, Reynolds delivered a long harangue against the World Court. For him, entrance into the World Court meant entrance into the League of Nations because the court was an offspring of the league. Reynolds did not want to enter the league in any manner—whether by the back door, the side door, or through the basement. The League of Nations was a political organization, thus it could never promote peace—witness its lack of action when Japan invaded Manchuria. The league, continued Reynolds, was so helpless in stopping war and winning the peace that it could not even prevent a wanton attack by Italy on Ethiopia.

Our Bob was convinced that eight out of ten Americans were opposed to entrance into the World Court. He informed his listeners that Tar Heels were against the World Court because for years foreign countries had taken American money without paying any interest or ever showing any gratitude for American help. Reynolds asserted that citizens of his state did not care about "spending money and time and energy and life and blood for the interest of Estonia, Ethiopia, Latvia, Liberia."

Reynolds continued his diatribe by referring to the court as a "court of intrigue." Instead of achieving a universal peace, membership in the league would merely get the United States into a foreign war because the nations of Europe were preparing for a bloody conflict.[145]

Josiah Bailey, Reynolds' colleague, made a speech strongly supporting American entrance into the World Court because the United States should not reject the principle of justice in international relations. Although he made no specific reference to Reynolds, Bailey clearly directed some of his remarks to his colleague. In becoming a member of the court, explained Bailey, the United States merely agreed to submit controversies to the court and to abide by its decision. Bailey asserted that it was a false argument to equate joining the court to joining the league, because they were separate organizations.[146]

Reynolds promptly replied to Bailey by claiming that Americans did not want "international justice. They want American justice, they are tired of fooling with those 'furriners' because they have been stung too much already." He then tried to read a list of the names of the World Court justices but said that the names were so foreign that he could not twist his tongue in a manner sufficient for correct pronunciation. Reynolds warned that the "furriners" in the court, who were going to deal out justice to Americans, spoke "so many different languages that any American there would not know what was going on." Although Senator King pointed out that the only two languages used by the World Court were English and French, Reynolds persisted in calling it the "Court of Babel."[147]

Reynolds later made a radio speech during which he referred to the court as a "court of babble, ballyhoo and bunk." He insisted that entrance into the court would lead to cancellation of World War I debts and the breaking down of American immigration barriers. Reynolds predicted defeat of the court proposal by two votes.[148] Although committed to the defeat of the court, Reynolds did not appear on the floor on the final day of debate because he was busy organizing a gym class for twenty-two senators.[149]

When the Senate voted on the World Court resolution on January 29, the vote was 52–36 in its favor but seven votes short of the two-thirds majority needed for approval. Despite President Roosevelt's strong advocacy, Reynolds, following his "sincere and honest convictions," voted no.[150] Democratic majority leader Joe

Robinson regretted the failure of the proposal and blamed the defeat on inflammatory statements that implied that joining the court would involve the country in foreign entanglements.[151]

The reaction to Reynolds's vote varied. The *Asheville Citizen* expressed surprise at Reynolds's position, especially because joining the court was part of the 1932 Democratic Party platform.[152] The *Greensboro Daily News* charged Reynolds and his isolationist friends with opposing a gesture that would lead toward international accord and understanding.[153] The *News and Observer* noted that Reynolds had now voted against Roosevelt on both the prevailing wage agreement and the World Court and that these votes would hurt a "political free lance" such as Reynolds come election time.[154] Conversely, John W. Hinsdale, a Reynolds supporter, wrote Reynolds and applauded his position. Hinsdale could not see the United States joining the court with a lot of nations that had "defrauded us during the last few years."[155]

The defeat of the World Court resolution was a smashing victory for the isolationists in the Senate and a severe blow to Cordell Hull's plans for international cooperation. Stunned by the defeat, the advocates of court membership knew that this setback foreclosed the question of American entry into the court for an indefinite period. The isolationists, encouraged by their success, turned their attention to the Neutrality Act of 1935.

The debate over the Neutrality Act developed against a backdrop of war between Italy and Ethiopia, the resurgence of an armed Germany, an ambitious Japan seeking to expand its power in Asia, and deepening pacifism at home. The act outlined a firm position of neutrality in the war between Italy and Ethiopia, warning Americans not to travel on vessels from either country and also declaring an arms, munitions, and trade embargo against both nations. The legislation also prohibited the carrying of munitions in American ships either to belligerent nations or to neutral nations for transshipment to belligerents. The act represented a decisive departure from American policy before World War I, when the government had insisted on freedom of the seas.[156]

Roosevelt accepted the neutrality legislation even though it did not provide him as much discretionary control as he desired. He hoped that Congress would pass a more flexible bill in 1936. Reynolds and the isolationists, however, were wary of giving too much power to Roosevelt lest he begin designating aggressors and passing sanctions based on determinations made by the League of Nations.[157]

In two separate speeches, Reynolds "flat-footedly" opposed any involvement with any nation under any circumstances.[158] "The world has gone crazy," explained Reynolds, "but it shall not get the wealth and flesh of this country in a war."[159] Reynolds, now a committed noninterventionist, voted for the Neutrality Act of 1935.[160]

Throughout 1934 and 1935 Reynolds characteristically worked for reelection. People continued to crowd into his office for jobs and favors partly because, once a visitor got in to see the senator, Reynolds treated his guest as if he had no other interests.[161] Perhaps a more selective process of choosing possible job seekers would have improved his efficiency in obtaining positions, but this was simply not Reynolds's way. He hoped that the people who visited him would remember his concern during election year. He constantly wrote letters to Marvin H. McIntyre and Louis M. Howe, secretaries to President Roosevelt, on behalf of constituents in search of federal positions.[162]

During this same period Reynolds set out to flatter Federal Bureau of Investigations director J. Edgar Hoover in hopes of getting Hoover's imprimatur for his reelection campaign. Reynolds proposed to Hoover that decorations for meritorious service in law enforcement be awarded to officials of the federal government. Hoover agreed that the award would serve a worthwhile purpose in acquainting the general public with the work of the federal government.[163] When traveling around the country making speeches, Reynolds frequently praised Hoover as "the finest law enforcement officer throughout the entire world." Reynolds wrote Hoover that he never forgot his friends and would continue to laud Hoover for the marvelous work he was doing.[164]

In January 1935, Reynolds sent Hoover a copy of an editorial that demanded more funds for the Department of Justice in order to fight crime more effectively.[165] Senator Reynolds also sent the FBI director a copy of "Demand It," an article he wrote for *Master Detective* magazine, in which he made a plea for improvement of law enforcement through the expenditure of greater funds and praised Hoover and the FBI.[166] Hoover and his agents treated Reynolds with courtesy because Hoover was assembling a group of publicists to enhance the bureau's image as an effective crime-fighting machine, and any publicity and support on Capitol Hill helped.[167]

Reynolds, trying to enhance his reputation, appealed to such individuals as Hoover or Roosevelt who could help him garner votes, but he spent most of his time in North Carolina on personal visits. At the end of July he spent four days in the state and made six speeches. "I can get a whole lot more votes now [1935]," explained Reynolds, "than I can just before I run again."[168]

On an earlier visit to the state, Reynolds was the last in a long line of speakers at the dedication of a new airport at Rocky Mount. The other speakers had rambled on at length about their reasons for being present—to pay tribute to the town or bring greetings from some department. Reynolds opened his speech with, "Ladies and gentlemen, I'm hungry as hell"—and proceeded to make only a brief talk. He did not mince words in explaining why he was at the dedication. "You know [why] I'm here. I can't fool you and I'm not going to try. I'm here to shake a lot of hands because I'm going to run for re-election within a few years. That's what I like to do and I hope you like it too." The crowd loved it.[169]

One-on-one campaigning proved to be most profitable for Reynolds, the master of the hearty handshake and the flowery compliment. One of the political pundits of the day observed him at work: "It is always a joy to see Bob do his stuff. He is the State's outstanding artist in applesauce. The beauty of his work is that he puts out his line with a label. No pretense about it. He likes to spread it on thick, and apparently, people like it. Every time Bob Reynolds is seen in a crowd doubts begin to rise about whether he can be beaten as readily next time as some people think."[170]

After Congress adjourned in 1935, he decided to tour the United States under the auspices of the United States Flag Association to extol patriotism and speak against crime.[171] While in New York, Senator Reynolds telephoned President Roosevelt at Hyde Park and asked for the opportunity to visit with him while passing through. Reynolds paid a short visit to the president's home and proceeded on to Boston,[172] where he praised Roosevelt, Governor James M. Curley, and historic Boston. As was his custom, he had a friend send the newspaper clippings to Roosevelt's personal attention so that the president would know that Reynolds had been praising his administration all over the country.[173]

Reynolds had agreed to be present in Washington on September 8 to meet with Governor Ehringhaus and other state officials to present North Carolina's case for additional funds from the Public Works Administration. Reynolds wired the governor from Niagara Falls to express his regrets at his failure to attend the meeting. Reynolds's excuse was that he was "providing North Carolina with a great deal of publicity on this national tour."[174] The *Asheville Citizen*, disturbed by his excessive wandering, commented that the senator's real purpose was not publicity for North Carolina but self-publicity. "Congress has adjourned," editorialized the paper, "but the junior senator is still in session and the whole country is finding it out."[175]

At this juncture, Reynolds began a pattern of behavior that would characterize the remainder of his Senate career. At a crucial meeting where his attendance was necessary to secure badly needed funds for his constituents, he was traveling around the country under the pretense of seeking publicity for his state. Reynolds seemed to be interested in traveling, publicity, women, and reelection, not necessarily in that order.

Reynolds's nationwide tour ended in Charlotte, North Carolina, on October 4, 1935, after visits to thirty-two states and fourteen governors. On his trip through America Reynolds had learned that the people had no desire to get into a foreign war and that Roosevelt would be reelected in 1936 despite the opposition of Wall Street.[176]

Reynolds, still motivated by wanderlust, was ecstatic when he learned of his selection as part of the United States government's official delegation to the inauguration of Manuel L. Quezon, the first democratically elected president of the Philippines in four hundred years.[177] Accompanied by his daughter Frances, Reynolds left from Seattle with the official party of seventy-five persons. After Manila, he joined Senator Burton K. Wheeler and others aboard the USS *President Grant*.[178]

Reynolds, ever the bon vivant, flirted with a lovely Chinese woman and, although very attentive to her, was happy to escort her off the ship. Senator Burton K. Wheeler decided to teach the amorous Reynolds a lesson and arranged for a fake cablegram to be delivered to Reynolds while he was dining. The cablegram was from the Chinese lady announcing that her mother and father had consented for her to meet Reynolds in Bombay and accompany him to the United States as his wife. Reynolds, according to the amused Wheeler, blanched and perspired heavily throughout the meal. After dinner, the shaken Reynolds announced his intention to return home immediately by plane. He was in the process of soothing his nerves with alcoholic beverages when Wheeler finally let him in on the joke.[179]

Reynolds returned home by early January 1936 but had missed the opening of Congress on January 3, the only member of the North Carolina delegation to do so. By returning late to Congress, Reynolds missed the president's address to Congress and the Senate debate on two issues crucial to Reynolds—the Soldier's Bonus Bill and the Neutrality Act of 1936. Reynolds had been traveling more or less since August 6, and during that time he did very little of the people's business except to attend the inauguration of Quezon.

CHAPTER FIVE

[Movie Stars, Aliens, and Neutrality]

During the second three years of his first term, Reynolds ended his "apprentice-ship" in the Senate. Our Bob continued his support of Roosevelt's New Deal but became increasingly vociferous in the area of foreign policy and developed a strong base for his reelection bid in 1938.

When Reynolds returned to Washington in early 1936 from his trip to the Philippines and the Far East, he received an enthusiastic reception from hundreds of friends who had gathered in his Senate office. Surrounded by a bevy of lovely women, the beaming Reynolds effusively greeted the well-wishers. One of his office staff observed: "Ain't he grand? I'll bet he doesn't know half of these people. Yet he makes them feel perfectly at home." Reynolds willingly posed for photographers but refused to stand up on a chair, stating, "I never rise above my audience."[1]

Few politicians better understood the value of publicity, and few were more adept at getting it. Determined to gain President Roosevelt's approbation, Reynolds kept him apprised of his activities while abroad. In a letter to FDR, he included a picture of Reynolds with his foot on a dead elephant labeled GOP and another photo of Reynolds in boxing trunks and gloves with the caption, "Training for the battle of 1936." Reynolds assured the president that the Democrats would win in 1936, "but we have some hard work before us."[2] One could never imagine Governor Hoey or Senator Bailey posing in boxing trunks, but it was natural and expected for Reynolds to engage in such antics. One can imagine Roosevelt's bemused reaction to the flood of letters and outrageous photographs from Reynolds, but Reynolds seldom passed up an opportunity to curry favor with Roosevelt.

Because of his great penchant for publicity, Reynolds managed to appear frequently in public in 1936. The Sioux Indians from South Dakota chose him as a chief for their tribe and performed the ceremony on the Capitol steps. The Sioux bestowed on Reynolds the title "Oyate-Wawecajiceji," which meant, "He stands for his people." Reynolds, pleased with his new title, thought it would be an excellent campaign slogan for 1938.[3]

In July 1936, while on a Mexican vacation with his daughter Frances, Mexican bandits robbed Reynolds and several carloads of tourists traveling between Mexico City and Acapulco.[4] The *Charlotte News*, which occasionally referred to Reynolds as the "Bounding Basque of the Mountains," suspected that Reynolds was among the group robbed in Mexico because "whenever you find as many as seven cars loaded with tourists, one of them is likely to contain Senator Reynolds. The law of averages, reinforced by the axiom of the rolling stone, almost guarantees it."[5] Despite his economic loss, Reynolds was ecstatic over the incident because of the publicity he derived from it.

On the day that he returned from his trip to the Far East, the senator, realizing that he needed to turn his attention to more weighty matters, held a long discussion on foreign policy with reporters. Reynolds's travels had convinced him that "the United States must take steps, drastic if necessary, to keep this country from being embroiled in any turmoil of a foreign character."[6] The war between Italy and Ethiopia was an excellent example of a serious international situation that might involve the United States. Reynolds viewed that war as a conflict between British and Italian imperialism, and the worst thing America could do would be to become involved in any way.[7]

Reynolds noted that the United States need have no fear that Japan would make war on it because Japan was America's third best customer and could not afford to lose its trade.[8] His assessment was, of course, correct for 1936, but he erred badly in not anticipating Japan's expansionist impulses.

Reynolds believed that the United States could "maintain peace with all countries as long as we have a policy of neutrality that is open and above board and is neutrality in its strictest sense." The senator, as he would from 1936 to the end of his senatorial career, advocated increased preparedness as the best insurance in the drive for peace.[9]

When not debating America's neutrality, Reynolds devoted most of his energy to the alien problem and to limiting immigration to the United States. In February 1936, along with Congressman Joe Starnes of Alabama, Reynolds introduced Senate Bill 4011 (the Reynolds-Starnes Bill). The bill required the registration of all aliens in the United States within six months of its passage, required the immediate deportation of all habitual criminal aliens, and reduced immigration to 10 percent of the present quotas. The number of new immigrants permitted to enter the country each year would be reduced from 153,000 to 15,300.

Reynolds introduced his bill in a two-hour Senate speech. He announced that there were between five and seven million aliens in America and complained that not even the commissioner of immigration knew exactly how many resided here or how many entered illegally. In Reynolds's mind, all aliens automatically owed political allegiance to another country, and without naturalization these foreigners were economic and political threats to America. Alien residents did not attempt to become naturalized citizens and were not interested in upholding the principles on which America was founded. Reynolds claimed that his bill would not only close the gates to undesirable immigrants but would also expel unwelcome aliens who occupied jobs that should be filled by Americans. It was unthinkable, he roared, that immigration would be increased at a time when one of six Americans looked to the government for assistance owing to unemployment. His bill, claimed Reynolds, would relieve overburdened taxpayers and would keep America for Americans.

In the same speech, Reynolds denounced the Kerr-Coolidge Bill sponsored by the administration. The legislation would allow the deportation of aliens with criminal records but would waive deportation if the aliens had been in the United States for ten years or if they had wives or parents who were legal residents. Reynolds saw the bill as making "two holes in the immigration barrier for every one it plugs" and complained that it would not really expel alien criminals.[10]

The *Asheville Citizen* approved of Reynolds's bill and agreed that there was a close connection between immigration and unemployment and that immigration had to be reduced during a depression.[11] Knowing that the issue played well at home, Reynolds, in a press briefing and a radio address, promoted his own bill by attacking the Kerr-Coolidge Bill for permitting "dangerous aliens to remain in the country for sentimental reasons." He urged all patriotic Americans to follow the American Legion and 110 other patriotic organizations by wiring senators to oppose the un-American Kerr-Coolidge Bill.[12]

On March 17, 1936, both the House and Senate Immigration Committees favorably reported the Kerr-Coolidge Bill out of committee and onto the floor of the Senate.[13] Reynolds immediately launched a two-and-one-half-hour filibuster against the bill and said he was willing to speak for days if necessary. In his opening foray, Reynolds accused the Department of Labor of failure to act on 2,862 alien deportation cases and maintained that the department was guilty of concealing the true facts on the status of these aliens.

After a thorough study of the files, Reynolds ascertained that the information presented to the Senate by the Labor Department was quite different from the material he had read. Moreover, carped Reynolds, the department described the hardship cases as being so saintly that "they came from the clouds above and with wings had alighted on our fertile soil." The senator concluded that the Labor Department had been harboring despicable criminals, a practice that would encourage other aliens to enter the country illegally.[14]

Our Bob continued his filibuster the next day and spoke energetically for almost three hours. He claimed he was "for America first, last and all the time, after which I can permit my heart to beat and my tears to flow for those beyond the wide waters of the blue Atlantic and the wind-swept Pacific oceans." Reynolds denied he was hard-hearted; rather, he simply felt that too many aliens were detrimental to the welfare of America and should be deported. Most senators, while somewhat impressed by the flood of mail received from patriotic organizations in support of Reynolds's bill, had no time for such fulsome oratory and departed the chamber early, leaving Reynolds with his own echoes.[15]

As Reynolds resumed his filibuster, he found himself in a dilemma. Acutely aware of the strength of tobacco farmers and manufacturers in his home state, he favored the passage of the tobacco section of the Agricultural Adjustment Act of 1933 known as the Kerr Tobacco Bill, also under consideration. This legislation would allow individual states to enter into compacts to restrict tobacco acreage and production and thus raise prices.

Reynolds was forced to give up his filibuster against the Kerr-Coolidge immigration bill when Senator William H. King of Utah threatened to filibuster against the Kerr tobacco bill in retaliation. Reynolds hated to step out of the limelight and relinquish his only weapon against the alien bill, but he had no choice. North Carolina was a big tobacco state, and he had already received unfavorable mail from constituents who thought he opposed the Kerr tobacco bill rather than the Kerr alien bill. As part of his agreement with Senator King, Reynolds agreed to limit his speech against the alien bill to three hours. King would then forgo his filibuster against the Kerr tobacco bill.

After the passage of the Kerr tobacco bill, Reynolds leaped to his feet to explain to constituents that he had done everything humanly possible to bring about the passage of the tobacco bill, sacrificing his most potent weapon against the alien bill to serve the farmers of his state.[16] Fearful that the Kerr immigration bill might be passed without his filibuster, Reynolds tried to wriggle out of his bargain with Senator King by claiming that his remarks on subjects other than aliens, such as world trade and international affairs, should not count against his allotted three hours.

An angry Senator King made a point of order that the North Carolinian had violated their agreement, and he threatened to reconsider the Kerr tobacco bill. Senator Sherman Minton, presiding over the Senate at the time, delivered a stinging rebuke to Reynolds and ruled that no matter what subject Reynolds discussed, he was exceeding his time under the agreement. After consultation with Vice President John Nance Garner, however, Minton stated that Reynolds had a right to break the accord because it was a gentleman's agreement between two senators and not binding according to Senate rules.

Now on the defensive, Reynolds angrily declared that he would never repudiate any agreement he made with another senator and ended his speech. Before retiring Reynolds again reminded his colleagues that he had entered the agreement against his will in order to serve ninety-seven thousand tobacco farmers. Finally,

Reynolds made a motion that the Kerr-Coolidge Bill be recommitted to the Immigration Committee, but the Senate adjourned before a vote could be taken on his motion.[17]

During the height of the alien controversy, Reynolds, in a talk to the Daughters of the American Revolution (DAR), declared that the country had to "Americanize the alien before the alien alienizes America." Reynolds favored an annual census of legally admitted aliens and would see that they had the chance to become citizens if they were worthy. "If they proved unworthy I would send them whence they came." Under this system, the government would have little trouble "weeding out the illicit immigrant, the smuggled Oriental, and the apostle of destruction who has found his devious way to America to preach the downfall of American institutions." In conclusion, Reynolds cried that America could have no double loyalty. "An American must be for America against all the world."[18] The DAR loved the speech and cheered Reynolds loudly. Their approbation encouraged him to return to Washington and fight the Kerr-Coolidge alien bill with renewed vigor.

Senator Lewis B. Schwellenbach of Washington effectively answered all Reynolds's criticisms of the Kerr-Coolidge Bill. Schwellenbach opposed recommitting the bill to the Immigration Committee because the committee had already reported the bill out and it should now be voted on by the full Senate. He believed that the Kerr bill would be fairly enforced, protecting the interests of both the American public and the immigrants. This country could not afford to be cruel, unfair, or inhumane to aliens when it had been built by immigrants. He then criticized Reynolds for selecting only 4 or 5 out of 2,862 cases handled by the Department of Labor. Reynolds's charges that all 2,862 cases were of bad moral character were simply untrue, said Schwellenbach, and the few examples Reynolds picked were the only ones that could be criticized. The Kerr bill, concluded Schwellenbach, strengthened deportation laws yet allowed the authorities some discretion and humanity in its decisions.[19]

Eventually, owing to opposition from Reynolds and many patriotic groups, plus the impending adjournment of the Seventy-fourth Congress because of the national party conventions, the Senate postponed a vote on the Kerr-Coolidge alien bill. Reynolds immediately announced that he had "won a great victory." His delaying tactics helped prevent the Kerr bill from being considered, but he did not achieve a great victory because no alien control legislation had been passed and he had done very little to aid in the passage of his own bill.[20]

On the last day of the session, emboldened by his perceived success against the Kerr bill, Reynolds railed against the Labor Department for keeping 2,862 hardship aliens in the country. He threatened to prevent the adjournment of Congress unless the Department of Labor acted immediately to adjudicate these cases. During his speech, Reynolds flailed his arms so much that Senator Minton, sitting next to him, asked if the speech were being made under the Marquis of Queens-bury rules. In citing the hardship case of one Adolph Lipschitz, Reynolds badly mangled the pronunciation of Lipschitz's name, prompting Senator Tom Connally to ask how many aliens were involved in the case. When Reynolds replied that only one person was involved, Connally said that from the "pronunciation of the Senator, I thought there were three or four." Another senator, for the added amusement of his colleagues, playfully asked Reynolds to repeat the name.[21]

Reynolds's flowery oratory and loose interpretation of the facts indicated once again that he rarely thought deeply or carefully about what he was saying. Al-though his Senate colleagues thought him affable, he was often viewed as a light-weight, his remarks were frequently ignored, and, worst of all, he had become a target for their jibes.

The press did not ignore Reynolds's filibuster against the Kerr-Coolidge legisla-tion and excoriated him for his attacks. The *Raleigh News and Observer*, which favored the Kerr bill, disliked Reynolds's intemperate remarks.[22] The *Washington News* charged Reynolds with "vanity, stubbornness and stupidity" in filibustering the Kerr-Coolidge immigration bill. His opposition, noted the paper, led the Department of Labor to deport twenty-four hundred aliens of good and moderate character who would leave families dependent on the federal government for relief and survival. "That is the logic of a man who thinks nothing of exploiting the misery of thousands to stand before misguided zealots as the savior of our institu-tions."[23] The *New York Times* also advocated passage of the Kerr-Coolidge Bill, indicating that if the hardship cases were deported, irreparable damage would be done to the aliens and to the country's reputation for fair play.[24]

The criticism by the *Washington News* and other papers stung. Reynolds re-sponded by saying that *his* position was supported by the Veterans of Foreign Wars (VFW) and many newspapers including the Hearst papers.[25] Reynolds understood that immigration control was an emotional issue in American politics but thought that the average American agreed with his views. Anson W. Betts, in a letter to the editor of the *Asheville Citizen*, praised Reynolds for protecting America from unwanted aliens. Betts thought the government was selling American children into the slavery of debt to sustain millions of foreigners who had sneaked into the country.[26]

After Congress adjourned, Our Bob attended the North Carolina Democratic Party convention, where the state pledged its twenty-six votes to Roosevelt[27] and chose Reynolds as one of the twenty-six delegates to the national convention in Philadelphia.[28] Before the convention, President Roosevelt had expressed a desire to end the two-thirds rule (which required a two-thirds vote of delegates at the Democratic convention to nominate a president), but Reynolds opposed the at-tempt to abrogate the rule. He maintained that the two-thirds rule had to be continued "if the South desires to retain any semblance of voice in party nomination." Reynolds was one of nine North Carolina delegates to vote against the elimination of the two-thirds rule. The Democratic Party, promising southerners increased convention representation in the future, voted to scrap the traditional party rule, and Roosevelt was renominated easily.[29]

Excited about Roosevelt's candidacy, Reynolds campaigned vigorously and forcefully for the president's reelection and for all Democratic candidates. At every stop he lavishly praised Roosevelt and the New Deal, identifying FDR as the best friend North Carolina ever had. Reynolds claimed that he delivered 75 speeches, visited 97 of the 100 counties in his state, and traveled over 6,000 miles on behalf of the Democratic ticket.

When asked if his campaign activities were always devoted to the president's reelection, Reynolds replied, "I do support the President and my party, but, of course, I will admit that I am not unmindful of my friend Robert R. Reynolds."[30] He constantly wrote his friends and leaders in the party about his campaign efforts on behalf of "our Democratic nominees" and "our beloved President" in the hopes that his party loyalty in 1936 would be rewarded when he ran for reelection in 1938.[31]

At the behest of the National Democratic Committee, Reynolds gave the keynote address at the Maine Democratic State Convention in March, where he credited Roosevelt with returning prosperity to the country. Reynolds urged New Englanders to keep the president in office.[32] Reynolds reported to Josephus Daniels that he had received an enthusiastic reception by the largest Democratic convention ever assembled in Maine.[33]

In his North Carolina appearances, Reynolds varied his approach but always delivered an entertaining speech. On one occasion, his suit soaked from a vigorous delivery and his usual arm flailing, Reynolds announced that the exercise he got while speaking "would save me the expense of a Turkish bath." He continually lambasted one of his favorite targets, big business, saying that the "egotistic, selfish, Wall street interests and capitalists who are opposing the New Deal can go to hell."[34] The business interests, said Reynolds, were crying "Hollywood tears" in fear of national bankruptcy when the reality was that Roosevelt had saved them from economic collapse and their criticism showed a lack of gratitude. Roosevelt's policies, pronounced Reynolds, placed human rights against property rights and had saved hundreds of lives.[35]

If FDR stayed in office, Reynolds predicted, the country would have the greatest economic boom in history.[36] To clinch his point, he again resorted to the purple prose for which he was rapidly becoming famous. "The storm over the seas of despair have quieted and the economic sun blazes forth its mellow rays of happiness and prosperity and contentment."[37]

When President Roosevelt came to North Carolina for a campaign visit in September, Reynolds met him in Knoxville, Tennessee, and accompanied him on an automobile tour of the Great Smoky Mountains National Park.[38] His close proximity to the popular Roosevelt, as Reynolds hoped it would, boosted Reynolds's reelection chances in 1938.

Roosevelt won a landslide victory over the Republican nominee Alf Landon with over 27 million votes and an electoral margin of 523 to 8. Roosevelt also led the Democrats to huge victories in both houses of Congress, including seventy-five Democrats in the Senate.[39] Reynolds's efforts on behalf of the president and his party had increased his popularity in North Carolina. His colleague, Senator Josiah Bailey, indicated that on a recent tour of the state in November 1936 he found Reynolds in "mighty good standing" and had heard many say that Reynolds's fences were in good shape.[40]

As soon as Congress convened in January 1937, Reynolds and Congressman Joe Starnes reintroduced a series of five immigration and alien bills.[41] The legislation, similar to that submitted in 1936, included such provisions as empowering the president of the United States to deport any alien whose presence was inimical to the public interest of the country and required mandatory deportation for any alien on relief for more than six months. Another bill would register and fingerprint all aliens in the United States and require them to report their residences to the Department of Labor. Reynolds also proposed mandatory deportation for habitual alien criminals who were convicted of a crime carrying a penalty of one year or more in prison, for espionage, or for carrying a concealed weapon. The Labor Department could delay deportation in some hardship cases for one year but had to report to Congress in each case. Senate Bill 1366 would permanently cut immigration from quota nations by 90 percent, and Senate Bill 1195 provided for the preferred employment of American citizens by the federal government and would prevent the employment of any alien in any department or agency of the federal government.[42]

To insure the success of their bills, Reynolds and Starnes issued a statement that clarified their aims. The two legislators alleged that during the previous ten-year period of quota restriction of immigrants, over three million aliens entered the United States, and at least one of every eight persons on relief was an alien. The two men warned citizens that as many nations prepared for war in 1937, America was foolish to spend millions for defense while allowing aliens to remain in the country when they could become "potential spies and enemies to bore from within."[43]

Reynolds, forging ahead on his mission to eliminate "alien criminals, racketeers, gun toters, and mental and physical defectives" from America, formed the American Coalition, an organization designed to coordinate the efforts of patriotic and civic societies to keep America for Americans. In his American Coalition flyer of February 12, 1937, Reynolds claimed that thousands of aliens crowded American jails and asylums. He asked supporters to help him deport these undesirables.[44]

Despite Reynolds's efforts to promote his bills, leading newspapers and administration officials, principally Secretary of State Cordell Hull, opposed his legislation. Secretary of Labor Frances Perkins believed that the measures were unnecessary and would tie the hands of the Labor Department.[45]

The *Raleigh News and Observer* agreed with Reynolds on the need to register aliens but argued that such registration fever rarely stopped with aliens and eventually all citizens might be investigated and fingerprinted by an overly zealous bureaucracy.[46] The *New York Times* again attacked the legislation as inhumane and costly. The *Times* advocated the bill sponsored by Martin Dies in the House as preferable to Reynolds-Starnes because the Dies bill provided for deportation of alien criminals but gave discretion to the secretary of labor in hardship cases.[47]

Reynolds pounced on the Dies bill with the same criticism he leveled at the Kerr-Coolidge legislation. He called the Dies proposal un-American and charged that it would increase taxes by retaining indigent aliens. The Dies bill was not a deportation bill, cried Reynolds, but an alien importation bill. By permitting aliens to remain, the bill would encourage others to enter. Dies, a militant right-winger, characterized Reynolds's criticism as "the most amazing statement ever uttered by anyone. Here is a bill which will rid this country of a large group of vicious criminals and yet it is denounced as un-American."[48]

Reynolds watched and fretted as the Dies bill gained support from the Roosevelt hierarchy and from newspapers. He feared that Martin Dies was stealing a politically significant issue from him and would ultimately threaten his own position as the number one alien baiter in the country.

Continuing his fight against the Dies bill, Reynolds, on January 6, gave a talk over the National Broadcasting Company titled "Criminal Aliens in America." He repeated his list of criminal aliens in the United States and indicated that no one on his list, all of whom were guilty of felonies and moral turpitude, would be deported by the Dies bill.[49] On January 12 the senator gave another speech, which was titled "The Alien and the Relief Problem," in which he once again decried the "maudlin sympathy" exhibited on behalf of these "alien parasites."[50]

In the closing hours of the Seventy-fifth Congress, Reynolds threatened to filibuster the Dies bill, already passed by the House and approved by the Senate Immigration Committee. To Reynolds's delight, the Dies bill never came to a vote, and the Department of Labor did not get its long-awaited discretion over hardship deportation cases. Reynolds's four years of opposition helped undermine the Dies bill, but negative comments from patriotic organizations whose members thought the Dies bill was too soft played a larger role. In the end the Roosevelt administration turned against the Dies bill because it would undermine the administration's Good Neighbor policy.[51]

From 1936 to 1938, Reynolds, while devoting much of his time to the alien menace, faced other domestic issues of importance. He again voted for the Soldier's Bonus Bill, which called for full and immediate payment of bonus certificates. Roosevelt vetoed the bill, but Congress, including Senators Bailey and Reynolds, mindful of the political influence of veterans, voted to override Roosevelt's veto,[52] and the bill became law in 1936.[53]

Reynolds continued his unwavering endorsement of Secretary of Agriculture Henry A. Wallace's program to help farmers. Although originally opposed to production controls on cotton, Reynolds, in speeches to farm groups, favored the curtailment of crop production, especially tobacco. Overproduction of these crops would drastically lower prices and seriously damage the economic status of the small farmer. He urged the government to continue the soil conservation program and to provide insurance against crop losses from natural causes.[54]

Reynolds also renewed his interest in law enforcement and agreed to give an address to the Law Enforcement Officers' Association of North and South Carolina on June 20, 1937. In a speech written by the FBI, Reynolds proclaimed that crime was of national importance and called for a nationwide solution. The FBI did not want to supplant local law enforcement agencies, explained the senator, but would assist them in solving crimes. To achieve this goal, the FBI needed better pay, more efficient technical equipment, and better facilities. Reynolds praised Hoover for his honesty, devotion, and effectiveness in saving lives and property.[55]

A major concern for Reynolds and the country in 1937 was military preparedness. In an address to the American Legion, Reynolds pointed out that the United States Air Force was the sixth largest in the world at a time when every foreign nation was at America's back door.[56] The senator described defense as "America's greatest problem" and deplored the small army, the weak air force, and the general unpreparedness of the country. Reynolds was against war but believed that military protection was necessary for the preservation of some semblance of American isolation.[57]

Reynolds worried about America's ability to stay out of such foreign entanglements as the Spanish Civil War, because the Neutrality Act of 1935 did not provide any guidance for a civil war. As the expiration of the act neared, an intense national debate developed over trade to belligerents. Congress had to decide to what extent it was willing to forgo the profits derived from neutral trade in order to avoid involvement in a foreign war. President Roosevelt stood between the isolationists, who demanded a mandatory embargo on all materials useful in war, and the internationalists, who feared America's export trade in basic raw materials would be devastated. Roosevelt wanted to curtail neutral rights without endangering America's trading rights and economic well-being. Thus FDR favored a *discretionary policy* that would enable the president to restrict trade if necessary to prevent American involvement in foreign affairs.[58]

Roosevelt was clearly concerned about American involvement in a foreign war. "A point has been reached," he declared, "where the people of the Americas must take cognizance of growing ill-will, of marked trends toward aggression, of increasing armaments, of shortening tempers—a situation which has in it many of the elements that lead to the tragedy of general war." The president blamed the autocratic rulers in Asia and Europe who had reverted to the law of the sword. Roosevelt wanted to preserve neutrality by denying belligerents American arms and by discouraging them from using excessive amounts of other American goods that would facilitate their war machine. The Italian invasion of Ethiopia was a case in point. American oil was flowing to Italy and aiding its military activities. Roosevelt wanted the power to control oil exports to prevent the prolongation of foreign wars.

The debate over the Neutrality Act of 1936 was essentially over the question of who would control U.S. policy in wartime—the Congress or the president. Roosevelt proposed a neutrality bill that retained mandatory arms and loan embargoes but gave the president more flexibility in determining when and how the embargoes were applied. Isolationists William Borah and Hiram Johnson rejected Roosevelt's bill and prevented the Senate Foreign Relations Committee from acting on it. Fearing a filibuster by isolationists, FDR settled for what became the Neutrality Act of 1936.[59]

The act extended the arms embargo and travel restrictions adopted in 1935 but added a prohibition of loans and credits to belligerent nations. The 1936 act further curtailed the president's decision making in foreign policy by denying him the right to restrict trade in raw materials and forced him to apply the arms embargo to any new belligerents entering a war already in progress. Roosevelt was displeased with the act because he did not have discretionary power over oil and other raw materials. He nonetheless accepted the bill, which he called "a definite step towards enabling this country to maintain its neutrality and avoid being drawn into wars involving other nations."[60]

Reynolds voted for the 1936 act because it embargoed the shipment of arms, munitions, and implements of war to either side in the Spanish civil war.[61] Other isolationists applauded this move as a safeguard against American entry into this war.[62]

When the strident debates over neutrality subsided, Roosevelt realized that the "American people were not prepared . . . to risk the slightest chance of becoming involved in a quarrel in Europe which had all the possibilities of developing into a general European conflict."[63] Roosevelt worked assiduously to modify the 1936 act. The president wanted to avoid the danger of American involvement in a foreign war through the financing or shipping of goods purchased by belligerents while maintaining American trade. He cleverly adopted a concept advocated by Senators Bennett Clark and Gerald Nye—the principle of cash-and-carry. Foreign countries had to pay cash for the goods and had to ship the goods in their own vessels. This method preserved the profits of neutral trade and minimized the risk of foreign war by avoiding the type of incidents that had led to American entrance into World War I.[64]

In January 1937, with the administration's blessing, Senator Key Pittman introduced the Neutrality Act of 1937. The Pittman bill, as it was known, continued the prohibition of loans and credits to belligerents and made American travel on belligerent ships illegal. The mandatory arms embargo on shipments to all belligerents, including those engaged in civil wars, was extended. The cash-and-carry principle in the bill gave Roosevelt the discretionary power to prevent the sale of goods other than arms (but useful in war to belligerents), unless they paid cash for them and transported them in vessels not owned by the United States. This legislation, which passed the Senate by a 63–6 vote, gave the president some flexibility yet still included mandatory restrictions that were beyond the authority of the president.[65]

Unusually reticent during the debate over cash-and-carry, Reynolds did not vote on the Pittman bill because, after much soul-searching, he simply could not make up his mind. He was in favor of the essential elements of the bill—it achieved permanent neutrality legislation and banned arms, loans, travel, and the arming of American ships. Reynolds, however, had doubts about the cash-and-carry provision and hoped it would not get America involved in a war. He finally accepted cash-and-carry because it was limited to a two-year trial basis.[66]

The first real test of the new neutrality legislation came in July 1937 with the outbreak of an undeclared war between Japan and China. Reynolds looked on Japan's invasion of China with disgust and horror, but he thought that instead of trying to police the world, the United States should not imperil the lives of "American sons who bear arms." Reynolds noted that some critics said that if America removed her armed forces from China we would lose face. "Perhaps this is so. But I'd rather lose face than lose American lives." Reynolds opposed any boycott against such aggressor nations as Japan.[67]

On December 11, still alarmed over the crisis in the Far East, Reynolds predicted that if American gunboats were not withdrawn from Chinese waters during the Japan-Chinese war, there would be an incident similar to the sinking of the battleship *Maine* in 1898.[68] The very next day Japanese planes bombed the American gunboat *Panay*, on the Yangtze River, killing two American sailors and wounding thirty. The *Panay* crisis led to severely strained relations between the United States and Japan despite Japan's apology, an offer of indemnity, and assurances against further incidents. The United States did not apply the Neutrality Act of 1937 on the legal technicality that war had not been declared.

Immediately after the news of the bombing hit Washington, Reynolds reminded his Senate colleagues of his uncanny prognostication and repeated his belief that an incident of this type would eventually involve America in a war. Reynolds demanded, with other isolationists, that the Neutrality Act of 1937 be invoked and that the United States withdraw its armed forces from China. America, concluded the senator, had no business trying to pull British chestnuts from the fire in China.[69]

His hometown paper, the *Asheville Citizen*, agreed with Reynolds. The *Citizen* wrote that Reynolds voiced the majority opinion of Americans when he urged withdrawal of American troops from China. The paper saw most Americans as pacifists who, while sympathizing with China, were determined not to fight for anybody else.[70]

Reynolds, seeking a seat on the prestigious Foreign Relations Committee, reveled in compliments from his colleagues and the press on his speech about the *Panay* incident and his knowledge of foreign affairs.[71] His fortuitous prediction about the situation in China was an important factor in his eventual appointment to the Foreign Relations Committee.

In a copyrighted article for the United Press, Reynolds explained how Japan could not be a threat to invade Russia because it was busy occupying China. Japan's expansion in the Far East, ascertained Reynolds, threatened only Great Britain and France. Reynolds thought it was strange that American sentiment was against Japan when "she is fighting our own worst enemies, the Chinese and Russian communists."[72]

Roosevelt, believing that the failure to punish Japan for its invasion of China illustrated the inadequacy of America's neutrality legislation, decided to go to Chicago, the heart of the isolationist Midwest, to deliver a speech in favor of collective security. Roosevelt warned the nation that if aggression succeeded in other parts of the world, "let no one imagine that America will escape." Roosevelt told his audience that there was no refuge in neutrality because it was impossible "for any nation completely to isolate itself from economic and political upheavals in the rest of the world."

The president further explained that 10 percent of the nations were breaking down law and order and 90 percent of the world was doing nothing about it. Roosevelt then called on America to "quarantine the aggressors. When an epidemic of physical disease starts to spread," continued the president, "the community approves and joins in a quarantine in order to protect the health of the

community against the spread of the disease." War was a contagion, whether declared or undeclared, and FDR knew that war could engulf countries remote from
the scene of the hostilities. Roosevelt wanted his country to avoid war but recognized the fact that peaceful nations had to stop aggressors from breaking the law.[73]

Reynolds and other isolationists reacted unfavorably to Roosevelt's "quarantine" speech. Reynolds, however, did not want his demands for troop withdrawal
from Asia to be seen as a break with administration foreign policy. Rather than
criticize the policy, he called Secretary of State Cordell Hull a statesman who
sought to maintain American independence from foreign entanglements and
lauded Hull for favoring a strong national defense. The Tar Heel senator noted that
both Hull and Roosevelt were "bending every energy to keep America from becoming involved in any threatened war."[74]

Reynolds's praise of Hull came despite a speech given by the secretary of state
only two days earlier in which he said it would be dangerous, from the point of
view of preserving peace, for the United States to withdraw from the Far East.
According to Hull, the United States had to remain in China to uphold international order and the sanctity of treaty obligations. Reynolds had simply referred to
the sections of Hull's speech with which he agreed and ignored the rest. Reynolds
was obviously searching for a pretext to support the Roosevelt administration's
foreign policy, because the election of 1938 was imminent and Reynolds wanted to
be completely supportive of Roosevelt at this juncture. He also desired a seat on
the Foreign Relations Committee and did not want to provoke Roosevelt.

The senator's pragmatic attitude toward reelection was further illustrated by his
views on the Ludlow Resolution. Every year since 1935, Indiana congressman Louis
Ludlow had sponsored a constitutional amendment that would require a nationwide referendum before Congress could declare war. In several previous speeches
Reynolds had agreed with Ludlow and had championed the right of the American
people to express themselves in a national referendum. When the Ludlow bill came
before the House of Representatives in 1937 with a good chance of passing, President Roosevelt voiced vehement opposition to the proposal. Although public
opinion polls indicated that some 73 percent of the American people favored the
resolution, Roosevelt used his clout to prevent the bill from being debated or voted
on in the House.

Reynolds, recognizing a fait accompli, quickly changed his position on the bill.
Although he believed it to be fundamentally sound, Reynolds acknowledged that
he would not vote for it if came before the Senate because Roosevelt was opposed
to the bill. A smiling Reynolds reminded reporters that "I have always followed the
President on foreign affairs and shall continue that policy."[75] In one year Reynolds
would break with the president over foreign policy, but in early 1938 reelection was
his primary goal.

In April 1938, Reynolds spoke to a nationwide radio audience over the Mutual Broadcasting Company about "eliminating the profit of war." Still hopeful of an appointment to the Committee on Foreign Relations, Reynolds knew that this speech was crucial to his chances. He understood that Americans were naturally concerned about the "rash boasts and the dire threats of arrogant dictators hurled at peace-loving nations." Reynolds cited as examples Hitler's occupation of the Rhineland and aggressive invasions by Mussolini into Ethiopia and by Japan into China. America, urged Reynolds, had to stay out of "these boiling foreign political pots" as our entrance "would complicate an already strained situation, and we would only get our hands scalded."

Reynolds feared that even if the United States followed a cautious course, America could still be drawn into war because among munitions manufacturers there were selfish interests who desired to lead America into war. If America had to go to war to defend its honor, Reynolds proposed the conscription of money as well as soldiers for war purposes. "Let us draft the munitions makers as well as soldiers and sailors—why permit a small clique of manufacturers of war implements to grow fabulously wealthy while millions of our youths forfeit their lives in defense of the Republic. Let the government draft the owners of the factories in the next war and the next war will be long delayed in arriving." Because greed and tyranny lead to most wars, said Reynolds, all profits should be outlawed during wartime.[76]

While his idea of drafting munitions manufacturers was offbeat and impractical, his speech drew much praise from constituents who were enthusiastic about his attack on war profiteers. Josephus Daniels, former secretary of the navy, congratulated Reynolds on his statement that the government should conscript money as well as men for war purposes.[77]

After his "eliminating profits" speech, Reynolds kept a low profile on foreign affairs until he campaigned for reelection in September. He did request that Great Britain cede the Bahamas, Jamaica, Halifax, and Newfoundland to the United States to pay off its $6 billion World War I debt,[78] but Reynolds's colleagues dismissed this proposal as unrealistic and as simply another attempt at publicity.

In a world threatened by war, Bob Reynolds desired to shore up America's perimeter defenses. To this end he urged the military development of Alaska with air bases at Sitka, Kodiak, and Fairbanks as well as the construction of a United States–Canada–Alaska highway.[79] Reynolds hoped that Britain would pay part of its war debt by ceding Newfoundland and a strip across western Canada for the Alaska highway.[80] His proposals were ignored in 1938, but his farsighted concept of an Alaskan highway and a unified and properly defended North American continent was implemented by the U.S. government after the outbreak of World War II.

Reynolds then turned his attention to important domestic issues. The Fair Labor Standards Act (Wages and Hours Law) of 1938 was the last major enactment of the second New Deal. The bill, which Roosevelt first proposed and championed in 1937, established a minimum wage and a maximum workweek (eventually forty cents per hour and a forty-hour week). Any employer who required more hours per week than the standard would pay the worker time and a half for overtime. The law applied to enterprises that engaged in or affected interstate commerce. Labor by children under sixteen was prohibited.

Reynolds favored the bill despite vehement opposition from conservative southerners who feared government by fiat and thought higher wages would paralyze business growth in a region characterized by cheap labor. Reynolds, sensitive to these arguments, proposed an amendment that would exempt all employers of ten workers or less from operation of the bill. Reynolds insisted that small establishments in the South could not survive with higher wages. The Senate voted down Reynolds's amendment 52–31. But he then proposed an amendment exempting employers of five workers or less; this amendment was adopted.[81]

Reynolds, unlike most of his fellow southerners, had voted for the Fair Labor Standards Act in 1937, but southern attacks in the House killed the bill.[82] The final act in 1938 contained major concessions for the South. The act exempted occupations such as farmers, employees in intrastate retail businesses, domestic servants, and administrative workers from the minimum wage and maximum hours provision. Also southern congressmen received a sectional wage differential that preserved the cheap labor market in the South.[83]

Reynolds's probable opponent in the 1938 election, Congressman Frank Hancock, opposed the Fair Labor Standards Act because it would hurt organized labor and because he feared increased federal bureaucracy.[84] Reynolds, to counter Hancock's position, explained why he voted for the bill: "My position on a greater share of the fruits of labor for the masses has never changed. Labor has been exploited and everybody knows it so why blink at it." The Wages and Hours legislation, responded Reynolds, would end this exploitation and raise wages that were so low that nobody defended them. Reynolds, a consistent Keynesian, argued that the increase in purchasing power meant that there would be more money spent for the items farmers sold locally.[85]

A significant economic recession in the summer of 1937 threatened the nation's economic recovery. Roosevelt's main response was to plug loopholes in the income tax laws which permitted holding companies and property trusts to avoid tax payments. Reynolds agreed with this move wholeheartedly. He supported a broader tax base because federal taxes had lost all semblance of equity. The average citizen, declared Reynolds, had to pay property taxes as well as taxes on the basic necessities of life, whereas the wealthy used loopholes to avoid their rightful share of taxes.[86]

Reynolds denounced Wall Street for its continued opposition to the New Deal.

Big business had no confidence in New Deal policies as indicated by its selfish demands to modify the capital gains taxes. "Business," declaimed Reynolds, "hates the President because he has been going down into its pockets and making it share its profits with the men who earned the wealth."[87] Reynolds exhibited a genuine concern for the economic position of the lower classes, but it was good politics to blame big business for the recession just prior to his bid for reelection.

Reynolds continued to promote his two pet projects in North Carolina. The senator wanted the federal government to finish the Blue Ridge Parkway through North Carolina and Tennessee and also urged the completion of the Great Smoky Mountains National Park. Reynolds met with President Roosevelt in late February 1937 to request an executive order for an initial allocation of $750,000 to purchase land for the national park. Although Reynolds received no assurances from Roosevelt during the one-hour meeting, he did get an appointment to confer with Interior Secretary Harold Ickes about the funds.[88]

On April 9, 1937, to bolster his cause, Reynolds presented to the U.S. Senate a resolution from the North Carolina legislature urging President Roosevelt to expedite the completion of the Blue Ridge Parkway. The resolution explained that North Carolina needed the jobs and government appropriations to help with the recession. The state legislature agreed to spend $250,000 in state funds to advertise the state and the park.[89]

One month later, to Reynolds's chagrin, the House Appropriations Committee slashed the money for construction of the Blue Ridge Parkway from $5 million to $2.5 million. Reynolds vowed to fight in the Senate to restore the cut. Eventually, owing primarily to the influence of North Carolina congressman Robert "Muley Bob" Doughton, the House restored the funds.[90]

In cooperation with Senator Kenneth D. McKellar of Tennessee, Reynolds managed to get a bill passed through Congress allocating $743,265 in federal funds to complete the purchase of land for the Great Smoky Mountains National Park.[91] The park and the parkway would eventually prove to be a great boost for tourism in the region. Reynolds's highly publicized efforts seeking funds for the project helped his reelection chances.

The United States Supreme Court, the forgotten branch of government, became the center of national attention in 1937 when the president made a controversial nomination of Senator Hugo L. Black of Alabama to the high court. Roosevelt chose Black, his first appointment to the Supreme Court, because he wanted a lawyer, a southerner, and a steadfast supporter of the New Deal. Roosevelt did not consult his usual advisers in making this choice. If he had, he would have been alerted to the rumors that Black had once been a member of the Ku Klux Klan.

Reynolds approved of Roosevelt's choice and voted in favor of Black's nomination, declaring that his Senate colleague was exceptionally well-qualified for a seat on the Supreme Court. Reynolds, of course, did not want to vote against a fellow southerner, nor did he desire to oppose Roosevelt's selection.[92]

When Senator Burton K. Wheeler demanded an investigation of Black's past affiliations with the Ku Klux Klan (KKK), Reynolds dismissed such criticism as "a lot of spite and political propaganda."[93] Later, after Black was confirmed by a vote of 63–16, Reynolds rejected any suggestion that Black resign from the Court because of his relationship with the Klan. Reynolds predicted that Black would be a "great justice" and opposed any effort to embarrass him. Even if Hugo Black admitted to a Klan connection, Reynolds hoped that Roosevelt would not ask for his resignation.[94]

Although Senator Black had remained silent on the issue during confirmation hearings, he later, after his confirmation vote, admitted that he had been a member of the Klan. He asserted that he had long since disassociated himself from the KKK, deplored intolerance, and pointed to his congressional record in defense of civil liberties. A deeply disturbed Roosevelt reluctantly decided not to ask for Black's resignation.[95] Black stayed on the Court and became a distinguished defender of individual rights.

Before Black's confirmation as a new justice, Franklin Roosevelt made a political miscalculation of significant proportions. After the "horse-and-buggy" Supreme Court had invalidated some of FDR's New Deal legislation, he had dramatically proposed a reorganization of the federal judiciary. Known as the court packing plan, Roosevelt's Judicial Reorganization Bill increased the membership of the Supreme Court from nine to a maximum of fifteen, if justices who reached the age of seventy declined to retire. The plan also included the addition of not more than fifty judges to all levels of the federal court system and the assigning of district judges to congested areas to expedite court business. Roosevelt declared that crowded dockets and delays in legal business necessitated reform and asserted that the courts needed a new outlook and new blood. The president's real reason was to change the composition of the Supreme Court from the conservative views of the "nine old men" and force the justices to accept a social welfare state.

Overly sure of himself and his political power, Roosevelt expected full support from the huge Democratic majorities in both houses of Congress. He was stunned by the violent controversy his measure provoked and dismayed by the serious split in Democratic ranks. Roosevelt's critics accused him of attempting to subvert the Constitution and to establish a personal dictatorship.[96]

As usual, the stalwart Reynolds rushed to the aid of his beleaguered chief. Reynolds announced his approval of Roosevelt's court plan and declared that he had long felt that changes were needed, especially the addition of more federal judges to relieve congested court dockets. These reforms, parroted Reynolds, would reduce government expenditures and eliminate the great delay in the arrival of swift justice in the courts. "The number of Supreme Court justices has been increased before," Reynolds correctly stated, and because the amount of litigation before the courts had practically doubled, why should the number of judges not be increased? Reynolds, unaware of the resistance to the bill, incorrectly predicted that the plan would garner sufficient votes in the Senate to pass.[97]

Reynolds approached the Judicial Reorganization Bill as a loyal Democrat and as a pragmatic politician. He did not consider the constitutional implications, the impending split in the Democrat Party, or the escalating conflict between Congress and the president over political power.

Reynolds badly misjudged the powerful opposition to the president's plan in the Senate. His conservative colleague Josiah Bailey opposed the legislation as compromising the integrity of the judiciary and claimed to have forty senators supporting his view.[98] Recognizing the growing animosity toward his plan, Roosevelt took personal charge of the fight for the legislation. In a fireside chat to the American public, the president urged support for his court reform, claiming that it would restore a balance of power among the three major branches of the federal government.

Reynolds supported Roosevelt's speech by announcing that over 90 percent of the citizens of North Carolina were for the president's plan. Reynolds judged that the Supreme Court had been usurping the functions of Congress for the past ten years, and he did not believe that any nine men should be allowed to defeat the will of the American people.[99] Reynolds then went to the White House to present Roosevelt with a certified copy of a joint resolution passed by the North Carolina legislature endorsing Roosevelt's court reform.[100]

Later that month, in a speech in Miami, Florida, which he inserted into the *Congressional Record*, Reynolds insisted, in a monumental overstatement, that Roosevelt's court reform "may become a landmark on the path of human progress." He lauded the president for his efforts to end the evil of "judicial tyranny in this country." Reynolds thought Roosevelt had been unjustly attacked simply because he had the candor to propose needed reform and wondered why there was so much "hellabuloo and hullabuloo."

The wisest course, continued Reynolds, was to put new justices on the bench who would protect the rights of workingmen against judicial usurpation, which favored bankers and big corporations. Reynolds concluded his talk by saying that there was no truth to the charges that Roosevelt intended to become a dictator or that Congress had become a rubber-stamp legislature. The Congress had rejected the World Court and the St. Lawrence Seaway, both favored by Roosevelt, and had passed the soldier's bonus over his veto. The real purpose of reform, reasoned the senator, was not presidential power but to find a workable and efficient method of promoting the common good and material welfare for all Americans.[101]

Eventually Roosevelt lost control of Congress when the conservative wing of the Democratic Party joined with Republicans in the fight against growing federal authority. After five months of congressional opposition and the untimely death of Joseph T. Robinson, Roosevelt's floor leader, the president gave up the struggle for court reform. Roosevelt's court plan probably never had a chance of passing, especially as it was seen by many in the Senate as a power grab and a devious, evasive device to create a more liberal Supreme Court.

With the impending retirement of conservative justice Willis van Devanter, the Supreme Court began to reverse its position on New Deal legislation. Roosevelt then accepted a compromise to which all Democrats could agree. On July 22, 1937, the Senate recommitted the original court reform bill to the Judiciary Committee, where it died. The new, compromise Judicial Procedure Reform Act included badly needed procedural reforms but denied the president the power to enlarge the courts.[102] The failure of the court plan was a decisive defeat for Roosevelt, but he later claimed that he had lost the battle and won the war because he began replacing retiring conservatives with more liberal justices. Given the increased opposition from conservative Democrats, however, the end of the New Deal was in sight, and in the long run Roosevelt probably had lost the war.

During both sessions of Congress in 1937, Bob Reynolds adhered to the party line. On twenty-five roll call votes considered of major importance, Reynolds failed to be recorded on only four. Of his twenty-one votes, twenty were with a majority of the Democrats. He cast only two antiadministration votes on important bills. As a matter of contrast, his North Carolina colleague, Josiah Bailey, voted against administrative measures a total of fifteen times. Bailey's voting record was similar to the voting patterns of most southern Democrats. Except for Claude Pepper of Florida and Lister Hill of Alabama, no other southern Democrat supported so many liberal bills and showed such loyalty to Roosevelt's legislative program, especially on controversial and critical bills. This unswerving support for Roosevelt unquestionably helped Reynolds in his bid for reelection, as Roosevelt remained extremely popular in North Carolina.

Our Bob was acutely aware of keeping his name before the public prior to an election year and 1937 brought Reynolds some of his most enduring notoriety. Perhaps the most famous incident of his senatorial career occurred in January 1937, when Hollywood screen stars Jean Harlow and Robert Taylor visited Washington to promote interest in President Roosevelt's Birthday Ball, a charitable event the proceeds of which went to aid in the fight against polio. As Reynolds posed on the steps of the Capitol with Harlow and Taylor, photographers asked him to kiss the platinum blond beauty. At first, Reynolds was shy and hesitant, prompting Harlow to remark, "The trouble with this gentleman is that he doesn't seem to want to go through with it." With that, the manly Reynolds, undisturbed by the presence of the great screen lover Robert Taylor, planted a resounding kiss on Harlow's lips, using what he later referred to as "Hollywood technique."[103] It was a kiss seen around the country, and *Life* magazine featured a full-page photo of the embrace.[104]

Opinion differed as to the propriety of a senator being photographed in an embrace with an actress. Some thought it a violation of senatorial dignity, whereas others commended Reynolds for dropping the curtain of formality and demonstrating his acting ability. A Washington, D.C., commissioner said that the photo of Reynolds and Harlow was worth ten thousand dollars' worth of publicity for the president's ball. Reynolds, never at a loss for words, replied, "I am always glad to help a worthy cause."[105]

In one sense this incident changed Reynolds's career. He had always been a snappy dresser and a ladies' man who was frequently seen hobnobbing in Washington society, but now he had moved into a higher league. Many of his constituents, according to Jonathan Daniels, loved his flamboyance. "In our democracy he is sort of a poor man's peacock, strutting and kissing where the boys in the filling stations would like to strut and kiss, too."[106] Others saw his performance as self-serving and demeaning, and many critics never could take the playboy senator seriously after this event. Walter Brown, a North Carolinian, had been trying to get Reynolds's assistance on a legislative matter with little success. Brown wrote to a friend: "You know that he has been extremely busy trying to make Jean Harlow, or I should say, endeavoring to make her visit to Washington a more enjoyable one."[107]

On another occasion, *Life* pictured Reynolds holding a slingshot presented to him by an admirer. On one side of the slingshot, burned into the wood, were the words, "Bob 'Shur-shot' Reynolds." After commenting on Reynolds's views on the deportation of aliens, the magazine referred to him as the "alien eradicator." *Life* further described Reynolds as "a combination of a clown, dandy, and a playboy."[108]

One of his happiest days in the Senate came when the page boys voted Reynolds as the senator they liked best. One page marveled, "And can he make a speech about immigration."[109] Reynolds, who frequently laughed and joked with the boys, was so pleased that he gave a banquet in honor of the twenty-two pages. He invited the North Carolina congressional delegation and correspondents in Washington and had James Roosevelt, son of the president, as guest speaker. Reynolds also included a letter from President Roosevelt praising the work of congressional pages. Reynolds topped off the evening by showing motion pictures of his trip around the world in 1934.[110]

Reynolds's popularity in Washington extended beyond the pages, for he maintained good relations with his colleagues and the press. They enjoyed his company because of his friendly demeanor and his constant wisecracks. The tradition of the Senate impressed Reynolds very little, and he often laughed and joked in committee meetings and on the floor. As a member of the Currency and Banking Committee, the jaunty senator jazzed up a dull session by peppering a witness with a series of erudite, perceptive questions. His colleagues gaped in astonishment at the brilliance of the usually unprepared Reynolds until he whispered loudly to a financial reporter, "Hey, bud, slip me some more of those questions."[111]

Reynolds managed to keep his name before the public with a series of speeches and appearances. He was the guest of honor on the *Major Bowes Amateur Hour*, a radio program broadcast from New York City.[112] He made major speeches at the national convention of the Loyal Order of the Moose and at a celebration of the settlement of Roanoke Island in North Carolina. In every speech he praised Roosevelt. He then, as always, wrote Marvin McIntyre, Roosevelt's secretary, to explain his activities and to ask McIntyre to bring his speeches to the attention of the president.[113]

A more embarrassing incident occurred in March 1937 when Reynolds joined with nine other members of the United States Senate to do a testimonial on behalf of Lucky Strike cigarettes. Reynolds received one thousand dollars from the American Tobacco Company for his services. The ad pictured Reynolds saying: "Luckies are considerate of my throat. Two southern traditions are oratory and good tobacco. Lucky Strike shows me how to indulge in both. For this light smoke not only pleases my taste but leaves my throat in condition." Reynolds, seldom without a cigarette in his hand, was asked if he smoked Lucky Strikes exclusively. He grinned and replied, "Among others." The senator also jokingly noted that the testimonial would be good publicity for him because it would "show that the charges that I am mixed up with the Reynolds Tobacco company are not true."[114]

Officials of the International Tobacco Workers Union were not amused. They denounced the Tobacco Trust for its oppression of labor and farmers and attacked Reynolds for violating ethical standards by receiving money from a company with legislation pending before Congress. "If a gift of money to public officials interested in important issues before such officials is bribery," questioned the union, "what is this"?[115]

Reynolds had no comment on the charges by the Tobacco Workers Union and referred to his endorsement of Lucky Strikes as a joke on big business. When informed that Senator Gerald P. Nye had given his fee to charity, Reynolds said that he had also given his fee to charity. "Which charity is that, senator?" asked a newspaperman. Reynolds replied with a rueful smile, "Well, you all know that charity begins at home." Reynolds elaborated by explaining that he had used the money to pay off debts in North Carolina, and "I know all my creditors are glad."[116]

Reynolds's response delighted his rural constituents who thought Reynolds had slickered big business, but he did not impress the *Raleigh News and Observer*. The paper did not believe that Reynolds was guilty of accepting a bribe, because politicians did not take bribes for publication. There was, however, "plenty to be said about the bad taste, the impropriety, the indignity of the wearers of the American toga testifying to the virtues of a cigarette for a price. Certainly the business reflects far less than $1,000.00 worth of credit on those Senators who reached both for the Lucky Strike and the money."[117]

This particular editorial did not disturb the thick-skinned Reynolds, who continued to revel in any sort of publicity. He simply continued to prepare for the political wars of 1938.

CHAPTER SIX

Reelection

The main event of 1938 for Bob Reynolds was reelection to the Senate. Before launching his campaign, he first had to deal with the Wagner-Costigan Anti-Lynching Bill, which penalized local authorities who allowed a prisoner to be taken away from them by a mob and lynched. President Roosevelt, in his annual message of 1934, had denounced lynching and wanted a vote on the bill provided it did not delay other reform legislation. Roosevelt did not, however, push the antilynching bill for fear that conservative southern committee chairmen might retaliate and reject all his New Deal proposals.[1]

In national politics, the one issue that most concerned blacks was an antilynching bill, a goal long sought by the National Association for the Advancement of Colored People (NAACP). Lynching had declined in the 1920s, but between 1930 and 1934 over sixty blacks were hanged, shot, or burned by mobs. Southern Democrats, aided by Republican senator William E. Borah, launched a determined filibuster designed to prevent the antilynching bill from coming to a vote in 1938. They also threatened to revolt against the administration's legislative program if the bill were forced on the South.[2]

Bob Reynolds, one of the floor leaders of the filibuster, referred to the antilynching bill as a "legislative monstrosity" that had been brought forth by northern and eastern states to attract black votes. Reynolds argued that the Senate was giving time to a nonexistent problem, because lynching was no longer a significant crime. The South was the safest place in America, continued Reynolds, and the section of the country where law-abiding blacks had their greatest number of friends. Reynolds noted that in 1936 there had been forty-four instances in which law officers prevented lynching, and thirty-nine of these had been in the South. Reynolds added that since 1882 only 4,673 people had been lynched in America, for him a number that hardly constituted a national problem. "Congress is endeavoring to make a legislative mountain out of a local mole hill." What Congress was doing, declared Reynolds, was to "lynch" the Constitution and its guarantee of states' rights.[3]

Despite Reynolds's remonstrances, the overwhelming majority of lynch victims in America were black, and lynching was a national problem. His cavalier dismissal of the 4,673 individuals who had been lynched showed his lack of compassion and judgment. Lynching, of course, was a disgrace both to the South and the nation. Reynolds, not known for racial diatribes, took a strong stand on the antilynching bill because he was up for reelection and felt he had to defend vigorously the traditions in the South. Had he not participated in the filibuster, Reynolds felt certain that his opponents would use that failure against him in his bid for a second term.

Reynolds's filibuster was neither anti-Roosevelt nor antiblack; it was simply an expedient designed to defeat the bill and keep him on good terms with both the administration and the voters of North Carolina. Reynolds held the floor most of January 6 and spoke primarily about foreign affairs, the American Civil War, Communism, preparedness, and the beauty of the mountains of North Carolina. Senator Barkley called his speech "entertaining and instructive." Reynolds took up the filibuster again on January 8 and for three hours rambled on about the cost of battleships, Mexican-American relations, and the strength of Jack Dempsey.

The North Carolina senator demonstrated a natural filibustering technique and spoke without strain, drawing most of his material from personal experience. He had a knack for stretching out roll calls and interruptions to the limit so that he did not have to spend all his time speaking. Twirling a pair of silver-rimmed spectacles and rocking back and forth on his heels, the dashing southerner delighted in expressing his opinion on a variety of subjects. Infrequently enlightening, often entertaining, Reynolds utilized every conceivable time-consuming device, primarily reading from newspapers and magazines.[4]

On January 27, 1938, the administration's attempt to invoke the cloture rule to end debate on the antilynching bill failed by a vote of 51 to 37. Reynolds voted in the negative and thus favored extending the filibuster.[5] The Wagner-Costigan Anti-Lynching Bill had been in trouble from the outset, and this vote ended any chance for its passage. The vote also demonstrated the effectiveness of the southern filibuster. The administration gave up its halfhearted support of the bill in order to end the legislative logjam. Roosevelt understood that the southerners, who by reason of seniority chaired most of the House and Senate committees, would block all his domestic legislation if he came out for the antilynching bill. By a 58–22 vote, with Reynolds voting aye, the Senate shelved the antilynching legislation.[6]

Despite his continued commitment to Roosevelt's domestic policies, Reynolds bucked the administration on two occasions. Roosevelt's housing bill, which lowered interest rates and insured mortgages to give poorer Americans a break in financing costs, passed by a vote of 42–40. The senator voted against the bill because it did not provide a prevailing wage amendment for construction workers on housing projects.[7] Reynolds also favored the repeal of the undistributed profits tax because he felt that business and industry should be allowed to use these profits to expand and increase employment and wages.[8] Congressman Robert L. Doughton of North Carolina blasted Reynolds's statement as a direct attack on Roosevelt's tax policies. Reynolds, in urging outright repeal, did not explain how the government would replace the $450 million that would be lost to the treasury. Doughton said that he knew of no supporter of Roosevelt who had asked for an outright repeal. Then, sarcastically, Doughton added, "I presume, however, that Senator Reynolds, as usual, has made a comprehensive and painstaking study of the subject."[9]

Reynolds, who since 1932 had denounced big business and its excess profits, offered no answer to Doughton and ignored the implications of his remarks. The *Asheville Citizen*, however, came to Reynolds's defense by declaring that the undistributed profits tax had deterred economic recovery and was partly responsible for the 1938 recession. Reynolds, argued the *Citizen*, was correct in opposing the tax, and his dissent should not be seen as disloyalty to President Roosevelt, "whom he has supported with extraordinary consistency."[10]

Reynolds returned to the fold and voted for the controversial government reorganization bill that would allow Roosevelt to reshuffle, transfer, and consolidate federal agencies in the interest of efficiency. The bill finally passed the Senate after a bitter struggle by a vote of 47–42, but it failed in the House when 108 Democrats, fearful that Roosevelt aspired to be a dictator, defected from the ranks and voted against Roosevelt.[11]

Elizabeth F. Clarke, a constituent, wired Reynolds to express disapproval of further government reorganization as it would give too much power to the president. Reynolds replied by stating that he always backed administration policies and would support the reorganization proposal. Clarke angrily wrote Congressman Lindsay Warren of North Carolina asking if such advance commitment by Reynolds "reflected a high order of intelligence and honesty or what he considers political expediency. It looks as if a large majority of our representatives are puppets who 'heartily approve' the most preposterous, unconstitutional legislative plans that come from the White House."[12]

Reynolds dismissed such criticism and announced his approval of all Roosevelt's national defense appropriation bills. He voted for the Naval Expansion Act of 1938, designed to make America the greatest sea power in the world.[13] In addition to naval power, Reynolds again argued for a stronger air force to protect American security. Airplanes were essential to national defense, he contended, because there was so much territory to cover.[14]

In 1938, as Adolf Hitler prepared to annex Austria, his expansionist policies posed a grave threat to the security of Europe. Mindful of the crisis in Europe, Reynolds reasserted his view that national defense was the most vital topic of the day. But he noted that the United States should prepare for a defensive war, not aggression. The purpose of the military buildup would be to keep a foreign invader away from "these peaceful shores."[15] In a later speech, before Germany's invasion of Czechoslovakia, Reynolds characterized Hitler as a "pushover man" who had been bluffing all the time. If Hitler's bluff were called, he would be unable to show the military strength of which he had boasted.[16]

Reynolds had been perceptive in many of his comments on foreign policy in 1938. He had correctly predicted the growing power of the Rome-Berlin axis in Europe and forecast the German annexation of Austria. He also had the foresight to see that Hitler would force Hungary and Czechoslovakia into the Nazi camp and then invade Russia through Poland. But he was wrong in assuming that Hitler could be bluffed. That might have been a correct view in 1934, but by 1938 Hitler had moved forcefully to fulfill his vision of a Third Reich.

As Hitler continued his march toward the domination of Europe, the American public became increasingly alarmed at his brutal totalitarianism and his militarism. The Japanese attack on China and Mussolini's invasion of Ethiopia had shocked Americans, but it was Hitler's Nazi Germany that most frightened them.

Reynolds, in the guise of a savior, believed it was his duty to find the most effective way to keep America out of war. He therefore proposed a policy of "watchful waiting" in Europe.[17] The *Asheville Citizen* editorially commended Reynolds for his careful survey of the world situation but found a great fallacy underlying his argument: "We in this country cannot dig a hole for ourselves and crawl into it without having the remains of civilization falling in on top of us." The *Citizen* declared that America could not allow the fascists to bluff their way into control of Europe or refuse its responsibilities and withdraw into isolationism.[18] Thus, in early 1938 the *Citizen* had framed the argument that Reynolds would face for the remainder of his Senate career. Reynolds, however, refused to budge from his rigidly held views on isolationism and felt certain that most Tar Heels agreed with him.

Despite the overwhelming importance of foreign affairs and the drift toward war, the daily activities of Congress had little interest for Reynolds as he spent most of his time preparing for reelection. He did, however, manage to introduce a joint resolution to establish a highway safety authority in the United States. The authority's purpose was to coordinate existing federal traffic safety activities, including the gathering of accident information and statistics, and to encourage the states to enact uniform motor laws and regulations.

Reynolds believed his bill to be far more important than the antilynching bill, as thirty-nine thousand people had been killed in traffic accidents in America in 1937. In North Carolina alone, 160 times more people were killed on the highways than were lynched in the entire country.[19] The bill did not pass, but the proposal marked one of the few times that Reynolds had offered constructive legislation during his first term in the Senate. Reynolds's concept of federal highway safety was a good idea but before its time. Only after the nation's highways became clogged with traffic did the government set up the National Transportation Safety Board.

Our Bob also found time to resume his tirade against aliens. On January 10, 1938, Reynolds discussed aliens in two lectures sponsored by the American Immigration Conference Board as part of an educational program designed to awaken people to the alien menace.[20] Reynolds saw the speeches as good publicity and surefire vote getters.

In April Reynolds gave a national radio speech titled "Registration and Fingerprinting of Aliens." Federal Bureau of Investigation director J. Edgar Hoover congratulated Reynolds on his "fearless and succinct discussion of the problem" and asked for additional copies to distribute to his agents.[21] Reynolds also announced that he had discovered over eight thousand Nazi storm troopers and sixty thousand members of the German-American Bund in America. Horrified at this subversive activity, Reynolds said that no other country would allow such behavior in the interest of a foreign power.[22] Although there was an active German-American Bund, the numbers were grossly exaggerated, and the claim of eight thousand Nazi storm troopers was patently absurd. Reynolds made these statements to get publicity for reelection. In view of his later affiliations with Nazi front organizations, these comments seem very hollow.

But the senator stayed focused on the main goal. In 1937, over a year before the Democratic primary, Reynolds had intensified his search for votes. He began making more frequent speeches in North Carolina in anticipation of a hard-fought campaign. Whenever a group of Tar Heels got together and offered Reynolds an invitation to speak, they could be assured that he would be on hand wearing his nattiest suit and smiling brightly.[23]

Reynolds worked hard at getting votes, and he knew what it took to entice voters to his banner. As he once explained to a friend, "Politics is a profession, a career. You have to practice politics just like you'd practice medicine or law."[24] He told Josiah Bailey the secret of being a good senator: "Answer all correspondence promptly, and do not fail to acknowledge every letter from every friend who is supporting you, because I know that the people appreciate that more than anything else."[25]

On one campaign foray, Reynolds arrived in Kinston, North Carolina, to introduce Senator Kenneth McKellar of Tennessee, the guest of honor. Reynolds, as usual, stole the show. Within five minutes of his arrival, Reynolds had made dozens of acquaintances, had patted young children on the head, and had posed for pictures with his arm around a noted prohibitionist. Reynolds held court in the

Kinston Hotel and greeted all comers as long-lost brothers. He courted women's votes by announcing that the lips of North Carolina women, not the lips of Jean Harlow, were the sweetest in the world. "And I ought to know."[26]

As an incumbent senator, Reynolds felt positive about his chances for victory in the Democratic primary of 1938. He boasted that he would "welcome any opponents who care to oppose me. It is a free country and anyone can run."[27] Despite his comments, Reynolds knew reelection was not guaranteed—he took no chances and campaigned vigorously. On one trip to North Carolina he delivered two commencement addresses, spoke at an automobile show, and addressed an American Legion rally. He then visited Lexington and Asheville and made three speeches in Charlotte.[28]

By late 1937 there was much animated discussion in North Carolina as to Reynolds's possible opponent. Cameron Morrison, Congressman Robert L. Doughton, former governor O. Max Gardner, Governor Clyde R. Hoey, Congressman Frank Hancock, and R. Gregg Cherry, former speaker of the North Carolina House of Representatives and current state party chairman, were mentioned as the most prominent possibilities.[29] Hoey, who earlier had thought of running against Reynolds, had been elected governor in 1936. Since he already had a job, he did not intend to get involved in a Senate race that might imperil his legislative program in the 1939 state General Assembly.[30]

The conservative wing of the Democratic Party encouraged R. Gregg Cherry to run. The conservatives saw Cherry as a formidable candidate because he was dry, could gain the support of business in the state, and was tough enough to engage in a rough-and-tumble campaign against Reynolds.[31] Cherry gave serious consideration to running but in the end decided not to announce. He refused the blandishments of his friends because he was chairman of the state Democratic Party, wanted to attend to his law practice, and thought he might not be able to defeat Reynolds.[32]

Reynolds was too liberal and too much of a maverick for the conservative wing of the Democratic Party, and they hoped to see him defeated in 1938. But they knew that his personality and his record of support for Roosevelt would be a hard combination to beat.[33] Also, Reynolds had been a dutiful senator and had escaped major scandal. Without a strong candidate (Cherry or Hoey), the conservatives recognized that it would be difficult to oust Reynolds. In a letter to the editor of the *News and Observer*, James H. Holloway, a Tar Heel voter, best summed up Reynolds's position in 1937. Holloway wrote that it would be a difficult job to relieve Reynolds of his senatorial toga. Many people might oppose him because they disapproved of his antics, but Reynolds was one of the most sensational campaigners in the state and would win unless opposed by Hoey or Gardner.[34]

George Creel, writing in *Colliers*, also discussed the dilemma of the Democratic leadership in North Carolina. The split in the party, argued Creel, was between the progressives who accepted Reynolds and the conservatives (Bailey, Hoey, Gardner) who desired a strong opponent for Reynolds but did not want to wage a costly and losing battle. Creel thought that Bailey, who disagreed with much of Roosevelt's legislative program, might be inclined to oppose Reynolds's reelection.[35]

Although correct about the conflict between the liberal and conservative wings of the party, Creel erred in his evaluation of Bailey. Bailey did not respect Reynolds and disagreed with most of his votes but would take a "friendly neutral attitude" during the contest. In private correspondence Bailey explained that he saw no reason to take sides in any senatorial contest, regardless of the candidates.[36] In public, Bailey denied that he was involved in getting an opponent for Reynolds and claimed the two men had a good relationship.[37]

By spring 1937, there was no announced opponent for Reynolds, and speculation centered around Congressman Robert L. "Muley Bob" Doughton and Congressman Frank Hancock, who was "strongly considering" making the race. Doughton said that there would certainly be an opponent for Reynolds "because so many people want somebody to run."[38]

Doughton had been approached by several people urging him to make the race. Ernest M. Green thought that Doughton was the only man in the state who could defeat Reynolds: "Thinking people in North Carolina feel it is just as necessary to redeem North Carolina from the Bob Reynolds type as it was his Republican counterparts in the old [Reconstruction era] days."[39] Doughton had never been anxious to get into the race but agreed that a change would be desirable. In letters to friends, the congressman complained that Reynolds was absent from Congress much of the time and had undertaken a desperate, defensive campaign even before he had any announced opposition."[40] Doughton told the newspapers that he thought he could beat Reynolds but would immediately withdraw his name from consideration should any acceptable opponent announce. In the absence of any such announcement, Doughton would continue to ponder a possible candidacy for several months longer.[41] Newspaper writers thought the contest between Reynolds and Doughton would be a natural—"Playboy vs. Plowboy."[42]

President Roosevelt urged Doughton to stay on as chairman of the powerful Ways and Means Committee to expedite meaningful New Deal legislation, while other friends urged him not to run because Reynolds would be hard to beat.[43] Doughton, however, was determined to see Reynolds defeated. If everyone in Congress, wrote Doughton, "took their duties no more seriously and worked no more at their jobs than Reynolds does his we could not do anything. Conservatively speaking, he is not here more than one-half of the time and when he is here, I am told, pays little attention to his public duties." Doughton noted that

Reynolds was currently absent from Washington campaigning while Congress was in session considering important legislation.[44] Reynolds knew of the burgeoning opposition to him but ignored his critics and did everything possible to stay in the public eye.[45]

Cameron Morrison thought Reynolds could be beaten. He seriously considered running against Reynolds to avenge his defeat in 1932 but could not decide if his candidacy would be the wisest course of action.[46] Few observers thought he could win, for he was sixty-eight years old and state surveys indicated very little support.[47]

Several influential party leaders, including Tyre Taylor, urged O. Max Gardner to make the race. Taylor believed that Gardner could win easily, but "more important than anything else—North Carolina needs an honest-to-goodness senator."[48] Gardner, a highly successful Washington attorney, replied that a large number of friends had asked him to enter the contest but that he was not in the least interested in making the race because politics no longer held any fascination for him.[49] With no credible opponent for Reynolds by midsummer 1937, conservative Democratic Party leaders in Raleigh reluctantly decided to accept his renomination. They thought it safer to allow Reynolds to run unopposed than to create a split in the party in a race they could not win.[50]

On October 13, fifth district congressman Frank Wills Hancock of Oxford, a capable opponent and a liberal proponent of the New Deal, announced that he would seek Reynolds's seat. He declared on his own initiative without the support of any key party leaders other than Bob Doughton. Hancock said that he would run on his record of public service and would wage a dignified but aggressive campaign. A World War I veteran, Hancock had served in the state legislature before being elected to Congress in 1930.

When he heard the news of Hancock's announcement, Reynolds appeared shocked, as he had predicted that he would be renominated without opposition. But he was philosophical: "Well, it'll simply mean that I'll get a little exercise. And I need the exercise anyway."[51]

Immediately after his announcement, Hancock rushed to Shelby to enlist the aid of the Gardner machine. Max Gardner eventually voted for Hancock, but he bluntly told Hancock that he could not beat Reynolds; Gardner also chose not to campaign for Hancock.[52] Hancock sought support from Bailey as well, but Bailey replied that he intended to continue his neutral stance.[53]

The following day, however, Congressman Doughton declared his support for Hancock and said that he had favored Hancock's candidacy all along. Doughton knew that Hancock had a difficult race on his hands, but he thought that because the congressman was so much the better man, in the end "the thoughtful people of

North Carolina will rally to his support."[54] Hancock wrote Doughton that he was elated at the response to his announcement and reported that he had been receiving letters from all over the state offering assistance.[55]

Political prognosticators expected a lively primary. Reynolds had a distinct advantage because of name recognition, but Hancock had many contacts in the state and had been effective at helping his constituents. Since both men were liberal New Dealers, it seemed unlikely that Roosevelt would have any impact on the primary.[56]

Josiah Bailey and others thought Hancock too liberal and hoped that a third, more conservative candidate might enter the race.[57] Because he still entertained the idea of running, Cam Morrison had openly opposed Hancock's candidacy,[58] but eventually he declined to run for "personal reasons" (read age and inability to attract support). Morrison suggested that Governor Hoey be "drafted" to make the race. Hoey declared that he already had a job.[59]

In the end, the conservative Democrats sat out the election. They simply could not come up with a strong candidate and were unwilling to risk time and money in a losing cause. They hoped Reynolds and Hancock would destroy each other politically and the conservatives could then pick up the pieces.[60] Had either Gardner or Hoey chosen to run, the conservative wing of the party would have unleashed all its resources and energy to defeat Reynolds. Based on their political prowess plus the aid of the Gardner machine, it seemed likely that either Gardner or Hoey would have beaten Reynolds in a one-to-one contest.

Hancock formally filed for the Senate seat on January 21, 1938, stating that "Senator Reynolds has said he wants some exercise. I intend to give it to him." Hancock filed only after conferring with James A. Farley, who apparently agreed that the national administration would adopt a hands-off policy for the Democratic primary.[61] Roosevelt did not think of Reynolds as a heavyweight, but he promised to stay out of the race because Reynolds had been a loyal New Dealer.[62] Had Roosevelt entered the fray on the side of Hancock, Reynolds's reelection would have been in jeopardy.

As the campaigning commenced, Reynolds and Hancock were so similar in their political positions that the contest quickly became one of personalities rather than issues. Reynolds, basking in his incumbency, publicly showed very little concern for Hancock's candidacy. He confided to reporters that he had no plans to leave his job in Washington to tour the state and would limit his campaigning to weekends.[63] This from a man who had been energetically running for reelection since 1933. Reynolds knew that he did not have a strong opponent, and because Hancock had no support from V. O. Key's "progressive plutocracy," Reynolds expected an easy victory. Reynolds's chances for victory increased when Bernard Baruch, a powerful, wealthy businessman who was both friend and adviser to

Roosevelt, visited Reynolds's office. Without asking for any favors, Baruch plunked down five thousand dollars in cash as a contribution to Reynolds's campaign.[64]

William B. Bankhead, speaker of the U.S. House of Representatives, comment ing on Hancock's chances in the Democratic primary, said that there was no clear-cut difference between the two candidates and regretted that Hancock had announced for the Senate. "Of course, I would be very much pleased to see him win, but I imagine that Reynolds will be difficult to beat."[65]

Despite a weaker opponent, the heavily favored Reynolds still planned to run hard and to take no chances. To this end, he changed his campaign tactics from those he employed in 1932. Aware of the criticism by Doughton and others, Reynolds decided to pay much closer attention to his Senate duties in order to blunt the charge that he was a playboy. He became more dignified and subdued on the stump without losing any of his effervescent personality. He adopted Roosevelt's technique of frequently using the radio for speeches and concentrated on foreign affairs—as befit a United States senator. Hancock, not as well known as Reynolds, found it necessary to crisscross the state making speeches, meeting people and attacking Reynolds.

In early January 1938, Reynolds struck the first blow by circulating "Renominate Bob Reynolds" cards among North Carolinians on the federal payroll, asking them to canvass other government employees with pledge cards. This tactic brought a quick response from Hancock, who charged that Reynolds put the federal workers on the spot: if they did not sign the cards pledging their support, "the plain inference is that their jobs may not be safe." Hancock called the move "political intimidation" and noted that the "kindest thing I can say about such tactics is that they are cheap and little and beneath the dignity of any man who presumes to hold the office of United States Senator." Hancock promised to protect the workers who refused to cooperate with Reynolds.[66] Reynolds made no comment on Hancock's charges.

Determined to avoid an upset, Reynolds solicited the approbation of Gordon Gray, publisher of the *Winston-Salem Journal*,[67] and set up a committee of friends in Craven County "to look after my interest."[68] Reynolds's activities in Craven County were typical of his statewide pursuit of victory. He wrote W. C. White of Vanceboro, asking him to place fifty campaign placards "in the most advantageous places,"[69] and followed up by writing a letter requesting assistance from all the election officials in Craven County.[70]

Meanwhile Congressman Hancock began attacking Reynolds in much the same way that Reynolds had attacked Morrison in 1932. Hancock concentrated on Reynolds's war record, his around-the-world junkets, and his failure to give priority to state and national legislative matters.[71]

On April 12 Hancock gave a satirical speech that became the basis for most of his negative oratory against Reynolds. He claimed that Reynolds clothed the high office of senator with the "accouterments of a clown" and that democracy was too serious to entrust to "uncertain and flippant hands." The congressman then announced a ten-point platform of what he would *not* do as a senator.

Hancock said he would *never* sell the name and dignity of the Senate to anybody, especially for "a brand of cigarettes I may or may not smoke." As senator, Hancock would not follow the sensationalism of William Randolph Hearst, would not belittle the dignity of the Senate by "bouncing around the country advertising myself," would not repudiate promises to veterans and other groups, would not be the most costly senator North Carolina had ever had, and would not be a resident of the world for five years and a resident of North Carolina for one year. Hancock closed his stock speech by saying that citizens had the right to expect honesty of intellect and honesty of purpose from their elected representatives. Voters should not believe that a vague program of national defense and a policy of keeping aliens out of the country would solve America's economic ills.[72]

As he did throughout the race, Reynolds wisely refused to respond to Hancock. He stated that he planned to make nonpolitical speeches and "disseminate information to my friends" whenever he could get away from his pressing duties in the Senate.[73]

Reynolds could afford to ignore Hancock, as all reports indicated that he was running far ahead of his challenger. Charles A. Webb wrote Reynolds that he would support the senator for reelection because of his heroic loyalty to Roosevelt. Helen R. Wohl, another supporter, in her travels around the state, reported that she had heard numerous times that citizens planned to vote for Reynolds because he stood by Roosevelt and because he was the friend of the farmer, worker, and veteran. John Easton, a farmer near Wilson, had suffered during the depression but had great faith in Roosevelt: "I'm a Democrat; I stand for the New Deal and Roosevelt. I am for the WPA, the NYA, the NRA, the AAA, the FHA and crop control."[74]

Hancock had no choice but to stay on the hustings and continue his attacks on Reynolds. After a two-week tour of the state, Hancock said he found very little support for Reynolds and predicted that Reynolds would go down as "the worst licked man in the history of North Carolina politics." When asked if he approved of kissing movie stars on the Capitol steps, Hancock produced a picture of his wife and seven children and said, "Right there is all the kissing I want."[75]

Hancock knew that few people disliked Reynolds personally but "nearly all of them question his senatorial capacity." He was positive that voters were determined to end "this five year senatorial vacation which was slipped over on them in a mad moment of political muddleness. The people were fooled once and they have paid the price without getting even second-rate comedy in return." The voters, deduced Hancock, would not be fooled again and would turn Reynolds and his coterie out of office to practice their buncombe on sources less intelligent than the citizens of North Carolina.

Hancock charged Reynolds with preferring India, China, Russia, and the Virgin Islands over North Carolina and of being on the West Coast during the fight for the Great Smoky Mountains National Park. When North Carolina peanut farmers were fighting for their bill in Washington, continued Hancock, Reynolds was off "studying divorce in Russia or the liberalization of the liquor laws in Shanghai." Hancock surmised that after five years of world travel he should at the very least have been an expert in foreign affairs, but nobody except Reynolds would take such a claim seriously. The administration did not put this "phony expert" on the Foreign Relations Committee but placed him on the Banking and Currency Committee, which was "beyond his faintest comprehension," and on the District of Columbia Committee where he could do little harm. In his radio speeches Hancock constantly referred to Reynolds as a "counterfeit statesman" and "a playboy senator."[76] The challenger kept predicting that he would win a landslide victory over Reynolds, calling him "an accidental senator."[77]

Despite Hancock's claim that Reynolds "was beaten already," Reynolds's confidence was boosted in May 1938 with the overwhelming victory in Florida by Claude Pepper, a 100 percent New Dealer. The press interpreted Pepper's victory as a mandate for Roosevelt. Although Roosevelt had formally endorsed Pepper and had not given his blessing to Reynolds,[78] Reynolds saw Pepper's victory as a positive omen.

Reynolds waited until May 18, only two weeks before the Democratic primary, to open his reelection campaign. In a radio address, a subdued Reynolds cited his seniority in the Senate and asserted that a win for Reynolds would also be a victory for President Roosevelt. He claimed that every vote he had cast on the floor of the Senate had been in the interest of the wage earner, the veteran, the farmer, or the aged. He also maintained (incorrectly) that he had been present on the Senate floor to vote for every important piece of legislation. He closed his address with a plea for the need to deport alien criminals, but he did not attack Hancock or answer his opponent's charges. Observers were surprised by the mild tone of his speech and astonished by his failure to criticize Hancock.[79]

Reynolds saw no useful purpose in attacking Hancock and intended to take the high road. This less aggressive attitude did not mean that he was not hard at work gathering votes. During the latter part of the race, Reynolds mailed out a series of seven campaign bulletins to the chairmen of the Reynolds Reelection Organization. The bulletins asked his supporters to arrange local newspaper publicity for his radio addresses, to call their neighbors and encourage them to listen, and to raise funds for ads. The mailings included campaign cards, pamphlets, and handbills to be distributed in the local area. Reynolds also wanted three of his most important speeches—"Keep America Out of War," "Eliminating Profits of War," and "Alien Criminals in America"—distributed to people living on rural mail routes. The speeches would be paid for by the government because Reynolds claimed it was government-printed matter pertaining to government business. The senator again warned against overconfidence and wanted a poll watcher at each voting precinct to insure a fair vote.[80]

The *St. Louis Star-Times* saw the North Carolina race as totally different from other southern races in 1938 given President Roosevelt's efforts to purge conservative, anti–New Deal senators. In the North Carolina race, noted the paper, the Democrats would get a New Dealer no matter who won. The *Star-Times* thought Reynolds would be the winner because of his unwavering support for Roosevelt. As one conservative Tar Heel told the paper, "The state is not for the New Deal, but it is for Roosevelt."[81]

In mid-May, the state Democratic Party held its convention in Raleigh. The convention put Governor Hoey and party conservatives in an awkward position because they did not want to endorse either Reynolds or Hancock. Max Gardner provided a solution by proposing that the party endorse all candidates and then Hoey would not have to choose between Reynolds and Hancock. Hoey, desirous of staying neutral and avoiding disharmony, followed Gardner's advice.[82]

Bob Reynolds arrived in Raleigh bursting with confidence and set up headquarters at the Sir Walter Hotel, long the center of political activities in the state. His headquarters, according to the *Charlotte Observer*, resembled the midway of a state fair. The *Observer* described the large crowds milling about, shaking hands with the senator, drinking the free soda pop, and wearing "I am for Reynolds" ribbons. There were full-sized likenesses of Our Bob plastered on each of the four walls in the lobby, and friends of the senator handed out yellow and white candy canes bearing the inscription "Stick with Reynolds."[83]

Reynolds made his grand entrance into the convention just as Chairman R. Gregg Cherry introduced the keynote speaker, Congressman Lindsay Warren. When Cherry said, "I now take pleasure in presenting a distinguished North Carolinian," in popped Our Bob, accompanied by cheers and a rebel yell. With a retinue of admirers at his heels and the broadest of smiles, Reynolds strode aggressively to the front of the hall. He then acknowledged the cheering by raising his arms above his head in the manner of a prize fighter. It was several minutes before the junior senator took his seat and order could be restored.[84]

Immediately after the conclusion of the convention, Hancock resumed his assault. He questioned Reynolds's loyalty to Roosevelt and wondered why, if Reynolds were as close to Roosevelt as he claimed, the president refused to indicate a preference for either candidate. When Reynolds was not sure of Roosevelt's popularity in 1933, continued Hancock, he opposed the president on the St. Lawrence Seaway, the World Court, and other matters. Hancock accused Reynolds, in a telling riposte, of being "closer to the headlines of Hearst [William Randolph] than to the heart of Roosevelt." As a congressman, Hancock averred that he had done something to further Roosevelt's programs and had not been just a "yes" man or a "coat-tail candidate." Reynolds had not been called to the White House for consultation on important legislative matters because he had no serious conception of the grave problems facing the country. Citizens of the state, asserted Hancock, should have difficulty reconciling "the action of a man who has no serious thought for five years, with a man who on election eve pretends that his duties are so great that he cannot even come back home to campaign."[85]

After a brief visit to Washington to attend to legislative matters, Reynolds and Hancock roused themselves for a final flurry of campaigning. Reynolds wrote letters to supporters thanking them for their help and encouraging them to work to the end.[86] He made a few radio addresses similar to his earlier speeches but added a defense of his travel around the United States in 1935: he had made his trip during a congressional recess, and the travel had been "at my own expense."[87]

On May 28, a desperate Hancock launched his final offensive. He knew his only chance was to continue to belittle Reynolds and hope that the thoughtful voters in the state would flock to his banner. The congressman declared that while he was working day and night for the farmers, "our playboy senator was spending his time in the night clubs of Baghdad."[88] Hancock criticized Reynolds for "religiously avoiding" answering Hancock's many charges. The only reason that Reynolds had given for why voters should reelect him, according to Hancock, was his seniority. Hancock described Reynolds's tenure in the Senate as "five years of the most glorious vacation mortal man ever had."[89]

At the last minute, former governor J. C. B. Ehringhaus endorsed Hancock, but there was little support by administration forces other than Ehringhaus.[90] Major L. P. McLendon, a power in the Democratic Party, appealed to voters on Hancock's behalf in a radio address. McLendon said that Hancock was "more interested in the condition of the tobacco and cotton crops in North Carolina than in the political and social conditions of the Virgin Islands." McLendon thought that the people of the state did not want to return a senator who had earned the reputation of "never having read a single proposed piece of legislation in the almost six years he has served as senator."[91]

In his final speech of the campaign, Hancock emphasized that he had not "attacked" Reynolds but had merely cited the "cold and merciless record." Reynolds, noted Hancock, had not provided "one iota of defense or explanation" for his legislative record. Hancock expected a huge victory and predicted that he would win sixty-nine counties.[92]

Bob Reynolds, as in 1932, returned home to Asheville at the head of a motorcade from Charlotte and held a "Mammoth Homecoming Celebration" at the courthouse, where he predicted a winning majority of 175,000.[93] The *Asheville Citizen*, obviously agreeing with Hancock's charges, refused to recommend native son Reynolds for reelection. The paper merely commented on the importance of the election, while urging everyone to vote.[94]

The election results, in what insiders called the quietest election in the state's history, were closer than Reynolds predicted, but he still won easily by a vote of 315,316 to 197,154.[95] Hancock's late support from Ehringhaus and McLendon had helped, but he carried only seventeen out of one hundred counties. Hancock ran very close to Reynolds in the large urban counties such as Forsyth, Mecklenburg, Wake, and Guilford, but Reynolds's great margin of victory came in the western part of the state, where he ran up huge majorities in many counties.[96]

Hancock conceded to Reynolds the next day, promised not to "sulk in my tent," and pledged to help Reynolds pursue the economic and social welfare of the people of the state.[97] Reynolds thanked the voters for their "renewal of confidence."[98]

The press commentary indicated that Reynolds's triumph was not as wonderful as the senator imagined. The *Asheville Citizen* congratulated him for a victory margin that was "amazing to political observers." The *Citizen* argued that Hancock had made a severe tactical mistake in keeping his campaign so negative but conceded that Reynolds's triumph was inevitable.[99] Other papers were not so charitable.

The *Charlotte News* was distressed that Reynolds had been returned to office, because "once you have conceded his personal magnetism and impressive platform presence, you have run the gamut of his qualifications to hold office." The *News* thought that it was not so much that Reynolds lacked the ability to be a capable public servant—he lacked the disposition. His first six years in office, declared the paper, were diligent only in terms of his own reelection, and reelection alone explained his ardor for the New Deal. Perhaps the voters, surmised the paper, knew that Reynolds, as a good fellow who meant no harm, was likely to inflict less enduring mischief than one who wanted to reform the world.[100] This latter view was upheld by W. J. Armfield III, who wrote Senator Bailey that the conservatives he knew supported Reynolds because "he would do nothing one way or the other," whereas Hancock might do something destructive.[101]

Tom Bost, writing in the *Greensboro Daily News*, maintained that the election proved that Reynolds held power tenuously. He won by tradition and by the grace of Roosevelt's popularity. If someone such as Doughton, Cherry or McLendon had run, Reynolds would have been badly beaten. "The magic of Our Bob is gone," announced Bost.[102]

Reynolds had been both extraordinarily lucky and shrewd in his 1938 campaign. He was fortunate that a strong politician from the west did not announce against him, and the decision of the Hoey-Gardner-Bailey conservative wing of the party to stay neutral helped immeasurably. Roosevelt's willingness to stay out of the contest hurt Hancock's chances, plus Hancock's voting record was so similar to Reynolds's that he did not offer the conservatives a real choice.

In 1938 Reynolds ran a race opposite in style, tone, and technique to his 1932 triumph. Hancock tried to adopt some of Reynolds's former tactics, but he lacked Our Bob's eloquence and flamboyance. Hancock also acknowledged that he had been handicapped by a lack of funds and pressing congressional duties. Reynolds never bothered to answer any of the charges fired at him by Hancock—a wise decision, as many of the charges were unanswerable. Any dialogue between the two would have created more interest in the election than Reynolds desired.

Reynolds won partly because of his charisma and partly because of the lingering aura from 1932 when he had presented himself as a champion of the people. By playing the role of the concerned statesman, Reynolds no longer appeared to be the clown and buffoon of 1932. He presented himself as a New Deal senator who supported legislation to help the people of his state. Perhaps more significant, Reynolds had campaigned hard for five years and had done a marvelous job of addressing constituents' needs. In addition, he had the strong support of labor and veterans,[103] as well as many votes from women. His daughter, Mamie Spears Reynolds, later talked about her father's courting of women's vote and their impact on his race. "He loved to have them around him. In return they loved him back. I believe the women elected Dad."[104] Finally, the alien issue, although a small part of his campaign strategy, helped get him votes. As Reynolds told Senator Millard Tydings, also up for reelection, "Talk about the alien within our gates. That's the stuff that gets the votes. It worked like a charm for me."[105] This statement did not mean that Reynolds was insincere in his views on aliens. A nativist, he believed firmly in his anti-immigration bills and the alien menace, but he also recognized that these issues were potent campaign topics and reminded voters of them whenever possible.

In the end, Reynolds's reputation took a severe battering in the primary. Hancock had correctly pointed out many of the senator's faults and foibles. Reynolds had prevailed, but damage had been done to his credibility and prestige.

Shortly after the contest with Hancock, Reynolds returned to Washington. He spent the time between the Democratic primary and the general election practicing law in Asheville and by taking a two-month trip to Alaska to study national defense. While in Alaska, he went walrus hunting and boasted that he had bagged "seventeen of the critters."[106]

Charles A. Jonas, a capable Republican, was Reynolds's adversary in the November election. Jonas planned to run a campaign of goodwill rather than attack Reynolds, although he did promise that when elected senator he "would not engage in public kissing on the Capitol steps."[107] As promised, Jonas ran a low-key campaign in which he urged a realignment of political parties. Jonas tried to soften the ideological lines between the parties because he was aware that the Republican Party in North Carolina was weak and had an ineffective state organization. Jonas thought that there was enough anti–New Deal sentiment in the state to defeat Reynolds if the Republicans could somehow organize disgruntled Democrats.[108] He charged the Roosevelt administration with excessive spending that would eventually lead to bankruptcy and warned of the danger of regimentation and loss of liberty under the New Deal.[109]

Reynolds expected an easy victory in November, but O. Max Gardner worried about the size of the Democratic victory—farmers were upset about the low price of cotton, and it was an off-year election with apathetic voters. Gardner also feared that many voters in the state were dissatisfied with Roosevelt because of his attempted purge of the Supreme Court and his 1938 campaign against conservative southern senators. Gardner thought that voters were becoming more conservative and might strike a blow against Roosevelt by voting against Reynolds and other Democratic candidates.[110]

Because the White House had a vital interest in Reynolds's success in November, Roosevelt persuaded Gardner to become an unofficial adviser to Reynolds. Although Gardner had voted for Hancock and valued the ability of both Hancock and Jonas over that of Reynolds, he heeded the call. Reynolds wisely accepted Gardner's guidance.[111]

Gardner told Reynolds to acknowledge the fact that some people were upset with Roosevelt's policies but to stress that the good far outweighed the evil. Gardner wanted Reynolds to recall the futility and hopelessness of the Hoover years when people were hungry and unemployed. Gardner said the people "must remember the evils that Roosevelt eliminated from our national life before we fall back into the error of turning our Government back into the hands of those who made such a miserable failure in the 12 years preceding." Gardner wrote several speeches for Reynolds sounding this theme.[112]

Reynolds followed Gardner's counsel throughout the race. A typical speech had Reynolds declaring that for the twelve years preceding Roosevelt, "this nation was over-fed at the top and under-fed at the bottom and squeezed to death in the middle. When the storm struck in 1929," stated Reynolds, "the whole fabric of business toppled like a house of cards. Roosevelt had only two alternatives. He could let the country go to the dogs or he could save the country. Thank God Roosevelt saved the country."[113] Reynolds pictured Jonas as a friend and supporter of Hoover and said that owing to the practical blessings received by North Carolina from the New Deal, he was certain that a majority of citizens would express a renewal of faith in Roosevelt.[114]

Bob Reynolds meets with his staff shortly after his return from Europe in December 1938.
(Courtesy *Raleigh News and Observer*)

Just before the election, Reynolds wrote President Roosevelt, reporting that the president was as popular with the people of North Carolina as ever before and praising Max Gardner for his admirable assistance. Reynolds predicted a victory margin of 250,000 votes.[115] Josiah Bailey, more careful in his calculations, thought Reynolds would win by 150,000.[116]

On election day a light rain and voter apathy in a nonpresidential year held down the number of participants and produced the smallest turnout since 1926.[117] Nonetheless, Reynolds and the Democratic Party won easily. Reynolds received 316,685 (63.8 percent) votes to 179,650 (36.2 percent) for Jonas—a plurality of 137,035.[118] J. Edgar Hoover sent congratulations on Reynolds's reelection.[119]

Senator Reynolds won a clear victory but did not achieve the overwhelming triumph he envisioned. Nonetheless, his vote total was generally consistent with Democratic majorities during nonpresidential years.[120] Republicans made very few inroads in the South in 1938 (although they made some heavy gains nationwide) even though Roosevelt was less popular than in 1932 and the party out of power traditionally gained in an off-year election. One can conclude that Roosevelt still had the confidence of a distinct majority of North Carolina voters. Reynolds had capitalized on that popularity, plus rather bland Republican opposition in a one-party state, to win another six years in the Senate.

Before the final tally had been posted, the most widely traveled senator had thanked the voters and had departed on a tour of Europe. On this particular trip, Reynolds outdid himself by becoming the first United State senator to visit Albania. He arrived in the country on November 29 and was greeted by the American ambassador. Reynolds had an audience with King Zog and discussed the crisis in Europe. He left on December 1 for Athens, Greece.[121]

When he finally returned to Washington in January 1939, two events had occurred which would set him in direct opposition to Franklin Roosevelt. First, Roosevelt appointed Frank Hancock, instead of Reynolds's candidate, to a seat on the Federal Home Loan Bank Board. The president's decision outraged Reynolds and set off an angry struggle over patronage. Second, Reynolds made a series of controversial statements while abroad. He praised economic gains in Italy and Germany, said we had nothing to fear from Hitler, and urged Americans to cease their "hate wave" against European dictators. These two events precipitated a dramatic split with Roosevelt.

CHAPTER SEVEN

[Neutrality, 1939]

As Franklin Roosevelt's New Deal came to a close and the nation shifted its attention to the world stage, Bob Reynolds did an assessment of the impact of New Deal legislation on North Carolina. He concluded that the Roosevelt-sponsored bills had had a significant and profound impact on the state. He was proud of his support for most of the legislation because it put people back to work and increased purchasing power.

Reynolds was certainly aware of some of the tangible benefits North Carolina received in the 1930s, but it was not until much later that historians would make a comprehensive and analytic study of the New Deal in North Carolina. Anthony Badger, in his fine work *North Carolina and the New Deal*, and Hugh Lefler and Albert Newsome, in their book *North Carolina*, found that the Federal Emergency Relief Administration (FERA) had provided relief for as many as three hundred thousand clients a month. The Public Works Administration (PWA) gave work to over two hundred thousand Tar Heels; expended billions on hospitals, public schools, airports, low-cost housing, playgrounds, and conservation; and built the Blue Ridge Parkway. The Works Progress Administration (WPA) expanded work relief programs with a WPA tourist guide, while founding a symphony orchestra and sponsoring artists, plays, and concerts. The Civil Works Administration (CWA) provided emergency jobs.

Lefler divulged that in the first five years of the New Deal, North Carolinians received $428,053,000 in federal aid. The Agricultural Adjustment Acts (1933 and 1938) made benefit payments for limiting crops and for soil conservation. The Rural Electrification Administration (electricity for farmers), the Farm Security Administration (aid to tenant farmers) and other agencies helped the farmers weather the storm. By 1940 crop prices had risen, and the total income of North Carolina farmers had increased.

Other New Deal bills that Reynolds voted for—the Social Security Act and the Wages and Hours Bill—as well as the Tennessee Valley Authority, had increased the security and well-being of the people of the state. By 1939 every important state service, except for education, had been restored to the 1930 level of financial support. What Reynolds did not know or ignored was that from 1933 to 1938, despite federal largesse, North Carolina received the lowest per capita amount of spending of all the states.

By 1939, however, many of the business and political leaders of the state had come to dislike the liberal economic and social reforms of the New Deal. Some critics saw work relief as a great boondoggle with costs out of proportion to benefits and believed that these projects reduced incentive and led to dependence on an enlarged, inefficient federal bureaucracy—a social welfare state.

Although the New Deal had saved many North Carolina banks and the Reconstruction Finance Corporation had loaned huge sums to businesses, the businesspeople in the state retained their traditional hostility to federal government intervention. Both Governor Clyde Hoey and O. Max Gardner turned against Roosevelt because of his ill-advised purge of southern senators in 1938 and because of the growing power of the federal government. Hoey disliked FDR's attempt to reform the Supreme Court, opposed the federal minimum wage and maximum hours legislation, and blamed the Wagner Act for labor troubles in North Carolina. The state, controlled by rural farmers and Piedmont businesspeople, did not continue the trend toward welfare liberalism. The citizens of North Carolina had overwhelmingly supported FDR and were grateful for his intervention, but by the gubernatorial election of 1940, New Deal issues were conspicuously absent.

Professor Badger concluded that New Deal legislation of the 1930s left the basic social, political, and economic infrastructure of the state largely unchanged. There were still low wages, inadequate spending for education, low per capita income, and limited public services, and workers still had difficulty unionizing. What remained, argued Badger, was a conservative, business-oriented ideology that had survived the dramatic changes of the New Deal largely unaltered.

Badger also viewed Reynolds as a conservative politician of the Josiah Bailey type and asserted that his support for the New Deal was purely political.[1] Badger's interpretation did not provide a full understanding of Reynolds's motives. Bob Reynolds favored New Deal programs for two reasons, both equally important. First, New Deal legislation alleviated the worst aspects of the depression, put people to work, and helped save the economic structure of the state. Second, he knew Franklin Roosevelt was wildly popular in North Carolina and that support for Roosevelt's programs would help him get reelected. There were occasions, such as court reform and the reorganization act, when Reynolds simply voted the way Roosevelt asked him to vote. On most of the social legislation, however, the senator voted aye because he believed in the efficacy of the bills, although he certainly knew that these acts would be greeted with enthusiasm by his constituents.

Thus, in 1939, when Reynolds broke with Roosevelt, it was not over New Deal legislation but over a patronage conflict and foreign policy issues. Reynolds's reelection gave him six more years of security, and he felt he no longer needed to rely on Roosevelt's popularity. But he did not change his political views or his isolationism. He had opposed FDR on the World Court, the Ludlow resolution, and neutrality legislation during his first term and would continue to cling to his isolationist views, to his political detriment, during his second term.

Frank Hancock, recently defeated by Reynolds, announced in September 1938 that he desired a seat on the Federal Home Loan Bank Board. The former congressman indicated that he had the support of Governor Clyde Hoey and the majority of North Carolina congressmen.[2] Reynolds had already promised to support Hancock for any federal position, as long as it would not cause Reynolds any embarrassment. Despite this statement, the News and Observer commented that Reynolds refused to push Hancock's candidacy and preferred someone who had supported him in the election.[3] Sure enough, Reynolds endorsed George W. Coan, a former mayor of Winston-Salem, North Carolina state director of the WPA, and a strong backer of his in 1938.[4]

President Roosevelt, with the advice of James Farley, controlled the appointment to the bank board, and they had agreed to give the position to those who had been loyal to the administration. Roosevelt's decision on whether to appoint Hancock or Coan was a major test as to how Reynolds stood with the administration. Reynolds made a special trip to the White House to urge Coan's appointment, while Congressman Bob Doughton, a powerful New Dealer, followed the next day to advocate for Hancock.[5] Reynolds thought he should be rewarded for his efforts in behalf of Roosevelt from 1932 to 1938 and flatly predicted that Coan would get the position.[6]

On December 22, 1938, the confident Reynolds was stunned to learn that Hancock, not Coan, had been appointed to a six-year term on the Federal Home Loan Bank Board.[7] Reynolds refused to comment on the appointment except to say that he would not oppose Hancock's confirmation in the Senate.[8]

Not only was Coan's failure to get a seat on the board a blow to his political prestige, but Reynolds regarded the decision as a personal rebuff. He knew that he had been assiduously loyal to Roosevelt and perceived the president as ungrateful for his past services. His failure to secure the position for Coan, especially after publicly predicting that Coan would be nominated, was humiliating for the senator and alienated him from Roosevelt. The sting was greater because not only had Roosevelt not supported Reynolds's reelection bid in 1938 but he also had named his defeated opponent to the post.

President Roosevelt, however, had recently supported Reynolds (an isolationist) for a seat on the Senate Foreign Relations Committee, an assignment long coveted by Reynolds. Roosevelt perhaps thought that the Foreign Relations Committee appointment was reward enough and apparently did not see the Coan selection as a major issue for Reynolds.

Because of his anger toward Roosevelt over the Coan matter, the security of a six-year term, and his isolationist views on foreign policy, Reynolds became more independent in the Senate and felt little obligation to support the Roosevelt administration. He immediately began, albeit subtly as first, to criticize both Roosevelt and his policies.

Shortly after the November 1938 elections, Reynolds departed on a trip to Europe, an event that would dramatically impact his political career.[9] Nothing was heard from Reynolds until December 23, 1939, when he arrived in New York after a six-week European journey. Clad in a red flannel shirt and a rumpled suit, the gregarious traveler informed the press that he had formal talks with Premier Edouard Daladier of France, Prime Minister Neville Chamberlain of England, and high officials in all the countries he visited, with the exception of Germany.

At this point, Reynolds made a series of statements to reporters that were among the most controversial and most misinterpreted of his Senate career. Reynolds began his discourse on foreign affairs by saying that the United States had to cease its "hate wave" against European dictators, because it could not get anywhere by hate. It was none of America's business how other countries conducted their internal affairs. "What we should do," maintained Reynolds, "is to open our eyes and find out what's going on in the world. We sit over here and knock Hitler and Mussolini and everyone else who differs with us in how a government should be run." The United States, Reynolds stated, would rightly resent interference from other nations in our internal affairs.

Reynolds had been impressed with the economic gains in Germany and Italy during the depression and praised the newly built German autobahns as the finest in the world. Reynolds announced that there were no unemployed people in Germany. They "all have jobs and food and they seem happy." Reynolds believed that America need have no fear of Germany except economically. Yet the senator made it clear that he did not approve of Hitler and Mussolini or their philosophy of government—he was satisfied with the American system of government. Although Reynolds personally observed no persecution of Jews, he nonetheless, trying to avoid any possible controversy, expressed sympathy for Jews and other minorities in Germany.

The senator reported that any talk of war in Europe was "all nonsense." Reynolds knew that Hitler already owned Europe and there was nobody to fight, as France was a secondary power and Britain had too many problems. "Chamberlain did the only thing he could do in negotiating the Munich settlement. Paris and

London would have been razed to the ground by German airplanes if he had not done so."[10]

As soon as Reynolds ended his impromptu remarks, the wire services began disseminating his statements. Reynolds had earlier characterized Hitler's campaign of aggression against Austria as bloodless and efficient and one that would lead to needed reforms.[11] This previous statement, together with his more recent comments, led to an immediate and vociferous reaction from many Americans. It appeared to many that because Senator Reynolds had praised Hitler and Mussolini, he must be a fascist sympathizer.

Reynolds's off-the-cuff remarks were made with little thought and no concern about negative political consequences. Nonetheless, Reynolds had given a generally accurate appraisal of European conditions, and his comments reflected his views on the world situation. His fulsome praise of Hitler's economic accomplishments should not have been interpreted as pro-Nazi or that he advocated a dictatorship for America. A loyal American, Reynolds rejected fascism as a system of government. But the newspaper coverage overlooked his defense of the American system and exaggerated his praise of the German economy. Thus it appeared to some readers that the isolationist Reynolds had suddenly, in the critical year of 1939, become pro-Nazi.

His hometown newspaper, in a series of editorials, agreed with Reynolds in warning citizens of the evil effects of an American hate wave directed against people rather than a system. The *Citizen* urged Americans not to hate all Germans and Japanese, while continuing its loathing of dictators and dictatorial methods.[12] Reynolds, however, had difficulty making the same distinction, and his failure to provide a clarification of his remarks hurt him badly with the press and constituents.

Two influential commentators, Drew Pearson and Robert S. Allen, writing in their widely disseminated column "Merry-Go-'Round," claimed that "the wisecracking Reynolds took a trip to Germany last summer and was wined, dined and flattered by moguls of the Goering-Goebbels clique. He came back singing their praises and acclaiming Hitler as a great man." Pearson and Allen wondered "what influences prevailed on him in Berlin, and whether his move to get appointed to the Senate Foreign Affairs Committee was not inspired by the Nazis. Already some of Reynolds colleagues are derisively calling him 'The Tar Heel Führer.'"[13]

The "Merry-Go-'Round" article was quoted time and again by Reynolds's detractors and gave added impetus to the image of Reynolds as pro-Nazi. There was, however, no evidence that Reynolds was entertained by the German high command. His daughter Frances, who was on the trip, emphatically stated that they did not travel to Germany.[14]

In fact, Reynolds did go to Germany on this trip. He observed little unemploy-

ment and was impressed by the autobahns, but there is no proof that he visited
Nazi officials while in Germany. The American ambassador to Germany, William
E. Dodd, made no reference in his personal diary to an official visit by Reynolds,
and Dodd would probably have made some comment on the arrival of a U.S.
senator. The records of the American embassy did not have any references to a visit
by Reynolds. His daughter Frances probably denied that they had been in Germany because of possible damage to her father's reputation.

In addition, the insinuation that Nazi Germany was behind his appointment to
the Foreign Relations Committee was sheer nonsense. Germany had no influence
over such a decision, and Reynolds's appointment had been made before his European trip. In short, the Pearson-Allen article was inflammatory and untrue in its
insinuations and charges. The muckraking authors, sensing a big story, made their
charges based on hearsay information.[15] Nonetheless, serious harm had been done.

In another article in February 1938, Pearson and Allen again discussed Reynolds's trip to Europe. The authors alleged that Reynolds had wired the American
legation in Budapest, Hungary, that he wanted a report on political conditions
ready for his arrival. The staff stayed up all night preparing the report, but Reynolds failed to arrive at the appointed time. Because the report seemed important,
a diplomatic secretary camped out at the Gellert Hotel to await Reynolds's return.
The senator finally arrived with a "blonde on one arm and a brunette on the
other." When offered the report he had ordered, Reynolds, at this point uninter-
ested in the political affairs of Hungary, told the astonished secretary to "forget it"
and walked away.[16]

Following Pearson and Allen's lead, other periodicals and newspapers began to
portray Reynolds as pro-Nazi. Reynolds was featured in a *Life* picture layout titled
"Fascism in America,"[17] and *Ken* magazine published an article critical of Reynolds
titled "Patriotism Incorporated." The *Ken* piece referred to Reynolds as a "fledgling
Fuehrer" who waved the flag of 100 percent Americanism but "carried the tune of
fascism." Overnight Reynolds had "barged into the national spotlight with a Jekyll-
Hyde transformation from mountebank to demagogue." When Reynolds praised
Hitler and Mussolini, continued *Ken*, he was mouthing the line of the German-
American Bund and the propaganda of Joseph Goebbels, who urged America to
remain isolationist and leave Europe to its fate. Reynolds, according to the magazine, apparently believed that democracies, not dictatorships, were the real aggressors in the world.[18]

The *Asheville Citizen* candidly acknowledged that Reynolds's opinions on the
crisis in Europe did not represent the views of the majority of North Carolinians.
The people of the state, judged the *Citizen*, agreed that the best way to prevent a
world war was through economic and diplomatic pressure on Hitler and Mussolini. "Senator Reynolds," asserted the paper, "may find much to praise in the

regimes of Hitler and Mussolini. The people of North Carolina do not. Senator Reynolds may distrust and even hate Britain and France. The people of North Carolina do not."[19]

These criticisms and the recurring pro-Nazi charges dominated the remainder of his Senate career. From early 1939 until the end of his second term in 1945, Reynolds was constantly maligned for his isolationist views and for his alleged pro-fascist stands. Yet despite all this criticism, Reynolds never wavered from his basic isolationist views and fought back against his critics, whom he called anti-American.

In assessing Reynolds's views on isolationism, one must understand his background and the attitudes of his state and region toward international affairs. Charles O. Lerche Jr., in his book *The Uncertain South*, helped illuminate Reynolds's views by defining isolationism in terms of the southern mind and culture. For Lerche, isolationism meant that the United States should withdraw completely from international affairs. Because few would deny the inevitability of American participation in world trade and world affairs, the majority of Americans, argued Lerche, would have to be labeled internationalists. Lerche indicated that the difference between isolationists and internationalists was not one of the quantitative level of international involvement but had to do with the terms and conditions under which these international contacts were carried out.

One group of Americans had long denied that the United States had any permanent or vital stake in any international order. They insisted that the United States retain the right to be independent in its policymaking without having its destiny inextricably entwined with that of all humankind. Lerche referred to this concept— that America retain the absolute maximum of national freedom of choice regardless of the circumstances—as "unilateralism." The opposite position—that American foreign policy be built on a recognition of the interdependence of all countries for mutual security and economic well-being—Lerche labeled "*multilateralism*."[20]

Lerche and others, including Alfred O. Hero, author of *The South and World Affairs*, depicted the South as favoring a unique brand of internationalism. One of the significant characteristics of southern internationalism was its full commitment to free trade. The southern view, noted Hero, also included a fervent Anglophilia and the support of a strong national defense. During the years 1939–41, the support of southern congressmen for seven important military bills outstripped that from any other region in the country. The military tradition was deeply rooted in the South, which historically stressed the defense of its home and institutions against outside threats. Thus the South overwhelmingly favored peacetime conscription and military preparedness in general and was willing to pay higher taxes for a stronger defense.[21]

Lerche explained that although the South was internationalist in terms of military preparedness and trade, the region did not believe in multilateralism (the interdependence of countries and people). The South was unable to transcend its provincialism and inherently refused to approve any general ideal of a world order such as the World Court.[22] Nonetheless, by favoring free trade, the South was more internationalist than unilateralist.[23]

Another aspect of southern thought about international affairs included what Lerche called "demagogic unilateralism." In this concept, the politician became the voice of social and economic protest rooted in the discontent of the poor-white element in southern society. The southern demagogue, wrote Lerche, in the course of continually sharpening the hostilities of "his" rural, unsophisticated, racist constituency, "tended to level his heavy guns at all outsiders." For Lerche, the southern demagogue had a standard set of scapegoats that he attacked as the root causes of the ills in the South. Included in this list were foreigners, big business, aliens, and Communists.[24]

Lerche described Reynolds as a practitioner of "demagogic unilateralism" who was adept at playing on the fears and hostilities of his poor-white constituents. Reynolds, declared Lerche, was a spokesman for a shortsighted and belligerent nationalism identified in the popular mind as "isolationism." Reynolds and his fellow demagogues "painted a dark picture of the perils awaiting the nation on the international scene. Each saw entrapment, impoverishment, and mongrelization as the inevitable outcome of American entry into world affairs." They professed to be "striving to spare the long-suffering American taxpayer the burden of subsidizing hordes of greedy, envious, slothful and wily foreigners."

Lerche did not see Reynolds's "demagogic unilateralism" as a matter of personal belief or intellectual argument. He believed Reynolds preached "isolationism" because his constituency demanded it. A demagogue could keep his power only so long as he attacked foreigners in the same way that he attacked blacks and high taxes. Such attacks, theorized Lerche, were extremely useful in agitating "the always tender psyche of the poor white." Lerche surmised that poor whites responded to such attacks because their basic beliefs were threatened by "alien" ideologies.

In presenting his doctrine of noninvolvement in foreign affairs, Reynolds, wrote Lerche, argued that the world could be kept forever from America's doorstep if the people remained alert and avoided the perils of international problems. The overall effect of this policy, concluded Lerche, was to deny the possibility of the United States conducting anything like a real foreign policy.[25]

Many circumstances and events influenced Reynolds's views on foreign affairs but perhaps most important were the attitudes fostered by the mountain environment in which he matured. Isolationism was very popular in western North Carolina when he grew up, and the locals strongly opposed American entrance into World War I. The prevailing view in Buncombe County was that Americans should be for America only. Reynolds, after his brief stint as a member of the National Guard during World War I, developed a real and personal fear of having to fight. Although he never entered combat, his daughter Frances believed that his brief, unpleasant military experience may have influenced his negative attitudes toward war.[26]

Reynolds traveled widely, but his sojourns abroad did not open his mind to the wonderful diversity of the world. His trips merely convinced him that most countries in the world did not appreciate American aid or assistance. Based on these travels, Reynolds became convinced that American involvement with such ungrateful recipients would lead only to misfortune and war. His long-time secretary, Wesley E. McDonald, shared Reynolds's unilateralist views and undoubtedly strengthened Reynolds's adherence to these views.[27]

Thus Bob Reynolds was a "demagogic unilateralist" by virtue of birth, attitude, and experience and because he reflected the views of the lower-class constituency instrumental in his election to high office. Lerche correctly characterized Reynolds's overview of foreign affairs but erred in concluding that Reynolds's unilateralism was politically motivated rather than a matter of personal belief.

Reynolds's isolationist views were politically wise in North Carolina prior to 1941, and Reynolds naturally took advantage of the popularity of these views during elections. After Pearl Harbor and American entrance into World War II, however, his views were anathema to most Americans. Reynolds, while supporting the war effort, never renounced his isolationist position, and his votes were so unpopular that he chose not to run for reelection in 1944. In these instances, Reynolds could not be accused of political expediency.

Reynolds's foreign policy positions were also influenced by anti-Semitism coupled with a fervent support of Anglo-Saxon culture. His daughter Frances claimed that her father was not anti-Semitic prior to his sponsorship of immigration control legislation but became anti-Semitic after Jews vigorously opposed his immigration bills and attacked him for his views.[28] Senate aide Hubert Rand indicated that Reynolds had always been anti-Semitic. Despite having many Jewish friends, Reynolds thought that Jews took advantage of him and frequently would remark that "you can't trust Jews."[29]

A difficult problem for Reynolds and his unilateralist views developed over the issue of southern support for military preparedness. During the 1930s southern voters sent to Congress a disproportionately large number of representatives who were pro-British and who increasingly favored active intervention in foreign affairs. After 1938, with the impending threat of war, many southern politicians tried to overcome the provincial isolation of their constituents by voting for most forms of economic and military aid to other countries. Southern representatives were willing to help the Allies defeat the Axis powers even if it meant getting into a war.

Reynolds was the only southerner who consistently voted with the twenty-five northern and western isolationists in Congress. This group opposed the majority of Roosevelt's measures designed to strengthen the Allies against German, Italian, and Japanese aggression and to prepare America for the coming war. Reynolds voted as an isolationist on nine of the eleven most crucial foreign policy bills sponsored by the administration before December 7, 1941.[30]

By early 1939, war in Europe seemed inevitable. Both isolationists and internationalists realized this and intensified their efforts to influence the course of American diplomacy. At this critical juncture, President Roosevelt set out to unite both conservatives and liberals behind a program of national preparedness. Roosevelt knew that American military preparedness alone would not be enough to deter Hitler. He therefore attempted to secure repeal of the restrictive features of American neutrality legislation to warn Hitler that in case of war, the United States would throw its economic and military might behind Britain and France.[31]

In January 1939, Senator Reynolds, adamantly opposed to any tinkering with neutrality legislation, took his place on the Senate Foreign Relations Committee. Reynolds hoped that his membership on the Foreign Relations Committee would "give his voice more prestige" and would provide a pulpit from which to expound his worldviews.[32]

It was at this juncture that Reynolds broke with Roosevelt over the future of American foreign policy. In a two-hour speech, Reynolds chided the president for leading America directly toward war. He claimed that America's hatred of other nations and their forms of government "can have no other effect except to crystallize their hatred for us. I ask you and I ask the world what business it is of the United States what government they have in Germany, Italy, and Japan." If these countries were satisfied with their system of government, declaimed Reynolds, then it was "no damn business of ours."[33] Reynolds hastened to add that he was not defending fascism, only reiterating his policy of isolationism.

Reynolds was shortsighted in referring primarily to fascist countries. His constant demand that we stop hating and criticizing Germany and Italy made it appear as though he was defending their form of government. At this point Reynolds either did not understand the dire threat that fascism posed for the world or he chose to ignore the reality of world politics.

An article penned by Reynolds, "Stick to Your Own Knitting or Mind Your Own Damned Business," appeared in the *Voelkischer Beobachter*, a German newspaper, on February 2, 1939. Reynolds wanted to know what Germany had done to America that "we should hate it." He thought the United States should solve its own problems first and, with ten million unemployed, was in no position to criticize other countries. His anti-Semitism was evident when he announced that he was absolutely opposed to the idea that America "go to war for the sake of protecting

Jews of any country whatever." Reynolds wondered why there was never any criticism of the Communist dictators in Russia who had persecuted and murdered more people than the Nazis had.[34] Reynolds did not understand that in 1939, the fascist nations, not the Communist nations, posed the greatest threat to world peace.

The *Winston-Salem Journal* took Reynolds to task for his views. According to the *Journal*, the senator's position was equivalent to saying that a homeowner would not rush out to protect his neighbor's daughter from a mad dog, because it was not his dog. The neighbor should have kept her daughter at home. Incidents that take place on the other side of the world had a direct effect on the lives and welfare of Americans, declared the paper, thus "it is sometimes necessary to kill the mad dog who attacks the neighbor's child."[35]

Shortly thereafter Senator Reynolds procured and denounced a confidential report to the Military Affairs Committee on the current state of European affairs. Reynolds jeered at the report's prediction, prepared by William C. Bullitt, ambassador to France, and Joseph P. Kennedy, ambassador to England, that there would be an early war and that appeasement had failed. The report's expressed fear of a large increase in German armaments did not change Reynolds's views about rearmament in America. All that was needed, surmised Reynolds, was the means necessary to protect the country from invasion by foreign enemies. "What if it is true that Germany does have 9,500 airplanes? That's no reason for us to match it."[36]

Reynolds continued to expound on his isolationist views. He delivered a speech over the National Broadcasting System, which he had reprinted in the *Congressional Record*, titled "Uncle Sam Should Keep His Nose out of the Internal Affairs of Other Nations." Reynolds finally admitted that Hitler had persecuted minorities and claimed that his heart and sympathy went out to them, but that was not a cause for war. The German government, asserted Reynolds, had not done anything to warrant the United States virtually severing diplomatic relations with it. If the United States severed relations with Germany, then Reynolds urged the government to do the same with Russia and Mexico, as both these countries were persecuting minorities, stealing American property, and opposed to the American form of government. Reynolds closed his talk by asking the administration to abandon attempts to pass "Sunday blue laws policing the political morals of the world."[37]

On January 25, Reynolds launched yet another shortsighted tirade against Roosevelt's foreign policy. On this occasion, he warned that nonimportation agreements against the dictators would lead to serious economic losses for the United States and would work a great hardship on the South, which depended on a profitable cotton trade with Japan.

The United States, maintained Reynolds, had to concentrate its efforts on improving conditions at home. Hitler, said Reynolds, was doing what we should be doing—that is, looking out for the people of Germany. Uncle Sam, however, had been running all over the world attending to other nations' business. Reynolds insisted that he was not praising dictators but warning the American people of the threat posed by the dictators.[38] The senator placed numerous letters from citizens praising his isolationist stance in the *Record*. These adulatory letters obviously reinforced his belief that his cause was just.

The press had been relatively quiescent during Reynolds's discourses on foreign policy, but finally the *Raleigh News and Observer* could take it no longer. The paper agreed that there was some validity in Reynolds's thesis that Uncle Sam should wash behind his own ears before sticking his nose into other peoples' business. The problem was, opined the paper, that Reynolds "stuck his own neck . . . pretty far out when he declared 'Hitler is doing what we should be doing.' "

The *News and Observer* continued by asking America to pray to God for help in escaping the evils of Adolf Hitler, who mistreated minorities, attacked democracy, and threatened world peace. Reynolds's absolute isolation could be accepted at face value, declared the Raleigh paper, but Reynolds himself had borrowed a chapter from Hitler. He had used the foreigner in America as the whipping boy just as Hitler had used the Jews in Germany. Reynolds's nationalism, judged the *News and Observer*, sounded very much like fascism. The editorial concluded that Reynolds had to make it clear that he had no sympathy with the ruthless nationalism that denied the rights of minorities—otherwise people would see Reynolds as a fascist.[39] Reynolds unfortunately ignored this criticism and was unable to persuade either his constituents or his critics that he did not support fascist doctrine.

By 1939 fascist dictators were on the move all over the world. Francisco Franco's Nationalists had captured Madrid, Hitler had gobbled up the rest of Czechoslovakia, and Mussolini had invaded Albania. Roosevelt feared that a European war was imminent and tried to prepare America for a vital part in assisting its allies. A bitter conflict between the isolationists and the interventionists ensued over America's role in providing military and economic security for the world against the encroachment of dictators.

Just as FDR launched his campaign to awaken America to the harsh realities of the world, the crash of a new Douglas Aircraft experimental bomber near the Los Angeles Municipal Airport presented his administration with a sticky problem. One of the injured passengers, a representative of the French Air Ministry, had been sent to America to arrange the secret purchase of American military aircraft. The United States government initially admitted that France was seeking American planes but insisted that no planes would be sold to any foreign power. Finally, under the glare of public scrutiny, Roosevelt admitted that the United States had secretly approved the sale of a number of modern warplanes to France without consulting Congress. Reynolds (along with Senator Gerald P. Nye and others), angered by Roosevelt's secret dealings with France, threatened a full probe of the administration's military and foreign policies. Reynolds thought that the proposed sale of planes smacked of a military alliance between France and America.[40]

Roosevelt tried to sidestep the crisis by explaining that the French need for the planes was both obvious and urgent, given that America's neutrality laws would prevent the purchase of these planes if France were to go to war. Roosevelt said the main reason for the sale, however, was that many aircraft companies in America were idle and an investment by the French into these companies would increase employment and help America's own expansion plans. Furthermore, said Roosevelt, the plane that crashed was "a manufacturer's plane" and had not yet been accepted by the American government. Roosevelt's devious explanation further angered the isolationists.

In an attempt to defuse the controversy, Roosevelt invited the entire Military Affairs Committee to the White House on January 31 to discuss the real reasons for the proposed sale of six hundred modern airplanes to France. Roosevelt asked the conferees to keep his remarks "confidential," because he did not want "to frighten the American people." The president then told his audience that he expected a war that would engulf all the nations of Europe and would directly threaten the peace and safety of the United States.

The president rejected the idea that the United States could draw a line of defense around itself and "live completely and solely to ourselves." Because the Axis powers were dedicated to world domination, Roosevelt explained, America's first line of defense was the independent existence of France, England, and other countries in Europe and South America. Roosevelt felt it necessary to sell planes to France to help overcome the vast superiority of the German air force. "It may mean the saving of our civilization," Roosevelt said. When asked if that meant the American frontier was on the Rhine River, Roosevelt said, "not that. But practically speaking, if the Rhine frontiers are threatened the rest of the world is too." Roosevelt closed by assuring the committee that "the last thing this country should do" was to send any American troops to Europe.[41] Senator Nye, Senator Reynolds, and other isolationists were deeply disturbed by Roosevelt's views and by his emphasis on secrecy. Nye was convinced, as was Reynolds, that Roosevelt intended to ignore the neutrality law.

The next day an unidentified senator disclosed to the press that FDR had placed America's frontier on the Rhine. Roosevelt's remark led to an uproar, and Reynolds told the newspapers that he disliked the thought of America's frontier in Europe.[42] President Roosevelt tried to calm the fears of the isolationists by denying that he had made such a statement and by asserting that America's foreign policy still rested on unchanged foundations. The president also referred to recent attacks on his policy as appeals to ignorance, prejudice, and fears and, therefore, un-American.

Reynolds quickly made it clear that the president could not have been referring to him when he decried the recent attacks on the White House. "My program is 100 per cent American and the President could not be talking about my speeches in the senate."[43] Roosevelt did not mention any names when denouncing attacks on his policy, but Reynolds, with good reason, felt that the charges were directed at him.

Reynolds attempted to blunt the pro-fascist charges made against him by lashing out against the Communist menace. He sincerely believed that the Communist dictatorship in Russia posed a more serious threat to the United States than the fascists and that the Communists wanted America and Germany to go to war so that they would destroy each other. Reynolds said that the Communists had murdered more people and cursed God more than any other dictators in the world. What was amazing to Reynolds was that the press filled its pages with the horror of fascism but ignored the "thousands of Communists termites boring from within."[44]

In February 1939, Reynolds asked the Roosevelt administration to recognize the regime of Francisco Franco, the fascist victor in the Spanish civil war. Reynolds was interested in selling cotton to Spain, and Franco's political leanings and dictatorship was of no concern to him. For Reynolds, this suggestion was a practical way to carry out diplomacy; for his detractors, it was another example of Reynolds's approval of a fascist regime.[45]

One wonders how Senator Reynolds could continue to make such ill-considered statements without realizing how much accumulated damage resulted from his comments. To some degree Reynolds was naïve about how such speeches were received by the press and his critics. He had just won reelection without support from the press and perhaps felt invincible. On the other hand, his statements reflected his chauvinism and unending hatred of Britain and France.

Despite numerous warnings from friends and advisers to tone down his rhetoric, Reynolds refused to listen. When Roosevelt stated that war could be avoided if the free nations of the world united and used a show of force,[46] Reynolds immediately responded. He judged that there had been too much talk of war and that the president's attitude increased the chances of American involvement in a European conflict. Reynolds did not think that Roosevelt was deliberately leading America into war, but the senator dreaded the consequences of a policy designed to convince European nations that the United States was willing to fight for democracy and peace.

Reynolds said that he wanted to allow Hitler the freedom to do as he pleased. After all, when Hitler seized land in Europe, he did it "in the same way that sometimes the boys in Texas and in North Carolina used to move a fence with the aid of a shotgun, instead of doing it legally by way of the surveyor. That is all that Hitler did." When Roosevelt used the words "quarantine the aggressor," Reynolds hoped that he did not mean the application of economic sanctions, because that would lead to war.[47] With this speech Reynolds had once again stepped in manure. Everybody else could smell the odor, but Reynolds blithely carried on as if nothing adverse had transpired. He had approved of and justified Hitler's brutal expansion in Europe. No wonder many observers saw him as a staunch defender of fascism.

Reynolds's conflict with Roosevelt became more personal when he inserted two inflammatory articles into the *Congressional Record*. The articles implied a connection between Roosevelt and the Communist Party of America. This charge was not new; Gerald L. K. Smith, the American Liberty League, and others had frequently branded the New Deal as communist in both theory and practice. One article, from the acerbic pen of Westbrook Pegler, a bitter critic of Roosevelt, charged that Communists had "disproportionate influence" in the Roosevelt administration. The other article quoted Earl Browder, head of the Communist Party in America, as pledging support for Roosevelt in the election of 1940.[48]

Reynolds did not accuse Roosevelt of succumbing to communist influence, but his ill-advised sponsorship of the two articles was politically foolhardy. According to his aide, Hubert Rand, Reynolds peevishly published the letters to get revenge for the Coan patronage fiasco.[49]

In April 1939, Reynolds shifted his anger and invective toward Great Britain. A dedicated Anglophobe, Reynolds lambasted England as the "bloodiest aggressor the world has ever known."[50] He feared that British propaganda would create a climate for American involvement in a European war. The senator saw no reason why the youth of America should fight to save "the so-called democracies of Europe—imperialistic Britain and Communistic France."[51]

Reynolds harped on Britain's and France's failure to pay their war debts. They had, argued Reynolds, "defrauded Uncle Sam out of the billions he loaned them when their backs were to the wall." He then proposed that the State Department send a special debt envoy to the exchequers of Europe to collect the unpaid debts, surmising that the payment of the war debts would almost instantly cure many of America's economic ills. If Britain refused to pay the debt, then Reynolds suggested that the United States force England to cede to America her island possessions in the Atlantic. If Britain refused to give up the islands, warned Reynolds, America could then seize property in the United States belonging to British citizens. Reynolds hastened to add that he did not actually want to seize British property and

America would not have to resort to that tactic if the State Department would firmly pursue the collection of the debts.[52]

It did not occur to Reynolds that the United States had not won World War I singlehandedly, nor did he understand that the people of Europe had suffered far more than the United States in that conflict. Many citizens of the Western democracies deeply appreciated American assistance during the war but found it economically impossible to repay their war debts during a worldwide depression. To do so in 1939 could lead to the economic dislocation of the entire European financial structure, as had happened in 1930, and would in turn imperil America's financial stability. Reynolds's shortsighted, nationalistic isolationism, as well as his hatred for England, prevented him from viewing the problem objectively.

Reynolds's anti-British sentiments reached a rather absurd peak when he heard that King George VI and Queen Elizabeth planned to visit the United States in June 1939. The senator surmised that the royal couple were coming to America to persuade the United States to save Britain once again, and he would have none of it.[53]

As the day of the royal visit grew near, diplomats feared that Reynolds would launch into a tirade condemning the British "imperialists." The State Department worried that such an outburst might hurt British-American relations and would embarrass President Roosevelt as well as the British monarch.[54]

As a member of the Foreign Relations Committee, Senator Reynolds received an official invitation to a garden party, a congressional reception, and a White House dinner in honor of the king and queen. Undecided about accepting the invitations, Reynolds eventually responded favorably in case he later decided to go. When accepting the invitations, he explained that something "might come up which will prevent me from attending. There might be some friends here from North Carolina that I ought to see."[55]

Three days before the royals' visit, Senator Reynolds approached Josiah Bailey, who was engaged in conversation with several North Carolina news reporters. Reynolds told the group that there was nothing personal in his criticism of England for not paying its debts and, to prove his point, announced that he would attend the lawn party for the king and queen at the British Embassy. The unpredictable Reynolds, clad in his best white linen suit, kept his promise and appeared at the lawn party. The isolationist senators, despite their political inclinations, were uniformly courteous and on their best behavior, and the royal couple made a highly favorable impression on the American politicians.[56]

Reynolds was conspicuously absent when the king and queen came to the Capitol to greet each member of Congress. He also missed the White House dinner. In a formal press statement, Reynolds explained his absences by stating that he had a commitment to entertain two North Carolinians and their wives who were visiting Washington—and "my friends from North Carolina can vote." He did manage to compliment the royal visitors by saying that from his observations at the garden party they were "charming and gracious people."[57]

If Reynolds thought that his clever explanation for snubbing the king and queen would help him back home, he was badly mistaken. There was an immediate backlash, and the *Asheville Citizen* got in the first volley by accusing Reynolds of being discourteous to the royal visitors because "they can't vote in North Carolina." The *Citizen* argued that while Reynolds might have gained four votes, he forfeited the respect of thousands of North Carolinians who thought that America's guests should be accorded respect by the nation's leaders. "If they had been movie stars," wrote the *Citizen*, "Reynolds would have headed a one-man procession to greet them."[58]

Nell Battle Lewis also denounced Reynolds for being discourteous. "Who could fail to be proud of such stalwart and unabashed republicanism which flung in the faces of visiting royalty a quartet of Tar Heel ballots?" The king and queen had to wonder, continued Lewis, if their visit were worthwhile "when Blatant Bob of Buncombe rated them less than four votes."[59]

Other letters to newspaper editors around the state expressed anger at Reynolds's mistreatment of the royal couple. S. B. Adams wrote that he did not expect Reynolds to bow down and worship royalty but did expect him to treat the visitors with ordinary respect and courtesy. "Reynolds deliberately snubbed them on the pretense that he could drum up votes by such tactics. If he had the courage to tell the truth his main reason was that he had been a vitriolic critic of England and he was ashamed to face them." On the other hand, Adams thought that "if it had been Chancellor Hitler instead of the King and Queen, the Senator would have been the first to greet him. Fine business for a Senator from this state to be denouncing the greatest republic outside our own, and at the same time courting the friendship of the worst dictator since the days of Nero. His actions leaves [*sic*] no doubt in the minds of the people that his sympathy is on the side of Hitler and Nazism. If a man with such a record can whoop up votes in this state we are in a sad plight."[60]

Reynolds had badly misjudged public opinion when he casually rebuffed the king and queen. He expected isolationists to approve of his actions but did not realize that most Americans would enthusiastically embrace the royal family and that his disrespect would be derided in his home state. The torrent of criticism, further eroding his declining popularity, prompted Reynolds to issue a detailed press release clarifying his activities in regard to the royal visit. He claimed that reporters had misinterpreted his "joshing remark" explaining his failure to attend the reception and dinner. Reynolds said he did attend the garden party as a token of respect for the royal couple and planned to attend the congressional reception but had an engagement with some friends from North Carolina. He thought he had time to make the reception but got caught in heavy traffic and arrived after its conclusion. He had been unable to attend the White House dinner because he had dinner with his friends. A defensive Reynolds blamed all the criticism on his enemies who grasped at any straw to smear him.[61]

Reynolds's weak excuse for his unpopular behavior failed miserably. If he had been delayed in traffic, why did he wait twenty-two days before presenting this excuse? His attempt to place the blame for his discourteous actions on his enemies, instead of taking responsibility for his actions, further alienated North Carolinians.

As criticism rained down on him from all directions, Reynolds finally seemed to realize the unpopularity of his recent actions and statements, and he began to temper his pronouncements about Hitler and fascism. In a series of speeches designed to repair the damage, Reynolds asserted that he looked "with horror upon the chaos in Europe" brought about by the encroachment of the dictators, and he roundly decried the activity of "the Berlin-Rome axis because we condemn the strong taking advantage of the weak."[62]

Reynolds also had granted an interview to two North Carolina reporters in May 1939, in an earlier attempt to repair his reputation. Unfortunately, he alienated the two men from the outset by complaining about how the press had misinterpreted his activities in Congress, especially given that 90 percent of the letters he received approved of his isolationism. Reynolds, "to set the record straight," explained that his speeches were designed solely to keep America out of war. However, if "you fight to keep your country from entangling in foreign alliances which will lead to war you are denounced as a Fascist."

The senator then launched into a strong attack on Hitler, blaming him for all the troubles in Europe. The American people, stated Reynolds, were getting fed up with dictators, and if "Hitler keeps on running roughshod over everybody, he is going to wake up some morning and find his bluff called." The senator's statements astonished the two reporters, for this was a Bob Reynolds entirely different from the one they had covered since early January.[63]

In spite of this attempt to modify his views and change the public's perception of him, the damage had already been done, and Reynolds eventually gave up on his attempt to satisfy his critics. In fact, one observer saw his attack on Hitler as merely a cover-up for his real views and pegged Reynolds as just another politician trying to avoid a catastrophe.[64]

Reynolds's isolationist principles faced a stern test when President Roosevelt asked for repeal of the restrictive features of American neutrality legislation. Roosevelt's proposals revealed a deep division in both Congress and the nation. Reluctant to engage openly in a fight for revision, the president chose to let the Senate Foreign Relations Committee, rather than the State Department, frame the new legislation.[65]

As the United States began consideration of modifications in its neutrality policy, the world situation changed dramatically. On March 15, 1939, the German army invaded the Sudetenland, the German-speaking portion of Czechoslovakia. Roosevelt criticized Hitler's move as a flagrant act of aggression and urged neutrality revision as soon as possible. Senator Key Pittman, chairman of the Senate Foreign Relations Committee, quickly drew up a bill satisfactory to Roosevelt. The Pittman bill would repeal the arms embargo, adopt cash-and-carry for all trade with belligerent nations, and continue the other provisions of the 1937 Neutrality Act. Pittman had specifically designed his bill to allow arms shipments to European democracies threatened by war.[66] Senator Reynolds urged caution in revising or repealing the neutrality laws, because they worked well so far in keeping America out of war.[67]

The Foreign Relations Committee opened public hearings on the neutrality issue on April 5, 1939. Henry L. Stimson, secretary of war under Roosevelt, was the first witness. Stimson vigorously advocated a repeal of the rigid neutrality act. The president, insisted Stimson, needed greater discretionary power in foreign relations because the threat of overseas aggression directly imperiled American security. Stimson proposed that the president be given the authority to designate aggressor nations so that the United States could bar shipment of materials to them.

Both Senator Hiram S. Johnson and Senator Reynolds took issue with Stimson and said his proposals would lead the United States into war. Reynolds asked Stimson if there were any conflict in the world at that particular moment which threatened America's security. Stimson replied that at that hour there was no danger to America but emphasized that continued aggression by Germany, Italy, and Japan would eventually endanger the Western Hemisphere.

Stimson and Reynolds then engaged in a heated exchange. Reynolds asked Stimson if it were not a fact that "the same thing Japan, Germany, and Italy are now practicing has been practiced by Great Britain and France except it was on a larger scale?" Stimson demurred, but Reynolds pressed his point and wanted to know how Britain secured her overseas possessions, if not by aggression.

Stimson acknowledged that it could be argued that America had come into being as a result of aggression against American Indians, but times had changed and countries had adopted policies opposed to aggression. The reason for this, shot back Reynolds, was that Britain and France had all they wanted and did not desire new territories by aggressive means. Britain, Reynolds asserted, was currently propagandizing America in order to drag the United States into another war. Stimson tersely replied that he had no knowledge that Reynolds's charge was true.

Next Reynolds questioned whether the president was in a better position to designate aggressors than Congress. Stimson explained that the chief executive had better foreign sources and more experience in foreign affairs, and under the constitution, the president operated the foreign service. Arms embargo discretion, concluded Stimson, would allow the president to "act quickly" in emergencies.

Reynolds continued the interchange by stating that he had frequently heard that the United States had to cooperate with and assist Britain and France in order to prevent Hitler from attacking the United States. "Do you think," asked Reynolds, "that there is any danger of Hitler attacking us here in the next six months or even years?" Stimson answered, "A good deal depends on the success of the nations against whom you seem to be prejudiced." Reynolds flushed at this remark and angrily admitted that he was prejudiced against Britain and France because they had lured America into one war and were about to do it again.[68]

An irate Reynolds then accused the Roosevelt administration of inflaming the minds of the people with talk about war. Reynolds said that some people had "gone crazy" in trying to get the United States involved in a war but admitted that neither the president nor Congress wanted war.

Colleagues began to question Reynolds about his views on the world crisis. When asked about Italy's occupation of Albania in April, Reynolds replied that it was "perfectly natural" for Mussolini to take over Albania in light of Italy's economic investment in that country. When asked if he would send troops to protect an invasion of South America, Reynolds said certainly, for he believed in the Monroe Doctrine, but he would never send troops to Europe. In response to a question as to whether he would defend the Philippines from a Japanese invasion, Reynolds replied that he would not give one American son to save the Philippines.[69] By approving of Mussolini's invasion of Albania, Reynolds had once again, despite numerous attempts to deflect Nazi charges, condoned aggression by fascist dictators. Reynolds was incapable of making a distinction between the imperialism of Britain and France and the brutal expansion of the fascist dictators.

When the hearings ended in May 1939, no consensus on neutrality had emerged, and Pittman had failed to rally a majority of the committee behind his bill. Even the isolationists were split, with Nye and Reynolds favoring rigid neutrality, while William E. Borah and Hiram Johnson wanted total repeal of the law. Congress had failed to take a productive step toward Roosevelt's goal of neutrality revision.[70]

President Roosevelt still believed that the most effective answer to Hitler's aggression was support for Britain and France through revision of the neutrality law, but he resisted entering the debate directly for fear of creating more opposition from Congress. He decided to press his case behind the scenes, counseling undecided senators that repeal of the arms embargo was the best way to keep the peace.

Secretary of State Cordell Hull, upset by Italy's invasion of Albania and fearing that war might break out in Europe at any time, joined Roosevelt in urging repeal.

The United States, argued Hull, encouraged aggressors and endangered its own safety through retention of the arms embargo. When Roosevelt declared a state of war, continued Hull, the present neutrality legislation made it mandatory for the president to embargo arms and munitions shipments to all belligerent countries. Hull believed that the denial of arms to France and Britain, if they were attacked by Germany, would be disastrous for the United States. Hull and Roosevelt still favored retention of the majority of the provisions of the Neutrality Act of 1937, including restriction of travel by American citizens in combat areas; prohibition of American ships entering combat areas; restrictions on loans and credits to nations at war; and the cash-and-carry provision for the sale of goods.[71]

Roosevelt, weary of the determined isolationist opposition, finally committed the administration to an all-out effort to repeal the arms embargo. The president, conscious of the critical needs of Britain and France, risked defeat in the Senate in an effort to reshape the nation's foreign policy. He again called on the Senate to rescind the arms embargo and threatened to keep Congress in session until the administration bill was passed.[72] Roosevelt's appeal failed when thirty-four isolationist leaders publicly opposed any modification of the 1937 neutrality law and threatened a filibuster.[73]

On July 11, 1939, the Senate Foreign Relations Committee finally voted, by a 12–11 margin, to put off further consideration of neutrality legislation until the next session of Congress. On this crucial vote, five Democrats, including Reynolds, joined with seven Republicans to vote for postponement. Even though the Democrats held sixteen of the twenty-three seats on the committee, the administration could not command a majority, and six months of intense effort by the White House had been for naught. Many isolationist senators, led by Senator Borah, voted to postpone because they believed there was no danger of war in Europe. Bob Reynolds, on the other hand, combined his dislike for England and a fear of involvement in war to vote for postponement.[74]

O. Max Gardner, a close observer of national events, disapproved of Reynolds's opposition to Roosevelt's policies and thought his opposition to neutrality revision could threaten America's security. In an attempt to embarrass Reynolds, Gardner asked Julian Miller, editor of the *Charlotte Observer*, to use his paper to remind Reynolds that if he did not support Roosevelt's foreign policies, he would be violating the deep convictions of the people of North Carolina who were horrified with the ruthless attacks of Adolf Hitler. Gardner wrote that Reynolds had to realize that the country was against Hitler, and he asked Miller to apply a little pressure to get Reynolds to change his stance.[75]

Two days later, an editorial addressed to the senators from North Carolina, South Carolina, and Georgia appeared in the *Charlotte Observer*. Miller's editorial contended that the present arms embargo did not satisfy the will and conscience of

95 percent of the citizens of the three states. Because the embargo was unfavorable to Great Britain and an aid to Germany, argued Miller, it would make America's entrance into the war more likely rather than less likely. The *Observer* asked the senators from the three states to amend America's neutrality policy to give America a realistic, intelligent, and practical neutrality.[76]

Reynolds did not see the editorial, for he had left on another tour of Europe with his daughter Frances. Prior to his departure he nonchalantly predicted that there would be no war in Europe and repeated his opinion that the war scare was merely European propaganda to get America to change its neutrality laws.[77]

Reynolds had barely reached the European continent when Hitler attacked Poland on September 1, 1939, and World War II began. President Roosevelt issued a proclamation of neutrality as required by law. Roosevelt explained that he wanted to keep the nation out of war, but he could not ask all Americans to remain neutral in thought, as morality and self-interest compelled America to aid Britain and France.[78]

Because of his status as a United States senator, Reynolds managed to secure passage on the United States liner *Washington* leaving from Le Havre, France. A total of 1,746 passengers (of whom 1,487 were American citizens) shared cramped and crowded quarters on the ship. The ship's capacity was only 1,040, thus the passengers had to eat in shifts, stand in line for a bath, and sleep in cramped quarters during their six and one-half days at sea. Reynolds's fellow passengers included Sara Delano Roosevelt, the president's eighty-four-year-old mother, impresario Sol Hurok, novelist Thomas Mann, violinist Fritz Kreisler, and Mrs. Joseph P. Kennedy, wife of the ambassador to Great Britain, accompanied by her children Eunice, Kathleen, and Robert.[79]

The *Asheville Citizen*, having learned of Reynolds's pell-mell retreat from Europe, crowed that the senator was "fleeing from the terrors of the very war which he hooted as an impossibility." The paper hoped that Reynolds had a speedy and safe return but also expected him to "drop his pose as an international expert who knows more about foreign affairs than even the President and the Secretary of State. Events have proven that as an international student, he has not progressed beyond the primary class."[80]

Reynolds arrived in New York on September 18, and as soon as he stepped off the boat, he complained that the Roosevelt administration had "fallen down miserably" in providing transportation and protection for Americans stranded in European war zones. He claimed that the liner *Washington* carried a large contingent of aliens (which was true) and that their accommodations should have been taken by American citizens—especially given that some of the aliens were traveling on German passports.[81] The next day Cordell Hull denied the allegations by accounting for 1,747 passengers (this number varied significantly with the *New*

York Times figure of 1,487) who were American citizens, leaving only 214 possible aliens on the ship. Hull explained that the government did the best it could in returning American refugees from Europe and did not fall down on the Job.[82]

While speaking to reporters, the peripatetic Reynolds admitted that he had been drastically wrong in predicting that there would be no war in Europe in 1939. He called for national unity, a military and moral rearmament, and a will to peace. Frightened by a war he thought would never come, he was forced to change his view on preparedness. Instead of adequate preparedness, Reynolds now believed that America could best be kept out of war "by making ourselves so strong that no nation will seek a quarrel with us." Reynolds continued to plead for a sincere and honest neutrality. America, as the repository of a great civilization, had a duty to safeguard this inheritance: "If we are drawn into the vortex of another war, we may lose those precious things for which our forefathers fought and died."[83]

President Roosevelt, hoping that the outbreak of war in Europe would provide an impetus for the repeal of the arms embargo, called Congress into a special session on September 21. He anticipated that Britain and France would benefit from the repeal because they were in a position to purchase American goods and carry them across the Atlantic. In a moving speech before a joint session of Congress, the president noted that this action would provide a way to peace, not war.[84]

With the help of the Hearst newspapers, the isolationist bloc began an intense effort to persuade the American people to reject the president's program. In a surprising move, Bob Reynolds announced that he had an "open mind" on the repeal of the arms embargo and refused to take part in any filibuster, because the American people were entitled to an early decision. He was conspicuously missing from the meeting of the Senate antirepeal coalition that had been counting on him for several lengthy speeches. Reynolds even went so far as to assure administration leaders that he would vote to report the bill out of committee but would reserve the right to support or oppose the bill once it reached the floor.[85]

Although temporary, this was quite a shift for Reynolds, who until July 1939 had been unalterably opposed to any change in the neutrality law. There were three possible explanations for his new stance. First, he finally realized, with the beginning of World War II, that his position as a unilateralist had become increasingly unpopular in North Carolina and the country. A Gallup poll in September 1939 showed that 62 percent of the American people favored repeal of the arms embargo. American citizens did not want war, but they did not want to see France and Britain crushed by Hitler. Second, Reynolds faced considerable pressure from Roosevelt, Democratic leaders in the Senate, and constituents. His mail had been running 60 percent in favor of repeal.[86] Third, his trip to Europe, the unprovoked attack by Hitler on Poland, and the events that had transpired since that time had forced him to rethink his views on neutrality revision.

On September 26, Key Pittman presented a revised neutrality bill that eliminated the arms embargo and set up a strict cash-and-carry provision on all articles,
not just arms. Two days later the Senate Foreign Relations Committee reported out
the measure by a vote of 16–7. As promised, Reynolds voted to send the bill to the
floor.[87] But he worried that the cash-and-carry plan might become the "credit-
and-carry" plan. Once America became a creditor to European nations, declared
Reynolds, we would be more likely to go to war to protect our investment. The
crucial issue for Reynolds was whether the United States wanted neutrality or
trade. To Reynolds, "selling goods must not be given first thought if it means
sending our sons later."[88] To destroy Hitler, stated Reynolds, the United States
would have to go to war and sacrifice the lives of millions of Americans. Before the
United States attempted to destroy Hitler, Reynolds thought it had "better destroy
Nazism and Fascism and Communism in the United States."[89]

Reynolds once again called for Britain to pay her war debts and proposed that
America accept Bermuda, the Bahamas, Trinidad, Labrador, and Newfoundland in
payment of the debts.[90] Here Reynolds made a practical proposal that later bore
fruit, but he startled colleagues when he conjectured that Hitler was anxious to call
off the war by the end of October. The fighting that Hitler had done to this point,
theorized Reynolds, was primarily to repel a French invasion of German territory.[91]

Reynolds had once again embarrassed himself with his bizarre defense of Germany. No one, not even Hitler, argued that France had invaded Germany. His
latest gaffe angered Joe L. Lee of Laurinburg, who complained about Reynolds's
"silly antics" in the Senate. Lee wrote that Reynolds had got him "vomiting sick"
and wanted him banished to some isolated spot "where Reynolds cannot be heard,
seen, felt, or smelt."[92]

On October 21, Reynolds pronounced the repeal of the arms embargo to be an
unwise and dangerous decision. "Why should we gamble when there is no necessity that we gamble?" Reynolds disclosed that he had been repeatedly warned by
close friends that "ninety per cent of the people of my state favored repeal" and if
he valued his political hide he had better vote to lift the arms embargo. Reynolds
had nonetheless reached his decision without regard for political consideration,
prompted only by the "dictates of my own conscience."[93]

Bob Reynolds disapproved of selling arms to any nation because the United
States would become an indirect party to the wholesale destruction of human
beings.[94] The senator also pointed out, correctly, that when America chose to help
Britain and France, the country was no longer neutral but practicing a "modified
form of belligerency."

The North Carolina senator reminded his colleagues that the Monroe Doctrine
had been violated only twice in the past one hundred years, both times by Great
Britain. Reynolds did not see Germany as a menace to the security of the Western

Hemisphere. In response to the theory that a Germany victorious in Europe would cast covetous eyes toward America, Reynolds said: "All evidence now available indicates that this theory is pure moonshine, lacking even the kick that our South ern moonshine produces on occasion."[95]

The four-week debate on neutrality legislation ended on October 27 when the Neutrality Act of 1939 passed the Senate by a vote of 63–30. Reynolds and John Overton, a Democrat from Louisiana, were the only southerners to vote against repeal of the embargo. The final bill abolished the arms embargo, permitting weapons of war to be purchased by all belligerents (in reality, only Britain and France) on a cash-and-carry basis. As a sop to the isolationists, American ships were forbidden to enter certain "combat zones," and American citizens could not travel on belligerent ships. Roosevelt did not gain as much discretionary power as he had desired, but compromise was the only way the bill could have been passed, and Cordell Hull crowed that the administration had "won a great battle."[96]

Bob Reynolds, despite pressure from constituents, had continued his consistent unilateralism and voted against the end of strict neutrality. He knew that his vote had hurt him politically, and he disappeared from Washington to lick his wounds. He later surfaced in Miami, Florida, unwilling to return to his home state for fear of a negative reaction from his constituents.[97]

CHAPTER EIGHT

[Vindicators and Nazis]

The four-story brick and frame apartment building at 1 Second Street, N.E., Washington, D.C., stood in the shadow of the Supreme Court building and served as the headquarters of the Vindicators Association, Inc., a new nationalistic organization founded by Bob Reynolds on January 31, 1939. An eight-page tabloid titled the *American Vindicator*, the official organ of the association, appeared for the first time in March 1939.

Reynolds organized the Vindicators as a patriotic society dedicated to 100 percent Americanism. The motto of the group was "Our Citizens, Our Country First." The first issue of the *American Vindicator* featured an interview with Reynolds about the origins of the association. Reynolds revealed that shortly after the founding of the association, he had received thousands of letters and telephone calls from all over the country expressing encouragement. In order that those participating in the movement might be advised of the activities and progress of the organization, Reynolds decided to edit and publish a monthly tabloid, announcing that "the bugle call for the assemblage of the patriots of America has been sounded." He claimed immediate success, with 118,000 subscribers in the first six months.

Reynolds priced the newspaper at one dollar per year (later raised to two dollars), and the sales of the newspaper were to be the only source of revenue for the Vindicators. Reynolds did not hire paid organizers, nor did he accept advertisements or contributions. Each subscriber and member received, in addition to the *American Vindicator*, a red, white, and blue feather to be worn in one's hat as well as a button of red, white, and blue with the yellow letter *V* in the center. The button featured the dome of the nation's Capitol and American flags in the background. According to Reynolds, the color red stood for courage, white for liberty, and blue for loyalty—"true blue." The official flag of the Vindicators showed a rattlesnake and the motto "Don't tread on me."

The Vindicators Association listed its five basic objectives in the first issue:

1. Keep America out of war.
2. Register and fingerprint all aliens.

3. Stop all immigration for the next ten years.

4. Banish all foreign isms.

5. Deport all alien criminals and undesirables.

Reynolds explained that he chose the word "vindicators" (which meant to defend) because America urgently needed defenders to combat alien enemies and alien propaganda. These alien enemies, warned Reynolds, were boring ceaselessly from within, and his organization would defend America from both within and without. Reynolds noted that as the national president of the Vindicators Association, he was prohibited from receiving any salary for his services. Hubert H. Rand, however, later disclosed that Reynolds did make money from the enterprise, but the main reason for the organization was to serve as a forum for Reynolds's views.[1]

Reynolds touted the Vindicators as a nonsectarian and nonpolitical order without any resort to secrecy, but any implication that the association was an open society was badly misleading. One had to be an American, either native born or naturalized, to become a member. Although neither color nor creed supposedly entered into the requirements for membership, blacks and Jews were not allowed to join. As Wesley McDonald Sr. made clear to one subscriber, "There are absolutely no Jews attached to the membership of this organization."[2]

Reynolds urged his readers to set up a seven-member group of Vindicators in their neighborhood, to be known as the Circle of Seven. These groups, made up of friends sharing similar ideas, would meet once a month to aid in the preservation of America. To attract young members, the Vindicators set up the Border Patrol, which was open to those between the ages of ten and eighteen. Each member had a badge covered with stars and stripes, and the eager neophytes could win twenty dollars for catching alien crooks.[3]

In the rather sparsely furnished offices of the organization, a visitor observed an American flag, an old confederate flag, and a blue banner with the words, "The Vindicators—America for Americans." Bob Reynolds wrote most of the editorials for the *American Vindicator* and approved the final copy for printing. As he stated on the floor of the Senate: "I know what is in the Vindicator because I do not have anyone to edit it. I pick out the material, I edit it myself."[4]

Wesley McDonald served as the national secretary of the Vindicators. The association employed approximately twelve other workers, including a managing editor, for general office chores. Reynolds usually spent at least one hour per day at the Vindicators' office, but when discussing organization business he frequently called members of the staff to a private entrance in his Senate office, where they had to knock five times before entering.

Publisher Reynolds had the personal goal of setting up at least one self-supporting chapter of the Vindicators in each of the thirty-two hundred counties

Page 8   THE VINDICATOR   April, 1939

THE AMERICAN VINDICATOR

Published monthly at Washington, D. C.

The official organ of The Vindicators.

A national patriotic organization, the objectives of which are:

1. Keep America out of war.
2. Register and fingerprint all aliens.
3. Stop all immigration for the next ten years.
4. Banish all foreign isms.
5. Deport all alien criminals and undesirables.

* * *

This paper is not competing with any other newspaper in the field — at least that is not its intention. It is designed to meet a specific need arising from certain definite trends operating in all sections of the land. It hopes and will faithfully endeavor to be the central connecting link in making more effective the efforts of all groups and individuals who seek to advance the objectives of The Vindicators.

What It's All About

In the beginning let's get this straight: The Vindicator's organization is an organization of American people. It is an organization in the interest of the people of America.

There are no paid organizers and there won't be any. The responsibility is definitely the responsibility of the American citizens themselves who organize units of the Vindicators in the more than 3,000 counties of the United States.

If in your county there is at present no organization of Vindicators, then it is up to you as an American citizen, believing in the principles of the Vindicators as enumerated, to get together five, ten, or twenty persons as a nucleus and form yourselves into a unit of Vindicators.

Each unit of the organization of Vindicators must of itself be self-supporting. Neither your unit nor any other unit will be called upon to contribute to any national organization, because this is not a money-making scheme; it is merely a movement on the part of American citizens to save America for Americans.

It will be the purpose of the Vindicator, this publication issued monthly, to provide the various units throughout the United States with news in its columns as to the progress being made North, East, South and West.

The Vindicator solicits no contributions, nor will it receive any. It has nothing for sale in the form of equipment or regalia of any description.

It will function as a forum for the one hundred and thirty-odd millions of people in the United States of America.

Each unit of the Vindicators will be in the form of county units exclusively, and each unit will meet monthly in public and serve as a public forum for the discussion of American problems of interest to the American people.

If you believe in the objectives of the Vindicators as enumerated, then take it upon yourself as a citizen of the United States interested in America's problems to organize a unit of Vindicators in your county. Do it today!

THAT'S THE STORY AND THAT'S WHAT IT'S ALL ABOUT.

Now — when you get your group together — proceed with the election of officers of your local group, set the date for monthly meetings and then send us all information pertaining to your local organization and a county unit number will be provided your group.

As you will note there are no advertisements in this newspaper — the Vindicator depends entirely upon its subscriptions.

REMEMBER, there is not one penny of profit to anyone anywhere connected with this publication — every cent is devoted to the cause of Americanism and in carrying out the objectives of the Vindicators — every penny received from subscriptions will be used in distributing the Vindicator — disseminating literature, compiling statistics and meeting only legitimate expenses incident to our principles and objectives.

Why Not Now

contribute to saving America by sending in 100—200—300—400 or 500 subscriptions to the VINDICATOR?

These Insignia Are Waiting For You

This is the banner of the Vindicators, a coiled rattler upon a yellow background. The symbol—the emblem of the Vindicators. *Slow to get aroused are the American people and just as slow are they to calm down.*

The button, which is to be worn in the coat label, is of red, white and blue.

The drawing shows in outline the red, white and blue feather which is being worn as the emblem of the Vindicators.

It designates active membership. Send for yours.

Banner, buttons and the feather emblems will be supplied without cost upon application by members to the National Headquarters of The Vindicators, in Washington, D. C.

Slow to Fight

Various explanations are given for choice of the rattlesnake as a favorite flag symbol in the Colonial days. Its choice may have been suggested by the habits of the reptile, slow to get into a fight and slow to get out of one.

The device was defended by Benjamin Franklin who noted that:

The rattlesnake is found only in America; that the ancients believed serpents possessed of wisdom and attack without first giving warning and that the number of rattles increases with age. The latter was especially appropriate then as it forecast expected growth and strength of America.

Although the rattlesnake appeared in various forms on the flags of that time—sometimes coiled ready to strike, and sometimes depicted as undulating across the field of the flag—each rattlesnake banner bore the unmistakable warning:

"Don't tread on me."

The emblem was flown by the illustrious John Paul Jones from the "Alfred," one of the early Colonial warships. It had previously been adopted as the flag of the Commanding Officer of the Navy.

The Rattlesnake Flag has frequently been confused with the national ensign of that time—the Continental Flag.

Let Us Have Peace

THIS COUNTRY IS DELUGED WITH PROPAGANDA: Propaganda to promote American participation in war, Propaganda to overthrow the Government of the United States, Communist propaganda, Nazi propaganda, Fascist propaganda pour from a multitude of spigots and pollute, with their intellectual poison, the thinking of the unwary in every element of our body politic!

TAKE WARNING BEFORE IT IS TOO LATE!

Your fears are being played upon, Your pride assailed, Your passions whipped by spokesmen for foreign interests, by dupes of alien guile, by secret minions of the Communist International and sinister agents of racial minorities, for one ulterior purpose, which is THE PLACING OF YOUR SONS ON EUROPEAN BATTLEFIELDS: Battlefields to wreak vengeance for enmities not ours, Battlefields to determine not so much the fate of democracy as the ownership of lands won for foreign nations by American intervention which cost us 350,000 casualties and — according to the last available figures — an expenditure of over $41,000,000,000.

With provocative utterance and insulting phrase, persons in high places of this nation have flicked the sensibilities of rulers of friendly states upon the raw. THEY HAVE DONE SO FOR NO CAUSE CONCERNING THE VITAL INTERESTS OF OUR PEOPLE — THE SOVEREIGN PEOPLE OF THE UNITED STATES.

THE SALVATION OF POPULAR GOVERNMENT IN AMERICA RESTS NOT IN FOREIGN WARS! HOSTILITIES IN WHICH WE MAY ENGAGE WILL BRING THE DOOM OF OUR FREEDOM.

If you doubt this assertion, read legislation recently proposed to socialize our country upon the declaration of a state of war.

THE FRONTIERS OF FOREIGN STATES CONCERN US NOT!

THE FORM OF GOVERNMENT PLEASING TO ALIEN PEOPLE IS THEIR AFFAIR, NOT OURS!

WOULD YOU SACRIFICE YOUR SONS TO RECTIFY A MAP, OR IMPOSE DEMOCRACY BY FORCE OF ARMS UPON A PEOPLE TO WHOM IT IS REPUGNANT?

THINK THIS PROBLEM THROUGH!

To do such things means to dedicate a conscript army of millions of Americans and the industries of the nation to the God of War!

AMERICANS! RISE IN YOUR MIGHT!

Assert your power to demand that the United States and the Government thereof be purged of dupes of alien interests, adherents of un-American political dogmas, inciters of class hatred, and fomenters of foreign wars!

THE TIME TO ACT IS NOW

THE CONGRESS OF THE UNITED STATES IS IN SESSION. CALL ON YOUR SENATORS AND REPRESENTATIVES TO RESTORE THOSE PRINCIPLES OF PUBLIC BEHAVIOR FOR THE PROMOTION OF DOMESTIC CONCORD AND INTERNATIONAL FRIENDSHIP LAID DOWN BY GEORGE WASHINGTON IN HIS GREAT FAREWELL ADDRESS!

JOHN B. TREVOR, President,

American Coalition, an organization to coordinate the efforts of patriotic, civic and fraternal societies to Keep America American, Washington, D. C.

Jefferson's Creed

Jefferson's creed, as promulgated in his inaugural address on March 4, 1801, was as follows: "Equal and exact justice to all men, of whatever state or persuasion, religious or political; peace; commerce and honest friendship with all nations, entangling alliances with none; the support of the State governments in all their rights, as the most competent administration for our domestic concern and the surest bulwarks against anti-republican tendencies; the preservation of the general government in its whole constitutional vigor, as the sheet anchor of our peace at home and safety abroad; * * * freedom of religion; freedom of the press; freedom of person under the protection of the habeas corpus; and trial by juries impartially selected — these principles form the bright constellation which has gone before us and guided our steps through an age of revolution and reformation."

One thing is clear, however—the flag has an honorable and unblemished history. Brave men believed in the principles for which it stood and fought wrongs inflicted upon them from across the sea.

Why not read this again? There's nothing new in it, of course, but too many of our fellow sojourners seem to have forgotten or have become confused by old sophistry under new names.

The insignia of Reynolds's Vindicator organization featured a red, white, and blue feather and a banner reading "Don't Tread on Me." (From *The American Vindicator*, April 1939)

in America and aimed for a total membership of one million by January 1940. Reynolds planned for a national convention to be held in St. Louis in the summer of 1939, at which time delegates from around the country would draw up a consti-tution for the organization. Although the convention never took place, Reynolds claimed to have three hundred units organized by September 1939, with subscrip-tions increasing by three hundred a week.[5]

During its first two years the *American Vindicator* focused on the elimination of communism in America and the eradication of criminal aliens. In a form letter seeking new members, Reynolds noted that North Carolina had fewer aliens and communists than any other state and he wanted to keep it that way. Reynolds announced that his "chief enemies are the communists, against whom I am waging an unrelenting war."[6]

While Reynolds jousted against aliens, communists, and foreign isms, leading newspapers and journalists castigated his new organization. Marquis Childs, an influential national columnist, claimed that Reynolds, who "preached a kind of Ku Kluxism, while undoubtedly of the purest native dye, was nevertheless a timid echo of Goebbels."[7]

The *Asheville Citizen* saw no need for the Vindicators and did not approve of Reynolds's radical and extremist methods of fighting aliens.[8] The *Citizen* inter-viewed several local citizens and asked their opinion of the association. Two men said that such extreme, mass nationalism as practiced by the Vindicators was dangerous and unhealthy. Ronald Green, another citizen interviewed by the paper, sarcastically pointed out that the potential of such an organization was enormous, given the expected membership of 5 million by June 1939. At that rate, said Green, there would be 120 million members in ten years, and even with nominal dues the club would be well off financially. Eventually, predicted Green, with patriots being plumed and buttoned at the rate of one million a month, the Vindicators would "include the entire electorate and Roosevelt will either join the Vindicators or be the only one left and have to be vindicated."[9]

The *Raleigh News and Observer* called Reynolds's new organization a con game by a master flimflam man. The paper puzzled over the purpose of this "new vindication scheme. Doubtless we will just have to wait until in his own good time Bob lets us know who wants to be vindicated with him, how a red, white, and blue feather will turn the trick, and whether some good old friends like precinct chair-men can get in on the ground floor with local concessions for V pins and fancy feathers." The only hint Reynolds had given for the purposes of his new group, alleged the *News and Observer*, was to get the minds of America back on their own business. There are many North Carolinians, smirked the paper, that "wish Bob had inaugurated this movement of tending to business a long time ago."[10]

According to *Newsweek*, the Vindicators' platform put Senator Reynolds "about

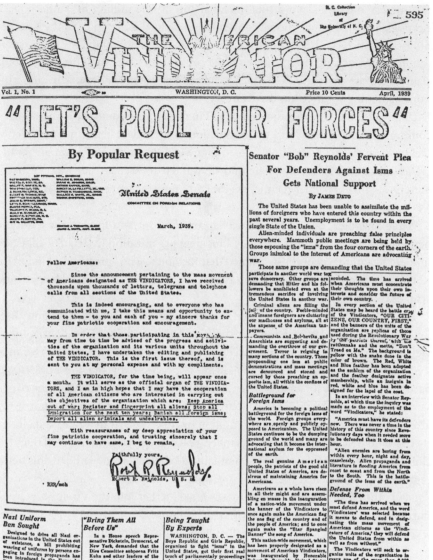

"Let's Pool Our Forces," volume 1, number 1 of *The American Vindicator*, April 1939. This first issue advocated the registration and fingerprinting of all aliens, halting immigration for ten years, deportation of all alien criminals, and staying out of World War II.

as much out of step with the Administration as he is with the American Legion." *Newsweek*, however, warned that "Reynolds is neither the fool nor the Fascist menace his enemies make out."[11]

Ken magazine thought Reynolds a "shrewd salesman" who might be successful with his new organization. Reynolds told the magazine, "I've worked very hard getting a program nobody in public life will dare to oppose. We're for 100 per cent Americanism and against war. Everybody is. I tell you, the man who criticizes us takes his political life in his hands." *Ken* called Reynolds "the greatest coat-tail rider in the Senate," since he got the idea for the Vindicators from Martin Dies and took his orders from the Hearst newspapers. Reynolds, however, would be the willing lackey of shifting political interests only while it proved politically profitable. In the end, wrote the magazine, Reynolds was "the sincere follower of no cause except the cause of Robert R. Reynolds."[12]

The *American Vindicator*, despite harsh denunciations by its critics, lasted from March 1939 until December 1942, during which period it was published forty times. Six issues of the publication did not go to press because of either financial difficulties or the absence of editor Reynolds. In the September 1941 issue, Reynolds admitted that the paper had not received the necessary support from patriotic Americans and he had no money in the treasury. Reynolds therefore reduced the number of pages in each issue from eight to four. The paper contained four pages until the final publication in December 1942. Reynolds gave no explanation or warning that the December 1942 issue was the last printing of the paper, but fewer subscriptions had reduced his financial base, and Reynolds did not want to finance the newspaper on his own.

In reviewing the three-and-one-half-year publication history of the *American Vindicator*, one finds the paper filled with Reynolds's old speeches, letters praising his views, and friendly quotations from other members of Congress. The initial offering contained an address on patriotism by Monsignor Fulton J. Sheen, and later issues featured articles by John B. Trevor, president of the American Coalition, an umbrella organization encompassing over one hundred patriotic groups. Over its lifetime, the paper consistently attacked aliens, communists, Jews, and the Roosevelt administration and advocated an isolationist foreign policy.

A letter from "K. C." of New York City reflected the rather shrill, xenophobic content of many published letters. This writer thought "there should be no Polish-Americans, no German-Americans, no Irish-Americans. Let's get rid of the HYPHENS. We're Americans and not Hyphenated Hybrids. Once this vital evil is attacked and cleared out there will be less trouble for America."[13]

The *American Vindicator* generally printed letters, articles, and editorial comments by those who sympathized with the aims of the organization—there were seldom any critical or dissenting letters unless Reynolds provided a rebuttal. The following is an example of some of the metaphoric, sophomoric verse found in the paper's pages:

> If alien enemies do not like us
> And would flaunt our Patriotic song
> Then let's promptly give them passports
> And deport them to the lands where they belong
>
> We want no part of other nations
> But to our own Colors we'll be true
> Prepared to protect every star in Old Glory
> The Red, White and Blue.[14]

The June 1939 issue of the *American Vindicator* pictured a lineup of five alien criminals wanted by the Justice Department for charges ranging from murder to gambling. The paper offered a reward of twenty-five dollars for the capture of any one of the men. Reynolds adopted this feature to illustrate the constant violation of American laws by alien criminals and the need to deport these criminals.

The same issue encouraged boys to join the Border Patrol with the promise of a "swell badge waiting for real hustlers." To become a member a boy had only to get one subscriber to the newspaper and then he could purchase his patrol badge for the paltry sum of two dollars. According to the *American Vindicator*, it was time for every red-blooded American boy to defend his country against the communists and the Nazis who were tearing the country apart. America belonged to Americans, not to foreigners who could not even speak English. For new members the "real fun for you will be in setting up a Patrol in your home town. And, you should become Chief patrolman there at home. Just think of all the fun that will be." Reynolds urged the kids to catch the alien crooks pictured each week and win the twenty-five-dollar reward because "over and above the fun you've had out of the money, you'll be doing your country a real service and would be growing up to protect the American way."[15] Reynolds did not specify the exact technique the young boys were to use in capturing and holding these crooks.

Reynolds informed his readers that he remained constantly vigilant against all of the isms threatening America. He said the difference between fascism, Nazism, and communism was the same as the difference between theft, burglary, and larceny: "I'd like to see the leaders of all other isms frying in hell."[16] Despite this fervent but impractical wish, Reynolds's earliest issues were strongly anticommunism with very little mention of the danger posed by fascism or Nazism. Reynolds's virulent stance against communism, coupled with his more lenient approach to fascism, undoubtedly encouraged the view that he was pro-fascist.

With a technique that would have done Joe McCarthy proud, the *American*

Vindicators's anticommunist bent led to the characterization of many liberal organizations in America as "pink" and un-American. Reynolds opposed the Works Progress Administration theater project because it was one of the most effective methods used by communists to spread their propaganda—and it was done at the expense of American taxpayers. "Remember," wrote Reynolds, "a play by Voltaire brought the French revolution."

The *American Vindicator* described the International Labor Defense, a communist front organization, as "that weird gutter stew of communist agitators and literary intelligentsia, the parlor pinks of the New Revolution, which brazenly instructs aliens to refuse to obey the laws of the U.S." The paper denounced the "utter flouting of our law" by a "rat-like organization" that "would haul down the Stars and Stripes and run up the death sickle and bloody red rag of Soviet Russia over the dome of the capitol building."[17]

In November 1939, the paper began its version of the Red Scare with the publication of a series of articles citing Earl Browder, head of the Communist Party in the United States, as America's number one enemy. Harry Bridges, the communist head of the International Longshoremen's Association, was comfortably ensconced in second place. Fritz Kuhn, head of the German-American Bund, Adolf Hitler, and Benito Mussolini were not even mentioned. The paper congratulated Martin Dies's House Un-American Activities Committee (HUAC) for revealing that there were more than twenty-eight hundred Communists occupying key government positions. The *American Vindicator* demanded that all communists in government be removed immediately.[18]

The paper appealed to such individuals as Mr. C. Wilson of San Antonio, Texas. Wilson wrote to Reynolds, Martin Dies, and J. Edgar Hoover praising the tabloid "as the most outstanding and popular publication of its kind in the U.S.A." Wilson could not understand why a Congress interested in the security of America did not get busy with concentration camps, prisons, and electric chairs to get rid of the "underground nests" of aliens and radicals in America. Wilson wanted Congress to pass a law so that Reynolds's *Vindicator* could be distributed free of charge throughout the country.[19]

The obsessive anticommunism of Reynolds's tabloid, his neofascist Border Patrol, and his consistent anti-Semitism increased the frequency of the charges that Reynolds was pro-Nazi. That the paper was anti-Semitic was unarguable. In addition to denying Jews membership in his organization, Reynolds carried on a constant attack against the *Jewish Examiner* for its disapproval of his opposition to immigration. Reynolds claimed that the *Examiner* wanted all the refugees (read Jews) from Germany to come to America and take jobs away from English-speaking Americans. In the same issue of the *American Vindicator*, Reynolds commented on a scholarly survey by a Dr. Cohen which concluded that American immigrants had enriched the nation's cultural, economic, and social life. Reynolds advised Mr. Cohen that America already had "enough merchants, motion picture producers, crooners like Eddie Cantor and entirely too many Cohens who are at the head of government departments."[20] Reynolds flaunted his anti-Semitism in his newspaper, and his public speeches often contained praise for fascist dictators coupled with a plea for America to leave them alone. He not only ignored the evils of Nazism but also misread public opinion, and he blatantly rejected criticism in the certainty that his position was the correct one.

Reynolds best illustrated his anti-Semitic and right-wing proclivities in his association with such individuals as Gerald L. K. Smith, Fritz Kuhn, Father Charles E. Coughlin, George Deatherage, Gerald B. Winrod, and other right-wingers, fascists, and crackpots. Reynolds seldom bothered to find out any details about the activities of these rabble-rousers, although he certainly knew of their general views. If they praised his views on aliens and subscribed to his paper, then Reynolds returned the favor. His frequent interchanges with these right-wingers proved to be the most damaging pieces of evidence that Reynolds harbored fascist views.

Despite Reynolds's protests that he was merely pro-America, the criticism of Reynolds as pro-Nazi continued. In his book *The Illustrious Dunderheads*, published in 1942, Rex Stout censured isolationists such as "the Ham Fishes, the Nyes, Wheelers, the Reynoldses and the rest of the illustrious dunderheads who bent the national eardrum in Congress with their bellowings that the country could never be invaded, that it was no use lifting a finger to help Britain, China or any nation struggling against tyranny, because their cause was hopeless. Shicklgruber was invincible." Stout described the isolationists as "they whooped it up and down the country, attended by that fantastic malodorous retinue of crackpots, Bundists, Kluxers, British-haters, Fifth-columnists, Roosevelt-haters, anti-Semites, Christian Fronters, *Social Justice* barkers, William Dudley Pelleys and hysterical old maids." In his book he also denounced the isolationists for either intentionally or unintentionally spouting Nazi propaganda in their speeches. The isolationists, insisted Stout, thereby gave publicity to writings designed to incite class warfare, separate the United States from her allies, and generally bring about the defeat of America.[21]

Although *The Illustrious Dunderheads* was not a scholarly work, Reynolds came under reproach by more worthy detractors. The distinguished urban planner and historian Lewis Mumford, speaking at a meeting of the American Foreign Policy Association in March 1939, stated that the war between the fascist states and America had already begun and that America had no choice but to support the democracies of France and England. Most Americans did not realize the gravity of the situation, said Mumford, owing to the effective German propaganda disseminated through members of known fascist organizations and other "powerful support-ers." Mumford listed Reynolds as a "powerful supporter" and described his utter-ances as "distinctly pro-fascist." This type of Nazi advocate, concluded Mumford, was a great detriment in the American fight against totalitarian governments.[22]

Drew Pearson and Robert Allen continued their disparaging remarks about Reynolds by divulging that Hitler had followed the controversy in America over the sale of six hundred planes to France. The authors revealed that "one very confidential report received in high places" stated that Hitler was "pleased by the speeches of Senator Reynolds, Clark and Nye," who opposed the sale of the planes.[23]

The House Un-American Activities Committee, often praised by Reynolds, unearthed documentary evidence that Nazi agents were in the United States with orders to conduct a campaign to smear Roosevelt and defame democracy. The committee also reported that members of the German-American Bund had been instructed by the Nazi Party "to subscribe to and distribute copies of 'The Vindica-tor,' fascist weekly [sic] launched by Senator Reynolds of North Carolina with mysterious financial backing."[24] The insinuation that his paper was backed by the Nazi Party caused an additional outcry on the part of Reynolds's critics. Reynolds, of course, was outraged that his favorite committee, HUAC, had turned on him.

An even greater furor ensued when Fritz Kuhn attended an address given by Reynolds in May 1939. Speaking to the American Defense Society, Reynolds made his usual speech, warning Americans of the danger within and asking citizens to take a "sleeping powder" so that they would not have to listen to the clamor about conflicts abroad. Kuhn, who had not been invited by the society and had been denounced by its chairman, claimed that the meeting was public and any visitor was welcome. In regard to Reynolds's speech, Kuhn said: "I liked it very well. I would underline everything."[25] One could hardly imagine a more damaging endorsement.

Heywood Broun, in his nationally syndicated column, did a piece on Reynolds's talk and the "loud applause" supplied by Fritz Kuhn. According to Broun, the approbation of Kuhn was not actually necessary, because Senator Reynolds "has been all the way to headquarters on his own." Citing a speech in which the senator had praised Hitler's achievements in Germany, Broun claimed that Reynolds had completely taken over Hitler's racial and nationalistic theories.[26] Vito Marcan-tonio, a United States congressman, later called Reynolds the "Number One Nazi spokesman in the United States" and also accused him of openly praising Hitler in Congress.[27]

The disapprobation of influential national writers and politicians was signifi-cant, but the condemnation at the state level was more caustic. His North Carolina constituents, while racially conservative, were overwhelmingly opposed to fascism and appeasement and wrote derisive letters about Reynolds's views. In the *Greensboro Daily News*, Belle Logan asserted that Reynolds was no longer Our Bob but "Hitler's Bob"—he was not representing North Carolina because he was too busy praising Hitler and criticizing Roosevelt. Moreover, Logan believed that the Vindicators was an organization run by Hitler.[28]

Although there were some laudatory letters praising Senator Reynolds's courage and isolationism,[29] the majority of the letters cast aspersions on his loyalty and ability. Some reactions were very discerning. In a Mother's Day sermon delivered at the United Church in Raleigh, the Reverend Mr. Robinson said that like Senator Reynolds he too wanted to spare mothers the necessity of sending their sons into a futile war. But the reverend felt that Reynolds did not "seem to realize that isolationism of the brand he is offering is part of the very spirit that threatens to send our world into new chaos." The minister then continued: "Poor Mr. Reynolds, we knew before you said all those hard words about Germany that you were not in that foreign government's employ. What you haven't convinced us of is that in your defense of America you will not cultivate a spirit that will give us our own brand of Fascism right here. I agree with Mr. Reynolds when he says 'the danger is from within.' What tragically he does not see is that men like himself constitute part of the danger, for they will have us mimic the things we hate. If Fascism comes to America it will have some nice American name. American Nazis might even choose to call themselves Vindicators."[30]

More devastating still was an article by Ulric Bell titled "Senator Reynolds Saves America," published in the November 1939 issue of *American Mercury*. Bell claimed that Reynolds, once known as the "Tar Heel Toreador," used to amuse his Senate colleagues. At this earlier stage of his career, recalled Bell, Reynolds was an "exemplar of hillbilly tomfoolery" and performed "as the shameless politico, filling the Senate record with turgid pages on his favorite subjects—himself, his travels, his slickness." His colleagues, wrote Bell, dismissed him as a "wayside Barnum" or "perhaps a Jeeter Lester who could read and write and exhort in the fashion approved of in his native habitat."[31]

But Reynolds, theorized Bell, had undergone a metamorphosis, and his self-righteous infallibility carried him to the position of the country's most voluble and ambitious "merchant of menace." Reynolds's tenets were merely "mildewed leavings of ancient nativism." Bell cast him as the nation's foremost demagogue—"the Duce of the Senate haranguers."

Bell noted that Reynolds had complained mightily about being unjustly linked with fascists and had developed a bitter persecution complex. Bell thought the fault lay not with his detractors but with Reynolds himself because of his association with other self-appointed American saviors.

Turning to the Vindicators, Bell realized that Our Bob had discovered that any dolt could find enough oafs to respond to the generalization "I am for the Americans." Reynolds had "draped himself in the American flag, and concocted a fantastic hocus-pocus of banners, badges, and patrols—in short, he dusted off all the standard tricks of patrioteering." Bell declared that one of the penalties of democracy is "that it often heaves up catch-as-catch-can statesmanship like 'Babbling Bob Reynolds.'"

Bell concluded that the phenomenon of Bob Reynolds was not so much in his platform as it was in the quality of his attacks—eternal demagogic flag-waving, shrill invective against aliens, and hysterics about foreign hordes. Reynolds's emphasis was not so much a love of country but a hatred of aliens.

National organizations also vilified Reynolds. The American League for Peace and Democracy, a communist front group, distributed copies of an open letter addressed to Reynolds, asking, "If you are an opponent of Nazism, why did you praise Hitler and the Nazi government as you did on the floor of the Senate January 17?"[32] The Non-Sectarian Anti-Nazi League described Reynolds as "an actual leader in the semi-Fascist movement in this country" who was "more than friendly to the powers whose machinations we are pledged to defeat."[33]

As the criticism peaked, the *Durham Morning Herald* surmised that Reynolds was beginning to realize his lone-wolf campaign to save the American people from foreign isms was not paying off. In his attempt to oppose all isms, Reynolds had "become entangled with Fascism and therefore lost caste as an exponent of Americanism. More seasoned politicians than Reynolds have played the same risky game and lost. Some have gone on to rectify self-invented blunders. How Mr. Reynolds comes out depends in no small measure on the turn of events in Europe. And, of course, how he plays his cards from now on."[34]

By the time the *Morning Herald* published its editorial, Reynolds had shifted gears. He finally seemed to understand his predicament and realized that he had to correct his blunders before he ruined his political career. He announced that he would rise to a point of personal privilege and make a speech in the Senate to answer all the "malicious and under-handed charges" made against him.[35]

Earlier, in January 1939, Reynolds had tried in vain to answer the pro-Nazi charges. He said that he had no anger toward Pearson and Allen, only toward those who supplied them with erroneous information. An agitated Reynolds decried the charges that he was pro-Nazi. He announced that he was still 100 percent for America and wanted only to advise America about world events in a frank and honest manner—"if that be treason," declaimed Reynolds, "why, then, let them make the best of it."[36]

Reynolds's January attempt to persuade Americans that he was a modern-day Patrick Henry had failed, and the attacks had increased. Although urged by friends not to get into a shouting match with powerful newsmen such as Pearson and

Allen, Reynolds decided that the charges were so serious that if he did not answer them, "they will destroy me." Reynolds then alleged that Pearson and Allen were trying to ruin him because they could not force him to end his fight to keep America out of war and to keep aliens from America's shores. Reynolds cried, "The only way they can stop me, the only way they can shut my mouth is to shoot me."[37]

Senator Reynolds continued his rebuttal to the frequent attacks on him in a bitter, four-hour response on the Senate floor on May 11. He concentrated his attack on columnists Pearson and Allen. Reynolds called the two men purveyors of untruths who would "eventually destroy the confidence of the American people in the American press." He also denied their insinuation that the Vindicators Association received financial support from the Nazis.

Reynolds maintained that he believed in freedom of the press but that this freedom did not include the freedom to libel and "to slander." He attributed the attack to the fact that Allen worked for the *Philadelphia Record*, published by Abraham Stern, a Jew who opposed Reynolds's fight to keep America out of war. Reynolds pointed out that very little of what Pearson and Allen wrote about anybody was true, quoting Cordell Hull as saying that Pearson and Allen "tell the truth only one-fourth of the time and only one-fourth of the truth two-thirds of the time."

Reynolds was angry because Pearson and Allen had virtually branded him "as a scoundrel and a traitor and a representative of a government that the American people hate worse than any government on the face of the earth." Their denunciation had inspired many of Reynolds's constituents to write him and condemn his beliefs. It was unfortunate, lamented Reynolds, that his opposition to foreign entanglements and advocacy of strict neutrality had caused him to be labeled pro-Nazi and pro-fascist.

Time and again Reynolds denied being wined and dined by Nazis in Germany and demanded that the two columnists prove their allegations or withdraw them. To disprove the insinuation that his newspaper was financed by the Nazis, he presented a statement of his financial position and the money spent on the paper. Reynolds himself paid for the first printing of 18,000 copies, but because 160,000 copies were sold, the paper became self-supporting. Members of the German-American Bund may have subscribed to his newspaper, for anyone could subscribe, but if this were so, no one on Reynolds's staff knew anything about it. Reynolds realized that Fritz Kuhn had heard his speech in New York, but Reynolds was glad Kuhn was there since he wanted *everyone* to hear what he had to say. The senator hastened to add that he did not personally know a single member of the German-American Bund.

Throughout his speech Reynolds explained that he never had and never would condone the practices of dictators. He reminded his listeners that he had denounced the inhuman treatment of minorities in Germany and other European countries but knew that America had to remain aloof from these problems or else the country would be dragged into another war.

At this point Reynolds shifted his attack to the North Carolina press. He was angry that the state press had opposed his candidacy in 1932 and 1938 and continued to oppose him as an elected official. Particularly sensitive about the disapprobation of his hometown papers, he claimed that the Asheville press hated him because he would not vote the way they wanted him to vote. Reynolds shouted that he was going to get revenge on the North Carolina press: "I'm going to crucify them. I'm warning them to get busy, because six years from now I'm going to beat the hell out of them, I'm going to lick them worse than ever before."

Reynolds's speech was one of the longest orations delivered during that session of Congress. The senator had notes scattered over six desks and marched about the chamber speaking at the top of his voice. When he began, there were a large number of senators present, but both the Senate and the galleries quickly thinned out. Lack of an audience did not deter Reynolds from a strong finish. He stated that he was tired of fighting for isolationism and restricted immigration when no one appreciated his efforts. But Reynolds swore that he would never change his views: "As far as all the foreign nations are concerned, they can all go to hell."[38]

In spite of his lengthy defense in the Senate, Reynolds did not succeed in refurbishing his tattered image as he had waited too long to deny the erroneous pro-Nazi charges by Pearson and Allen. Although his defense was effective, his response was too emotional and bombastic. The senator's tirade was marked by neither poise nor good temper.

In response to Reynolds's ill-considered threat to "crucify" the press, North Carolina newspapers unleashed a series of derogatory editorials. The *Raleigh News and Observer* featured a picture of Reynolds wearing boxing gloves and striking a pugilistic pose. The paper got a kick out of the performance of the Reynolds entourage on speaking tours—"the flying advance party to create the atmosphere for a regal entry; the ever-ready applause when the Senator spoke; the ever-watchful shepherds to rescue the Senator from overindulgence." But Reynolds had had no handlers on the floor of the Senate during his recent diatribe. The Raleigh paper denied that the press had persecuted Reynolds. They could not help it "if Buncombe Bobby strikes a negative chord when he stumbles over the keyboard of public opinion."[39]

The Raleigh paper's derisive rebuke reflected the opinions of other editorials around the state, but the most complete and devastating answer came from the paper closest to the conflict, the *Asheville Citizen*. Referring to Reynolds as "occasionally of North Carolina but more frequently of foreign parts," the paper stated that its earlier criticisms of Reynolds had been dignified and temperate and there was no justification for "the stream of abuse which flowed like lava from the erupting Senator." The senator, opined the *Citizen*, should have been able to define his views without recourse to cursing and vulgarities. As for Reynolds's threat "to crucify" the state newspapers, the *Asheville Citizen* stated that they owed neither their existence nor their freedom to him and would survive long after he passed out of the political picture. The only person that Senator Reynolds could crucify, responded the paper, was his own "imprudent self and he is rapidly achieving a first-class job in self-crucifixion."[40]

The other Asheville paper, the *Citizen-Times*, regretted the use of space to discuss a senatorial representative for whom the people of the state were constantly apologizing. But when Reynolds used the epithets of the gutter in reference to those who disagreed with "his strange, fantastic, and wholly un-American policies," then the paper had to answer lest its silence be construed as consent. The *Citizen-Times* wondered if Reynolds's "inordinate craving for the sunlight caused reason to give way to folly? Have his antics in the Senate and elsewhere so far deluded even himself that he no longer cares for the friendship and respect which once were his for the asking?" The paper had heard almost universal criticism of Reynolds and was disappointed that so promising a career had ended so ingloriously. The *Citizen-Times* pitied rather than censured the "lonely, solitary figure" of Reynolds but was not sorry for its criticism of him, only for the necessity of having to write it.[41]

Reynolds quickly realized that he had made a serious mistake in antagonizing the state press. When the senator returned to Asheville for a visit, he arranged an interview with both Asheville papers to try and restore a good relationship. Yet, as he had done in similar situations, Reynolds continued in the same vein as his Senate speech and ended up doing more harm than good. He insisted that he was not pro-fascist and declared that those who charged him with being a Nazi were the ones opposed to his immigration bills. He then chastised the Asheville papers for advocating the admission of twenty thousand European refugee children into the country. Reynolds thought that the admission of children would open the floodgates and that millions of refugees would come pouring in.[42] One reader of the *Citizen* wrote to the editor that Reynolds's position against admitting refugee children who were victims of Hitler's cruelty was not patriotism but inhumanity.[43]

Reynolds should have known that the opprobrium directed against him was not due to his immigration bills but because the press and constituents interpreted his speeches and actions as pro-fascist. Reynolds never seemed to grasp the basis for the public's displeasure, and his many attempts to clarify his views were abortive failures. Perhaps the foremost reason that Reynolds failed to win over public opinion was his continual relationship with many individuals who were either pro-fascist or unsavory right-wing radicals. Constituents found it hard to accept Reynolds's protestations of innocence when he constantly cavorted with the likes of Gerald L. K. Smith. In an article on fascism in America, *Life* listed Reynolds as a "man to watch," along with George van Horn Moseley; Father Charles Coughlin; William Dudley Pelley, founder of the Silver Shirts; Gerald B. Winrod; and others.[44]

The most damaging accusations linked Reynolds with Fritz Kuhn, leader of the German-American Bund. The bund's meetings featured Nazi uniforms and salutes as well as the singing of the Horst Wessel song. By 1939, Nazi propaganda minister Joseph Goebbels desired to cultivate a favorable attitude toward Germany in America and exhorted the operatives of his American propaganda machine to use the utmost caution in masking the sources and the intention of the propaganda.[45] Members of the German-American Bund sold Reynolds's *American Vindicator* at its meetings because its rabid antialien and Jewish bias, its virulent attacks on Great Britain, and its opposition to all war measures was made to order for them.[46]

The bund insisted that it was a patriotic American organization and even went so far as to hold a pro-America rally in Madison Square Garden on February 20, 1939.[47] The bund, however, remained an American branch of the German Nazi Party, and members had to swear allegiance to Adolf Hitler. Instead of gaining sympathy for Germany, the openly militaristic and pro-Nazi stance of the bund led to an investigation by the U.S. Congress.

The House Un-American Activities Committee concluded that the bund, with direction and funding from Nazi Germany, had trained hundreds of spies and saboteurs. According to the HUAC, the bund had also constructed an intricate network of American fascist organizations that included George Deatherage's Knights of the White Camellia, William Dudley Pelley's Silver Shirts, and the Christian Front.[48]

In late 1939, the Nazi government directed all of the bund's efforts toward the exploitation of the isolationist sentiment in America. Germany wanted to ensure American neutrality by making the isolationist position credible. The Nazis planned to develop several themes to bolster their case: an emphasis on the great burden of public debt left over from American participation in World War I, Britain's cynical role as World War I debtor, and the impact of the munitions industry as a large war profiteer. The Nazis also wanted to persuade Americans that they had nothing to fear from the rise of Germany, which had neither the desire nor the ability to conquer the United States.[49]

The Germans used George Sylvester Viereck as the point man to carry out their propaganda mission. Viereck, an intelligence agent for the German Foreign Office, was the editor of and a writer for a weekly newsletter called *Facts In Review*. Viereck's biographer referred to him as the most prominent and sophisticated of all the German propaganda agents, while the German Foreign Office considered him "their most valuable liaison agent."[50] Viereck's purpose was to influence members of Congress, divide opinion in the country by spreading confusion and chaos, and provide secret intelligence when possible. Viereck created a network of confidential informants and developed close ties with a number of lawmakers whose isolationism and anti-Roosevelt bias made them easy prey.[51]

Viereck circulated isolationist speeches, written by German propagandists, by persuading congressmen to print the speeches in the *Congressional Record*. He then had reprints of this material sent out by the hundreds of thousands at taxpayers' expense under the congressional franking privilege. With the imprint of the *Congressional Record*, Viereck had a document that was as genuinely American as one could wish. As an added benefit, German influence was not visible, and the cost of this campaign was negligible. The large number of speeches printed due to the influence of Viereck and his agents verified "the astonishing exploitation of American isolationists."[52]

Viereck managed to cultivate cordial relationships with such influential isolationists as Senator Ernest Lundeen and Representative Hamilton Fish, and he used their offices for his Washington operations. Viereck then created the Make Europe Pay War Debts Committee and the Islands for War Debts Committee to serve as vehicles for his efforts to strengthen isolationist, anti-British, pro-German sentiment in America. Both committees, which existed on paper only, demanded that America seize British and French possessions in the Western Hemisphere and apply these possessions toward the payment of war debts. Viereck hoped that by calling America's attention to the war debts, he could divert interest from German aggression.

Prescott Dennett, a paid German agent, was the secretary-treasurer for the Make Europe Pay War Debts Committee, established in December 1939. He worked closely with George Hill, an assistant to Congressman Fish, and obtained from Hill reprints of suitable speeches and articles for insertion into the *Congressional Record*.[53]

Dennett offered Senator Reynolds, among others, the opportunity of becoming a vice chairman of his committee. In a letter to Dennett on March 4, 1939, Reynolds agreed to accept the position. On the same day, Reynolds introduced in the Senate a joint resolution for the acquisition of British islands to pay England's World War I debts. At Dennett's request, Reynolds put press releases announcing the formation of the Make Europe Pay War Debts Committee into the *Congressional Record*. Dennett reprinted all this material and sent out seven thousand copies under Senator Reynolds's congressional frank. Dennett had used Reynolds's influence to promote Nazi goals.[54]

Eventually, in 1944, Prescott Dennett was indicted under the 1940 Smith Act, which forbade any organization advocating the overthrow of the government of the United States. In the so-called great sedition trial of 1944, Dennett appeared in the dock with thirty other alleged Nazi agents. Another defendant at that trial was Lois de La Fayette Washburn, who served as a secretary to Reynolds in 1944 when he organized a new political party, the Nationalist Party. Both these individuals went free owing to a mistrial, but there was no question that both worked for the Nazi government. Viereck was later convicted of violating the Foreign Agents Registration Act and spent five years in jail.[55]

Did Bob Reynolds cooperate with Viereck and Dennett with the knowledge that they were Nazi agents? The available evidence indicates that Reynolds did not know that they were Nazi agents, nor did he understand that the Make Europe Pay War Debts Committee was a front for Nazi propaganda.

O. John Rogge, chief of the Justice Department's Criminal Division and prosecutor for the government in the 1944 sedition trial, was convinced that Reynolds and nineteen other politicians were used by Viereck and did not collaborate with him.[56] For example, Senator Gerald Nye refused to reprint articles when approached directly by Viereck, but when the request was made by the Make Europe Pay War Debts Committee, Nye permitted one hundred thousand copies of an isolationist speech to be printed and distributed under his frank.[57] Other authors who wrote about these circumstances, such as Michael Sayers and Albert Kahn in their Plot against the Peace, believed that most of the isolationists were unwitting tools of the Nazi propaganda machine.

Although George Viereck's sentiments and previous activities for the German government were rather widely known through HUAC investigations, it was possible that Reynolds was unaware of Viereck's connections with the Nazi Party because he seldom carefully investigated anyone with whom he worked. Reynolds cooperated with Dennett and Viereck through the Make Europe Pay War Debts Committee without realizing that it was a front for Nazi propaganda. Reynolds, who had been urging Britain and France for years to pay their war debts, simply could not resist joining such a committee. There was no conclusive proof that Viereck approached Reynolds personally, and there was no reason for Reynolds to suspect Prescott Dennett as a German agent. Viereck and Dennett may have fooled Reynolds as they did other isolationists such as Nye and Lundeen. Wayne S. Cole, in Senator Gerald P. Nye and American Foreign Relations, concluded that Nye, Reynolds, and others were used by Viereck without knowledge of Nazi connections.[58] The trial testimony did not directly implicate Reynolds, nor was he cited by any government investigations. Nonetheless, Reynolds's association with Nazi agents Viereck and Dennett, even if unintended, proved to be a huge embarrassment.

Reynolds, however, simply did not want to learn a lesson from his damaging associations, nor did he try to hide these associations. He continued to attach himself to leaders of avowedly anti-Semitic and antidemocratic organizations, which were considered fascist by many Americans. An FBI report indicated that

August T. Gausebeck, an investment banker and Nazi sympathizer, was on "close and friendly" terms with Reynolds.[59] According to *New Masses*, a leftist paper, Reynolds associated frequently with most of the anti-Semitic and fascist groups in America, and Reynolds's *American Vindicator* had a "full blown Fascist program" replete with thinly disguised Jew-baiting propaganda.[60]

The *Jewish Examiner* claimed that such fascist groups as the Christian Front and the Silver Shirts had increased their antialien rhetoric as the international situation approached a crisis in 1939. The brightest star of the antialienists, according to the *Examiner*, was Bob Reynolds. The paper noted that the most staunch leaders of the antialien group enthusiastically endorsed the Nazi movement and that it was a short step from antialienism to anti-Semitism.[61]

Reynolds answered the criticism from *New Masses* and the *Jewish Examiner* with a rejoinder in the *American Vindicator*. The senator claimed that he was not anti-Jewish and that the *Examiner* and Jewish groups were attacking him simply because he would not stand aside and permit all European refugees and foreigners to flood America.[62]

One right-wing leader who knowingly cooperated with the spread of fascist propaganda in America was George E. Deatherage, who set up a white supremacy group, the Knights of the White Camellia, as an anti-Semitic, antiforeign organization. Deatherage worked assiduously sending out fascist material from Italian and German sources.[63] On February 22, 1939, Deatherage distributed a patriotic speech by Reynolds under Reynolds's franking privilege. Edwin M. Curry, who had seen hundreds of copies of the speech, then wrote Reynolds for an explanation about the senator's association with Deatherage. Wesley McDonald Sr. answered the letter by merely stating that Reynolds had "some correspondence with him [Deatherage] and it appears that he is thoroughly acquainted with what Senator Reynolds is trying to accomplish."[64] Reynolds's and McDonald's admission of an association with Deatherage reflected the extraordinary bad judgment both men possessed. Reynolds *had* to have known what the Knights of the White Camellia believed, and his willingness to provide franking privileges to Deatherage demonstrated approval of their anti-Semitic and racist viewpoint.

Father Charles Coughlin, a radio priest from Detroit and a fierce critic of the New Deal, organized the secret Christian Front group for the apparent purpose of overthrowing the United States and eliminating all Jews from key positions in the government. The Christian Front compiled a remarkably odious record, attracting many violent and unstable members.[65]

For several years Father Coughlin's newspaper, *Social Justice*, a stridently anti-Semitic organ, loudly praised Reynolds. *Social Justice* reprinted Reynolds's speeches and on two occasions published signed articles by him. Between February 27, 1939, and August 19, 1940, the paper quoted the senator on his isolationism, on his anti-

British feelings, and on various other subjects at least eighteen times.[66] In July 1940, Reynolds sent a letter of commendation to *Social Justice* praising its antiwar position.[67] In 1942 the postmaster general barred *Social Justice* from the mails, and the attorney general warned that Father Coughlin could face formal charges of sedition if he did not cease his public activities. It was abundantly clear, from his speeches on the floor of the Senate and in conversations with the press, that Reynolds knew the views of *Social Justice*.[68] Yet he not only refused to denounce Coughlin but continued to praise him.

In 1933, in Asheville, North Carolina, of all places, William Dudley Pelley organized a fascist group known as the Silver Shirts. Pelley's newspaper, *Liberation*, praised the founding of Reynolds's Vindicators and printed a statement allegedly made by Reynolds. When asked about Pelley's Silver Shirts, Reynolds said, "There is room enough in this for all of us."[69] *Liberation* later applauded Reynolds for exposing the dangers of immigration.[70] In testimony before HUAC, a writer for *Liberation* indicated that he gained data for some of his articles through the assistance of Senator Reynolds.[71] It should be noted that the *American Vindicator* attacked the Silver Shirts on occasion, and *Liberation* amazingly accused Reynolds of being "a Gentile front for Jews."[72] There was no evidence, although both men were from Asheville, that there was any personal relationship between the two.

Reynolds also had a friendly relationship with John Trevor, head of the American Coalition, as well as G. Allison Phelps, author of several anti-Jewish and antidemocratic pamphlets published in California, who charged that Hollywood was controlled by aliens, Jews, and communists. Reynolds inserted excerpts from Trevor's and Phelps's articles into the *Congressional Record* and the *American Vindicator*.[73]

Senator Reynolds also placed speeches by right-wing fundamentalist minister and anti-Semite Gerald B. Winrod into the *Congressional Record*. Winrod saw Jews as responsible for all the evils in the world and fought against a perceived Jewish plot to control the world.[74] On July 7, 1939, after Winrod's speech attacking Jews, Catholics, and communists, Reynolds telegraphed Winrod as follows: "Your most excellent address entitled 'Keep America Out of War' delivered by you was inserted in *Congressional Record* yesterday by me. Consider it a high privilege and honor to be provided opportunity of bringing to attention of American public such a marvelous address. Thank you for your patriotic cooperation." Reynolds and Winrod also exchanged letters praising each other. In his newspaper, the *Defender*, Winrod commended Reynolds on his effort to stop immigration: "Ever increasing numbers of Christians and patriots are thanking God for your insight into true causes behind our nation's plights and the courage you are manifesting in combating these evils."[75]

Winrod wrote Gerald L. K. Smith that he had received a letter from Reynolds

complaining that reporters from *Life* had been snooping around his office, secur-
ing copies of the *American Vindicator*. Reynolds feared that he, Smith, and others
were about to be victims of a smear job from the magazine.[76] Winrod warned
Reynolds that there was a concerted effort to mobilize public sentiment against
persons who did not approve in every detail of the foreign and domestic programs
of the present administration. Winrod claimed that the snooping activities by *Life*
were part of the process to inflame public passion against those who stood up for
America.[77]

In addition, so as not to discriminate against other fascist nations, Reynolds
inserted material into the *Congressional Record* from the official Franco propaganda organ in America, *Spain*.[78] He also put in a bitter antialien, anti-Semitic
article from the pro-fascist Italian paper *Il Grido Della Stirpe*, which was edited by
Domenico Trombetta, later arrested and indicted for sedition. Reynolds, despite
Trombetta's arrest, said he would not hesitate to reinsert the material supplied to
him by Trombetta into the *Congressional Record*.[79]

The most significant relationship for Reynolds was his association with the
Reverend Gerald L. K. Smith, former lieutenant for Huey Long in his Share Our
Wealth program. According to Glen Jeansonne, Smith's biographer, Smith was
Reynolds's closest friend on the far right, and Reynolds shared Smith's bigotry as
well as his opposition to internationalism.[80] In July 1940, Reynolds praised Smith
for getting 1.2 million people to sign a petition to outlaw communism, fascism,
and Nazism and to keep America out of foreign wars. Reynolds paid high tribute
"to the Americanism, the patriotism, and the worthwhile activities" of Smith and
wished that there were more people working to keep America out of war.[81] When
Smith began the publication of his newspaper, *The Cross and the Flag*, Reynolds
wrote a letter of endorsement: "Let me congratulate you with my full heart upon
your first edition. It hits the bulls-eye with every paragraph; it is straight from the
shoulder; it is gotten up in a conservative manner; it speaks the truth. America
must be saved for Americans."[82]

When radio commentator Walter Winchell reported that he was appalled to
learn that Smith had the confidence and friendship of Senator Reynolds, Reynolds
replied that he had "no apologies to offer for endorsing the program of any
individual or group standing for the things that I have stood for many years."[83] He
also wrote to a woman who had doubts about Smith and told her that Smith,
"insofar as I know, is a real, genuine American who loves his country better than
any other country in the world, and I do not believe I could pay a man a higher
compliment than that."[84] Smith, in his paper, frequently touted Reynolds as one of
the leaders in the isolationist movement and complained that the senator had been
smeared by the same people who fought *The Cross and the Flag*.[85]

In 1941 Smith shifted from antiwar crusading to anti-Semitism, and by 1942 his

Committee of One Million had a substantial following of over one-half million. Smith stepped up his attacks on Jews and increased his contacts with Gerald Winrod, Elizabeth Dilling, William Dudley Pelley, George Viereck, and the other leaders of the radical fringe. His move toward extremism cost him the support of Senators Gerald Nye and Arthur H. Vandenberg,[86] but not that of Bob Reynolds. It seems incomprehensible that Reynolds would continue to laud and support an individual such as Gerald L. K. Smith, whom Jeansonne labeled the "Minister of Hate." Reynolds might not have understood the relationship of George Viereck and Prescott Dennett to the Nazi Party, but he surely knew the goals and ideas of Smith, Coughlin, Winrod, Pelley, and Deatherage. Reynolds found common ground for association with these varied groups because of their strong isolationist views and their attacks against aliens and Jews. As with the Nazi propagandists, Reynolds helped and supported those individuals who were in agreement with his basic beliefs.

Unfortunately, these groups used Reynolds's position as a United States senator to lend credibility to their organizations. Reynolds ignored the inherent evil in these racist groups and did not consider the adverse public reaction to his association with them until too late. When such people as Gerald Winrod lauded Reynolds for his courage and sound judgment, he should have known he was in bad company and that the public would associate him, correctly, with Winrod's opinions. He could have easily presented his isolationist position, without associating with the Winrods of America, simply by joining America First, a legitimate, intellectually sound organization that opposed war.

Pelley, Smith, Winrod, and lesser prophets inundated the country with hate mail, Nazi propaganda, and anti-Semitic literature. They managed to reach an audience of millions, and their aims were bolstered by a small coterie of isolationists and racists in Congress. Although disloyal and potentially dangerous, they did not undermine the democratic system, nor did they hamper the war effort in any significant way. They were little more than fringe groups, and the majority of Americans recognized them as rabble-rousers and ignored their message. Nonetheless, their rantings and ravings stirred up hatreds, fears, and frustrations during a tense period in American history.

In the end, Reynolds was a misguided nationalist who believed that isolationism and immigration restriction would save America. He had hoped to use his Vindicators Association to create publicity and promote his political career. The unintended result, however, was exactly the opposite. His affiliation with the right-wing radical groups and his unwillingness to criticize their excessive racism and hatred demonstrated that Reynolds not only shared but approved of many of their ideas. His beliefs in putting America first and in isolationism could not hide his underlying anti-Semitism and his appeals to prejudice.

CHAPTER NINE

[
1939–1940
]

In his State of the Union Address in 1939, Franklin Roosevelt discussed the economic recession of 1938 but focused on the dangers that the forces of aggression posed to international peace and democracy. Reynolds decided to comment only on the domestic portion of the president's speech, waiting for another day to find fault with his foreign policy. Reynolds lauded Roosevelt for recognizing the necessity for continued economic recovery and found the speech "constructive, patriotic, and filled with hope."[1]

Although the New Deal had been essentially completed by 1938, Roosevelt tried to alleviate some of the distress caused by the recession of 1938. He urged Congress to restore a $150 million appropriation to the Works Progress Administration which had been cut by the House. The Senate defeated the appropriations bill by the narrow margin of one vote, 47–46, with Reynolds uncharacteristically voting against the increase. Alben Barkley, majority leader of the Senate, said that Reynolds's vote surprised him for he had counted on that vote to give the administration the margin of victory.

Reynolds consistently favored inflationary spending and rarely voted against a bill of this type. His explanation indicated just how strongly his dislike of aliens influenced his thinking. He had determined that North Carolina, with fewer aliens than any other state, had received less relief per capita than any state in the nation, while New York had received much more money per capita. Reynolds complained that in New York State they had "the biggest foreign element in the country. The people can't even speak English that you can understand. New York gets $69.40 relief money per capita in a year. In North Carolina they have the finest, purest racial strain in the union, and North Carolina gets only $13.30 per capita. Why should I vote these hundreds of millions for those aliens in New York?"[2] Reynolds's drift toward a more militant antialienism, coupled with a need to demonstrate his independence from Roosevelt, meant that his vote on domestic issues could no longer be taken for granted by the Democratic Party.

With the alien threat foremost on his agenda, Reynolds proposed an amendment to the revised social security pension bill. Reynolds's amendment excluded from social security benefits all foreign-born aliens who had not taken out American citizenship papers by January 1, 1941, or who did not become American citizens within six years after entering the United States. The amendment also included a provision that required American employers who used alien laborers to pay a "special privilege tax," since the aliens were in economic competition with American citizens. The Senate, to speed passage of the bill, accepted Reynolds's amendment without a record vote.[3] Reynolds voted for the revised social security pension bill, stating that America could "certainly afford to open up our hearts and take care of the old people of the country."[4]

The *New York Times* had urged the defeat of Reynolds's amendment because its very wording revealed an appeal to prejudice. The amendment discriminated against older people who might have failed to take out citizenship papers because of circumstances beyond their control. The levy of a gratuitous penalty tax for hiring aliens, observed the *Times*, was bigoted and malicious.

Abraham Epstein, executive secretary of the American Association for Social Security, in a letter to the *New York Times*, asked the House and Senate conferees to strike out the Reynolds amendment because it was "contrary to all established social policy, is inhuman and vicious as well as most uneconomical." The amendment, argued Epstein, sought to discriminate against human beings at a time of their greatest need. Especially affected would be women and older immigrants who "have contributed by their labor to the welfare of the nation, have paid their just proportion of taxes and have every right to seek the protection of their government."[5] The House and Senate Conference Committee, meeting to reconcile two different versions of the social security bill, eventually eliminated Reynolds's amendment.[6]

In early January 1939, Reynolds astonished the Senate by momentarily abandoning his perorations on foreign affairs and aliens to speak out against the inequities of the beer and liquor merchants in the country. Although he had won election to the Senate partially on a "wet" platform, Reynolds now attacked the liquor forces in America as "drunk with power" and predicted that unless drastic steps were taken to promote temperance and reduce the number of saloons, then the American public might decide to resort to prohibition again. The liquor interests had been given an inch, alleged Reynolds, and they had taken a mile. They had advertised over the radio and in newspapers and magazines—"advertising their liquor, God's worst enemy and the devil's best friend, to the children of America."

Reynolds's outburst had been triggered by the annual speech by Senator Morris Sheppard of Texas commemorating the adoption of the Eighteenth Amendment. As soon as Sheppard complained that most male saloonkeepers had been supplanted by barmaids, Reynolds leaped to his feet to denounce barmaids. If anyone were not aware of the large number of barmaids in Washington, Reynolds volunteered to "take him down here in the District of Columbia and show him hundreds of barmaids. I know where they are." This last remark brought loud laughter from the Senate floor and the galleries.

Reynolds quickly recovered and stated that he hoped that there was "no inference here that I drink." Again the gallery and the Senate roared with laughter. Reynolds admitted that he had taken a drink in the past but had given it up. "I have learned better. I know that it will give you a little excess energy for the minute, but it is very destructive of the physical cells."[7]

Reynolds, at this juncture, was on one of his temperance kicks. Reynolds, according to his secretary, Wesley McDonald, had been a rather heavy drinker for several years. After a particularly difficult drinking bout he would repent and, full of guilt and remorse, would swear off alcohol forever. Reynolds's resolve would last for eight weeks or so, and then he would return to his old habits. When in one of his dry periods, he righteously denounced demon rum, but no one took him seriously.[8]

While on his temperance kick, Reynolds advocated federal control of drunk driving, which he believed was one of the most serious hazards to life and property. Reynolds designed a bill to provide for scientific means to determine the exact degree of intoxication of an automobile driver. A special committee of the American Automobile Association studied the bill and found it so inadequate that its passage would be harmful. The bill did not clarify such important areas as to whether the test would be administered forcefully or taken voluntarily or whether drugs, in addition to alcohol, would be considered. Because of these defects the committee rejected Reynolds's bill.[9] In this instance, Reynolds had called attention to an important problem badly in need of reform, but he did such a sloppy job with the bill that it was dismissed out of hand.

While Reynolds occasionally lost his resolve and flirted with the pleasure of alcohol, he was usually one of the most health-minded men on Capitol Hill. An article in Bernarr Macfadden's magazine, *Health Review*, featured pictures of a very fit Reynolds working out on a punching bag and straining at a rowing machine. The article explained that Reynolds, with an athletic physique that was the envy of his more corpulent colleagues, had proposed that the senators build a gym at their own expense. The senators chipped in thirty dollars each to purchase weights, punching bags, and a rowing machine. They then took over an unused portion of the Senate office building for their workouts.[10]

In addition to setting up a gym for politicians who wanted to exercise, Our Bob got into a minor imbroglio with Hollywood when he called on moviemakers to stop butchering the southern accent in films. Reynolds wanted the directors to stop making southern characters indulge in "vaudeville honey chile talk." He patiently explained to Hollywood, in his own rich drawl, that "you-all" never meant one person but always referred to more than one person.[11] Unfortunately for Reynolds but luckily for movies such as *Gone with the Wind*, which premiered in Atlanta in December 1939, Hollywood directors ignored his advice.

Already one of the most talked-about senators in Washington, Reynolds blithely acknowledged that he welcomed newspaper comments whether they were good or bad, because if one received no attention from the press, then the individual might as well be dead. But he certainly did not welcome the widespread publicity given to an article written by Joseph Alsop and Robert Kintner in the *Washington Evening Star*.

The authors referred to Reynolds as "the most conspicuous mountebank-statesman of our day. He has the loudest voice, the lightest heart, and the lowest estimate of his responsibilities of any member of the Senate." Alsop and Kintner believed that few men enjoyed themselves as much as Reynolds, who devoted much of his life to eating, drinking, junketing, playing the ladies' man, and performing antics for the news camera. The authors continued: "He is not a very deep thinker and his own significance has certainly escaped him. It is, quite simply, that things can't be very bad in the United States if the people are willing to sacrifice their franchise for a joke. Bob Reynolds is so entertaining that one seldom doubts whether the joke is worth $10,000 per year."[12]

No one, particularly a politician already in trouble, needed that kind of press attention. Reynolds immediately asked for help from the North Carolina Democratic Club of Washington, D.C., a political club of Reynolds's supporters controlled by Wesley McDonald. The club responded to the senator's plea by adopting a resolution requesting that the *Washington Evening Star* issue a statement of the real facts about Senator Reynolds's ability. The club felt that the article was neither fair nor constructive and reflected badly on Reynolds and North Carolina. Although Reynolds's office actually released the statement, the club denied that Reynolds had anything to do with it.[13] Reynolds had obviously orchestrated the rebuttal, and his feeble attempt to gain a retraction from Alsop and Kintner compounded his embarrassment.

The press attacks were insignificant when compared with Reynolds's anguish over the death of his mother, Mrs. Mamie Reynolds, on July 29, 1939. Mrs. Reynolds had been in declining health and became seriously ill three weeks before her death. Reynolds remained constantly at her bedside the last ten days of her life and was grief stricken at her death, as mother and son had been extremely close.[14]

Reynolds, without a father since childhood, had been devoted to his mother, as Frank Graham confirmed in a letter of condolence: "Your devotion to your mother and your constant companionship during her last days must now be a consolation to you as it was to her." Franklin Roosevelt also sent Reynolds a note of sympathy, as did J. Edgar Hoover, who wrote "if the sympathy and understanding of a friend can help, there is a wealth of it in my heart for you."[15]

Mrs. Reynolds left an estate that included three large buildings occupied by business firms on Patton Avenue in downtown Asheville, a large lot at Woodfin and South Liberty Streets, and other personal property. The annual income from the rental property amounted to approximately ten thousand dollars per year. Reynolds received half of the revenue, with the other half divided equally among five grandchildren.[16] After his mother's death, Reynolds canceled all speaking engagements and left on August 6, 1939, to travel to Europe, as he had on other sad occasions.[17]

Although momentarily distraught by his mother's death, Reynolds returned to his crusade against aliens and his fight for immigration control. Aware of the South's long-held suspicion of foreigners, Reynolds understood the popularity of persisting in his opposition to aliens at a time when America feared involvement in a world war. Charles O. Lerche, in *The Uncertain South*, explained what Reynolds knew intuitively. Southern whites, wrote Lerche, tightly knit by homogeneous mores and traditional social ties, had experienced very little intercultural contact with individuals of different origins, customs, and values. Thus the majority of southerners desired to preserve their culture against immigration, and in the crisis atmosphere of 1939, they consistently opposed increases in the number of immigrants allowed to enter the United States.[18]

Thus at a time when his popularity had declined significantly, Reynolds pushed the alien issue for all it was worth. He once again submitted the same five immigration bills he always proposed but on this occasion forcefully pointed out that the critical world situation should awaken citizens to the need for alien control. He said that he had high hopes for the passage of his bills.[19]

Shortly after Reynolds dropped his bills in the congressional hopper, the verbose senator addressed the nation over NBC radio. He disclosed that foreign countries kept their best citizens at home and sent their undesirables to America for jobs or relief. Some immigrants, admitted Reynolds, were persons of high character who helped build America, but most were job seekers, "weaklings, some criminals, and the majority unwanted." America, instead of stopping the parade of criminals and illegal immigrants, continued to "play Santa Claus for many thousands of undesirable aliens" who owed their allegiance to another country and who had even attempted to mold the American government on the lines of foreign dictatorships.[20]

As usual, the Tar Heel's immigration proposals and speeches drew violent criticism and lavish praise. The *New York Times* regretted that Reynolds wanted to change the concept of the United States as an asylum of the oppressed.[21] The Federal Council of Churches of Christ in America denounced Reynolds because they had a responsibility for the suffering of human beings. The council believed that immigrants would be economic assets as producers and consumers and urged America to continue its historic policy of friendliness to refugees.[22]

On the other side of the coin, the *Huntington (W. Va.) Advertiser* favored Reynolds's proposal to fingerprint all aliens as it would greatly assist in the enforcement of deportation laws at a time when many aliens were agitating against the government.[23] The state senate of Maryland and the Oklahoma legislature adopted resolutions praising Reynolds for sponsoring alien-control legislation. The Maryland senate called his stand "patriotic and inspiring." Reynolds referred to these resolutions as evidence of "vast popular support" for his program.[24]

Finally, after many years of agitation and pleading, Reynolds won a victory when the Senate Committee on Immigration reported favorably on his bills to stop immigration. The subcommittee took key features of all five bills and codified them into a single piece of legislation but limited the bill to five-years' duration instead of the ten years originally proposed.

The final immigration measure reported out of the committee had more drastic restrictions than the Johnson Immigration Act of 1924. The committee described the codified bill as a measure "to prohibit the immigration of aliens into the United States during the period of abnormal unemployment." The bill prohibited the issuing of an immigration visa to any alien for a minimum of five years and for an additional period until such time that the president could determine that the number of unemployed persons in America over eighteen years of age did not exceed five million.

More significant, the act provided for the Census Bureau to obtain information on all aliens residing in the United States, including name, address, place of birth, date and port of entry into the country, and whether an intention of citizenship had been filed. An Alien Registration Board would administer the procedures, and all aliens had to apply for registration at U.S. post offices, pay a registration fee of one dollar, and notify the postmaster of any permanent change of address. Any alien failing to register could be punished by a fine of not more than five hundred dollars or one year in jail or both. The government could deport any alien unlawfully in the United States.[25]

Senator Reynolds called the bill a "step in the right direction" and found it "encouraging that my colleagues have adopted my position in principle."[26] Despite this progress, Reynolds made it clear that he intended to fight on the floor of the Senate to restore the ten-year ban on immigration and to retain the fingerprinting provision of his original bills.[27] Newspapers such as the *Bogalusa (La.) News* and the *Roanoke Rapids (N.C.) Herald* approved of Reynolds's bills. The *Herald* de-plored the fact that every national group in the country, "running hand in hand with every foreign spy, sympathizer, and traitor," would fight against the bill.[28]

Senator Robert F. Wagner Sr., Democrat from New York, challenged the ba-sic philosophy of Reynolds's immigration restriction by offering the so-called Wagner-Rogers bill, which would admit twenty thousand refugee children under the age of sixteen (most of whom were Jewish) from Germany, over a two-year period, as nonquota immigrants. The adherents of this bill stressed the humanity of saving children regardless of their race or religious creed and reminded listeners that America had traditionally succored the persecuted of Europe.[29]

Predictably, the main opposition to the Wagner-Rogers bill came from Bob Reynolds, now the chief spokesman for the restrictionists. Strongly supported in his stand by the American Legion and other patriotic groups, Reynolds made a radio speech opposing *any* legislation that would lower immigration barriers, especially because the twenty thousand children would be on the labor market in a few years. Influenced by his anti-Semitism, Reynolds also feared that the bill was designed to create sympathy for the European immigrant and would be used as an "entering wedge" to force open America's immigration gates. Reynolds asked his listeners to cast their eyes southward and picture the sons and daughters of eight million sharecroppers "who live in hovels and sleep in rags. They derive their meager nourishment from gravy and biscuits as a year-round diet. From out of these huts of tragedy comes a reeking army of destitution, while the false idea of humanitarianism and internationalism is wailed by many."[30]

In a letter to Rufus C. Holman, Reynolds expanded his comments. If the Ameri-can people were willing to accept twenty thousand refugee children, wrote Rey-nolds, "why don't these same big-hearted rich friends take care of the thousands upon thousands of orphans and American children who are now in our asy-lums?"[31] The same question, of course, could be asked of Reynolds. Other than voting for New Deal legislation, he had done very little to aid the poverty-stricken people of his own state.

Reynolds and other patriotic groups undermined the Wagner-Rogers bill by amending it to allow the twenty thousand children to enter only as quota immi-grants. When Senator Wagner refused to accept this amendment, the bill died in committee.[32] Senator Wagner's attempt to liberalize immigration laws on behalf of needy refugees failed, in part due to Reynolds's dissent and also because FDR declined to support the bill.

In April 1940, Reynolds proposed legislation that would restrict the number of Mexicans living in America to the number of Americans living in Mexico. All Mexican aliens in excess of the prescribed number were to be deported from the United States within one year. Early in his Senate term he had been very friendly toward Mexico but by 1940 had come to think of the country as a "colony for Soviet Russia." The senator also accused Mexicans of "usurping" jobs that should be held by Americans and insisted that all illegal immigration from Mexico had to be stopped.[33] His bill, a precursor of future attempts to limit Mexican immigration, did not gain sufficient support for passage.

Reynolds continued to pursue his goal of immigration restriction with two amendments to the Civil Liberties Bill, which was designed to forbid the use of oppressive tactics by employers against laborers. His first amendment limited individual employment of aliens to 10 percent of the total personnel of any company coming under the law. His second amendment forbade the employment of any known Nazi or Communist. Failure to comply with either amendment would result in five years in prison or a ten-thousand-dollar fine or both. The Senate approved these two amendments without a recorded vote.[34]

The New York Times, in another angry editorial, denounced Reynolds's 10 percent amendment as "a deadly blow at the civil liberties of several million law-abiding residents of the United States. It was drawn with a fine disregard for the Americanism which it pretends to defend." The amendment, railed the Times, carried with it the mark of bigotry and injustice and fueled the flames of irrational prejudice at the very time the country needed to be calm.[35] In spite of opposition, the Civil Liberties Act passed the Senate by a vote of 47–20. Reynolds, pleased with the amended version of the bill, voted in the affirmative.[36]

In his book Six Million Died, Arthur D. Morse condemned Reynolds for his venomous antialien statements and characterized him as a person of "virulent racial views."[37] Secretary of the Interior Harold L. Ickes, in his Secret Diary, also expressed concern about public figures hunting down aliens in America as spies or traitors, "while in Congress we have blatherskites like Senator Reynolds and Congressman Dies inspiring them to greater endeavors." Ickes wrote that men like Dies and Reynolds "who aren't capable of discriminating or logical thinking, would tar every alien with the same brush"—regardless of whether or not the individual was loyal.[38]

Certain that aliens were acting as foreign agents and spies, Reynolds wrote J. Edgar Hoover in January 1940, requesting data on the number of cases of espionage and sabotage investigated by the FBI and the results of these investigations.[39] In June 1941 Reynolds also asked Hoover for the names of the one hundred most dangerous aliens in America and requested complete details about their criminal backgrounds.[40]

Hoover refused to accede to Reynolds's requests, after the first of which he wrote the senator a vague, rambling response. He indicated that the number of specific cases of espionage and sabotage was not very large but the cases made up in danger what they lacked in number. Hoover reported that the FBI always received a large

number of complaints about alien sabotage, most of which were without foundation.[41] The response from the FBI did not satisfy Reynolds. He wanted hard evidence of alien sabotage to bolster his charges. When Reynolds heard that there
were twenty-six accidents in twenty-eight days at Langley Field, Virginia, he immediately announced that the accidents were due to sabotage.[42]

President Roosevelt pleased Reynolds when he issued an executive order trans-
ferring the Bureau of Immigration and Naturalization from the Labor Department to the Department of Justice. Roosevelt told the press that he approved this
reorganization in order to strengthen the machinery for combating subversive
alien influences and fifth-column activities, but he assured Congress that there
would be no infringement on the legal rights of aliens.

Reynolds hailed the transfer as absolutely necessary for the welfare and safety of
the country. He criticized the Labor Department for failing to enforce the immi-
gration laws and hoped that these laws would receive more attention from the
Justice Department. While acknowledging that Roosevelt's action was a first step,
Reynolds claimed that more needed to be done because "there are many herds of
Trojan horses grazing in the fertile fields of America." He also urged the passage of
a Senate committee report that favored the deportation of Harry Bridges, whom
Reynolds characterized as one of the "stallions in the herd of Trojan horses."[43]

Reynolds pressed his attack on radical groups by introducing a bill in the Senate
which would outlaw the German-American Bund, the Communist Party, and all
groups that sought to overthrow the government by force and violence. Penalties
were ten years in prison and a ten-thousand-dollar fine or both. In addition,
Reynolds's bill, which clearly violated first amendment rights, prohibited attendance at meetings sponsored by such groups, penalized those who owned buildings in which such meetings were held, and punished publishers for publishing
any material sponsored by these groups. (Publisher Reynolds and the Vindicators
would, of course, be in violation of the law.) Another bill offered by Reynolds
barred Communists from holding office in labor unions.[44] Reynolds hoped the
legislative proposals outlawing the German-American Bund would undermine
the charges that he was pro-Nazi. Surely a sympathizer would never advocate the
elimination of one of the Nazi Party's most important propaganda groups in
America. Reynolds's critics, however, dismissed his proposal as a grandstand act to
get the senator's enemies off his case.

In June 1940, Congress put aside Reynolds's bill but used some of his language in
passing the Alien Registration Act (also known as the Smith Act). This act strengthened existing laws governing the deportation and admission of aliens. No alien
seeking to enter the United States could get a visa without being registered and
without fingerprinting. Convicted smugglers, those who aided others to enter the
country illegally, and those who impaired the loyalty or morale of the armed forces

of the United States were added to the list of deportable aliens. The measure was designed not so much to control immigration as to check subversive activities. The bill followed Reynolds's reasoning and made it unlawful for any person to advocate or teach the overthrow or destruction of the government by force or violence or to become a member of any organization teaching such doctrine.[45] Overjoyed with the passage of the Smith Act, Reynolds now perceived himself as a major player on the national scene.

Bolstered by the recent success of his alien control bills, Reynolds announced that he planned to go to the 1940 Democratic National Convention in Chicago to urge the adoption of a plank in the party platform outlawing the Communist and Nazi Parties in America. He declined an invitation to go to the convention as a delegate but appeared personally before the Resolutions Committee to plead his case. In his testimony, Reynolds repeated his proposal for deporting alien criminals and ending immigration for ten years. Since totalitarian countries would not accept aliens deported from the United States, Reynolds suggested the creation of detention camps near federal prisons or on an island outside the country. The Resolutions Committee listened patiently to Reynolds's views but did not incorporate his ideas into the platform.[46]

Undeterred by his failure, Reynolds continued his diligent fight against sabotage and Communist infiltration into America. When Reynolds received a letter from Bart Logan, the secretary of the North Carolina State Committee of the Communist Party, he had proof of a Communist conspiracy in his home state. Reynolds immediately showed the letter to the press, explaining that, unlike Don Quixote, he had not been tilting at windmills when he warned the people against a rising tide of Communist influence. This letter, asserted Reynolds, proved the existence of a working Communist Party in North Carolina and demonstrated the unfairness of all previous criticisms of his attacks on aliens and Communists.

The *Raleigh News and Observer* did not take Reynolds's statement seriously. The paper admitted the existence of the Communist Party in the state but explained that the Communists were few, unimportant, and no cause for alarm. With all the massive problems in the world, "Senator Reynolds' fears about Communism in North Carolina because one wrote him a letter may hardly be expected to give his country-men the jitters—here is another case where he should be permitted to jitter all by himself."[47]

In an attempt to assess his political standing in the state, the senator gave a speech in January 1940 on the campus of the liberal University of North Carolina in Chapel Hill on his favorite subject, "Americanism." An unusually large crowd of fifteen hundred students listened to his address, titled "Threats to America become Realities." In a typical performance, Reynolds lashed out at aliens and Communists while praising J. Edgar Hoover and the Dies Committee. He defended his

Vindicators movement and insisted that the Vindicators had the same program as the American Legion. Reynolds attributed all the criticism directed at him as coming from vicious minorities, aliens, and radical camp followers. The students generally received his speech sympathetically and applauded his frequent references to keeping America for Americans. But there were boos mixed in with the applause, and on occasion, laughter greeted serious passages.[48] Reynolds judged his speech as effective, and if he could survive at Chapel Hill, his success elsewhere was assured.

The next day the *Daily Tar Heel* commented on a "typical speech" by Reynolds, full of ranting against aliens and tireless repetitions. The paper criticized the speech and Reynolds's performance as a senator but gave him high marks as a showman and a master politician. The *Daily Tar Heel* voiced the opinion that Reynolds, despite his obvious loss of popularity in the previous year, would be difficult to defeat in 1944.[49]

America's neutrality was put to the test when, on November 30, 1939, the Soviet Union invaded Finland. Roosevelt denounced the invasion as a "wanton disregard for law" but refused to antagonize isolationists by asking for an unrestricted loan to buy arms to assist Finland. Senator Reynolds pointed out the inconsistency of American policy, given that the United States sold munitions and arms to Russia and these arms were now being used by the invading Russians to crush Finland. On the other hand, Reynolds reminded his colleagues, the proposed Senate bill for aid to Finland stated that the Finns could not use the funds to buy arms and munitions to defend their country against Russia.

Reynolds voted against this legislation because it would keep America from strict neutrality. While expressing sympathy for Finland's people and their plight, Reynolds rejected assistance to any government actually engaged in war, because the United States would then buy a part of that war.[50] If the purpose of aid to Finland was to stop Communism, said Reynolds, then the place to start was America.[51]

When Finland capitulated to Russia on March 15, 1940, Reynolds declared that all America had received for its assistance to Finland was a "kick in the pants." The *Asheville Citizen* criticized Reynolds's view and insisted that America's aid to and sympathy for the Finnish cause was a noble effort in behalf of democracy.[52]

A more controversial issue was how to respond to Japan's campaign to subdue China and its desire to establish a "New Order" in the Orient. The United States government would have to consider retaliation with tariffs or an embargo if Japan continued to discriminate against U.S. commerce or to expand in Asia.

Reynolds questioned the wisdom of placing an embargo on Japan or of taking any punitive action specifically directed at any one country. If America had a policy on embargoes, it should be applied equally to all countries whether they were in Europe or in Asia. Reynolds thought it foolish to cut off trade with a good customer such as Japan, for it was the largest foreign buyer of southern cotton. Reynolds believed that if "we play ball with Japan, they will play ball with us." Reynolds also favored the continued sale of scrap iron to Japan, because it served to clear up the backyards and junk piles in the United States.[53]

Buncombe Bob had once again demonstrated his ignorance of public opinion by proposing that America "play ball" with a brutal fascist power. His naïve observation favoring the sale of scrap iron for the purpose of cleaning up American junkyards ignored the fact that Japan used the scrap metal to make weapons for use against China and other Asian countries.

President Roosevelt, however, refused to embargo goods to Japan. The president wanted to help the moderates in Japan in hope of avoiding a military conflict with that country. America, believed FDR, was not prepared to fight a two-front war.[54]

Not only did Reynolds desire economic embargoes applied uniformly around the world, but he also wanted to know why the United States did not use economic reprisals against Great Britain for its recent embargo on American cotton and tobacco. Reynolds also decried England's policy of inspecting, censuring, and seizing U.S. mail. These British activities, a clear snub to the American policy of "benevolent neutrality," reinforced Reynolds's view of Britain as high-handed and arrogant.[55] His wish to apply the embargo equally to all countries made no sense. Britain and France were not dictatorships bent on conquering neighboring countries.

Throughout 1940, Reynolds constantly expressed disapproval of the administration's foreign policy. He believed that he was immune from retaliation from Roosevelt because he did not have to run for reelection until 1944, and by then FDR would be out of office. Senator Reynolds assumed that Roosevelt would respect the two-term tradition and not run for reelection in 1940.

Another crisis occurred when a German foreign policy statement (white paper) alleged that the U.S. ambassador to France, William C. Bullitt, had promised American war aid to Poland. The German white paper also indicated that in the final analysis the United States would join Britain and France in the war against Germany. The Nazi government published these documents to strengthen the American isolationists' case against Roosevelt.

Reynolds and Congressman Hamilton Fish expressed outrage over these allegations and urged Ambassador Bullitt, in America for consultation, to delay his return to Paris until the charges were investigated. Reynolds insisted that Bullitt appear before a Senate inquiry panel and introduced a resolution to that effect in order to put a "red light" on the road to American participation in the war. Senator Reynolds argued that the executive branch did not have "unlimited powers to conduct the foreign relations of the United States as it sees fit" and that Congress should have a voice in setting policy.[56]

Reynolds's resolution had little support because Bullitt had twice denied the charges. Secretary of State Cordell Hull felt satisfied with Bullitt's categorical denials of the German white paper allegations and said that it was not in the public interest to delay Bullitt's departure to France, where he was needed to carry out his duties. Senator Key Pittman explained that the Foreign Relations Committee would ignore Reynolds's resolution as the majority of its members were convinced that an attempt to force Bullitt to make an explanation of his conduct would be an unwarranted invasion of the president's power to conduct foreign affairs.[57]

The *Asheville Citizen* continued its ongoing feud with Reynolds by criticizing his attack on Bullitt. All participants, pronounced the paper, had denied the charges, and most thoughtful Americans believed the white paper to be a crude attempt by the Germans to discredit Roosevelt. Reynolds knew very little about foreign policy, and the *Citizen* concluded that he was "as useful to his state when he is lost in the wilds of India as when he is with us in person."[58]

President Roosevelt continued to reassure the public that the United States was going to stay out of the war, but he reminded citizens that there was "a vast difference between keeping out of war and pretending that war is none of our business." Roosevelt hoped that there would be "fewer American ostriches" burying their heads in the sand now that the intentions of the European aggressor nations were so clear.

To protect national security and to unify the country in a time of world crisis, Roosevelt surprised fellow Democrats by nominating two Republicans, Henry L. Stimson and Frank Knox, as secretary of war and secretary of the navy, respectively. Not only had Roosevelt nominated two Republicans, but he had chosen two outspoken interventionists. Stimson, for example, favored universal military training and aid to Britain.[59]

Despite his misgivings over Stimson and Knox, Senator Reynolds did not oppose the nominations. He said that he did not know of any two men who were more thoroughly in favor of getting the United States into war, but he recognized the president's right to appoint anyone he desired to his cabinet and declared both men eminently qualified.[60]

Some of Reynolds's colleagues in the Senate, tired of his inaccurate prognostications and isolationist rantings, decided to have a little fun with the North Carolina senator. One senator quoted his speech of April 8, 1940, in which Reynolds stated that Norway, Sweden, and Denmark would escape the European war. At almost the precise time that Reynolds made this statement, continued his colleague, Germany launched an attack on Norway and Denmark. This, it was noted, was the second major prediction by Reynolds that had been far off the mark, for the senator had also predicted in early 1939 that there would be no war in Europe.

Reynolds hastily arose to defend himself. In an amazing distortion of the facts,

Reynolds argued that Norway had made every effort to remain neutral but charged that England had precipitated the German invasion by mining Norway's territorial waters, thus violating Norway's neutrality. Naturally, deduced Reynolds, Germany had to retaliate against Britain's violation by sending troops into Norway to protect German interests. For Reynolds "it was a race between the British and the Germans as to whom would be the first to establish troops on the Scandinavian front."

Reynolds's position happened to be exactly the same line taken by the German government to justify its invasion of Scandinavia. Senator Wiley noted that Reynolds apparently agreed with Hitler. Reynolds quickly responded: "Oh, I certainly do not agree with Hitler, I do not agree with Hitler at all," and then proceeded to condemn aggression by any power against a weaker nation. When Reynolds finished an inadequate and confused explanation of his position, Senator Alva B. Adams of Colorado said sarcastically, "I knew the Senator would vindicate himself."[61]

Reynolds had, again without reflection, taken the same position as the German government. His colleagues were correct in taking him to task for such ill-informed statements. The *Asheville Citizen* added insult to injury by commenting that Reynolds's extensive travels armed him with the courage to predict impulsively but failed to endow him with the understanding to predict accurately.[62]

As the ranking member of the Military Affairs Committee, Reynolds inevitably became heavily involved with the buildup of American defense forces. In July 1940 the committee began consideration of the controversial Burke-Wadsworth Bill, which required one year of compulsory military training for all males between the ages of twenty-one and thirty. The introduction of the first peacetime conscription bill in American history led to a long and loud debate.

Reynolds favored the bill because voluntary training simply would not suffice and because of his belief in the Fortress America concept. He especially liked the section of the bill that required the registration of all males, because it would supplement the Alien Registration Bill. Reynolds thought it would be "asinine" for Congress to vote $18 million for national defense unless America had sufficient staffing to utilize the equipment.[63]

The Burke-Wadsworth Act eventually passed the Senate by a vote of 58–31, but only after prolonged and determined opposition from the isolationists. The isolationist bloc in the Senate was in full cry, claiming that since America was not in peril, a peacetime draft could only be a step toward involving America in the European war. Burton K. Wheeler, Gerald P. Nye, Hiram Johnson, Robert La Follette, and other isolationists voted against the legislation. Reynolds abandoned his isolationist colleagues on this issue. He voted for the bill because he had always supported a strong defense as the best way to prevent America's involvement in a war.[64]

During the height of the debate over selective service, Reynolds received a wire from Frank P. Graham, the president of the University of North Carolina, which urged the senator to support the proposal for sending old American destroyers to Great Britain to help save freedom and democracy.[65] Reynolds replied, as he was to do on many occasions, that he adamantly opposed turning over any American naval vessels to Great Britain or to any warring powers.[66]

To increase his knowledge of America's defense capabilities, Reynolds embarked on a four-week tour of newly acquired naval bases in the Caribbean. Reynolds stated that he expected to investigate fifth columnists, Nazis, and communists while there. He planned to visit Bermuda, Nassau, Bimini, Trinidad, Cuba, Puerto Rico, and Panama. Before his departure, Reynolds told the press that he was taking the trip at his own expense to collect data that would be valuable to him as a member of the Foreign Relations Committee, the Military Affairs Committee, and the Committee on Territories and Insular Affairs.[67]

Despite all his justifications, Reynolds was off on another junket, and everyone knew it. D. Hiden Ramsey, writing to Senator Josiah Bailey, noted that "the unusual sense of duty which our junior senator possesses has compelled him to return to Latin America," at a time when the state of North Carolina was desperate for national largesse.[68]

The happy wanderer returned on October 26 and reported that South American countries were still pro-American and favored cooperation with the United States despite much activity and pressure from Germany. Reynolds had found strong fifth-column activities in every South American nation, with most of the propaganda disseminated by German legations via newspapers.[69]

His Latin American trip limited Reynolds's participation in the campaign of 1940 to seven days. But once Roosevelt announced he would seek reelection, Reynolds immediately embraced the president and declared him a cinch for a third term.[70] The presidential election of 1940, however, posed a dilemma for Reynolds. He had broken with Roosevelt over foreign policy, patronage, and other issues. As of early January 1940, it had appeared that Roosevelt might not run for a third term.[71] And although he had expected the president to stay on the sidelines, Reynolds had remained noncommittal until he knew Roosevelt's plans. When questioned about the presidential race in March, Reynolds refused to comment on a third term for Roosevelt except to say that he favored a third, fourth, fifth, or even a sixth term for himself. "As for other persons running for office [read Roosevelt]," exclaimed Reynolds, "well I'll let the conventions decide."[72]

Reynolds finally had no choice except to support Roosevelt, but he chose not to attend the National Democratic Convention as a delegate and did not openly take sides in the convention, which chose Roosevelt for a third term. Reynolds, although very unhappy with Roosevelt's foreign policy, accepted him as the party

Reynolds, pictured here on a trip around the world while serving as a newspaper correspondent and magazine writer in 1923, never gave up his desire to visit exotic locales and was the most traveled U.S. senator. (Pack Memorial Library, Asheville)

nominee. For Reynolds to oppose the head of his party during such a critical period would have been a political disaster for the North Carolina senator.

Although Reynolds had not actively supported Roosevelt for the Democratic nomination and despite previous criticisms of and disagreements with the president, Reynolds, a loyal Democrat, campaigned briefly for Roosevelt. For him, any Democrat was better than a Republican—especially the Republican nominee, Wendell L. Willkie, whose international concept of one world was anathema to Reynolds. Also, Reynolds did not want to compound his mistake of not promoting Roosevelt for the nomination by failing to campaign for him in the general election.

When President Roosevelt journeyed to North Carolina to take part in the dedication of the Great Smoky Mountains National Park, Reynolds accompanied him from Washington and rode in Roosevelt's car to the ceremony. Roosevelt could not resist teasing Reynolds before the home folk about his isolationist views. During his speech, Roosevelt turned to Reynolds and said, "Most Americans realize now that the danger can no longer be met with pitchforks and squirrel rifles." This remark brought a roar of laughter from the crowd and a sheepish grin from Reynolds, who, a few weeks earlier, had said that the great shooting ability of mountain squirrel hunters was an aid to national defense.[73]

Reynolds, smarting somewhat from his encounter with Roosevelt, gamely took to the stump and predicted Roosevelt's reelection.[74] He even went so far as to buy a pair of red, white, and blue suspenders emblazoned with Roosevelt's name and to give the suspenders several snaps for the benefit of photographers.[75] Although he made only four speeches for the party in his state, he believed that he had discharged his obligation to the Democrats.[76]

Reynolds made no formal statement after Roosevelt defeated Willkie by 449 electoral votes to 82. He had expected Roosevelt to win and was not disappointed. Senator Reynolds did not, however, plan to change his opposition to Roosevelt's foreign policy.

CHAPTER TEN

[Guns and Diamonds]

While Bob Reynolds never wavered in his commitment to isolation and his pursuit of enemy aliens, domestic issues began to dominate his time. In early January 1941, Senator Reynolds became chairman of the Senate District of Columbia Committee and thereby assumed the title of "mayor" of Washington, D.C. Reynolds was assured of the post when Senator Pat McCarran, who had first call on the position owing to seniority, declined the opportunity. Senators Millard Tydings, John Bankhead, and Carter Glass also declined the appointment. Reynolds, next in line, promptly agreed to take the position. Reynolds said that because McCarran and others had refused the job, "I'll take it. I think it is about time somebody did something for the District of Columbia. . . . It has never been properly promoted or expanded in the manner in which it should be. It should be made the model for every town in the country."

Senator Reynolds, known chiefly in the district for his unsuccessful attempts to legalize horse racing, immediately advanced a five-point program designed to improve the District of Columbia.

1. Give residents of the district the right to vote.
2. Relieve traffic and parking congestion by requiring garage facilities in apartment houses, office buildings, and theaters.
3. Reduce real estate taxes.
4. Increase federal contributions to the cost of city government to compensate for withdrawal of federal property from local tax rolls.
5. Devise a means of taxing the transients and temporary residents who enjoyed the benefit of local government without paying taxes.[1]

The *Raleigh News and Observer*, as usual, commented on Reynolds's new post. The paper acknowledged that the junior senator now had his most important assignment since arriving in Washington and speculated that his days as a Senate playboy were now over—his new position would require a great deal of hard work. The *News and Observer* believed that Reynolds had shown a new seriousness in announcing his five-point program for the district, but "two hallmarks of the

Reynolds political pattern are in evidence." Reynolds, according to the paper, believed in "giving his constituents, whoever they may be, what they want. And the Senator has not forgotten his sense of showmanship." At any rate, Washington was "likely to have a lively time with its new 'Mayor' for the next four years. At the end of that time, North Carolinians, rather than Washingtonians, will determine whether or not the term is to be extended."[2]

On January 21, the Senate approved Reynolds as the new chairman of the District of Columbia Committee.[3] But Reynolds, in the hospital with a severe case of influenza, suddenly had second thoughts about accepting the appointment. He stated that he had not fully made up his mind about the job as his membership on other committees entailed such work that it might keep him from giving the necessary attention to district affairs.[4]

Civic leaders in the District of Columbia urged Reynolds to accept the position because of his interest in improving the district; they favored Reynolds because Theodore G. Bilbo, a southern segregationist from Mississippi and adamantly opposed to suffrage for the district, was next in line for the post. Two days later, after milking a little publicity from his indecision, Reynolds announced that he would definitely assume the chairmanship and hoped to make the most important city in the world one of the most beautiful, orderly, and law-abiding cities. Reynolds said he would have nothing to do with patronage and would not recommend any person for a job, because to do so might interfere with his desire to be a fair and impartial chairman.

Reynolds decided to keep his other committee assignments. He felt that with a proper systematizing of his time and with assistance from Washington business organizations and interested citizens, he could handle the job.[5] Although this was a perfect job for the glad-handing Reynolds, his good intentions for the capital city never came to fruition partly because of his lack of administrative ability and partly because critical developments in foreign policy demanded his time and attention. Nonetheless, some of Reynolds's proposals for the district were significant, especially giving D.C. citizens the right to vote in national elections and increasing federal financial aid to the city.

Throughout the crucial year of 1941, Reynolds continued to insist that he was not an isolationist but a nationalist interested only in the welfare of the United States. He urged the government to set up some sort of control over foreign propaganda, as America was being swept forward "into the cesspools of Europe and toward the abyss of death by propaganda."[6] He claimed that America's irrational fear of invasion by Germany had been instilled in the minds of the American people by newspapers, radios, and other mass media. Reynolds demanded that this divisive and false propaganda be stopped since Germany was incapable of attacking the United States.[7]

Reynolds hoped for a quick and lasting peace in Europe but feared that the war would last for many years. He opposed building warships to be sent to England because they would be sunk, blood would be spilled, and the country would be swept into a war with Germany. Reynolds knew that no American wanted war, and "none of us ever want to witness again the scene of American mothers standing by the side of graves prepared for the remains of their sons—graves to keep the bodies of boys who died in Europe."[8]

A speech to Women United, the women's auxiliary of America First, was one of several contacts between Reynolds and the America First Committee. This committee, founded by General Robert E. Wood of Chicago in September 1940, was the most powerful noninterventionist pressure group in America and strongly opposed Roosevelt's foreign policies.

Reynolds did not join America First, however, partly because of its inept and failed attempt to persuade southerners to oppose war. The committee's effort and activities left bitter feelings in the South against it.[9] Because of southern dislike of the *organized* viewpoint of the America First Committee, Reynolds felt it would be better to refuse membership even though many of his isolationist colleagues in the Senate were members. In addition, he apparently thought that he could be more effective as an independent voice. He therefore supported the views of the committee without becoming a member. He could derive some benefit from the organization without the onus of belonging.

Reynolds agreed with the basic principles of the America First Committee, which maintained that only by keeping out of a European war could American democracy be preserved. The committee, like Reynolds, denied the inevitability of American participation in the war and stressed the need to solve American domestic problems first. In 1941 the America Firsters advocated a national referendum on the issue of peace and war, but efforts to secure the passage of a resolution in Congress were unsuccessful. The America First Committee then considered conducting a referendum on war and peace in North Carolina under Reynolds's sponsorship, but the senator refused the proposal. He was convinced that both a statewide and a nationwide referendum would result in an embarrassing vote in favor of war.[10]

Despite Reynolds's refusal to conduct a referendum, the America First Committee frequently solicited support from Reynolds and wrote him on November 1, 1941, to ask for assistance in getting radio time for its broadcasts. William S. Foulis, head of the Speaker's Bureau, indicated that it would not be necessary to make any reference to America First; he merely wanted Reynolds to present the noninterventionist cause. Mr. Foulis also invited Reynolds to address America First rallies in Pittsburgh, Providence, and Rochester.[11]

Reynolds responded that he had a full schedule during December and could not make any speeches then but would be glad to discuss possible engagements after January 1, 1942. Reynolds congratulated Foulis on "the fine work the America First Committee is doing." Foulis discussed a possible speaking date on January 15, but the Japanese attack on Pearl Harbor on December 7 led to the cancellation of all speeches and the ultimate dissolution of the America First Committee.[12]

On another occasion, Earl C. Jeffrey, a spokesman for the America First Committee, announced that Reynolds had invited the staunch isolationist Colonel Charles A. Lindbergh to speak in Raleigh, North Carolina. Reynolds was quoted as saying that Lindbergh was "a great man, a great aviator, and a great patriot who knew what he was talking about." Reynolds told the *Raleigh News and Observer* that he knew many people disagreed with Lindbergh's views but that he wanted the colonel to carry the message of truth to North Carolinians and felt certain that the citizens of his state were eager to hear both sides of the neutrality controversy.[13]

When apprised of the strong resistance in the Tar Heel State to a possible speech by Lindbergh, Reynolds backed down and denied that he had asked Lindbergh to come to North Carolina. Reynolds had, he announced, in his most hospitable manner, merely invited an aide to Lindbergh to speak in North Carolina.[14] The beleaguered Reynolds disavowed his invitation to Lindbergh because he wanted to avoid any additional criticism from his constituents.

The America First Committee, like Reynolds, had been frequently attacked for associating with fascist organizations and for serving as a channel for Nazi propaganda. Lindbergh, although an American hero, had been labeled pro-Nazi and denounced for his views. Because Germany wanted to prevent American entrance into World War II, it was inevitable that there would be a striking similarity between the views of the America Firsters and Nazi propaganda. Nazi propagandists unquestionably used the committee to disseminate their message, but America First was never indicted for seditious or treasonous activities. The majority of its officers were patriotic Americans who sincerely believed in appeasement and a negotiated peace in Europe. It was doubtful, according to historian Wayne S. Cole, that any isolationist group of this type could have avoided the association with Nazi propaganda, nor could they have avoided the attacks by interventionists who delighted in discrediting the committee.[15]

A. Scott Berg, in his exhaustive biography of Charles A. Lindbergh, concluded that the aviator had never associated with any pro-Nazi or anti-Semitic organizations and had not consorted or consulted with the German-American Bund or with anyone who had connections to the Third Reich. Berg revealed that Father Charles Coughlin was Lindbergh's most ardent supporter. With his anti-Semitic agenda, Coughlin appropriated Lindbergh's likeness to promote his own message and his national weekly, *Social Justice*. Berg believed that the more Lindbergh "attracted such bigots, the more people judged him by his followers."[16]

Because of his publicly expressed views on isolation, Lindbergh came under vicious attack. The assault on Lindbergh, according to the *Christian Century*, "has pulsed with venom. If this man who was once the nation's shining hero had been proved another Benedict Arnold he could not have been subjected to more defamation and calumny." The FBI reactivated Lindbergh's file, he was called the spokesman for the fascist fifth column in America, and Robert Sherwood, Pulitzer Prize–winning playwright and speechwriter, charged him with being a traitor and the "unwitting (purveyor) of Nazi propaganda."[17] That Lindbergh, an articulate, authentic American hero, could be subjected to such vilification indicated the emotional state of mind prevalent in America during the pre–Pearl Harbor period. Journalists, spokesmen for the Roosevelt administration, and common citizens feared both American entrance into the war and fascist expansion. All these groups searched for scapegoats and traitors in their midst. If Lindbergh could be so mistreated, imagine the abuse directed against Bob Reynolds.

Bob Reynolds approved of Lindbergh's views because the colonel frequently pointed out that three groups had been "pressing this country toward war"—the Roosevelt administration, the British, and the Jews. Reynolds could not have said it better. Also Lindbergh, while not overtly denigrating Jews, occasionally made disparaging remarks about them, especially the power of Jews in the media. His xenophobic thinking was illustrated by references to Jews as "not American," "other people."[18] In essence, Lindbergh, who talked about guarding America's common heritage and urged an impregnable system of defense, and Reynolds were soul mates. Reynolds wisely kept his distance from the controversial Lindbergh, who was constantly attacked by such journalists as Dorothy Thompson. Thompson denounced him for his failure to criticize the perversion of Nazi doctrine.[19]

Franklin Roosevelt, realizing that Great Britain was running short of funds to pay for American arms, began to fight back against America First and the noninterventionists. Aid and assistance to Britain was of the utmost urgency, realized the president, for if Britain failed to survive a Nazi onslaught, democracy would be in danger worldwide. Roosevelt wanted a policy of all-out aid to Britain short of war, but the problem was how to accomplish this goal within the framework of American neutrality laws. The president had to persuade a reluctant Congress that America's security depended on furnishing goods and supplies to England. Roosevelt and his advisers then hit on the brilliant idea of lending and leasing these goods to Britain and thus circumventing neutrality laws.

Roosevelt undertook the task of educating the people about the necessity of sending large quantities of military hardware to England. In a press conference and a fireside chat, Roosevelt explained to the American people that the purchase of arms by Britain would help the United States economy and would create additional production facilities. Roosevelt noted that Britain's best defense was also

America's best defense and that by leasing arms to Britain, America would gain more benefit than if the arms remained in storage.

Roosevelt used the phrase "lend-lease" to describe the program, explaining that America was not giving the British money—only lending them some useful tools for which they would pay a fair price. He spoke of the impossibility of compromise with the fascist powers and the failure of appeasement. Roosevelt asserted that he did not intend to send American troops to war, but America had to support those nations fighting the Axis powers and had to produce the weapons of war quickly. America, insisted the president, had to be "the great arsenal of democracy."

The proposal for lend-lease came at a time when Americans were shocked and saddened by Germany's saturation bombing of London and other British cities. The idea appealed to people who were anxious to aid Britain without having to go to war. Roosevelt had assured American citizens that there would be no American convoys or American ships sent into the war zones, and public support swung noticeably in favor of Roosevelt's policy. In early January 1941, public opinion polls indicated that Americans supported lend-lease by two to one and that a majority would even help England at the cost of entering the war.

Roosevelt continued to stress "national unity" and implied that dissent from his policies was disloyal; represented irresponsible, pro-Nazi partisanship; and would amount to treason. Roosevelt knew that favorable public opinion would not get the bill through the formidable isolationist bloc in Congress. Thus, using his unity theme, he set out to persuade Congress of the necessity of passing what eventually became the Lend-Lease Act of 1941.

The bill gave President Roosevelt the sole authority to permit the sale, lease, or lending of war materials and other supplies to any country whose defense the president deemed vital to the defense of the United States. Roosevelt would thus have unlimited power to supply Great Britain with guns, tanks, airplanes, and other armaments.[20]

Congress debated the Lend-Lease Bill (HR 1776) for two months and held numerous hearings on the subject. America Firsters, historian Charles A. Beard, Charles Lindbergh, and others protested the bill as suicidal for America because it would allow America to wage undeclared war. Lindbergh asserted his belief that America should not police the world and opposed an English victory because it would take many years of war and an invasion of Europe. This prolonged war would create poverty and destruction in both Europe and America. Reynolds, in a letter to his daughter Frances, described Lindbergh as the "best witness" he had heard. Unfortunately, complained the senator, the Foreign Relations Committee did not give Colonel Lindbergh enough time to speak, and Reynolds feared that the press would certainly "twist his testimony."[21]

Reynolds's questioning of witnesses before the Foreign Relations Committee indicated a continuing anti-British, unilateralist sentiment. As he had done with the Neutrality Act of 1939, Reynolds voted with the majority of his colleagues on the Foreign Relations Committee to report the bill to the Senate floor.[22] He had done so not because he was wavering in his opposition to the bill but because he was acutely aware of the strong and vociferous support for the bill by his North Carolina constituents.

As debate on Lend-Lease progressed, the isolationists did everything they could to water down the bill. They tried to drown it with numerous amendments restricting the power of the president. Reynolds offered an amendment to exclude Russia as a beneficiary of Lend-Lease aid as he believed that Russia would use American aid to destroy the United States and establish universal communism. Reynolds theorized that Russia was waiting for the time when America would go to war and be forced to devote all its resources and energies to defeat the fascist powers in Europe. Then Russia would increase communist agitation through spies and saboteurs in the United States with the goal of overthrowing a weakened government. Stalin, said Reynolds, believed that a destructive world war would lead to the collapse of capitalism, and America did not need to subsidize the communist conspiracy through Lend-Lease aid. Despite his impassioned plea, the Senate defeated Reynolds's amendment by a 56–35 vote.[23]

Meanwhile, Senator Josiah Bailey came out in support of Lend-Lease and announced that if the bill meant war then he was prepared to fight.[24] Despite mounting pressure from the administration, Democratic senators, and especially from his constituents, Reynolds chose to oppose the bill.

Reynolds was the initial speaker for the forces to stop Lend-Lease and gave a lengthy, anti-British speech in the Senate. Reynolds began by stating that the Lend-Lease Bill had implications more far reaching than any bill the Senate had considered since World War I. After conscientious consideration, Reynolds opposed Lend-Lease because the bill unnecessarily extended America to the point where it would be caught in a European war machine. American participation in World War I had proved futile and unjustified by the results—it was not the war to end all wars, and it did not save democracy.

The pending bill, continued Reynolds, should be titled "A Bill for the Defense of the British Empire at the Expense of the Lives of American Men and the American Taxpayer." He declared that the menace to America from Hitler was no greater than it was from Napoleon in 1808. The numerous millionaires of the British Empire should be called on to strip themselves of their castles, hunting lodges, dogs, falcons, and cash "before the one-gallused, overall clad farmer is called upon to pay increased taxes." Financial aid to Britain would lead to American bankruptcy, unemployment, chaos, and the destruction of democracy. Reynolds explained that he did not oppose aid to Britain according to existing neutrality legislation, but he opposed any circumventing or modification of these statutes.[25]

In a speech characterized by the same tired rhetoric and prejudices of the past, Reynolds remained consistent in his viewpoint. At this juncture, he surely realized that his unwavering unilateralist position was becoming increasingly unpopular in North Carolina, but he stubbornly held his ground.

The reaction to Reynolds's speech was immediate, predictable, and overwhelmingly negative. A few like-minded individuals praised Reynolds; Gerald L. K. Smith, for instance, called Reynolds's vote a courageous stand against a conspiracy to get America into war. Smith predicted that Reynolds would be subjected to persecution but that history would ultimately prove him correct.[26] E. Dana Malpass wrote Reynolds that he was delighted to learn of his vote against the "damnable Lend-Lease Bill" which demanded that Malpass offer up his only son for sacrifice on foreign fields.[27] Reynolds's longtime nemesis Jonathan Daniels defended Reynolds from the pro-Nazi charges. He told Americans that they should not mistake Reynolds's flag-waving and attacks on helpless minorities as fascism.[28] Almost everyone else denounced Reynolds's vote. Grady Withrow, speaking on the floor of the North Carolina House of Representatives, which had endorsed Lend-Lease, called Reynolds a disgrace to the state and labeled him pro-Nazi. "If he [Reynolds] were there [Germany] now, Hitler would put a purple robe on him, a ring on his finger, and everything else."[29] Other letters indicated the avid support for Lend-Lease in North Carolina. C. C. Duke wrote Reynolds that he was "utterly astonished and disappointed" that the senator opposed a bill favored by 90 percent of the state.[30] E. G. Flanagan wrote Senator Bailey that the large majority of people wanted Lend-Lease and chastised Reynolds for jumping to conclusions without studying the facts. "He must have been greatly influenced when in Germany by his ride in Goebbels' machine."[31]

The abusive letters continued. A missive to the editor of the *Raleigh News and Observer* accused Reynolds of undermining the security of the country when America was under a greater threat than ever before: "But whatever harm Senator Reynolds has done is counteracted by the fact that he has exposed himself to the ridicule of the nation more completely than at any other time. He himself has done the most to convince the country that he should not be taken seriously."[32] Even Reynolds's longtime ally in his fight against internal subversion, the Veterans of Foreign Wars, expressed resentment.[33]

Durham businessman George Watts Hill urged Reynolds to submit to the will of the majority of North Carolinians or resign his office. Hill predicted that the senator was headed for political oblivion. Hill admired Reynolds's blind courage but could not say the same about his political acumen or his attitude toward representative government.[34]

Reynolds admitted that most people in his home state favored passage of Lend-Lease and recognized that any legislator who voted against the bill might be committing political suicide. Reynolds told reporters that he preferred political suicide to the sight of America plunging into another nation's war. He explained that his stand was based on a robust love for America and that a vote against Lend-Lease was best for America. Reynolds announced that he already had a farm in North Carolina to which he would retire if vengeful voters failed to reelect him in 1944. Reynolds smilingly said he would be perfectly happy raising a few pigs and chickens and eating all the turnip greens and cornbread he wanted.[35]

One month after his speech against Lend-Lease, however, Our Bob began to backtrack. He attempted to justify his position by saying that sentiment in North Carolina and the nation was rapidly turning against Lend-Lease. While his early mail was 90 percent for Lend-Lease, a reaction had set in, and now his mail was running 50–50.[36] He also wrote a form letter to supporters around the country reiterating his belief that Lend-Lease was the final step leading to a war he could never support.[37] He admitted to William Cocke that he might have been wrong in his vote on Lend-Lease, but he was willing to let history judge whether his decision was right or wrong.[38]

The opposition to Lend-Lease eventually collapsed when administration supporters voted down all crippling and restrictive amendments.[39] The last great fight of the isolationists ended in defeat when the Senate passed the Lend-Lease legislation by a vote of 60–31. Although he said he was tired of being denounced in the North Carolina newspapers and the state legislature, Reynolds cast his vote against Lend-Lease, the only southern senator to do so.[40]

The initial appropriation requested for Lend-Lease was $7 billion, and Reynolds, in a shocking turnaround, said he would support the appropriation because the bill had already been enacted and the people had indicated their approval of the policy. Once the policy of the United States had been clearly defined, stated Reynolds, it should not be hampered by lack of necessary funds. Reynolds hoped that the supporters of the bill were correct in their belief that Lend-Lease was the only way to avoid war, but if the United States did go to war then it would be directly attributable to Lend-Lease. The Senate passed the appropriation by a 67–9 vote.[41]

On September 4, 1941, the American destroyer *Greer*, heading for Iceland, tangled with a German U-boat. The *Greer* tracked the sub for several hours and fired depth charges, and the U-boat also fired a torpedo. President Roosevelt announced that a German submarine had fired on the *Greer* without warning, which he characterized as an act of international lawlessness. Roosevelt did not want war with Hitler but advocated a policy of "active defense" and warned German and Italian warships that if they entered the waters considered necessary for American defense, they would do so at their own risk.

In September and October, American destroyers, in support of Roosevelt's "active defense" directive, increased their escort and protection of Allied convoys but could not cover all ships crossing the Atlantic. Unescorted vessels had no better than an even chance of surviving the trip. To remedy this situation, on October 9, 1941, Roosevelt asked Congress to modify the Neutrality Act of 1939 to permit the arming of merchant ships engaged in overseas commerce and to allow them passage through combat zones.

On October 17 a German submarine attacked the American destroyer *Kearny*, with the loss of eleven lives, and on November 1 a German U-boat sunk the *Reuben James* with the loss of one hundred lives. These incidents heightened tension and persuaded 75 percent of the American public to favor the arming of merchant ships. Although America was, in effect, at war with Germany, the isolationists fought vigorously against Roosevelt's request to arm merchant vessels.[42]

As early as September 1939, Reynolds had registered his opposition to any revision of the Neutrality Act of 1939 that would allow merchant ships to be armed and sent into the war zones,[43] and his colleagues expected Reynolds to continue this resistance. However, when the Senate began its debate on the revision of the Neutrality Act, Reynolds was conspicuously absent. Reynolds missed the crucial debate because on October 9, 1941, he had married for the fifth time and was in the middle of a seven-week honeymoon with the wealthy heiress Evalyn Washington McLean.[44]

Reynolds, enthralled with his twenty-year-old bride, did not even bother to follow the debate over neutrality revision. He certainly could have arranged a one- or even two-week honeymoon or could have postponed his trip to a less auspicious time. His absence for such a long period from an important debate indicated a clear unwillingness on the part of Reynolds to accept his responsibilities as a senator. He had been absent from Washington on numerous occasions before, but never during such a momentous debate on an issue so dear to his heart. His action also indicated a lack of commitment for his professed unilateralism, as his presence in the Foreign Relations Committee might have prevented the bill from getting out of committee, given that one vote had been crucial in past discussions on neutrality. On November 7, 1941, by a vote of 50–37, the Senate repealed the restrictive measures of the 1939 Neutrality Act. The new measure authorized the arming of American merchant vessels and permitted them to carry cargoes to belligerent ports. Reynolds, of course, did not vote but paired with Senator Robert Wagner and if present would have voted nay.[45]

While Reynolds had spent much of the year wrestling with neutrality legislation, he had earlier become the center of a significant struggle over seniority in the United States Senate. The drama began on April 9, 1941, when Senator Morris Sheppard of Texas died of a cerebral hemorrhage in Walter Reed Hospital. With the passing of Sheppard, Bob Reynolds, by virtue of seniority, was slated to succeed Sheppard as chairman of the powerful Military Affairs Committee. Despite Reynolds's isolationism and his opposition to administration foreign policy, it seemed certain that the Senate's traditional seniority rule would prevail and would limit serious opposition to his selection.

Reynolds initially refused to discuss the chairmanship out of respect for Senator Sheppard but later stated that he intended to accept the position. He also explained that he had long been an advocate of preparedness and national defense and would make a good chairman.[46]

The impending elevation of a confirmed isolationist and alleged pro-Nazi as chairman of the Senate committee most concerned with military affairs at a critical point in history set off violent reactions across the country. Some critics believed that Bob Reynolds, a fervid opponent of administration foreign policy, would be in a position to sabotage administration defense measures. All defense bills went through the committee, and the chairman had the responsibility for steering them through to a final vote. For many observers, Reynold's appointment would be a disaster.

The Roosevelt administration realized that Democrats and Republicans who held leadership positions based on seniority would support Reynolds in a Senate vote. Unwilling to override the ingrained tradition of seniority, the White House tried to persuade Senator Reynolds to stay on as chairman of the District of Columbia Committee and waive his right to be chairman of the Military Affairs Committee.[47] This attempt failed.

The *Greensboro Daily News* speculated that while there would not be strong initial objections to Reynolds from administration supporters in the Senate, the president's friends might try to circumvent Reynolds's influence when he did become chairman. The Greensboro paper concluded that a White House decision to block Reynolds's elevation to the chairmanship seemed unlikely as the tradition of seniority would prevail despite Reynolds's conflicts with Roosevelt.[48]

The Military Affairs Committee deferred the selection of a new chairman until after Senator Sheppard's funeral. This brief delay in choosing a new chairman allowed those opposing Reynolds to state their case and enabled the North Carolina press to train their journalistic guns on Reynolds. The *Raleigh News and Observer* cleverly attacked the inequity of the seniority system when it really questioned Reynolds's qualifications for the post. The paper wrote that "his selection on the basis of seniority alone seems a willingness to relegate leadership in important aspects of military affairs to luck at a time when the military affairs of this nation may be the first basis of its security." The *News and Observer* argued that Reynolds should receive the position only if he were judged the best qualified man. If offered on any other basis (seniority), advised the paper, the most patriotic thing Reynolds could do would be to decline the office. "If the Senate is disregarding the rule of safety for the country in order to safeguard its rule of seniority, Senator Reynolds does not have to be a party to such foolishness."[49]

The *Charlotte News*, at a later date, wrote that if Hitler had studied the entire membership of the Senate, "he could not have chosen a Military Affairs Committee Chairman better suited to advance the Nazi cause than Robert Rice Reynolds."[50] The *Charlotte Observer* agreed with the *New York Times* that the elevation of Reynolds was seniority at its worst. Reynolds, judged the paper, had no special qualifications for the post except that he had been in the Senate longer than the next Democrat serving on that committee. "It would be to laugh over such mockery were it not a matter of deep solemnity."[51]

National newspapers joined the onslaught. The *Cincinnati Enquirer* condemned Reynolds as "a genuine native Fascist" and hoped that the administration would have the courage to buck the seniority tradition and prevent Reynolds from taking over the committee.[52] The *Kansas City Journal* called Reynolds's elevation to chairman "a travesty of the first order" and contended that "Hitler would applaud his election."[53] The *Baltimore Evening Sun* noted that "it was hard to believe that enough senators could die to make Reynolds chairman" and urged the Senate to put aside precedent and elect someone whose views more nearly coincided with those of the country at large.[54] Even *Time* referred to Reynolds as "the Senate's Number One Clown,"[55] while the syndicated columnist Dorothy Thompson asserted that giving the chairmanship to a "small town Nazi" such as Reynolds was "worth ten divisions to Hitler."[56]

A huge influx of letters from Reynolds's constituents urging his withdrawal reinforced the press's rejection of his candidacy. A group of Chapel Hill citizens was terrified by the prospect that Reynolds, whose highest military rank had been that of captain of the National Guard in World War I, would now be in a position of great power.[57] In neighboring South Carolina, the state bar association adopted a resolution suggesting that the Senate not be bound by the custom of seniority in selecting a chairman of the committee. The resolution stated that in a time of national crisis it was essential to have a competent chairman of such a vital committee—not one who was committed to obstructing its work.[58]

Several citizens urged President Roosevelt to use his influence to prevent Reynolds's appointment. Tom Glasgow of North Carolina concluded that Reynolds had not demonstrated either the capacity or the patriotism to "warrant his being placed in so vitally important a position."[59] Isidor Shaffer asked Roosevelt to defeat

Reynolds or there "would be a national calamity."[60] Marvin H. McIntyre, personal secretary to the president, explained Roosevelt's official position on the controversy in a letter to Louis Lober, telling him that the executive branch of government had nothing to do with the selection of the heads of congressional committees and that the matter was solely for determination by members of the Senate.[61]

At this juncture, Roosevelt had decided that a hands-off policy was the wisest course of action. He did not wish to risk a conflict with Congress, a fight he could not win, over delicate matters such as seniority at a time when neutrality was an explosive issue and national unity was essential.

Senator Josiah Bailey received hundreds of letters assaulting Reynolds's ability and patriotism. The petitioners pleaded with Bailey to use his influence to prevent Reynolds from heading the Military Affairs Committee. One writer predicted that the appointment would create for the Democratic Party and the nation "a veritable Pandora's box of dissension, delay and trouble at a time when speed and unity are essential."[62] A doctor from Morehead City declared that Reynolds was "one hundred per cent discredited in this section of the country. He has no chance for re-election. If he were to come here to make a speech he would probably be mobbed. As a representative of several hundred thousand outraged and indignant Democratic voters of North Carolina, I ask you to reject this un-American excrescence."[63] W. J. Cash, author of *The Mind of the South* and associate editor of the *Charlotte News*, urged Bailey to thwart Reynolds as North Carolina bitterly opposed him.[64]

Senator Bailey replied to all complaints with a carefully reasoned explanation as to why he would not take any hand in the matter. Bailey explained that Reynolds was a duly elected senator from North Carolina and that seniority was an established tradition designed to avoid conflicts between senators. Bailey was not disposed to disturb this practice, particularly if it would antagonize a senator from his own state. "This would be unseemly and unwise." Bailey proposed leaving the matter in the hands of the Democratic Steering Committee in the Senate. He revealed to one constituent that Reynolds had given assurances to the Democratic Party that, as chairman of the Military Affairs Committee, he would go along with the president's wishes on defense issues. Bailey thought that in the absence of any charges that would disqualify him, Reynolds would be recommended by the Steering Committee.[65]

The case against Reynolds, however, escalated when the prestigious *New York Times* weighed in with a harsh indictment of the seniority system. In an editorial titled "Seniority at Its Worst," the *Times* denounced the obsolete and foolish policy of seniority. The United States, asserted the *Times*, was now in the position of having as head of an important committee a man who was completely out of sympathy with the majority of his party, the administration, the congressional majority, and the expressed public opinion of the country in the matter of public defense. "Length of service," declared the paper, "is his solitary qualification. Without entering into the question of his sincerity, one may say that throughout his eight years of service in the Senate he has not said anything that in a sensible legislative system would entitle him to this position."

Reynolds, continued the *Times*, had stirred up a foolish and unjust prejudice against aliens with his refusal to admit victims of dictators into this country. Although he denounced Nazis and communists by name, Reynolds followed their "line" in his opposition to the repeal of the arms embargo and the passage of the Lend-Lease Act. "To put the Military Affairs Committee under his thumb," concluded the *Times*, "is to violate grossly the principle of democracy which says that the expressed will of the people is binding on their representatives."[66] The New York newspaper restated its case against Reynolds on May 6. "The Senate is notably jealous of its prerogatives. If it is equally jealous of its public standing it will not make this egregious mistake."[67]

Estes Kefauver, a United States senator from Tennessee, maintained that the controversy over Reynolds's appointment in 1941 created a potentially dangerous situation. Kefauver recognized that since Reynolds had views opposed to a policy on which the country and Congress agreed, there was the chance that as a hostile chairman Reynolds could have impeded a constructive and vital military program on which the very survival of the nation might depend. However, Kefauver judged that the Senate membership was generally helpless to do anything about the inbred tradition of seniority.[68] Historian James McGregor Burns agreed with Kefauver's assessment. Despite the widespread protest against Reynolds from both inside and outside Congress, Burns concluded that the tradition of seniority could not have been overcome.[69]

Despite the Senate's customary adherence to seniority, several senators contemplated vigorous opposition to Reynolds's appointment. Senator Carter Glass of Virginia admitted disliking Reynolds. He acknowledged that he had replied to a correspondent from North Carolina who had protested Reynolds's promotion, informing her that he thought the matter would be settled to her satisfaction.[70] Senate Majority Leader Alben Barkley, however, was the one who would determine if a fight would be made against Reynolds. As late as April 21 the matter was still under discussion, and Barkley remained noncommittal.[71]

Reynolds, serving as acting chairman of the committee, launched a counterattack. He stated firmly that he desired the post and that he would "fight it out to the limit." Reynolds reminded everyone that he was entitled to the post on the basis of service and seniority, "a rule which has prevailed in the Senate down through the ages and which I insist shall be followed." The senator pronounced himself as favoring national defense and felt that he was "eminently equipped" to carry out the administration's program.[72] A few days later Reynolds wrote an open letter to many of his Senate colleagues and asked their support in any fight waged against him. He reiterated that he had voted in favor of every defense measure to come before the Military Affairs Committee and by virtue of his wide travels was personally acquainted with many defense problems.[73]

Protests against Reynolds flooded into the Democratic Steering Committee, the body responsible for selecting a new chairman. Senator Barkley and others had received many disapproving letters from North Carolina, including a telegram from Charlotte signed by one thousand citizens declaring their senator to be the wrong man for the post. Despite these protests, it appeared that Barkley did not intend to launch a fight against Reynolds's confirmation. By then Senator Josh Lee of Oklahoma, secretary of the Democratic Steering Committee, had come out in favor of the seniority rule, and the formidable isolationist bloc in the Senate said that it would stand by Reynolds. Senator Lee's stand and the fact that Senator James F. Byrnes, a confidant of President Roosevelt, had not entered the fight against Reynolds signaled that the Roosevelt administration would not oppose Reynolds.[74]

Both Frances Reynolds Oertling and Hubert H. Rand, however, believed that Barkley, following Roosevelt's orders, delayed Reynolds's confirmation in the hopes that negative public opinion would force the North Carolina senator to give up the post. Although Barkley had been a mentor of his when Reynolds first came into the Senate, the two had developed a strong dislike for each other. When Reynolds, unwilling to give up the post, insisted on a face-to-face meeting, the two men argued. Barkley told Reynolds that he was already chairman of the District of Columbia Committee and should be satisfied with that. Barkley thought it would not be appropriate for an isolationist to be head of the Military Affairs Committee and offered Reynolds another committee. An angry Reynolds told Barkley that if he were not appointed very soon, he would take his case to the floor of the Senate, and "there will be more blood on the moon than you fellows ever dreamed of."[75]

Some Democrats still wanted the Steering Committee to pass over Reynolds and to select New Dealer Elbert Thomas of Oklahoma, next in line for the vacancy, but a check of the Senate showed that twenty-eight Republican senators would vote to uphold Reynolds's selection if the decision were appealed to the full Senate. In addition, the canvass indicated that Reynolds retained the vote of those who were firmly wedded to the seniority system.[76]

The Democratic Steering Committee, however, demonstrated its opposition to Reynolds's views by subjecting the senator to an additional "cooling off" period before it would confirm him in the post. The Raleigh News and Observer declared that important committee chairmanships were usually promptly filled, and the delay in appointing Reynolds indicated doubts about the senator's qualifications.[77]

Senator Barkley, having accepted the inevitable, told Reynolds that he would speak for him in the Steering Committee if necessary. He assured Reynolds that he would be approved without any major controversy. Senator Byrnes also worked to make the vote unanimous. With these two stalwart administration leaders working for Reynolds, the vote was a foregone conclusion.[78]

Predictably, on May 15, 1941, the Steering Committee approved Bob Reynolds as chairman of the Military Affairs Committee by a vote of 12–3. Reynolds stated that he intended to discharge his duties to the best of his ability and promised to promote America's defense interests in the Western Hemisphere. But, cautioned the new chairman, no one should expect him to modify his views about American participation in war—he would continue to oppose involvement by word and deed.[79] The following day the full Senate formally accepted the recommendation of the Steering Committee, and Reynolds immediately vacated his position as chairman of the District of Columbia Committee to assume his new post.[80]

The three senators on the Democratic Steering Committee who voted against Reynolds were Theodore Green (Rhode Island), Carter Glass (Virginia) and Joseph Guffey (Pennsylvania). Glass and Green said they had nothing personal against Reynolds but thought that Elbert Thomas would have made a better chairman because of the defense emergency. Senator Guffey explained his action rather bluntly: "I voted against him; isn't that expression enough?"[81] Carter Glass had not attended the Steering Committee meeting but left explicit instructions that his vote be cast against Reynolds's confirmation. According to Drew Pearson, Glass returned to the Senate shortly after the vote and learned of Reynolds's nomination. A furious Glass glanced contemptuously at Reynolds seated nearby. When Senator A. B. Chandler asked what was the matter, Glass replied that he had learned "that Barkley and Jimmy Byrnes had just voted for that blankety-blank Reynolds. Fine leaders they are, selling out to the isolationists."[82]

By not challenging the immutable tradition of seniority, Roosevelt had wisely avoided a situation that could have caused grave difficulty for the country. Roosevelt and Barkley knew that they could not prevent Reynolds's elevation and finally accepted him because they believed that he was patriotic and would not actively obstruct the nation's defense program.

The president also knew that the maverick Reynolds, hardly a powerful or influential senator, could be controlled and manipulated by stalwart administration supporters on the Military Affairs Committee. The administration, by delaying Reynolds's confirmation and through warnings by senate leaders, had let Reynolds know that they expected him to cooperate fully with administration policy on national defense. In addition, Reynolds began slowly to recognize the significance of the grave world situation and his newly acquired responsibility to the country. The almost universal denunciation that he had suffered at the hands of the press and constituents had affected him significantly. He now realized how unpopular and disliked he was, and he began to modify his views.

Thus, for the most part, Bob Reynolds carried out the wishes of the Roosevelt administration. Because of his isolationist views, however, the White House consulted Reynolds as little as possible, told him only what it was imperative for him to know, and discouraged him from making policy.[83] Reynolds ran Military Affairs in name only. Loyal Roosevelt supporters led by Elbert Thomas controlled the committee, and Reynolds had very little influence either in the committee or in the Senate.[84] Since Reynolds did not use his position to obstruct vital defense legislation, he was seldom of any concern to the White House.

The first problem the new chairman faced was the extension of the Selective Service Act of 1940. The act registered all men between the ages of twenty-one and thirty-five and set up a one-year training period for 1,200,000 troops and 800,000 reserves.[85] At the request of General George C. Marshall, army chief of staff, Reynolds introduced bills to retain selective service trainees in the army beyond one year and to lift the ban against sending them outside the Western Hemisphere.[86] Although Reynolds dutifully introduced the bills, he did not favor the legislation and claimed that he was "embarrassed" by having to sponsor the bills. Reynolds objected to the legislation because he voted for the original Selective Service Act with the understanding that the men would not be sent out of the Western Hemisphere and would serve only one year. Reynolds firmly believed that the sending of draftees abroad would be tantamount to a declaration of war, and although he hated to vote against bills he had sponsored, he announced that he would have to do so on this occasion.[87]

A few days later President Roosevelt and General Marshall invited Chairman Reynolds to a White House conference to discuss the selective service extension. In spite of convincing and persuasive arguments by the president, Reynolds did not change his mind. Nonetheless, he promptly opened hearings on the bills the following day and even had the committee working overtime.[88]

On July 26 the Military Affairs Committee voted 9–1 (with Reynolds casting the only negative vote) to keep the present army in service indefinitely, but the committee refused to change the provision that prevented the use of draftees outside of the Western Hemisphere. The Selective Service Act of 1940 stated that the enlistment period of draftees could be extended if the national interest was imperiled, but the committee rejected the idea of declaring a national emergency. A cartoon in the *Washington Star* showed the Military Affairs Committee marching in formation with Chairman Reynolds stepping off with his left foot while the remainder of the squad lead off with their right foot. The caption read, "Everybody out of step but Our Boy Bob."[89]

The committee reported the Selective Service Act out to the full Senate, where it

"Everybody Out of Step but Our Boy Bob." This cartoon, originally published in
the *Washington Star*, shows the isolationist Reynolds casting the only vote against
the proposal to keep the U.S. Army in service indefinitely. (Reprinted in the
Asheville Citizen-Times, August 3, 1941)

gained immediate support, in part as a result of the Japanese invasion of Indo-
china. General George C. Marshall lobbied hard for the bill because when the
draftees' terms expired in October, he would lose 75–90 percent of his officers and
half of the enlisted men. Marshall complained that failure to extend selective
service would decimate the military and he could then not guarantee that the army
could protect America properly.[90]

Reynolds, trying to undermine the growing support for the bill, explained that
he had voted against it in committee partly because it appeared to give the president the power to prepare the army for offense rather than defense. Reynolds did
not consider the world situation an emergency and did not think that national
interests were imperiled.[91]

The Senate ignored Reynolds and passed a compromise bill to extend the enlistment of draftees on active service for eighteen months. The vote in the Senate was

45–30, with twenty-one members refusing to vote on the controversial measure. The bill passed the House by a vote of 203–202. By a single vote, the United States Army had not been disbanded and American mobilization remained on course. The close vote in the House did not signal a reversion to isolationism, merely the limits of interventionism.[92]

The *Raleigh News and Observer* once again flayed Reynolds for being the only member of the Military Affairs Committee to oppose selective service extension. The paper reluctantly gave Reynolds credit for not using his position to obstruct the defense program and for introducing the very bill to which he objected. The *News and Observer* did not expect a person to vote against his convictions, "but when this Senator finds himself at odds with an overwhelming majority of his constituents, all of his colleagues on the committee, and all of the military experts in the country, it would seem the time has come for him to re-examine his own thinking. The chairman of the Military Affairs Committee should be a leader in national defense. The present chairman will never lead as a dissenter."[93]

Although Reynolds did not obstruct American defense measures, he continued to oppose any aid to Russia.[94] Even after Germany attacked Russia in June 1941, Reynolds asked that the United States not be deceived by its propaganda or pleas for help, since Russia desired only to destroy our system of government. Reynolds was completely against providing Communist Russia with one penny of money from the American taxpayers.[95]

In the summer of 1941, Chairman Reynolds, under pressure from his colleagues, agreed to a request by Senator Harry S Truman to set up a special committee for investigating the National Defense Program so as to prevent waste and inefficient planning.[96] Harry H. Vaughan, then secretary to Senator Truman and later liaison officer for the Truman Committee, recalled how the committee was established. According to Vaughan, Truman had received hundreds of letters complaining about the great waste of manpower and materials in military construction. Truman investigated and found the charges to be true. He then went to Reynolds and asked him to look into these problems. Reynolds refused, stating, "Oh, I haven't got time for that now." So Truman, according to Vaughan, said to hell with Reynolds and proposed the new committee on the floor of the Senate. His colleagues accepted the idea, and Reynolds then agreed to appoint Truman as head of the subcommittee,[97] which became known as the Truman Committee. Frances Reynolds Oertling recalled that Truman had pestered Reynolds so much about a subcommittee that he gave Truman the least important subcommittee just to get Truman off his back.[98]

The Truman Committee, contrary to Reynolds's expectations, was very successful in its investigations. Its revelations, which led to savings and increased efficiency, gave Harry Truman a national reputation. Truman's loyalty, effectiveness, and integrity while working on the committee were factors in Roosevelt's choice of him for vice president in 1944.[99]

Otis Ferguson, writing in the *New Republic*, made an interesting assessment of Reynolds as chairman of the committee. "Some thought it laughable when the rigid seniority rule elevated clownish Senator Bob Reynolds to the chairmanship of the Military Affairs Committee. Others, lacking appreciation for nonsense, thought it tragic." Up to the present, wrote Ferguson, "Chairman Reynolds has not got or at least has not seemed to get, in the way of the national defense effort in spite of his isolationist convictions. Indeed he is so enthusiastic about riding around in combat cars for the benefit of news photographers that the Army is finding him a helpful publicity agent." The *News and Observer* added a postscript to Ferguson's story: while Reynolds was no expert at legislation, he was as good as any other senator in a jeep.[100]

Because of his duties on the Military Affairs Committee, Reynolds had less time to devote to the alien menace. He did manage to warn America of an impending threat in April when he divulged that thousands of communists were waiting in France to come to the United States in the guise of tourists and refugees. "What I'm afraid of," explained Reynolds, "is there are so many of these aliens arriving that they will take the country away from us, just like we did from the Indians."[101]

A series of labor strikes at Allis Chalmers and U.S. Steel frightened Reynolds and convinced him that communists had infiltrated labor unions and planned to undermine the American economy. He once again introduced a resolution in the Senate to make it illegal for labor organizations to employ aliens or persons with membership in communist, fascist, or Nazi bodies.[102] Nothing came of this proposal, and the resolution never cleared committee.

Reynolds received several angry letters from individuals upset with his resolution and his views on communism. James Pitteau wrote Reynolds that his bill to outlaw communists and fascists was "more vicious than anything a fascist dictator has even imposed upon his subjects. I have clear proof now that you are a fascist in mind as well as in action." An unsigned letter to Reynolds ended as follows: "you no good rotten anti-Catholic, anti-Semitic son of a bitch . . . you will get your yellow belly stinking guts blasted out of you before very long." Reynolds, worried about his personal safety, sent the letters to J. Edgar Hoover and asked him to investigate. After a thorough study, Hoover did not come up with any relevant information.[103]

By 1941 Reynolds's unpopular votes and speeches led to a nascent "Dump Reynolds in 1944" movement. The *Williamston (N.C.) Enterprise* urged North Carolinians to aid national defense by writing Bob Reynolds to ask him either to resign his seat or change his ways. The *Enterprise* declared that Reynolds had given little representation to the views of his constituents and had devoted most of his time to "disgusting publicity dished out by peroxide blondes, cigarette manufacturers, and big game hunting." The *Enterprise* admitted that Reynolds had pulled the wool over the eyes of the people when elected to two terms in the Senate but hoped "that the people will not be duped again when the time comes around for nominating and electing a Senator."[104]

Professor Kenneth Colgrove, upset with Reynolds's position on foreign affairs, wrote a letter to Frank Graham encouraging citizens of North Carolina to apply pressure to Reynolds by telling him that if he did not mend his ways they would vote against him in the next election. Graham assured Colgrove that North Carolinians had already expressed their disagreement with Reynolds and added that he believed that if Reynolds were a candidate for reelection at that time he would be defeated overwhelmingly.[105]

The *Asheville Citizen-Times* agreed wholeheartedly with Graham's assessment. The paper observed that when Bob Reynolds had recently received a clear bill of health after a checkup at the Mayo Clinic, he had announced: "There is nothing wrong with me." The Asheville paper wryly noted that Reynolds's reference was merely to his physical well-being as the Mayo Clinic did not "concern itself with the political health of its patients." The *Citizen-Times*'s diagnosis was that Reynolds was so ill politically that he would suffer a devastating defeat if he ran for reelection in 1944.[106]

Reynolds, not oblivious to the furor he had caused, was concerned about his political future. Nonetheless, he generally ignored the unfavorable outcry and concentrated on more important matters—his fifth marriage. The object of the fifty-seven-year-old senator's affections was Evalyn Washington McLean, the twenty-year-old daughter of Evalyn Walsh McLean, one of Washington's leading hostesses and granddaughter of wealthy prospector Thomas Walsh.

Thomas Walsh had discovered gold and silver in the Camp Bird Mine in Ouray, Colorado, and had turned his find into one of the great fortunes of the world. His daughter, Evalyn Walsh, married Edward Beale McLean, son of John R. McLean, multimillionaire publisher of the *Cincinnati Enquirer* and the *Washington Post*. The Edward B. McLeans built a fabulous home in Washington, D.C., called "Friendship," and Evalyn Walsh McLean became the proud owner of two of the world's most famous gems, the Hope Diamond and the Star of the East.[107]

Evalyn Walsh McLean gave sumptuous dinners served on a gold dinner service, and people seldom refused invitations to her parties. After dinner, guests were either treated to the latest movie on Mrs. McLean's private screen or danced away the remainder of the evening. Reynolds, first invited to a dinner party in 1939, became a frequent guest at Friendship. It was during one of the dinner parties that Reynolds first met young Evalyn Washington McLean (or Evie, as she was called).[108]

Evalyn Washington McLean was raised in luxury and as an infant slept in a golden crib given to her father by King Leopold of Belgium. After a quiet childhood, she shocked Washington society by announcing that she would not make a formal debut—an event that had been long awaited by Washington cognoscenti. Miss McLean said that instead of playing the role of a debutante, she planned to sing in a nightclub or get a job in radio.[109] The tall, attractive Evie McLean, however, gave up her career plans and decided instead to marry Bob Reynolds. When first interviewed by reporters, she shed very little light on her romance except to say, "I don't know how it happened—it just happened."[110]

In another interview she recalled that she met the senator at a party at her house a year before the engagement, but they were not particularly attracted to each other on that occasion. However, according to Evie, they met several times at other parties and became romantically interested in each other after they discovered that they had similar interests—nightclubs, parties, and flying. Evie said that the thirty-seven-year difference in their ages was unimportant and that she preferred older men. She also explained that she did not believe in any superstitions or curses associated with her mother's Hope Diamond and had worn the gem on several occasions. The engagement was announced in the newspapers on August 11, although the previous day Reynolds's son, Bob Reynolds Jr., had vigorously denied any engagement, saying that his father and Evie McLean were just friends.[111]

According to his aide Hubert Rand, Senator Reynolds was shocked to learn of his impending nuptials. He, like his son, thought he and Evie were just good friends. On reading the announcement, the agitated senator slipped by waiting reporters and called Mrs. McLean. Reynolds told Mrs. McLean that he and Evie were not engaged and that there was no truth to the newspaper story. Mrs. McLean said she wanted Evie to marry Bob because her daughter had a lot of money and Mrs. McLean wanted him to "take care of her money." She also said that Evie really loved Bob and admired his stories and travels.

Rand recalled that Reynolds, with visions of extraordinary riches dancing in his head, hesitated approximately one minute. He then asked Mrs. McLean, "What dates are you considering?" After agreeing to the marriage, Reynolds admitted to his staff that he had been dating Evie for some time, but "apparently I know that little girl better than I thought I did."[112] Another old friend, T. Lamar Caudle, recalled that Reynolds had been captivated by Evie but had hesitated to ask for her hand because of the difference in their ages.[113] Once Mrs. McLean indicated her approval of the match and informed Reynolds that Evie loved him, however, the marriage was a done deal. It was an absolutely splendid opportunity for Bob Reynolds: he captured a young, attractive, extremely wealthy wife and all the publicity and social activities he could ever dream of.

From the time Reynolds announced his engagement and modestly exclaimed, "I think I am a very lucky man," he faced numerous barbed comments from the state newspapers. The *Raleigh News and Observer* told its readers that this marriage would be the debonair senator's fifth such relationship and illustrated that he was one of the few men in public life "who could hold the hands of two ladies and also keep a third one happy at the same time."[114] The *Asheville Citizen* expressed its delight that Reynolds had finally acquired "social contacts, big cars, the Hope Diamond as a tie-pin, butlers and mansions," and enough money to become a true playboy. The paper hoped that Reynolds would quickly become a full-time play-boy and urged the senator to take a nice long rest as he had been working too hard. "Take a month off. In fact, take off all the time between now and 1944."[115]

Capitol Hill wits, unable to resist a dig at the often-married Reynolds, talked about sending the presiding magistrate at the wedding a Boy Scout handbook so that he could learn to tie a really tight knot. The press frequently referred to Reynolds as "Hope Diamond, Jr."[116] The *Raleigh News and Observer* ventured an appraisal of the forthcoming nuptials. "The union will place the city's most mar-ried Senator in a position enviable to some of his fellows. In addition to the power he has as Chairman of the Senate Military Affairs Committee, he will enjoy addi-tional influence when his $10,000 annual salary is augmented by the $80,000 yearly income which Miss McLean receives from the estate of her paternal grand-father. There is little doubt that Senator Reynolds, who is personality plus, will become part and parcel of Miss McLean's entertainment committee. This is a far cry from his humble beginnings, but not at all surprising. Bob Reynolds has been prepared for the unexpected and unusual all his life."[117]

Evalyn Washington McLean became the bride of Robert Reynolds in a simple ceremony at 11 A.M., October 9, 1941, at the McLean estate. Evie wore an inexpen-sive ring she had picked out at a shop in the Mayflower Hotel, while her mother wore the Hope Diamond. Evie's cousin and her mother were the only guests at the ceremony, and the only guests at the champagne reception were newspapermen and photographers. Reynolds laughed off any possibility of a curse on the owner of the Hope Diamond and said that it "brought me good luck. It brought me the privilege and the pleasure of meeting this charming daughter of its owner."[118]

Reynolds wanted to spend the first night of his honeymoon on the soil of his native state, so the couple motored to Raleigh, where they occupied the Governor's Suite at the Sir Walter Hotel.[119] Senator and Mrs. Reynolds enjoyed a seven-week honeymoon in Miami and Havana, Cuba,[120] abandoning his colleagues and his new committee, as previously mentioned.

A tanned, beaming Reynolds returned to his Senate duties on November 28, 1941, and announced that he and his bride were still "heavenly happy." When asked by reporters if America were headed for war, Reynolds stated his belief that every step America had taken was propelling the country toward war and that it would be very difficult to change course because "our momentum is so great and our brakes so weak that we can hardly stop."[121]

Barely one week after Reynolds made this statement, on December 7, the naval and air forces of Japan attacked Pearl Harbor. The American people quickly forgot all the partisan quarrels and debates over foreign policy and became unified in a firm determination to win the war that the Japanese had started.

Isolationism ended on December 7, and longtime opponents of Roosevelt's foreign policies, including Senator Arthur Vandenberg, immediately pledged their full support for the war effort. Other isolationists in Congress also called for unity among the American people and endorsed the goal of winning the war. Burton K. Wheeler, an outspoken critic of Roosevelt's policy, expressed the view of his fellow isolationists when he said that "the only thing now is to do our best to lick the hell out of them."

All the isolationists, save one, agreed with Wheeler's statement. Reynolds, who heard the news while attending a Washington Redskins football game, once again made an astonishing and ill-advised statement to the press. He declared that even after the Japanese attack he remained fully against war and wanted to know more about what was actually happening before he could say anything about declaring war. He blamed the Japanese attack on Britain's desire to get the United States to relieve British forces in China so that England could then send the troops elsewhere to fight.[122]

Reynolds had blundered badly. His unrehearsed statement had incorrectly blamed the British, instead of the Japanese, for the attack on Pearl Harbor. It was patently obvious to Congress and the majority of citizens, but apparently not to Bob Reynolds, that America could not ignore an unprovoked attack. The press and voters were disgusted and angry at his failure to support an immediate declaration of war. The *Asheville Citizen* wrote that no patriotic North Carolinian could read Reynolds's shocking statement without a feeling of deepest shame and anger. The *Citizen* asked that Reynolds be "ejected" as chairman of the Military Affairs Committee and asked voters of the state to make known their "complete contempt for his sinister views."[123]

Reynolds quickly tried to repair his error. During the evening of December 7, the senator issued a position paper markedly different from his previously expressed views. In his second statement, Reynolds told the nation that he would vote for a declaration of war against Japan and would support the dispatch of an expeditionary force to the Far East "if military necessity demanded it." Reynolds then denounced the Japanese for pretending to seek peace while they were "in reality two-timing and double-crossing us. We have been physically attacked without cause and without reason. In view of this unwarranted, deceitful, murderous, and uncalled for attack on us, there is nothing left to do but to go to it 100%."[124]

Reynolds also wrote to William S. Foulis that America was now at war, and "regardless of what our former opinions were, there must be nothing but national unity and we will all put our shoulders to the wheel and push together to bring about a victory."[125]

Although Reynolds had been a bit late rallying to the cause, he now enthusiastically backed the government and voted for a declaration of war against Japan on December 8. He also voted for similar declarations against Germany and Italy.[126] Reynolds admitted that he had said on numerous occasions that he would never vote to send Americans to foreign fields to prosecute another nation's war, but the violent assault on Pearl Harbor made it America's war, and it had to be won.[127]

The *News and Observer*, as expected, denounced Reynolds for his initial statement on December 7. According to the editorial, however, Reynolds should not now be condemned for his past opinions, for although they had been wrong, it did not mean that the senator was unpatriotic. The *News and Observer* thought that the real issue was not Reynolds's ideas but his abilities and wanted him removed as chairman of the Military Affairs Committee. "In peace perhaps America could afford the luxury of keeping in places of power men of less than first quality. But when America fights a war for its security such a luxury should be among the first abandoned. America cannot make its best fight unless in all branches of government, civil as well as military, it insists upon the leadership of its best men."[128]

Whether people were angry at Reynolds or thought him unpatriotic or incompetent, the incontrovertible fact remained that America was at war and Reynolds, as chairman of the Military Affairs Committee, had to do his utmost to insure an American victory. Reynolds's isolationism ended on December 7, and he was now faced with the most serious and the stiffest challenge of his career—helping to win a war he had never wanted to fight.

CHAPTER ELEVEN

The War Years

In *Washington Goes to War*, journalist David Brinkley characterized Washington at the beginning of World War II as a middle-class town totally unprepared to take on the global responsibilities recently thrust on it. The country, explained Brinkley, needed a new government bureaucracy "to get the tanks and airplanes built, the uniforms made, the men and women assembled and trained and shipped abroad, and the battles fought and won. The war transformed not just the government. It transformed Washington itself. A languid Southern town . . . grew almost overnight into a crowded, harried, almost frantic metropolis struggling desperately to assume the mantle of global power and to change itself into the capital of the free world."[1]

In the months after Pearl Harbor, chastened by his blunder in blaming Britain for Pearl Harbor, Bob Reynolds concentrated on his duties as chairman of the Military Affairs Committee. He constantly urged American unity in order to save the country and preserve democracy.[2] The isolationist Reynolds even changed the goals of his *American Vindicator* so that the paper's main objective was no longer to stay out of war but to win the war. The *Vindicator* stood fully behind the Roosevelt administration in its effort to obtain victory and favored the outlawing of strikes and the abolition of the forty-hour workweek until the war was won. Reynolds also encouraged all Americans to buy war bonds to assist in the war effort.[3] In the opinion of his colleagues, Reynolds had been a model of loyalty, cooperation, and industry since Pearl Harbor and had worked to transform the directives from the War Department into legislation.[4]

Since Reynolds had become acting chairman in May 1941, eighty-one general bills and resolutions had been referred to his committee. Hearings had been held on twelve of the measures, and eighteen had been enacted into law. Thirty-six of the bills were personally introduced into Congress by Reynolds. The legislation ranged from a bill to give the leader of the army band the rank of major to a bill extending the draft age. The latter bill passed after Reynolds read a letter from General George C. Marshall urging such a move. Reynolds claimed that he worked from 8:30 A.M. until 7:30 P.M., with two-thirds of his time devoted to committee work.[5]

Chairman Bob Reynolds presides over a meeting of the Military Affairs Committee, ca. 1942.
From left, across table: Senators Harold H. Burton, Henry C. Lodge, Harry S Truman,
Reynolds, and Elmer Thomas.

Surprisingly, one criticism of Reynolds was not that the chairman obstructed the war effort but that he was so impressed by army brass that he had made the committee a mere machine for grinding out requested legislation. Reynolds did not take a significant or independent role in the war effort, and his committee did very little to check on the efficiency with which the military carried on the war. Reynolds partially resolved the latter problem by requesting a high administration official to appear before the committee once a week to keep it posted on the progress of the war and by asking Senator Henry C. Lodge (a Republican from Massachusetts) to make personal inspection tours of military units.[6] Despite his cooperation with the military brass, Reynolds still did not have the confidence of the administration, and Roosevelt continued to control the committee.[7]

Reynolds's deferential responses to military requests can best be illustrated by a rumor that the War Department would propose to lower the minimum draft age to eighteen or nineteen years. Reynolds had not read the Gurney bill and refused to express a personal opinion until he learned exactly what the War Department desired. Reynolds said that America "must put implicit faith in our Army officials, who know more about their needs than I do or any other civilian does."[8] When the government eventually decided to support an amendment to the Selective Service Act to lower the draft age, Reynolds promptly opened hearings and encouraged its early passage.[9]

Senator Josh Lee of Oklahoma complicated matters with an amendment to the bill which would prohibit the sale of alcoholic beverages at military camps and surrounding communities. Chairman Reynolds immediately wrote Secretary of War Robert Patterson to seek his views on the Lee amendment. Patterson lauded the desire to promote temperance on the part of soldiers, but because prohibition in the country at large had failed to bring temperance, there was no reason to believe that it would be any more successful in this instance. In addition, Patterson thought the attempt to stop the sale of liquor in surrounding counties would bring the army in direct conflict with civil authorities and would thus pose grave problems.[10]

Armed with advice supplied by the War Department, Reynolds announced that he would vote against the Lee Amendment since the army was doing a good job of controlling liquor. He would, however, vote for the Gurney bill because the commander in chief and other military leaders had advised him to do so. "All they have to do is to tell me they want them (men aged 18 and 19 years), that they have to have them in order to win the war, and I am not asking why. I am perfectly willing . . . to take the word of those upon whom we are depending to win the war."[11]

The amendment was killed by sending it back to committee.[12] The Military Affairs Committee, encouraged by Reynolds, quickly completed hearings and then unanimously approved the Gurney bill, which passed the Senate a week later.[13]

General Edward Greenbaum, a liaison officer between Congress and the War Department, reported that despite Reynolds's acquiescence in War Department requests, the army disliked him because he had opposed the war and had no concept of what the war was all about. Reynolds, noted Greenbaum, had contempt for the military but knew he had to play ball with the War Department.[14] On the other hand, the War Department did appreciate Reynolds's willingness to accede to their demands and to expedite legislation.

Reynolds's eager advocacy of the administration's war policies may have been significantly influenced by the publicity accorded several of his neofascist colleagues, especially the trial of alleged Nazi agent George Sylvester Viereck on February 16, 1942. A federal grand jury heard evidence about the Make Europe Pay War Debts Committee, for which Reynolds had served as vice chairman. The grand jury indicted Viereck, and he was convicted on three counts and sentenced to jail.[15] Reynolds also was aware that William Dudley Pelley of the fascist Silver Shirts had been indicted for sedition; that Father Coughlin's magazine *Social Justice*, which Reynolds had praised, had been banned from the mail; and that two prewar isolationists in the Senate had been defeated for reelection.[16] Worried about the publicity over his relationships with Viereck and fearful of a backlash over his former associations, Reynolds wanted to be seen as loyal and patriotic on every occasion.[17]

Reynolds certainly knew that the pro-Nazi charges had put his political future in grave doubt. He realized the consequences of any opposition to the war effort, no matter how insignificant. If he were to have any chance at reelection in 1944, his best bet was to support the administration on all military matters. The *Raleigh News and Observer* observed that Reynolds, with several contenders lurking in the background, had to support the administration completely or lose in 1944.[18] Jonathan Daniels, writing in *The Nation*, agreed with this assessment, noting that Reynolds had never been "passionately interested in any problem outside his own hide" and that his voting for war legislation was less related to the welfare of the world than to the welfare of Bob Reynolds in 1944.[19] Reynolds naturally wanted to be reelected, but he remained a loyal American. Time and again in correspondence, Reynolds stated that "America must be saved, the war must be won," and he often opined that by working to pass bills, he was doing something to help his country.[20]

Fearful of continued Japanese aggression, Chairman Reynolds, as he had many times before, demanded that America beef up its national defense and advocated strengthening of U.S. outposts in Alaska and the Aleutian Islands as they would be key bases for the eventual military offensive against Japan.[21] He did, however, resist dramatic increases in the size of the army because it would withdraw too many men from war production and would harm the economy.[22]

Although busy with military responsibilities, Reynolds could not, for any length of time, restrain his reckless rhetoric. He made a long, impassioned plea in the Senate requesting that England give immediate independence to India. Reynolds cited the Atlantic Charter, which said that the United States was fighting to give people the freedom to choose their own government. For Reynolds, England's failure to grant India independence was a denial of the charter.[23]

Reynolds's speech caused a furor in the Senate. Six prominent senators rebuked his views and claimed that the North Carolina senator had caused disunity among the Allies, thus aiding the enemy. The senators expressed sympathy for the nationalistic aspirations of India and hoped that the country would achieve independence after the democracies won World War II.[24]

Senator Walter George insisted that Reynolds's speech could be interpreted as a denunciation of England and would be exploited by Germany and Japan. Tom Connally thought that any moves of this sort should originate in the executive branch and felt that anything that detracted from a unified effort by the Allies did not serve the national interest.

Senator George Norris asked Reynolds how he would feel if a member of the British House of Commons arose to demand that the United States abolish the antidemocratic poll tax and remove all bars, including color, to the right to vote. Reynolds, surprised and overwhelmed by this counterattack, was scarcely able to reply. He finally managed to blurt out that abolishing the poll tax would be all right if it contributed to winning the war. Otherwise, said Reynolds, the suggestion by Britain would be presumptuous. Reynolds then lamely declared that the only thing he wanted to do was win the war and, reverting to his obsequious posture, noted that he would vote for all administration proposals to that end.[25]

Senator Styles Bridges also took Reynolds to task for using personal impressions, newspaper clippings, and gossip instead of authoritative documents as the basis for his discussion of the delicate and difficult problem of Indian independence. The documents that Reynolds read into the record, chided Bridges, failed to disclose any material that showed evidence of an objective study of the Indian problem, nor did they discuss the difficulties of achieving independence during wartime.[26]

Our Bob's gaffe gave his longtime critics a new target. The New York Times accused Reynolds of speaking irresponsibly. "That such a statement ignores all the real problems in the Indian situation is less important than the fact that it will be hailed by the enemy as evidence of disunity between Britain and ourselves." Senator Reynolds, continued the Times, was hardly the person to deliver lectures on liberty or democracy since his record did not suggest a very profound grasp of either philosophy. The editorial cited Reynolds as an admirer of the Nazi regime and decried his attempts to halt immigration. "So much for his hospitality to the victims of totalitarian persecution."[27]

The Asheville Citizen, noting Reynolds's propensity for erupting at the most inauspicious moment, denounced his "indiscreet" speech as an embarrassment to the administration because it would upset Secretary Hull's quiet efforts to find a compromise solution for Indian independence.[28] The Right Reverend William T. Manning, the Episcopal bishop of New York, characterized Reynolds's anti-British propaganda as a "dangerous and despicable form of sabotage" and called his speech an "amazing and most reprehensible utterance."[29]

Reynolds tried unsuccessfully to answer these charges. He put the onus on his detractors by protesting that his rebukes by his colleagues and the press constituted a damaging blow to the Allied war effort. Japanese propagandists were now telling the people of India that England had no intention of ever giving them independence. Thus, Reynolds announced that he was not the sower of disunity, his colleagues were. He did not think it improper to speak for freedom for India, especially since he did not mean immediate freedom for India but intended his remarks only as a suggestion to the British to aid the war effort.[30] As usual, the senator's attempt to clarify his thoughtless comments confused the issue even more.

As it turned out, however, Reynolds happened to be more in tune with President Roosevelt's private views in regard to Indian independence than either he or the press knew. Roosevelt wanted to end colonialism around the world and had been secretly trying to negotiate independence for India since early 1942. Roosevelt even went so far as to challenge Winston Churchill on this issue, but the prime minister refused to yield. To maintain Allied unity, Roosevelt reduced his pressure on Britain but continued his indirect program for decolonization.[31]

Reynolds had nonetheless blundered by not consulting either the president or the secretary of state before making a speech on a delicate diplomatic subject. The senator's hatred of Britain was well known, and his reproachful speech was a possible source of discord. Reynolds acted irresponsibly with little real knowledge of the situation in India. In light of the administration's activities to end colonialism, however, the criticism of Reynolds's position was unduly harsh.

Already under fire for his India speech, Reynolds also had to respond to a resurrection of the Nazi charges. The syndicated columnist Dorothy Thompson accused Reynolds of being "an outright Nazi unless miraculously converted on December 7." Thompson wrote that Reynolds's hold on the Military Affairs Committee tended "to make the stomach of a patriot feel uneasy."[32] Reynolds quickly denied Thompson's charges and called her allegations ridiculous and untrue. Reynolds said that he had always condemned Nazi and fascist doctrines as they were "in direct opposition to our way of life. I am pro-America."

Reynolds included in his remarks a warning about Russia. Even though Russia and America were allies, Reynolds remained strongly opposed to Communism. "Just because we are partners with Russia," he said, "we don't have to share political opinions." When Russia defeated Germany, which was likely, Reynolds feared that it would then conquer all of Europe.[33]

The Raleigh News and Observer assured its readers that Thompson's charges were ridiculous and untrue. Reynolds, said the paper, would have been better off not to answer the charges. Thompson's remarks would have done little damage to Reynolds, whose political prestige was already at its lowest point. The trouble with Reynolds's answer, editorialized the Raleigh paper, was that once Reynolds started, he continued to talk until he had denounced Russia. Reynolds spoke as chairman of an important committee with a direct responsibility in the prosecution of the war. He should have been too busy to engage in loose predictions about future relations between Russia and the United States when an effective alliance between the two was absolutely necessary to defeat the Axis powers.[34]

As noted earlier, Dorothy Thompson and PM magazine had for many years

callously and erroneously accused Charles Lindbergh of being "pro-Nazi." In fourteen columns from 1939 to 1941, Thompson denounced Lindbergh and accused
him of wanting to be "the American Fuehrer," arguing that Lindbergh and his wife
supported several "American Fascists." She based her claim on the fact that such
rabble-rousers as William Dudley Pelley had endorsed Lindbergh's isolationist
views. Although Thompson admitted that she had no proof of her accusations, she
continued to make them.[35] She made the same charges against Reynolds, also
based on his associations.

Reynolds's attempt to focus on the issue of Indian independence and the evils of
Communism had some validity—after all, why was America fighting World War
II? However, his views on India and Russia, while accurate, were ill-advised during
wartime. Even when he was right, Reynolds lacked wisdom about how and when
to present his views.

Stung by the renewed charges of Nazism and disloyalty and unsure of his
political future, Reynolds filed a petition in Washington, D.C., in June 1942 for
dissolution of the Vindicators Association, Incorporated. Since one of the main
objectives of the association had been to keep America out of the war, Reynolds
thought it impractical and undesirable for the Vindicators to remain in existence.
The assets of the organization, which had been in financial difficulty for some
time, were turned over to the publication, the *American Vindicator*, which would
continue to be published once a month.[36] The June 1942 issue of the paper supported all necessary war measures; attacked aliens, communism, and labor unions;
and reported favorably on Australia's immigration policy, which prohibited all
nonwhites.[37]

Reynolds's main purpose in disbanding the Vindicators Association was to
disassociate himself from an alleged pro-Nazi isolationist organization in time of
war. One wonders why he waited until June 1942 to make the decision and why he
continued to publish the *American Vindicator*.

The *News and Observer* gleefully greeted the demise of the Vindicators Association. "The Vindicators Association has outlived its usefulness, if it ever had any,
and the founder has now realized that. The magazine is too closely associated with
the ill-fated organization to ever be an asset to the Senator. If he continues its
publication he will find it to be a liability."[38]

Eventually, in March 1943, Reynolds erased all vestiges of the Vindicators by
changing the name of the *American Vindicator* to the *National Record*. Published
by the Continental Publishing Company in Washington, D.C., the new publication
had the same format as the *Vindicator*, with a sales price of ten cents and no
advertising. Reynolds stated that his new paper was nonpartisan, nonpolitical,
nonsectarian, and independent (which, of course, was what he had said about the
American Vindicator). The major objectives of the *National Record* were similar to

those of the *Vindicator* with the exception of isolationism and the addition of a new plank on labor·

1. Win a decisive and complete victory over "the dastardly Nazis, the treacherous Japs and their murderous partners in arms."
2. Outlaw the Communist Party.
3. Abolish all isms except Americanism. "Sweep from our shores every alien ideology designed to destroy the very fundamentals of our own form of government."
4. Stop all immigration now.
5. Register all labor unions.

In addition to the basic aims of the newspaper, Reynolds adopted such patriotic features as "Uncle Sam's Lettergram," addressed to "My dear Nieces and Nephews," which urged unity and sacrifice in order to win the war. He frequently ran full-page ads asking readers to buy war bonds and solicited support for the American Red Cross.[39] He also wrote letters to "Fellow Americans," explaining the goals of the paper and urging their support in his drive to save America for Americans.[40]

The happiest event of an otherwise difficult period occurred on October 15, 1942. On that date a proud father announced the birth of a six-and-one-half-pound baby daughter, Mamie Spears Reynolds, named after Reynolds's mother.[41] The fifty-eight-year-old father was ecstatic at the birth of his daughter. He had not only demonstrated his virility but also seemed to realize that little Mamie would provide him with some of the happiest moments of his life.

Perhaps because the Roosevelt administration did not take him seriously as chairman of the Military Affairs Committee or because he believed that the New Deal had lost its popularity, Reynolds began to demonstrate a strident opposition to almost all Roosevelt's domestic legislation. He voted with the administration on only two of the eighteen major bills that Roosevelt proposed in 1943, a far cry from his voting record during the previous ten years. The *Greensboro Daily News* quoted Reynolds as saying the New Deal was dead. Reynolds further decried the increasing regimentation, the misuse of public funds, and the trend toward centralization of power in Washington. Having once wanted the government to control big business, Reynolds now wanted the government taken away from the New Dealers and restored to the American people.[42] The once ardent proponent of the New Deal had dramatically shifted positions. Facing reelection, Reynolds sensed a more conservative mood in North Carolina.

During the Seventy-eighth Congress Reynolds frequently missed Senate debates and roll call votes because he spent most of his time trying to mend his political fences for 1944. Unfortunately for the senator, he alienated teachers and educators by missing the debate and the vote on the federal aid to education bill. Reynolds had promised to vote for the bill but was in New York for four days on personal business. The educators charged him with being irresponsible, unprepared, and uncommitted to better education for American children.[43]

Reynolds also managed to anger organized labor. In a radio speech in February 1943, he lambasted labor for its failure to give the war effort its full support. He admitted that labor had made many deserved social and economic gains in the last twenty-five years, but labor would forfeit those advances unless it put an immediate stop to every form of strike, absenteeism, and tie-up of war production. Reynolds explained that he had consistently voted for legislation favorable to organized labor. Now, however, labor had to end all strikes and cleanse its house of the un-American influence of racketeers in order to gain Reynolds's continued backing.[44]

Reynolds introduced a bill in Congress designed to correct the aforementioned deficiencies of labor. The first part of the bill, Senate Joint Resolution no. 9, required the registration of labor organizations with the Department of Labor. The registration included the name and address of the organization, its officers and their salaries, as well as dues; initiation fees, and a detailed financial statement. Failure to register led to a fine and the union's disqualification as the representative of its workers in collective bargaining.

The second part of his bill prohibited the employment of aliens, communists, fascists, Nazis, and anyone who had lost privileges of citizenship owing to conviction of a felony. Violation of this provision was punishable by a fine of not more than ten thousand dollars.[45] The Committee on Education and Labor did not favorably report on Reynolds's bill, and it never came to the floor of the Senate.

Reynolds tried to elicit favorable reaction to his labor control bill with an editorial in the National Record. Since political parties and businesses had to register and show incomes, asked Reynolds, why not labor unions? Why should such alien criminals as Harry Bridges be allowed to come to America, join labor unions, and defy the laws of the country? Reynolds alleged that racketeers held key offices in labor unions and that the only opposition to his bill came from those very same racketeers.[46]

Senator Reynolds's problems with labor intensified on March 25, 1943, when Union #2598 of the Enka (N.C.) Rayon Workers adopted a resolution condemning his antilabor proposals. The resolution said that Reynolds, "always an opportunist rather than a statesman," had joined the ranks of labor baiters. The Enka workers wondered how Reynolds, "back from his most recent of many honeymoons" and "basking in the glittering reflection of the famous Hope Diamond," could ask labor to sacrifice all its gains. They apologized for ever supporting him for office and pledged to "relegate Senator Reynolds to the ash-heap of political oblivion, where he can retire and eat caviar in peace for the rest of his life."[47] C. A. Fink, president of the North Carolina Federation of Labor and a former Reynolds supporter, joined the attack by canceling the senator's honorary membership in the federation.[48]

Despite vigorous opposition from organized labor, Congress did pass bills incorporating some of Reynolds's suggestions. For example, in January 1944 Congress passed legislation requiring labor unions to file annual financial reports with the commissioner of internal revenue. Reynolds reached another objective in May 1943 when the Senate passed the Smith-Connally Anti-Strike Act by a vote of 63–16. This bill empowered the president to seize any war plant or other property where interference with war production was threatened by a lockout, a strike, or other major disturbance. Any instigation of strikes or lockouts in plants seized by the government would result in a fine or one year in jail or both.[49] President Roosevelt vetoed the bill, but the Senate overrode the veto by a vote of 56 to 25, with Reynolds voting to override.[50]

Reynolds explained that he had voted for the Smith-Connally bill because it was essential to keep production at the highest levels if America were to win the war. The bill became necessary, according to Reynolds, through the broken promises of labor. He resented labor's effort to pressure legislators into opposing the bill and accused labor of subordinating all other interests to that of labor. "Nothing more Nazi or Fascist has ever been advocated in the United States."[51]

Throughout the Seventy-eighth Congress Reynolds ostentatiously supported all efforts that would bring the war to a speedy end. He advocated a second front in Europe and insisted that America supply its troops with the best arms, clothes, and food.[52] As late as January 1945, he wrote Harry Truman calling for united action and a spirit of cooperation to win the war and the peace.[53]

When the Lend-Lease Act came up for renewal, Reynolds voted for the extension despite his adamant opposition to the original act. By 1943 Reynolds had accepted Lend-Lease as an instrument of war and understood that America had to utilize it effectively to win. In a Senate speech, Reynolds made it clear that he had never regretted his decision to vote against the lifting of the arms embargo or against the original Lend-Lease measure. He was convinced that those decisions were steps that led America directly into World War II and that without those steps the United States would not now be involved in the war. Reynolds brought up the matter to assure his colleagues that his isolationist views had not changed and that his vote for Lend-Lease extension was merely a matter of expediting the war effort.[54] In blaming Lend-Lease for America's entrance into World War II, Reynolds conveniently ignored Pearl Harbor and the fascist drive for world domination. His comments on the renewal of Lend-Lease illustrated once again that he remained uninformed when assessing foreign affairs.

Reynolds continued to warn America of the threat of internal subversion. He claimed that throughout the war fifth-column activities by alien enemies had hampered America's war effort, and he wanted to put all alien enemies into concentration camps until the war was over.[55] In a Joe McCarthy-like outburst, he advocated cleaning house by getting rid of those "wishy-washy, zig-zagging, pop-eyed pinks, reds, and Communists in high positions, bureaucrats galore, who are attempting to destroy here the very things for which our boys are fighting in every part of the world."[56]

Fearful of internal subversion by Japanese Americans, Reynolds in 1943 directed Senator Elbert D. Thomas of Utah to head a subcommittee of the Military Affairs Committee to investigate reported demonstrations and outbreaks in the Japanese American relocation centers in the West.[57] Reynolds had read reports claiming that these Japanese enemy-aliens were being pampered by the War Relocation Authority and were getting food, clothes, and housing while Americans received nothing. The Japanese Americans correctly responded that they were not being pampered. They invited Reynolds to come see for himself the barbed wire, sentries, rationed mess, outdoor toilets, and the other indignities that 112,000 loyal Japanese Americans had to suffer. Other than appointing a subcommittee to investigate, Reynolds ignored the situation except to say that the evacuees could not be pampered any longer.[58]

Earlier, in February 1942, Reynolds had become involved in the deportation of Japanese Americans from the West Coast. On February 19 President Roosevelt signed Executive Order 9066, which proclaimed that successful prosecution of the war required every possible precaution against sabotage of and espionage in defense installations. Roosevelt, as commander in chief, gave the War Department the discretionary authority to prevent individuals from entering certain military areas and to remove anyone considered to be a threat to American security. Although Japanese Americans were not specifically mentioned, the end result was to remove more than one hundred thousand Japanese Americans from the West Coast and to place them in relocation facilities. The removal occurred because of the irrational fear of a second Pearl Harbor, fanned by exaggerated press releases and the willingness of Attorney General Francis Biddle to surrender constitutional rights to the demands of the military.

To carry out Executive Order 9066, the War Department had to persuade Congress to pass a bill that would establish criminal penalties necessary to punish any violators of military orders. Chairman Bob Reynolds presided at a one-hour hearing before the Military Affairs Committee on Public Law 503. The committee approved the bill unanimously, and the Senate went on to pass the bill that same afternoon, March 13. Only two senators, other than Reynolds, participated in the debate over the bill, and Senator Robert A. Taft was the lone legislator who expressed any reservations about possible violations of individual rights.[59]

Reynolds, according to Peter Irons, "indulged his long-winded proclivities"

with a speech denouncing Japanese Americans as "fifth-column" agents and saboteurs. Reynolds reiterated, without questioning their validity, charges made by
Navy Secretary Frank Knox, that Japanese Americans had aided the attack on Pearl
Harbor with spying and sabotage. Without any proof whatsoever, Reynolds announced that in Hawaii "canefields were cut in the form of arrows pointing to
military objectives," that Japanese Americans had "wrecked cars and . . . obstructed traffic" near Pearl Harbor, and that "Japanese pilots shot down above
Pearl Harbor were found to be wearing Honolulu high school insignia and United
States college rings." Reynolds, as usual, had used erroneous press accounts for his
allegations. Had he checked with the FBI, he would have learned that they had
dismissed these charges as unfounded.[60]

Reynolds had no responsibility for the relocation of the Japanese Americans,
but he had very little sympathy for their plight. His outrageous charges of Japanese
American sabotage were totally unsubstantiated but understandable for Reynolds.
He considered them subversive seditionists who posed a serious threat to American security, and he wanted them rigidly controlled until the end of the war. The
idea that their civil liberties might have been violated never seemed to have crossed
the senator's mind.

By 1943, when it seemed likely that the Allies would win the war, many Americans were anxious about the shape of the postwar world. Reynolds, still a unilateralist, was well aware of how unpopular his previous isolationist stands had
been received in his home state. Thus, his votes on such important international
agreements as the United Nations were pivotal for Reynolds's political future.

The first test came in March 1943 when Reynolds announced his opposition to
the Ball, Burton, Hill, Hatch Resolution that called on the Senate to affirm the
intention of the United States to collaborate with other nations in the postwar
world. Reynolds rejected this proposition primarily because he feared that America would lose its independence and become part of a world government.

Reynolds, not wanting to state his views publicly so as to avoid providing
ammunition for his opponents in 1944, concealed his opposition to the United
Nations (UN) by pursuing a false issue. Reynolds said that it was an improper time
to get into a debate over America's postwar program since victory had not yet been
achieved. He wanted the country to devote all its energy to winning the war
because "we cannot do anything after the war until we win it." The senator also
noted that some significant problems such as the enslavement of people by other
nations had to be cleared up before international commitments were made. Certain that Stalin was "a Soviet Firster," Reynolds predicted that he would take
control of the Baltic states, Poland, Rumania, and Bulgaria at the end of the war.
Reynolds did not think that Russia would accept an international police force until
it had acquired all the territory it desired.[61]

By obscuring the issue, Reynolds tried to avoid taking a definitive stand on international cooperation after the war. His ploy failed. When Fred S. Hutchins wrote Reynolds that his isolationist beliefs were anathema in North Carolina and the citizens were strongly in favor of cooperation among nations at the end of the war, Reynolds changed course.

Hutchins's letter apparently jolted Our Bob into action. Hoping for political salvation, Reynolds dramatically altered his views on postwar cooperation. Citing Hutchins's letter in a Senate speech, Reynolds called for an early meeting between Churchill, Stalin, and Roosevelt to determine what was to be done in the postwar world. He argued that the best way to prevent future wars was to establish the machinery for the peaceful settlement of disputes between nations. Reynolds then voiced his approval of a United Nations and even favored the maintenance of a United Nations military force to suppress any attempt at military aggression. He insisted that he was still an isolationist and approved of the United Nations only because it offered the best course for peace.[62]

Reynolds's speech supporting a United Nations was an astounding statement for a man who had been unalterably opposed to such minimum international cooperation as the World Court and who had uniformly rejected any sort of international commitments by the United States. The only explanation for Reynolds's momentary aberration was politics. His speech was, in part, a trial balloon designed to test his constituents' reaction to his new stance on foreign policy. Unfortunately, his speech generated very little comment, either pro or con.

Those who did comment on his speech accused Reynolds of a blatant bid for reelection. The *Charlotte Observer* saw Reynolds's volte-face as an effort to get himself more in line with the sentiment of North Carolinians, but the paper thought that it was too late for Reynolds to change how most citizens viewed him.[63]

Reynolds decided that because he had failed to elicit popular support for his newfound position, he might as well return to his isolationist views. In a speech on June 25 over the National Broadcasting Company, he discussed the problems America would face at the conclusion of hostilities. The United States, announced Reynolds, would have to cope with 15–20 million unemployed, many wounded veterans, and a national debt of over $500 billion. Thus America, in Reynolds's opinion, should consider the welfare of America "before considering a world-wide WPA, a quart of milk every day to each of the two billion people on the face of the earth and probably the policing of the entire world at the expense of the American taxpayer."[64]

His shift back to isolationism came full circle in October 1943 when he opposed the Connally resolution favoring the creation of international machinery for peace. The Connally resolution urged that the United States, "acting through its constitutional processes, join with free and sovereign nations in the establishment and maintenance of international authority with power to prevent aggression and to preserve the peace of the world." The resolution explicitly endorsed American cooperation and recognized the necessity for establishing a general international organization at the earliest possible date. On October 22, the Senate Foreign Relations Committee voted to recommend the resolution to the full Senate. Although he was the only committee member absent from the vote, it was clear that Reynolds opposed the resolution.[65]

Nell Battle Lewis, his old enemy, rebuked Reynolds for his opposition. Lewis was pleased that he continued to spout his isolationist views because it would make him easier to defeat in 1944. Lewis wrote that there "isn't going to be any doubt about what we'll be voting against in voting against him—the blindest, most reactionary, most selfish isolationism which now is the greatest single obstacle to human welfare and the gravest threat to the future of the world."[66]

Reynolds, as usual, ignored Lewis and offered a prescient amendment to the Connally resolution. The amendment provided for the guarantee of the independence and territorial integrity of Latvia, Lithuania, Estonia, Poland, Greece, Yugoslavia, and other subjugated nations after the war ended. America, argued Reynolds, could not accept Russian annexation of these territories without betraying its pledge for freedom and free elections in the world.[67] Senator Arthur Vandenberg and other Republicans, fearing communist expansion in Europe, supported the Reynolds amendment,[68] but it was defeated by a voice vote.[69]

While the Connally debate proceeded, the United States, Russia, and Great Britain took part in the tripartite conference of foreign ministers in Moscow. The Big Three reaffirmed the decision to punish all Axis war criminals and advocated freedom for all states occupied by the Axis powers. They also agreed to the regulation of postwar armaments and the creation of a general international organization to maintain the peace. Reynolds expressed his surprise that Cordell Hull did not insist on guarantees of the political integrity of all subjugated nations, not just those controlled by Axis powers. Senator Reynolds protested that the resolution sanctioned the acquisition of subject territories by the Allies (meaning Russia) and would make World War III inevitable to prevent those injustices.[70]

On November 5, 1943, after two weeks of debate, the Senate voted 85–5 in favor of the Connally resolution. In deference to the isolationists, the final version specified that America should join into this agreement only with a two-thirds vote of the Senate. Reynolds was one of five hard-core isolationists (along with William Langer, Burton Wheeler, Hiram Johnson, and Henrik Shipstead) and the only southerner who voted against the resolution. Reynolds said he voted no primarily because it did not guarantee the freedom of countries in Eastern Europe, but he also feared the submergence of American sovereignty into some form of super world government not yet disclosed.[71]

According to Professor Wayne Cole, the role of the Senate isolationists in the vote on the Connally resolution "dramatized the enfeebled and discredited state to which they had been reduced since World War II." Most prewar noninterventionists had changed their view of the world and had voted for the Connally resolution. Of the five who voted no, all but Reynolds were western progressives on domestic issues.[72] The British Embassy political reports, which referred to Reynolds as an irresponsible and rabid isolationist, viewed the strong vote in favor of the resolution as a movement away from isolationism and were optimistic about the future of American foreign policy.[73]

Faced with one of the more difficult decisions of his political career, Reynolds, after a brief flirtation with interventionism, had voted his sincere convictions on the Connally resolution. He remained an isolationist to the end and believed that the country would return to isolationism after the war.[74] Other observers, including Senate colleagues and Breckinridge Long, the assistant secretary of state, thought that because Reynolds was doomed to defeat in the coming election, he had deliberately voted against the resolution "to give public excuse for his coming repudiation."[75]

Reynolds now focused attention on his bid for reelection in 1944. Although he had kept his political fences mended by diligently attending to constituent requests, he had spent very little time in North Carolina since the war began, and all indications were that he would face a tough campaign against a formidable opponent.[76]

As early as December 1942, speculation in North Carolina centered around either Clyde R. Hoey or O. Max Gardner, both former governors, as opponents for Reynolds.[77] The *High Point Enterprise* noted that both Hoey and Gardner were being urged to run and would get together to decide which of the two would make the race. As brothers-in-law and close personal friends, they would not run against each other. "Either, of course, would make a far better Senator than Reynolds but that statement doesn't mean much in itself for the same thing could be said about thousands of others."[78]

O. Max Gardner, the most likely candidate, had received numerous pledges of support from North Carolinians.[79] Gardner said he would not be interested in running "were it not for the fact that I am satisfied Bob Reynolds is not the man to represent North Carolina in the terrific period of transition that lies ahead." Senator Reynolds, according to Gardner, had not maintained his strength with the common people of the state and would be opposed by organized labor, business interests, and the churches. Even women, concluded Gardner, would not vote for him because of his five marriages.[80]

Gardner offered a further assessment of Reynolds's political viability to the columnist Tom Bost. "They say the Hope Diamond is the most valuable jewel in America, but it will not be valuable enough for Bob to pawn to retain his seat in the Senate. If there is anything certain, it is the fact that he is going to be defeated."[81]

As of early January 1943, Gardner had not yet made up his mind to run. He again told the press that he had no inclination to run for public office but "would not be afraid to run in 1944" if he were convinced that it was his duty and if he could contribute to world peace.[82] Reynolds seemed unconcerned about his burgeoning opposition. When advised that Gardner might be his opponent, he stated that he was too busy with government matters to comment.[83] Reynolds, according to Wesley McDonald, was not worried about a Gardner candidacy because they had been friends since university days and Reynolds did not expect Gardner to oppose him.[84]

Perhaps the most significant threat to Reynolds's reelection was the behind-the-scenes opposition orchestrated by his influential colleague Senator Josiah Bailey In February 1943, having lost patience with Reynolds and his views, Bailey wrote a harsh denunciation of his colleague, indicating his strong dislike of the man and all that he stood for. Bailey sent the diatribe, titled "Senator Reynolds Reminds Us," to D. Hiden Ramsey, editor of the *Asheville Citizen*, with a cover letter from Gardner. Bailey asked Ramsey to use the letter as the basis for an anti-Reynolds editorial but warned Ramsey that the authorship had to remain a secret.

It was unusual for a colleague to work so diligently to defeat a fellow senator, but Bailey's anger had peaked when Reynolds called Germany and Japan America's friends and had urged America not to do anything to upset them. Senator Bailey was convinced that Reynolds had been instrumental in causing friction between the United States and its allies, Britain and Russia, with the hope of bringing about a victory by the Axis powers. Bailey's embittered portrayal of Reynolds was the culmination of years of repressed anger and disgust with Reynolds as a senator.

The senior senator wrote that the Senate had given Reynolds the benefit of the doubt on many of his utterances, making "due allowance for his ignorance. We were not at war, and could afford to be patient, but patience has ceased to be a virtue." Bailey denounced Reynolds as a man not taken seriously by his fellow senators and reproached his colleague for "his thoughtlessness, for his habit of speaking without thinking, and his impulsive tendency to seize any subject and say anything to remind the public of his existence as a Senator." According to Bailey, Reynolds seldom had a sense of the consequences of his actions. Moreover, added

Bailey, Reynolds had been unchanged by the gravest circumstances in world history and had gone blithely on his reckless way—"as inconsequential as ever at a time when none can afford to be inconsequential."

Reynolds, concluded Bailey, apparently did not understand the great blunders of his past because he was planning to run for the Senate again. Bailey wanted the people of North Carolina to have the opportunity to vindicate themselves. "The time has come to deal seriously with Robert R. Reynolds."[85] Bailey's letter, a perceptive overview of Reynolds's Senate career by a close observer, dealt a devastating blow to Reynolds's place in history.

Hiden Ramsey, however, decided not to use the Bailey material because he believed that Reynolds was already a "political corpse. If we kick him too venomously we may kick him back to life." Ramsey wrote Gardner that he did not want to waste his best ammunition now but wanted to hold his strongest fire "until we can see the whites of Bob's eyes. Just now his eyes give forth only a glassy stare."[86]

Similar arguments were presented by other detractors. One unknown author called Reynolds a threat to America's future and claimed that he could no longer win votes by joking and grinning. The author believed that the citizens of the state would now discipline Bob Reynolds for a dozen wasted years.[87]

Gardner knew that he had strong support from the Democratic Party leaders in the state and from Josiah Bailey, but he had no burning desire for political office.[88] Gardner admitted privately to Josephus Daniels and to Hiden Ramsey that he had not seriously entertained the idea of running for public office again, "but the career of Reynolds in the Senate has so outraged my sense of pride and decency, combined with unsolicited tender of support from every section of the state, that I have about made up my mind to endure the ordeals of another political campaign in order to drive this fellow from his seat in the Senate." Despite hundreds of letters favoring his candidacy, a reluctant Gardner backed away from an official announcement.[89]

In mid-February 1943, Reynolds, now sufficiently worried about the incipient movement to unseat him, decided to return to North Carolina to shore up his support. He planned to make radio speeches in Raleigh and Greensboro as well as visits to Fort Bragg and the shipyards in Wilmington. Reynolds stated that he planned to talk about the war and claimed that his visit was nonpolitical. It was evident to the press, however, that Buncombe Bob wanted to rejuvenate his former adherents and perhaps head off Gardner's potential candidacy.[90]

While in Greensboro, Reynolds announced that he planned to be a candidate for reelection and would run on his record and the service that his office had rendered to the people of North Carolina. He also emphatically stated that he would not retract a single vote he had cast since he had been in Washington.

Reynolds's declaration scotched rumors that he might not run because of the substantial support already pledged to Gardner.[91]

The *Charlotte Observer* responded to Reynolds's "brazen" announcement that he was not ashamed of a single vote he had cast in Washington. "Well," the paper rejoined, "the people of North Carolina are ashamed of practically every stand he has taken, ashamed of the record he has made as it now stands and because of it they will relegate him and his abominable past to the shades of the unreturning past."[92]

Still undecided on his candidacy, Gardner had nonetheless begun accumulating ammunition to use against Reynolds. Gardner wanted to force Reynolds to defend his record as an isolationist and had no intention of permitting him to masquerade under the guise of pretended patriotism. In Gardner's mind, Reynolds "was the most complete isolationist I knew and if we had relied on his leadership, God only knows what would have happened to this country."[93]

Gardner learned that Reynolds had become very agitated about his political future and was having frequent conferences with friends. Since the senator had no semblance of an organization and public sentiment was against him, Gardner believed that Reynolds was now so unpopular that he could not carry a single county in his home district.[94] O. Max Gardner reported to Hiden Ramsey that he had gotten the approbation of Frank P. Graham, president of the University of North Carolina, and that the business leaders of the state were also in his corner. Gardner thought these developments offered evidence that "Bob is somewhat like Rommel in the Tunisian campaign. I think we have him encircled."[95]

Santford Martin, editor of the *Winston-Salem Journal*, predicted that Gardner would defeat Reynolds by a margin greater than Reynolds had defeated Morrison, as the voters were ready to atone for their mistakes in 1932 and 1938.[96] Congressman Lindsay Warren also was positive that Gardner would win easily, and Hiden Ramsey encouraged Gardner to bury Reynolds "beyond hope of resurrection. I am sure that you can do the job of providing Bob with the appropriate interment."[97]

On April 23, however, Gardner shocked his supporters by withdrawing from the contest because of ill health. Gardner had low blood pressure and became completely exhausted after a speech in Charlotte. His doctor advised him not to engage in a difficult campaign, because it would impair his health. Gardner regretted having to withdraw as he had never seen such a manifestation of confidence and loyalty for his candidacy. He did, however, pledge to do everything in his power to redeem the state from Bob Reynolds.[98]

After Gardner's withdrawal, pundits again speculated about possible candidates. The names of Clyde Hoey, William B. Umstead, Cameron Morrison, Frank Hancock, and Robert L. Doughton were mentioned most prominently. The immediate goal of many Democrats was to find a candidate behind whom the anti-

Reynolds forces could rally.[99] W. Kerr Scott, commissioner of agriculture, considered entering the race and wrote friends asking for advice. One respondent told Scott that it was too late. "Everyone was so anxious to see Reynolds defeated" that they had already pledged support to Hoey.[100]

Former governor Clyde R. Hoey had stated on several occasions that he had no desire for public office and would not oppose his brother-in-law. However, after Gardner bowed out, Hoey indicated that he would run if urged to do so by the people. On April 28, claiming that he had been contacted by citizens from eighty counties, Hoey announced that he would enter the contest against Reynolds. Doughton, Umstead, and Morrison quickly informed the press that they did not plan to oppose Hoey.[101] Although Hoey insisted that his call came from the people, Gardner had secured Hoey's promise to run prior to his own withdrawal.[102]

Hoey was a popular campaigner, and the Democratic Party organization promised to assist him.[103] Although the conservative Hoey was not a New Dealer, he was not an isolationist. The Roosevelt administration, surmised the *News and Observer*, was so opposed to Reynolds that they were expected to put forth considerable effort to help Hoey.[104]

The majority of the state's newspapers delighted in Hoey's announcement. The *Charlotte Observer* believed that Hoey was the one man most capable of beating Reynolds.[105] Although Reynolds had not commented on Gardner's withdrawal or Hoey's announcement, Josiah Bailey suspected that Reynolds supporters realized they were doomed. They knew of Hoey's popularity and "were whistling to keep up their courage."[106]

Reynolds, however, was not yet ready to give up the fight. In an effort to regain some prestige, he wrote a self-laudatory editorial and placed it in Hearst-owned newspapers around the country. The editorial depicted Senator Reynolds as a distinguished figure of vitality, honesty, integrity, and vast courage. His enemies, explained the editorial, were the communists and other subversive anti-Americans who had launched unwarranted attacks against him. The editorial praised Reynolds as "one of the most valuable men America has in her present hour of trial."[107] Reynolds then mailed the published editorial to constituents statewide. This abortive attempt to revive his popularity did not receive much favorable consideration.

A month later Reynolds followed up the Hearst editorial with a public speech that was a rehash of his previous views. Reynolds declared that he would place his political future squarely behind his belief that isolationism was the best course for America. The press generally ignored this speech as well. The *Greensboro Daily News* warned the people of North Carolina that a return to isolationism would be a greater tragedy than World War II and that Reynolds's platform was merely a compilation of all the prejudices for which he had stood in the past.[108]

When Bob Reynolds did not return to North Carolina during the summer recess of the Seventy-ninth Congress and did not appear to be mounting a serious campaign, rumors became rife that he would not run in 1944.[109] When confronted with those rumors, Reynolds seemed shocked and insisted that he was a candidate for reelection. He contended that he had not been active as a candidate because his duties as chairman of the Military Affairs Committee kept him too busy.[110]

In spite of Reynolds's halfhearted attempts to bolster his candidacy, most observers, including his Senate colleagues, knew that he was in serious trouble. Marvin McIntyre, private secretary to President Roosevelt, wrote Jonathan Daniels that North Carolina was strongly pro-Roosevelt and very decidedly anti-Reynolds.[111]

The *High Point Enterprise* concluded by mid-October that Reynolds was "a badly beaten man."[112] Drew Pearson, licking his chops at the prospect of Reynolds's demise, gave Our Bob credit for a generous amount of political shrewdness, but surely he realized that with his new wealth and a new wife, the reelection battle was too uphill to try. In 1943 it was Reynolds, not Cam Morrison, who was eating fish eggs, and the home folks knew all about it.[113]

On November 8, 1943, one year before the general election, Bob Reynolds, faced with insurmountable odds in his battle for reelection, announced that he would not be a candidate. Despite his public protests to the contrary, Senator Reynolds had been considering this move for some time but was reluctant to give up the benefits of his office. He insisted that he chose to forgo the campaign because of "the tremendous pressure of work" during wartime.[114]

Reynolds's decision, coming just a few days after he stated that he would be in the race, caught Washington and North Carolina by surprise. The *Raleigh News and Observer*, after many years of partisan sniping at Reynolds, was remarkably restrained and objective. The *News and Observer* surmised that Reynolds lost all chance for reelection by voting against the Connally resolution. The Connally vote climaxed a long series of actions disapproved by his constituency, and Reynolds's choice not to run showed that he correctly read the sentiment of the voters.[115] Nell Battle Lewis greeted Reynolds's announcement with "joyous relief. Better political riddance North Carolina hasn't had in many a long day, and I hail it with a succession of loud huzzahs." Her only regret was that Reynolds would never know how many Tar Heels rejected his misrepresentation.[116]

The *Greensboro Daily News* agreed with the *News and Observer* and thought that Reynolds had defeated himself. He did not stand a chance for reelection so he quit.[117] The British Embassy hailed the withdrawal of the "regular hero of the lunatic, i.e. fascist fringe" and saw the decision as a strong expression of popular opposition to isolationism.[118]

In a more demeaning vein, the *Durham Morning Herald* suggested that Reynolds's withdrawal, barring resignation, was the best contribution that the senator could make to his constituents. "The refreshing breeze generated by Reynolds's announcement," continued the paper, "is somewhat fouled by the attached prattle about sacrificial devotion to duty."[119]

The *Asheville Citizen* had surprisingly little to say except to note that it was gratified that Reynolds had retired. The paper would no longer have to apologize for the accidental circumstances that had placed him in the Senate.[120] One of Reynolds's constituents wrote Lindsay Warren of his delight at Reynolds's withdrawal: "I see that Bob does not choose to run. Bully for him. That removes one large carbuncle from the body politic of America."[121]

Newspapers outside of the state were generally pleased with Reynolds's decision. The *New York Times* carried the story without editorial comment,[122] but the *Chicago Sun* wrote a biting editorial. The *Sun* observed that Reynolds announced that he would continue to champion those principles to which his public life had been devoted—to wit, a fostering of race antagonisms and a ranting isolationist nationalism. The paper insisted that Reynolds had retired because his twin burdens—the Hope Diamond and his isolationist record—were too much for him to overcome.[123]

Although a large majority of newspapers hailed Reynolds's withdrawal, the Hearst press regretted his decision. Some of his loyal supporters, such as John G. Pecos of Raleigh, also came to his defense. In a letter to the editor, Pecos praised Reynolds as a fine senator who fought for the best interests of the common people in North Carolina and was always ready to talk with the people and provide his constituents a small favor.[124]

Why did Reynolds decide not to run in 1944? One explanation floated by Reynolds's pals portrayed him as a sincere isolationist who unselfishly gave up his seat to allow someone more favorable to a new world order to make the decisions. Reynolds, however, although a consistent noninterventionist, would never have given up his seat to accommodate the Roosevelt administration unless he knew he could not win. The official excuse provided by Reynolds—that the tremendous pressure of work in Washington would not allow him to take time out for campaigning—was simply an attempt to withdraw gracefully. He had not been concerned about his senatorial responsibilities in his previous eleven years of vacation jaunts, inspection tours, and worldwide excursions, and there was no reason to believe that he would have been in this instance.

T. Lamar Caudle, an old friend, claimed that Reynolds's wife Evie had threatened to leave him unless he got out of politics, as she wanted him with her all the time. Caudle believed that Reynolds had acceded to her wishes.[125] It is difficult to imagine Reynolds, who loved politics and his role in the limelight more than life itself, denying himself high political office to satisfy the desires of his fifth wife. Her wishes and her money might have been a minor factor in his decision.

The reason for his withdrawal was crystal clear. Reynolds knew that he could not win reelection in 1944 and decided not to subject himself to a humiliating defeat. Almost all the newspapers, political pundits, and even his advisers recognized that Reynolds probably could not win over one-third of the vote in a contest with the popular Hoey, who had the total support of the Gardner machine. Reynolds's popularity had reached a new low in 1943 owing to his vote against the Connally resolution, the opposition of labor and educators, and his failure, after twelve years in office, to build a strong political organization. Other factors included the accumulated anger of constituents over his isolationism during wartime, his "playboy" reputation, his infrequent visits to North Carolina, and a reprisal of the charges about his association with Nazis and fascists. Reynolds's daughter Frances Oertling said he did not run because of three factors—his unpopular isolationism, his wife's desires, but, most significant, his inability to win.[126]

Reynolds's political fortunes, at their lowest ebb on November 9, 1943, were briefly revived by Gerald L. K. Smith, the chairman of a newly organized America First Party.[127] Smith opposed the nomination of Wendell L. Willkie on the Republican Party ticket in 1944 because of Willkie's interventionist views. Smith predicted that the America First Party would be on the ballot in 1944 with a presidential candidate and said that "Bob Reynolds would suit me."

Reynolds was "flattered and honored" with Smith's invitation to be the presidential nominee of the America First Party "because to be spoken of as Presidential timber is a great compliment." Reynolds deferred acceptance of the nomination until after both the Democratic and Republican platforms were drawn up and their nominees chosen. Senator Reynolds thought that a third party might be necessary if the two parties did not base their platforms on solid American planks and did not put America's interests above foreign interests.[128] Smith hoped to persuade Reynolds to make a nationwide speaking tour under the auspices of the America First Party. Reynolds refused to make the tour but endorsed a strict nationalist program and believed that a majority of the people in America favored America First views.[129]

Long enamored with Smith, Reynolds continued his association with him throughout 1943 and 1944. He wrote letters to several individuals in defense of Smith and told one woman that Smith was a "real, genuine American who loves his country better than any other country in the world, and I do not believe that I can pay a man a higher compliment than that."[130] He decried Walter Winchell's charge that Smith was a Nazi propagandist. "Nothing could be further from the truth. I know of no better American in this country."[131]

Reynolds, while agitated over the charges by Winchell, did not take immediate action but agreed that Winchell was "doing a lot of harm to the war effort." When he heard that Smith had filed a defamation of character lawsuit against Winchell,

Reynolds expressed his pleasure as well as his anti-Semitism at a suit "against that rat-kike Winchell." When he returned to Washington, Reynolds planned to have Martin Dies and his House Un-American Activities Committee investigate and expose Winchell. Reynolds wrote Smith in disgust: "Good loyal native born American citizens being libeled by alien Communists, now isn't that something?"[132]

Reynolds also denounced the book *Under Cover*, by John Roy Carlson, as nothing but a recapitulation of a lot of false charges and lies made over the years.[133] Reynolds knew that the assault by Carlson contained enough damaging information that a revival of the charges would further deflate his political image. So Reynolds did nothing.

When the *Daily Worker* also attacked Reynolds for his support of Smith's *Cross and the Flag* and, by implication, his agreement with Smith's pro-Nazi program, Reynolds claimed that there was a communist conspiracy against him.[134] There was, of course, no conspiracy to "get" Reynolds because there was no need for such a plot. Reynolds was simply trying to gain sympathy as a victim of a communist attack, but his tactic did not work.

Despite all the negative publicity, as late as one month before he withdrew from the race, Reynolds continued to cozy up to Gerald L. K. Smith, who remained his closest confidant on the right. Throughout 1943, Smith praised Reynolds as a defender of American independence and published his speeches.[135] Smith wrote that wherever he spoke, his audiences hated the idea of a world government and that "the mere mention of your name brings tumultuous applause."[136]

Other organizations also admired Reynolds and touted him for president. A group in Boston, headed by attorney Albert R. McKussick had a similar goal and set up the Reynolds for President Clubs.[137] Edward J. Smythe, chairman of the Protestant War Veterans in New York, wrote the Reynolds for President Club in Boston for some flyers and announced that he would stand with Bob Reynolds to defeat the "Jew" New Deal.[138]

While Reynolds was flattered by all the attention, the talk of Reynolds for president brought an immediate response from his favorite journalist, Nell Battle Lewis. Lewis did not believe that anyone took Gerald Smith's third-party aspirations seriously and found the idea of Bob Reynolds as a presidential nominee "entirely fantastic." Lewis believed that Reynolds was about to bolt the Democratic Party but did not care which way he hopped—"into the arms of his buddy Smith or into the Republican bosom." The only important thing, concluded Lewis, was that he had relieved the state of further embarrassment by withdrawal from the Senate.[139] The *Asheville Citizen* dismissed his chances for the presidency since as a representative of the people he was a "disgraceful misfit."[140]

Lewis's prediction that Reynolds was about to depart the Democratic Party was verified by the November 1943 issue of the *National Record*. In this issue Reynolds blasted the Democratic Party, concluded that the New Deal was dead, and hoped for a Republican Congress and a Republican president in the November 1944 election.[141] Reynolds now completed his break with the Democratic Party after basing his career on the promise of the New Deal and the genius of Roosevelt. His negative comments on the New Deal and his friendship with Gerald L. K. Smith showed that at the end of his career, Reynolds had lost his way—he had self-destructed. Because he could not be reelected to the Senate, Our Bob planned for vindication on the national stage. Unfortunately, the only people interested in him were the disciples of right-wing fringe groups.

Rumors circulated in the corridors of the Senate that Reynolds, Burton K. Wheeler, and others who opposed Roosevelt's policies were preparing to launch a third party composed of all Republicans and Democrats who wanted the country out of international affairs after the war.[142] These rumors were well founded, and in 1944 Reynolds would form a third party called the American Nationalist Committee of Independent Voters.

CHAPTER TWELVE

[The End of a Career]

Despite his decision not to run for reelection, Bob Reynolds began his last year as a United States senator with the same jaunty demeanor that had characterized his previous eleven years. He had not lost his sense of humor and still enjoyed some prestige as chairman of the Military Affairs Committee.

In early January 1944, rumors circulated in North Carolina that Reynolds still might make the race.[1] Apparently Reynolds had breezed into a committee meeting complaining that his office was full of North Carolina constituents. When asked why he bothered with them if he were not running for reelection, Reynolds replied that he had not actually decided whether or not to run. A Senate colleague presented a logical explanation for the rumor. Reynolds had been dropping from the limelight since his announcement to forgo the race, and to regain the spotlight, he began hinting that he might change his mind. Reynolds, claimed his colleague, had no intention of running in spite of hints to the contrary and was just creating a little publicity for himself.[2]

Allen Drury, an astute news reporter, verified this view after overhearing Reynolds in conversation with Senator Henry Cabot Lodge. Reynolds, whom Drury described as "a pretty likeable character of a certain fulsome Southern school," had responded to Lodge's query about what had been happening in his life. Reynolds replied, "Nothin' much, Henreh, 'cept they's a lot uh pressuh bein' brawt to beah to make me run again." Lodge laughed, and then Reynolds paused a second before adding, "Of coahse, Ah'm the wuhn who'se puttin' on most of it, myse'f. Guess the on'y thing Ah can do 'bout it is bow to the pressuh and run."[3]

Drury, fascinated by Reynolds's display of charm and effusiveness, followed the North Carolinian as he went about his duties. Drury observed Reynolds talking with Senator Clare Boothe Luce and noted that Reynolds was always in his element when beautiful ladies were around. Reynolds, according to Drury, enjoyed constantly bowing, scraping, and playing the "gracious and fulsome squire." On one occasion, after the dapper Reynolds had appeared on the Senate floor, Drury remarked to a fellow reporter, "You've got to hand it to Honorable Bob. There's something about him." "There's something about him, all right," agreed Drury's companion, "but it isn't honorable."[4]

Drury got to know Reynolds well enough in two years of reporting on the Senate to offer an interesting assessment of the man. He saw Reynolds not as a clown but as a "shrewd, sardonic, clever man, who accepts the appellation of fop and the derogatory of 'Buncombe Bob' with impassive suavity, secure in the knowledge that they will induce in the public mind just the attitude of amused contempt he needs to foster his purposes."

During his final year in the Senate, Reynolds managed to introduce another alien bill and to speak out against some New Deal legislation. Otherwise, his legislative efforts were confined to his duties as chairman of the Military Affairs Committee. Reynolds remained committed to winning the war as well as converting America to a peacetime economy. Worried about the problem of unemployed veterans at the conclusion of the war, he cosponsored a veteran's bonus bill. His bill, however, was eventually discarded in favor of the G.I. Bill of 1944, which offered educational training, unemployment aid and insurance, loans for home purchases, and mustering-out pay.[5]

A key item on the agenda of the Military Affairs Committee was the Austin-Wadsworth Bill, which was designed to set up compulsory military training. Although the bill had little chance of passage, Reynolds held hearings and asked Joseph C. Grew, former ambassador to Japan, to appear before the committee. Grew supported the adoption of a national service law. Reynolds warned that the national service bill was a step toward creating a totalitarian state in America. Grew responded by admitting that the plan represented an effort to use total war production but that the process would not make the United States a totalitarian power. The bill eventually died in committee, and Reynolds did not have to vote against a bill that he considered dangerous to American democracy.[6]

Senator Reynolds persevered in pursuing the administration's military goals, but he continued to oppose any postwar commitments on the part of the United States. Reynolds strongly disapproved of a resolution authorizing $1.3 billion as the country's contribution to the United Nations Relief and Rehabilitation Administration (UNRRA), a program to provide aid to civilians in liberated territories. Reynolds thought that before America paid such a huge sum for European relief, the United States ought to rehabilitate its own people. Reynolds exclaimed: "Stalin is standing up for Russia. Churchill for Britain. Reynolds is for America."[7]

Senator Reynolds backed an amendment reducing the American commitment to UNRRA by $1 billion and placing the American Red Cross in charge of administering the fund. Reynolds, "with his face redder than ever . . . and flowing hair swinging from side to side in emphasis,"[8] unleashed a rip-roaring denunciation of the UNRRA. He complained that America would end up paying two-thirds of the cost of UNRRA and would be unable to care for its own wounded veterans when they returned home. His speech had little impact, and his amendment failed. The UNRRA measure, with the original appropriation, passed the Senate by a vote of 47–14, with Reynolds voting no.[9]

From August 21 until October 7, 1945, representatives of the United States, Great Britain, the Soviet Union, and China attended the Dumbarton Oaks Conference in Washington, D.C., to discuss postwar developments. The conferees drafted a charter for a permanent postwar international organization to maintain world peace and security. The tentative proposals (known as the Dumbarton Oaks Plan) served as the basis of the United Nations Charter.[10]

Breckinridge Long, the assistant secretary of state and a major player in the Dumbarton Oaks meetings, feared that the isolationists in the Senate would defeat any movement for an international organization. During the Dumbarton Oaks Conference, Long expected a partisan attack orchestrated by Senator Arthur Vandenberg, who could muster the support of at least fifteen to eighteen Republicans and five Democrats, including Bob Reynolds.[11]

Reynolds, however, waited until the Dumbarton Oaks Conference adjourned before attacking the plan as one that would "turn a war for liberation into an aftermath of subjugation."[12] Reynolds theorized that the internationalists would destroy national sovereignty and national self-determination by proclaiming a one-world government. Although Reynolds knew that the distances between cities could be quickly covered by an airplane, this did not mean that ideology, culture, history, and love of country could be so easily bridged. "All the swift flyers in the world," announced Reynolds, "cannot mongrelize the Yankee Doodle American or douse him in the stinking stew of compulsory foreign alliances AS LONG AS THE DISTANCE BETWEEN INDEPENDENCE HALL AND THE KREMLIN REMAINS INCALCULABLE."[13] Reynolds believed that the Dumbarton Oaks proposal placed too much power in the hands of the larger countries and would split the world into spheres of domination. The end result would surely be the imposition of unwanted political ideologies (read Communism) on certain smaller countries.[14]

The junior senator from North Carolina wanted the world to know that the Allies, by condoning Russia's demands for territory, were accepting the conquest and partition of smaller nations. These policies were helping to create a powerful Russia that might someday destroy the United States. America, charged Reynolds, was setting up Joseph Stalin, another great aggressor, in place of Hitler and had to stop Russia before it completely dominated Europe and Asia. Communism, said Reynolds, was strong and widespread, and the United States had to be on its guard.[15]

Despite his accurate assessment of the threat posed by Russia, Reynolds's warnings were ignored by the Roosevelt administration. Reynolds knew that very little could be done short of armed intervention to prevent Russian territorial gains, but he wanted to make certain that the government and the American people did not underestimate the threat of Communism.

Throughout 1944, radical groups continued to mention the Asheville native as a possible candidate for president of the United States. The Sons of George Washington and the Sons of the Far West endorsed Reynolds for president,[16] while Gerald L. K. Smith resumed his campaign to persuade Reynolds to announce for president. Smith wrote in January 1944 that he had recently returned from Chicago and found a strong sentiment among his friends for "Reynolds for President." A Roosevelt-Willkie race, surmised Smith, would certainly mean a third party, with Reynolds as the probable standard-bearer.[17]

Reynolds found the support for president "very flattering" and praised the work of Smith's America First Party in keeping alive the spirit that would save America. He again lauded Smith for his courage in speaking out on behalf of America when it was "being destroyed by internationalists, crack-pots, and communists."[18] Reynolds, however, had no intention of joining the America Firsters.[19] He did not plan to attend any of the conventions[20] but did hope to influence the foreign and domestic planks of both the Democratic Party and the Republican Party at their respective conventions.[21]

To that end, Reynolds sent a list of suggestions to John McCormack, chairman of the Platform Committee for the Democratic Party. These suggestions were a reprise of his political philosophy. He proposed an end to immigration to preserve jobs for returning veterans and opposed any alliances by which American sovereignty might be endangered. He also wanted all labor unions to be registered with the federal government and asked that all aliens, communists, Nazis, and any member of any subversive organization be prohibited from holding office in a labor union. Finally, he called for an end to waste in government and a reduction in taxes after the end of the war.[22] The Democratic Party generally disregarded his suggestions.

But Heinz Eulau, writing in the New Republic, reproached Reynolds for cultivating fundamentalist preachers such as Smith, Gerald Winrod, and Harvey Springer in order to tap into their army of believers for his nationalist cause. Eulau saw these fanatic, authoritarian fundamentalists as predisposed toward fascism. He described their beliefs as "anti-Soviet, anti-British, anti-New Deal, anti-Semitic, anti-international understanding, isolationist, chauvinistic and purposefully demagogic." The writer considered Reynolds and the fundamentalist preachers as dangers to American democracy and feared that they would join with the out-and-out fascists in America to create a formidable force.[23]

Reynolds resented the attacks on him, but the indictments merely strengthened his resolve. No longer beholden to voters, Our Bob pursued his beliefs with renewed vigor. He told Gerald Smith that he was "getting sick and tired of being called a rabble rouser and being smeared as pro-Nazi" just because he had tried to keep the country out of war and the aliens from America's shores.[24] Reynolds also defended Smith when he was called a rabble-rouser. Reynolds thought the attacks "were either lack of common sense, or just downright foolishness or perhaps it is jealousy."[25]

Strongly influenced by Smith and other splinter groups, Reynolds began to see himself as the national leader of the isolationists. To this end, in June 1944 Reynolds organized a bipartisan group called the American Nationalist Committee of Independent Voters. Serving as temporary national chairman, Reynolds planned to hold a national convention in 1944, when a permanent leader would be chosen.

The organization's purpose was to stop the drift toward internationalism by forming nationwide political clubs that would elect individuals with isolationist viewpoints to Congress. Reynolds denied any intention of setting up a third party, explaining that he merely wanted to give nationalists a voice in their government. He had been inspired to set up this group as a result of some "25,000 letters" that approved of his writings and speeches.[26]

The American Nationalist Committee of Independent Voters was made up of volunteers who were interested in putting America first. Pledge cards were circulated throughout the country, and Reynolds planned to have chapters organized in every city. The local units would be limited to ten members (a technique used by Reynolds's Vindicators) so that subversive elements would not be able to "worm" their way into the organization.

According to its official organ, the *National Record*, the committee

1. does not believe in any alliances that would interfere with the independent action of the United Sates.
2. does not believe in anything that will destroy the sovereignty of the United States.
3. opposes creation of a postwar international police force to maintain peace; when the war is won, all American troops should return home.
4. believes that the United States should help rehabilitate the world as much as possible without pauperizing itself.
5. believes that all countries should choose for themselves the type of government each desires.

Reynolds hoped his organization would rescue the country from the internationalists and the do-gooders who had pushed America to the brink of bankruptcy, radicalism, and destruction. Reynolds thought that America could be saved from autocratic government only by "the courage and fortitude with which

America holds fast to the things of past spiritual and tested values. The hour is here—WHERE IS THE MAN?"[27]

Obviously, "the man" was none other than Bob Reynolds, who, despite protestations to the contrary, did have visions of leading a third party in America. Reynolds's pipe dream had been fostered by the flattery and adulation of a few right-wing nationalists. In despair over the end of his political career, Reynolds simply could not bow out of the spotlight. He took the tattered bouquets of praise to heart and somehow pictured himself as the savior of America.

Reynolds sincerely believed that his message of Americanism would thrill his compatriots. They would then rally to his cause as he waved his banner of nationalism and raced about the land to thrust his sword into the flanks of alien enemies. Reynolds planned to deliver Americans from the abyss of internationalism and lead them into triumphant nationalism.

The North Carolinian's hopes for the resurrection of his political career were, at best, totally unrealistic. His new organization was merely a rehash of the discredited Vindicators. Eager to revive his political influence, however, Reynolds continued to fraternize with Gerald Smith, Gerald Winrod, and other fundamentalists. He was either too self-absorbed to get the message, or his desire for recognition was so great that it clouded his judgment. Reynolds apparently thought that he could succeed in a national election when he had failed at a state level. He assumed that the Midwest and other areas of the country were more isolationist and nationalistic and would be more receptive to his message. He could not have been more wrong.

Throughout 1944, still oblivious to criticism, Reynolds continued to promote his new organization. He intermittently published the *National Record* and inserted articles into the *Congressional Record*. Reynolds wrote frequent pieces warning of the menace of Communism, Nazis, spies, and fifth columnists. In March 1944, Reynolds claimed that he had achieved most of his political objectives. Aliens were now registered and fingerprinted, and the Communist Party, according to Reynolds, had recently announced that it would no longer serve as a political party. Therefore, according to Reynolds, the Party had been outlawed.

With these objectives achieved, Reynolds announced a major new goal—reducing federal taxes—which he hoped would appeal to a broad spectrum of Americans. Lower taxes would be achieved by dismissing several hundred thousand government employees (bureaucrats to Reynolds) and by spending only the money necessary to win the war. The federal government, declared Reynolds, should be prohibited from taking more than 25 percent of any individual's income.[28]

At this juncture, the short-time senator was searching for a popular national issue to boost membership in his organization. It was incongruous to see an old New Dealer, who built his career on getting jobs for constituents, advocate the firing of thousands of these individuals. Reynolds never objected to high income taxes before he married a millionaire and was personally affected by confiscatory taxes. When he was masquerading as a poor man of the people, he sang a different tune.

Reynolds did get some cursory support for his program from readers of the *National Record*. But with names and addresses omitted from the letters, it is entirely possible that Our Bob wrote some of them, for the letters often contained the same rhetorical flourishes used by Reynolds. A letter from G. P. of California was fairly typical: "*The National Record*, produced by Robert Rice Reynolds, Doctor of American Philosophy, is capable of sterilizing and healing the wounds and sores on the body of the United States which have been caused by the spread of the International Plague, a disease born and nurtured in the slums of Europe and carried into America in the unclean minds of refugees termed 'intellectual superiors' by alien-lovers, Communist coddlers, and foreign fawners, and the army of mountebanks who, while waxing fat on the blood, sweat, and tears of the American taxpayers, are gnawing, like rats, at the very foundation of this great independent republic."[29]

Despite a few congratulatory letters, public opinion once again turned against Reynolds. His old friends, the Veterans of Foreign Wars (VFW), launched an angry attack against him. The VFW, Department of California, conducted a formal investigation of the American Nationalist Committee of Independent Voters on August 9, 1944. A spokesman for the VFW said that it was an impartial inquiry and that Reynolds had been invited to attend but had chosen to send a statement in defense of his views.

The findings of the VFW investigation, which were made public, noted that there were articles in the *American Vindicator* and the *National Record* that condemned America's allies in the war and opposed selective service. These articles, according to the VFW, weakened America's war effort. The Board of Inquiry condemned Reynolds for his association with such men as Gerald Smith, for his pro-Nazi behavior, and for his "sly and devious" anti-Semitism. Reynolds, concluded the inquiry, continued to preach his racial and religious prejudice, and the American people had to be warned against postwar self-seekers who would exploit the unrest of returning veterans. The Board of Inquiry recommended that all members of the VFW and citizens of the United States reject Reynolds's new committee and oppose his "self-vaunted ambition."[30]

Reynolds gave a rather tepid reply to the VFW charges. He admitted his opposition to aliens and increased immigration and also agreed that before Pearl Harbor he did everything in his power to keep America out of war. However, since the war began he had fully cooperated with the government in its efforts to win the war. Senator Reynolds assumed that the pro-fascist charges resulted from his opposition to war and to Communism. He also said that he believed in tolerance and that the charges of racial and religious prejudice came from his campaign against aliens. Reynolds ended his reply by reminding the VFW that he had always been a friend and would continue to be one despite the "unwarranted charges" against him.[31]

Reynolds did not effectively answer the specific allegations against him. Rather, he restated his noninterventionist views and treated the entire episode as some sort of aberration. Reynolds simply could not face reality. When the VFW, an early supporter, turned against him with such an organized and telling broadside, Reynolds should have realized, at long last, how unpopular his views were.

To the contrary, in January 1945 he announced the formation of the Nationalist Party—a true third party. Reynolds said that the new party was necessary because the Democratic Party had been "taken over by Communists, Reds, and pinks" and the Republican Party, which had little to offer and mimicked the Democrats, was now dead.[32]

The fundamental purposes of the Nationalist Party were similar to those of Reynolds's other organizations—America first, maintenance of national sovereignty, no international commitments, an end to all immigration, and the combating of anti-American ideologies such as communism. Two notable additions to the list were opposition to free trade and the restoration of states' rights.[33]

Reynolds's Nationalist Party, however, was headed for trouble. On June 20, 1945, the *Raleigh News and Observer* reported that the magazine *PM* had uncovered Reynolds's plan to finance his new party with the assistance of large contributions from rich industrialists. *PM* reprinted a detailed story about one Jack Williams (an alias for Joe McWilliams, a notorious anti-Semite, pro-Nazi crony of Fritz Kuhn, who had been indicted for sedition) who visited several Cleveland industrialists to solicit contributions for the Nationalist Party. McWilliams produced a letter from Reynolds that requested a favorable hearing for his representative. Reynolds immediately denied any connection to McWilliams, but *PM* rejected his response and denounced Reynolds as a dangerous person.[34]

The *Chicago Sun* also reported that a flying wedge of professional, high-pressure salesmen had been putting the bite on Chicago businesspeople on behalf of the Nationalist Party. The *Sun* described the new party, which had the support of the Hearst newspapers, as offering a fusion of southern anti-New Dealers, midwestern isolationists, and the right kind of anti-Dewey Republicans. According to the paper, Reynolds's solicitors told businesspeople that the contribution would be tax deductible even though the organization was not recognized by the Bureau of Internal Revenue as a bona fide political party for tax purposes. Joe McWilliams, when interviewed by the *Sun*, said that he thought Reynolds's new party was a wonderful thing, but he denied having any connection with it. Although Reynolds again claimed to know nothing about solicitations, a Chicago entrepreneur made public a letter from Reynolds touting McWilliams.[35]

The *Worcester (Mass.) Daily Telegram* reported that the assistant attorney general of Massachusetts had investigated and found illegal solicitations for the Nationalist Party in Boston. Reynolds denied that his party was seeking funds,[36] but in Indianapolis, Indiana, the man asking for funds was J. Victor Malone, a persuasive, professional promoter and on the payroll as Reynolds's chief fund-raiser.[37]

Intrigued by all the stories of illegal solicitation reported in newspapers around the country, Eugene Segal, a staff writer for Scripps-Howard, published an exposé of Reynolds's fund-raising racket. Segal accused Reynolds of capitalizing on prejudice and discontent to weld dissident groups in the country into a powerful third party. Segal wrote that the Nationalist Party had fashioned a program of "racial hatred, exploitation of racial strife, and glorification of dictatorship."

Segal also disclosed that the Nationalist Party, in search of members, had infiltrated the ranks of labor unions, farmers organizations, veterans groups, and certain churches. They took over the National Farmer's Guild, a right-wing offshoot of the Farmer's Union. The Nationalist Party used the United Sons of America, a Ku Klux Klan clone, to organize labor unions with its "Old Glory" clubs. The Nationalists, continued Segal, were antiblack, anti-Semitic, anti-Catholic, and antialien. Gerald L. K. Smith; Mrs. Lyrl Clark Van Hyning, head of We, the Mothers Mobilized for America; the Reverend Gerald Winrod of Kansas, the "Jayhawk Nazi"; and the Reverend Harvey Springer were the individuals who championed the party, spouting the party line while retaining their autonomy.[38]

The Segal articles, although a badly written hatchet job, revealed the fund-raising irregularities of the Nationalist Party. There was just enough truthful information in the stories to discredit Reynolds's latest organization.

Readers in North Carolina were outraged by the disclosures. Charles J. Shields was ashamed that North Carolina "could spawn such an ingrate, such a clown, such a boob." Shields regretted that Reynolds was still running around the country with a mob of malcontents expecting the American people to fall "for his vitriolic vacuums again." He concluded that if Reynolds expected the American people to follow him, "his swell [sic] head is due for a bloated burst and let us hope the putrid political ideas he is trying to father in his constant dotage will pour down over him and become his shroud."[39]

Reynolds responded to the articles not in a public journal or newspaper but in the *National Record*. Reynolds said Segal's articles drew false conclusions and distorted facts and figures in an effort to smear the good name of the Nationalist Party. The charge that the Nationalists were anti-Semitic, asserted Reynolds, was without foundation, as many of his closest friends were of the Jewish faith. The majority of Jews in the United States, declared Reynolds, were opposed to immigration restriction and were prowar before 1941. These differences of opinion, protested Reynolds, did not make the Nationalists anti-Semitic.[40]

Reynolds also argued that not only was he not anti-Catholic, but he also had praised Catholics as doing more to combat ungodly Communism than any other religious organization. Reynolds condemned Segal for calling him antiblack, for the Nationalist Party was for all Americans, regardless of race, color, or creed. Reynolds had been brought up in the South and "admired as a whole the members of the colored race." Reynolds claimed to have been supported by a very large majority of black voters in every political race he ran. He had gained their confidence by treating everyone equally.

Reynolds's answer lacked credibility and detail. He neglected to mention that his companions in the Nationalist Party, such as Winrod, Springer, and Smith, were notoriously anti-Catholic and anti-Semitic. Reynolds himself, according to many sources, especially his writing in the *American Vindicator* and the *National Record*, proved he was an anti-Semite despite the fact that he had many Jewish friends. Reynolds had no strong personal animus toward blacks—although he refused to allow them in his organizations and opposed giving them equal rights—or Catholics.

On this occasion, however, Reynolds learned a lesson. When the HUAC began to investigate the Nationalist Party, Reynolds realized the jig was up. Although HUAC found nothing wrong with his group,[41] Reynolds obviously believed that the HUAC investigation, coupled with the California VFW charges and the articles by Eugene Segal, had done irreparable damage to his cause. On September 27, 1945, a contrite Reynolds ended publication of the *National Record* and refused to accept any more subscriptions to the paper.[42] Thus Our Bob's attempt to form a viable third party in America came to an inglorious and ignominious end.

Stymied in his effort to resurrect his political career, Reynolds spent the last days in the Senate whiling away the hours as chairman of the Military Affairs Committee. He was, concluded Allen Drury, at his fulsome best as his tenure came to an end. Drury described Reynolds as he bowed in all the witnesses appearing before the committee, telling them "how much we 'preciate havin' you with us, havin' you take youah valu'ble time to come up heah and give us the ben'fit of youah 'sperience."[43]

Reynolds courteously assisted his successor, Clyde R. Hoey, with his transition to the United States Senate. He offered to help Hoey with any matters in which Hoey might need assistance and followed through with great concern.[44] When Allen Drury saw the old-fashioned, businesslike Hoey in the Senate, he wrote that Hoey appeared to be "like a breath of fresh air after the effulgent blast of his dapper predecessor."[45]

On December 20, 1944, the junior senator delivered his final oration. He took a parting shot at international cooperation, stating that the Dumbarton Oaks agreement would set the world back 120 years. Reynolds ended his speech by noting that it made him very sad to depart from the Senate and disassociate himself from the members of that body, because he had enjoyed fine friendships with all his colleagues. They had often differed vigorously, but Reynolds recognized that the Senate was a great forum of debate for the benefit of the American people and there had never been any unpleasantness as far as personal relationships were concerned.[46] With these remarks, Reynolds ended his service as a United States senator.

Many voters and constituents were relieved to see Reynolds out of the Senate, but many of his colleagues were genuinely fond of Bob Reynolds. Even the *Raleigh News and Observer*, one of his most bitter critics over the years, had a kind editorial on his last day in office. The paper reviewed Reynolds's career from his early days as a staunch New Dealer to his stance as a fervent isolationist. The *News and Observer* praised his steadfast support of war measures after Pearl Harbor and lauded his spirit of courtesy and friendliness. "Nobody could fail to like the genial Senator Reynolds, for he has been the soul of kindness to all his constituents and served many in the years he has been in the Senate. North Carolinians wish for him happiness and hope before the shadows lengthen he will return to what 'Our Bob' calls the 'Land of the Sky.'"[47]

The *Winston-Salem Journal* also remembered Reynolds favorably. The paper insisted that his magnetic personality, a remarkable faculty for remembering names, and his strong loyalty to his friends made Reynolds one of the most popular men in Congress. As a fair-minded critic, the *Journal* admitted that Reynolds had performed some good services for his country while in the Senate. He had supported the relief, recovery, and reform bills of the New Deal and had cooperated with the administration as head of the Military Affairs Committee.[48]

His hometown paper, the *Asheville Citizen*, marked his passage from politics with the most vindictive and brutal editorial of Reynolds's career. The *Citizen*, in commenting on Reynolds's valedictory speech, wrote that he "was his faithful, intemperate self. He delivered a lecture fantastic for its narrowness of mind and paucity of information." The paper continued: "North Carolina rues the day it allowed its scruples to be overcome by a low-velocity politician who has consistently misrepresented the state. It remembers to its shame a record of obstruction, cynicism, and hate-spieling so discredible that the author dared not submit himself to the wrath of the electors." The *Citizen* summed up its harangue against Reynolds by saying that in his record in the Senate there was "not a glimmer of sober and constructive thought, not an original piece of legislation, not a single appeal to nobility of sentiment, not a vestige of that quality which gives the citizen pride in the stature of his elected representative no matter how much he may disagree with him."[49]

Thus Bob Reynolds left the Senate after twelve tumultuous years of service during one of the most critical periods in American history. His years in the Senate, 1933–1945, spanned the Roosevelt era and the New Deal, the Great Depression, and World War II. If he had not been a great senator, at least he had been colorful and entertaining. He had the ability, as did Will Rogers, to help America laugh its way through a depression. Reynolds, however, was not a comedian but a United States senator. When he left the Senate, he was so unpopular in his home state that he took up residence in Maryland to begin a new career in the practice of law.

CHAPTER THIRTEEN

[The Last Hurrah]

Bob Reynolds's first order of business after leaving the Senate, as one might expect, was a vacation. On January 20, 1945, Reynolds and his wife, Evie, visited Cuba and the Caribbean, finally spending three months at the McLean family's estate in West Palm Beach, Florida.[1] Although independently wealthy owing to his wife's fortune, Reynolds initially decided to return to the practice of law. Prior to his departure from the Senate, he agreed to open a law firm in Washington, D.C., with his former secretary, Wesley McDonald. They planned to practice general and administrative law, primarily representing clients before government agencies.[2] Reynolds, however, quickly became bored and applied himself to the law only intermittently.

Meanwhile, the former senator and his wife had been occupying a basement apartment in Washington. Mrs. Evalyn McLean had invited them to stay in her mansion, but Reynolds declined, declaring: "No southern gentlemen would live on a woman's money." But Reynolds then took Evie's money and purchased a twelve-hundred-acre farm near Waldorf, Maryland. Reynolds explained to reporters that the farm had lots of timber on it and he planned to harvest and sell the pulpwood—"I'm farming forests."[3] Predictably, Reynolds lost interest in his role as a gentleman farmer and moved on to other pursuits.

While searching for something to keep him occupied, Reynolds and his wife returned briefly to "Friendship," the McLean estate, to live with Evie's mother, who had recently fractured a kneecap in a fall. On September 20, 1946, Bob Reynolds had lunch with his wife, and she appeared in good spirits. Reynolds then left to go to their farm in Waldorf.

After he left, Evie returned to her room for her customary afternoon nap and asked not to be disturbed until her husband returned. She then locked herself in her room and took an overdose of sleeping pills. When her mother could not reach Evie by an internal phone system at 2:30 P.M., Mrs. McLean became alarmed and summoned Dr. B. W. Leonard, the family physician, who was already in the house on a routine call to examine Mrs. McLean. When Evie McLean did not answer their calls, Dr. Leonard and a butler broke down Evie's locked door and found her unconscious in bed. Dr. Leonard worked for over an hour trying to revive her and then pronounced Evie McLean Reynolds dead at 4:16 P.M. Mrs. McLean informed Bob Reynolds, who rushed back to the estate.

Dr. Leonard had noticed a bottle of sleeping pills next to Evie's bed and told investigators that death might have been caused by an overdose. Police officials, however, announced that the young woman had died of "apparent natural causes," and Coroner A. Magruder McDonald issued a temporary death certificate that listed congestive heart failure as the cause of death. McDonald, however, indicated that he would not issue a final certificate until he had done a chemical analysis of the sleeping tablets found near the body.[4]

After an autopsy, Coroner McDonald issued a verdict of accidental death on October 4, 1946. The cause of death, concluded McDonald, was "acute congestive heart failure due to barbiturate poisoning. Accidental overdoses taken by one who was in the habit of using this drug."[5] McDonald believed that Evie McLean Reynolds had not intended to kill herself. She was addicted to barbiturates and, in his opinion, had simply lost track of how many pills she had taken.[6]

Bob Reynolds's daughter Frances Reynolds Oertling corroborated McDonald's version of Evie's death. Oertling explained that Evie had developed an inferiority complex from living with her dominant, flamboyant mother. She had frequently been depressed and despondent. Her husband tried to get her to see a psychiatrist, but she had never agreed to seek professional help. Evie had been addicted to pills for some time, divulged Oertling, and had taken too many pills several times before.[7]

Before her death Evie refused to admit that she had any mental problems. On July 6, 1946, she had her lawyer, Abe Fortas, draw up a statement in which she asked her husband, mother, and doctors to continue medical treatment for a weakened physical condition until she had regained her strength. Evie wrote that it was understood that she would stay in her mother's home during treatment. "It is also understood," continued the statement, "that there is no question whatsoever of my mental condition. I am being treated solely for my run down physical condition."[8]

One finds it difficult to determine if Evie committed suicide, because there was no note. Despite her protestations, she had been having severe psychological problems for some time. According to Hubert H. Rand, because of Evie's addiction to barbiturates, her mother locked the pills in a safe at Friendship. The day Evie died, her mother inadvertently left the safe unlocked, which gave Evie access to the pills. Rand claimed that Evie had been extremely depressed and had decided to commit suicide when the opportunity presented itself. She died with a picture of Bob Reynolds clutched to her breast.[9]

T. Lamar Caudle, another close friend of Reynolds, saw the couple frequently. Caudle did not know what made her depressed, for they seemed to have a happy marriage despite their age difference. Caudle surmised that "whatever it was, it caused her to take her life."[10]

There was always the possibility that Evie took an overdose by mistake, but the fact that she had locked the door to her room and had died with Bob Reynolds's picture on her breast points toward a suicide. On every other overdose she had been found in time. Her previous attempts were probably cries for help—she wanted to be saved. On September 20, 1946, she apparently did not want to be rescued. Regardless of the final circumstances, Bob Reynolds had once again lost a wife and now had the responsibility for raising a four-year-old daughter.

Newspapers and the press trumpeted the fact that Evie Reynolds's death marked another tragic episode for the owners of the ill-fated Hope Diamond. The legend of the curse of the Hope Diamond began when the diamond was stolen from the eye of an idol in India. The theft caused the god to place a curse not only on the robber but also on all subsequent owners of the diamond. This story was pure fiction, but the legend of a curse or bad luck always followed the Hope.

The first recorded mention of the diamond was in 1830 when Henry Philip Hope, a London banker, purchased it from a London diamond merchant. The Hope, a fine blue diamond weighing forty-four carats, was surrounded by sixteen diamonds and was suspended from a necklace containing forty-six more diamonds. Eventually the gem found its way to the Cartier firm in Paris, which sold it to Evelyn Walsh McLean for the sum of $180,000 in 1918. In her book *Father Struck It Rich*, Evelyn wrote that initially she did not let her friends or children touch the gem because of the superstitions surrounding the stone. Later she took it to a priest to be blessed. From that day forward, Evelyn wore the diamond as a lucky charm. Although she considered the stone to be lucky, whenever bad luck befell her, she always thought of the curse.

Although Mrs. McLean's public life seemed happy and exciting, she had experienced her share of sorrow. Her brother Vinson had been killed in a car accident, and six years after she purchased the diamond, her nine-year-old son, named Vinson after her deceased brother, was struck by a car and killed. Owing to her unremitting anguish over the death of her son Vinson, Mrs. McLean became addicted to morphine. Then her marriage to Edward B. McLean ended in a bitter divorce, with Mrs. McLean accusing her husband of adultery. Edward McLean, deeply involved in the Teapot Dome scandal, eventually was declared insane and died in a mental institution in 1941. Finally, in 1946, Mrs. McLean had to face the tragedy of her daughter's death, from which she never recovered.[11]

Evie left an estate of $497,000. Since she died without a will, Bob Reynolds received one-third of the estate, and their four-year-old daughter, Mamie Spears Reynolds, received the remaining two-thirds. Mamie Spears also inherited her mother's one-third interest in a $10 million trust fund that had been set up by Mamie's great-grandfather John R. McLean. The trust fund brought her an estimated yearly income of $400,000. Reynolds was named administrator and guardian of his daughter's extraordinary wealth.[12]

John R. McLean's will provided no specific allowance for the support and maintenance of Mamie. Reynolds was allowed to disburse the funds but had to report his expenditures to the trustees of the will. Reynolds received a 2.5 percent commission on his daughter's guardianship funds (he was entitled to 10 percent but set the rate lower) and received approximately twenty-two thousand dollars as his commission in 1949.

On October 19, 1949, Reynolds reported an accumulated income of $282,526 in his ward's account. His daughter's gross income had been $313,041 in 1949. He also reported that he had been spending around twenty thousand dollars per year to provide his daughter with the appurtenances to which her financial and social position entitled her. He had hired a full-time governess, a cook, and at least one other servant to tend to her needs. And, one might surmise, her father's needs as well. He also spent money on food, the upkeep of an automobile, and swimming and horseback lessons.[13]

After his wife's death, Reynolds deserted Washington and returned to practice law and "raise apples" in his beloved Asheville. He and Mamie Spears took up residence in a rambling house atop Reynolds Mountain, named for his grandfather, Daniel Reynolds.[14]

Although retired from politics, Reynolds continued to give interviews and to express his unchanging views on the world situation. In 1946 Reynolds presciently identified Korea as the hot spot of the world and said he would not be surprised if a clash between the United States and Russia took place in Korea. He confessed to being upset that America paid for 90 percent of the cost of the United Nations. Uncle Sam is "already loaded with enough burdens without putting on his shoulders that task of caring for a snarling, bitter and ungrateful world."

Reynolds called Joseph Stalin a "great man" because he was looking after the Soviet people. Reynolds admitted that Stalin's dictatorship was as bad as Hitler's and that he did dominate Europe, facts that did not lessen Reynolds's admiration for his leadership.[15] Reynolds's approval of a brutal dictator was the same sort of muddle-headed thinking that had gotten him in trouble in 1944. Now, however, he did not have a Senate seat to protect.

Reynolds announced that America's entrance into World War II was a great mistake as it left the United States with a huge public debt. Reynolds remembered that his critics had said "that old Bob was a durn fool" for opposing the war, but World War II cost the United States many lives, much sorrow, and billions of dollars without achieving democracy, the Four Freedoms, or peace in the world. According to Reynolds, Stalin's domination of Russia indicated that America had substituted one dictator for another by exchanging Hitler for Stalin.

Reynolds also opposed the Marshall Plan (massive financial subsidies to countries in Western Europe to revive their economies and hold off the spread of communism) because it would deplete the resources of the United States—it would be like "pouring $20 million down a rat-hole." The plan would never work, because America could not buy people away from the communist ideology.[16] To the end, Reynolds persisted in his half-baked and illogical statements. Sure Stalin survived, but Europe had been freed from the scourge of Hitler. Democracy and freedom had been preserved, albeit at a great cost. One would think that a self-proclaimed patriot would have praised America's sacrifice, but Reynolds could focus only on the negative.

While pontificating on international politics, Reynolds learned that Evalyn Walsh McLean was gravely ill, and he rushed to Washington. McLean died of pneumonia at the age of sixty on April 26, 1947.[17]

Mrs. McLean's last will, dated November 13, 1946, gave Bob Reynolds use of her house (also named Friendship after her earlier estate) and all its furnishings at Wisconsin and R Streets in Georgetown. Reynolds could use the house during his lifetime, subject to the control of the trustees. If the house had to be sold and the income invested, decreed the will, then the income from these investments went to Reynolds. Mrs. McLean wrote that Reynolds had shown "such love and consideration for my daughter that he richly deserves to be fully considered in this matter."

The will provided that the greater part of her estate be left equally to her seven grandchildren. Her jewels were to be kept in trust until the youngest of her grandchildren, Mamie Spears Reynolds, reached the age of twenty-five. Mrs. McLean instructed trustees to provide adequately for Mamie Spears Reynolds until her twenty-fifth year and noted that Friendship and her jewels could be sold for this purpose.[18]

In a petition filed in Federal District Court by Thurman Arnold, her attorney, for probate of McLean's will, the value of her estate was estimated at $919,550, with debts of $174,000. The value of Friendship was put at $172,720, while the furnishings in her home were listed at $100,000. Her jewelry was formally appraised at $606,110.80, with the Star of India valued at $185,000 and the Hope Diamond assessed at $176,920.[19]

In March 1948, Reynolds sold the furnishings of Friendship at auction and also offered the house for sale or lease.[20] The house eventually sold, but the price received was not publicly announced. On March 27, 1949, district judge James W. Morris gave the executors permission to sell McLean's jewels so long as they sold for not less than $591,107. The trustees requested the sale to settle $300,000 in claims against the estate and because the gems were costing $12,000 per year in personal taxes. New York jeweler Harry Winston purchased the jewels for $611,500.[21] Winston donated the Hope Diamond to the Smithsonian Institution in 1958.[22]

Bob Reynolds regretted McLean's death, for he had been very fond of her. Her death made Reynolds a wealthy man, and he did not have to work for the rest of his life. The sale of Friendship and its furnishings, the commission he received for handling Mamie's money, and the extraordinary amount of money Mamie received yearly from her trust funds enabled him to retire to Reynolds Mountain and live the life of a country squire.

The old warhorse, of course, could never permanently leave the limelight. Few political observers believed that he could quit politics cold turkey and remain free of the opiate of electioneering. When Reynolds returned from Washington, D.C., to Asheville to practice law, both the *Washington Post* and the *Durham Morning Herald* reported to their readers that Reynolds's purpose in returning to North Carolina was to rebuild his political strength in order to challenge Senator Clyde R. Hoey in 1950.[23]

The two newspapers were right on target, because in 1949 Reynolds confided to his law partner, Irving C. Crawford, that he planned to run for the United States Senate in 1950.[24] He also tried to keep his Washington contacts open. He sent birthday greetings to President Harry Truman, his old Senate colleague, and the president responded with a thoughtful letter.[25]

Reynolds, at this juncture, planned to run against Senator Clyde R. Hoey, but fate intervened. On March 6, 1949, newly elected senator J. Melville Broughton, only two months into his term, collapsed and died from a massive heart attack.[26] Broughton's death had major political consequences for the state, and Governor W. Kerr Scott was faced with the unenviable task of appointing a new United States senator who would serve until the next scheduled election in May 1950.

Scott, a plainspoken, cigar-chewing dairy farmer from Haw River, knew that his appointment of Broughton's successor had implications far beyond that Senate seat. Broughton's untimely death had presented the maverick Scott an unrivaled opportunity to extend his influence in the state and the Democratic Party by naming a liberal senator friendly to his views. Scott intended to pick someone who would not only support his legislative program but also favor the national Democratic Party and the Truman administration.[27]

Whatever his choice, Scott would anger several political factions, so he delayed his appointment in order to consider all possible candidates. A political feeding frenzy then ensued, with candidates, their supporters, and press observers hungrily churning the political waters in quest of Scott's delectable prize.[28]

On March 23, 1949, in a move as unexpected as Broughton's death, Governor

Scott, who gloried in surprises, stunned all political observers in the state by appointing Dr. Frank Porter Graham, president of the consolidated University of North Carolina. The choice of Graham, a personal friend of Harry Truman and the foremost southern liberal of his time, was a move so astounding that for twenty-four hours nearly an entire generation of North Carolina politicians was struck dumb.[29]

Scott's decision drew commentary from nearly every national newspaper and journal of opinion. Within the state, the exuberance of Graham's supporters, who hailed the choice as brilliant, was partially nullified by the groans and lamentations of Graham's opponents—thus indicating that the governor's decision had the potential for spectacular political conflict. An overwhelming majority of North Carolina's press editorially endorsed Scott's selection, and hundreds of citizens, including Eleanor Roosevelt, President Harry Truman, and others, wrote to Scott in approval.[30]

As V. O. Key Jr. and W. J. Cash both observed, Frank Graham was a prominent educator and public servant who had contributed greatly to progressive reform in the South.[31] Kind and compassionate, Graham often stirred up controversy with his support of unpopular left-wing causes, and he joined scores of liberal and radical organizations. As a consequence of his public conduct and advocacy, he was a popular yet divisive figure, loved by his friends, besieged by his critics. Thus his candidacy would become, in part, a state referendum on his activist past.[32]

When Graham was sworn in as a United States senator on March 29, 1949, he immediately announced that he would be a candidate in 1950 for the remaining four years of Broughton's term.[33] Governor Scott pronounced Graham as unbeatable in the forthcoming contest and stated that he planned to take to the campaign trail in Graham's behalf.[34]

Unbeatable he might be, but unrivaled he would not be, as many commentators disagreed with Scott's assessment and thought Graham would have strong competition from conservatives in North Carolina. Potential candidates were already stirring. No less an authority than Bob Reynolds predicted that the forthcoming campaign would find "the woods full of candidates." Reynolds made it clear in March 1949 that he would not be among them as he was having too good a time living in seclusion on Reynolds Mountain, undisturbed by individuals seeking political favors.[35]

Reynolds, despite his denial of interest, planned to run for office again. Another law partner, Paul Teal, thought that the former senator was very lonely on Reynolds Mountain and desired once again to hit the campaign trail and press the flesh. Teal realized that for such individuals as Reynolds, who had been a prominent politician, it was difficult to withdraw from the attention and adulation of the public. Reynolds told Teal that "votes were the greatest compliment ever paid to me," and Teal maintained that Reynolds sought either public approbation or redemption after his embarrassing withdrawal from the Senate race in 1944.[36]

In April, Reynolds toured the eastern part of the state to test the waters for a possible candidacy. When he turned up in Raleigh, some reporters got excited about the possibility of a Reynolds candidacy in 1950. Buncombe Bob demurely explained that he had "no aspirations" for the office, but Wade Lucas of the *Charlotte Observer* said that "the truth of the matter is that Reynolds would like nothing better than to be back in the Senate."[37]

In July, Reynolds called a reporter from the *Charlotte Observer* and admitted that he was thinking seriously of making a bid for the Senate seat in 1950. He had been touring the state "seeing a lot of people," and many friends had approached him about running. Reynolds had not made up his mind what to do, but if he did announce he thought that he would "have a lot of fun running."

When asked if he planned to run against Senator Frank Graham, Reynolds answered that it was out of the question because Graham was from the east and Reynolds from the west. If Reynolds won, then both senators would be from the west, which would upset the tradition of having one senator from the east and one from the west.[38]

Ignoring Reynolds's March disclaimers that he was not a candidate, the *Charlotte Observer* argued in September 1949 that Reynolds was already actively campaigning despite the lack of a formal announcement.[39] C. Sylvester Green, editor of the *Durham Morning Herald*, agreed that Reynolds was toying with the idea of running against Hoey,[40] and Senator Hoey himself admitted that Reynolds was very anxious to make the race.[41]

In early December 1949, the *New York Mirror* announced that Bob Reynolds, "the marrying mountaineer," one of the "roughest, toughest campaigners" in American politics, was "about to come snorting back into the arena."[42] By late October Reynolds confirmed the various political rumors and said he might be prevailed upon to run against Hoey. "I'll tell you frankly and honestly, and every man, even a politician, ought to be honest. I'm getting a great deal of encouragement to run. And I might add that I am encouraging myself to enter the race."[43]

The political prognosticators thought that there was a better than even chance that Reynolds would run against Hoey, even though Graham was also up for election.[44] T. C. Johnson, commissioner of paroles in North Carolina, wrote Capus Waynick that many North Carolinians agreed that Reynolds would oppose Hoey, but they did not expect him to make much of a race. Johnson, however, was not willing to sell Reynolds short: "One never knows what so good a showman may be able to do."[45]

Doubtless Reynolds's competitive juices became charged when, by early January 1950, Graham had no serious challenger. Olla Ray Boyd, a pig-breeding political perennial from Pinetown, had entered the fray against Graham, but he was not considered a credible threat given that he favored bulletproof vests for combat troops, federal price supports for hogs, and "legalized lynching."[46] More significant for Reynolds, William B. Umstead, seen by many as Graham's most difficult challenger, withdrew from the race owing to poor health. Thus it seemed likely that Graham would have no serious opposition.[47] *The State* magazine, in fact, could not even think of a candidate other than Umstead who would have a chance against Graham.[48]

In mid-January 1950, Reynolds coyly told inquiring reporters that he had not yet made up his mind about running. "I've been so busy lately building myself some fences that I haven't given much thought to what I should do. And I don't mean political fences. I mean cattle fences." Reynolds noted that he had been encouraged to run by poor people fed up with high taxes and an intrusive federal government. As a states' rights man, Reynolds wanted to control the excessive power of the federal government. "You know," Reynolds intoned, "the federal government now takes the rich cream of a man's income, and the state comes along and takes the thin cream, then the cities and counties get the milk, and by George, when they're through the poor old taxpayer ain't got a thing left but blue-john [skim milk]." Reynolds made it clear to the reporters that he was not making a political speech, "just talking." He did not know if he would run but acknowledged that he enjoyed campaigns. "They're always good for me. I get around and see the folks and have a fine time. Campaigns suit me fine."[49]

Despite his comments to the press, Reynolds had already decided to run but was not yet sure of his opponent. Publicly he continued the charade that he was not yet a committed candidate, but his campaign had already been launched. His friends and advisers met on Reynolds Mountain to discuss campaign plans,[50] and in January 1950 he mailed letters urging an end to world government, hoping to update his isolationist views in a way that 1950 voters would embrace.[51]

Party officials and political experts were nonetheless surprised on January 30 when Reynolds announced he would run against Senator Frank Graham instead of against Clyde Hoey. Seasoned politico that he was, Reynolds always cocked an eye toward the main chance, and he had followed the Graham appointment and the resulting political controversy with great interest. Reynolds had thought about opposing Graham for some time but had kept his thoughts a secret because a surprise announcement would get more attention.

Reynolds acknowledged that he had originally planned to run against Hoey, but he realized that if he did he would be "running against Hoey and talking about Graham." Reynolds knew his differences with Graham on political questions were much sharper and more pronounced than his differences with Hoey. Also, Graham's liberal views would serve as a better target for Reynolds's type of campaign-

Reynolds's last hurrah—a campaign photo from the 1950 Senate race.
(Courtesy *Raleigh News and Observer*)

ing. According to Reynolds, Graham believed in "many things that are foreign to my thinking and not in keeping with the views of the voters of North Carolina."[52]

Reynolds knew, of course, that many Tar Heels disliked Graham's liberalism, whereas Hoey's conservative views were widely embraced. Reynolds's chances of victory were infinitely better against the controversial, inexperienced Graham than against the popular Hoey, who appeared invincible.[53] The newly announced candidate graphically expressed this sentiment in a memorable statement made to Irving C. Crawford: "I could never defeat Hoey. I can't beat a man who goes around the state with a Bible in one hand and his pecker in the other."[54]

Why did Reynolds decide to run? He was sixty-five years of age, had left the Senate in 1944 under extremely negative circumstances, and lacked the necessary organization to win. A critical reason for his announcement, according to his friend Hoover Adams, was that no one had announced against Graham. When Bill Umstead withdrew, there seemed to be no viable candidate on the horizon. Reynolds disliked Graham's views so intensely that he wanted Graham defeated. Adams affirmed that Reynolds lacked the will to run a strong campaign and did not think he could win, but he felt it was his duty to challenge Graham.[55]

Terry Sanford, however, believed that Reynolds ran because he thought he could win and a victory would vindicate his withdrawal in 1944. Sanford said that Reynolds expected that all of his friends would rise up and support him again but noted that in this view Reynolds was totally out of touch with reality.[56] Richard Thigpen, a lawyer in Charlotte, also maintained that Reynolds ran because at one time he had a good many friends and somehow thought he could win.[57]

Perhaps he hoped that he could win, but surely such an experienced politician as Reynolds knew better. He understood his liabilities when he withdrew in 1944, and little had changed since then. He certainly opposed the views of Frank Graham, but he and Graham were friends of long standing. Reynolds had neither the energy nor the funds to carry out the type of campaign necessary to defeat Senator Graham. Reynolds supplied the most logical answer for his decision to run when he stated that he enjoyed campaigns and admitted that he loved getting out to see the folks. This view is buttressed by his lackluster and limited campaign. Reynolds was lonely and wanted to be in the spotlight one more time.

Once he entered the contest, he couched his campaign platform in the conventional rhetoric of states' rights. His platform stated that fair employment practices and social equality were matters to be determined by individual states. As usual, he demanded a sharp curtailment of foreign expenditures, a reduction in the national debt, and reduced taxes. He remained firmly opposed to Communism and socialized medicine, although he advocated monthly pensions and adequate medical care to persons over sixty-five. The perennially paranoid Reynolds charged those labeling him as an isolationist with using smear tactics. Reynolds saw himself as a patriot who was merely following the advice of George Washington that Americans should look after their own affairs first. Borrowing a line from Asheville author Thomas Wolfe, Reynolds concluded that "the time has come to look homeward."[58]

Reynolds pledged a vigorous county-by-county campaign, but most Democratic leaders, irrespective of political philosophy, saw him as an embarrassing anachronism. Reynolds had always been a political outsider, a party crasher, and state Democrats greeted his reentry into elective politics with loud groans. Liberal Graham supporters, such as Jonathan Daniels, national Democratic committeeman, dismissed his candidacy outright. Daniels wrote that Graham simply was a "better citizen, a sounder man, and a better Senator" than Reynolds. Privately, Daniels was even stronger in his condemnation of Reynolds, referring to him as "a very persuasive jackass" and writing a friend that Reynolds's return to the Senate "would be a North Carolina shame and a national calamity."[59]

Governor Kerr Scott urged Graham not to take Reynolds lightly, for he was a showman who would undoubtedly attract voters. Were he Graham, Scott admonished his appointee, he would "run like I was shot at."[60] Others agreed with Scott. The *Dunn Dispatch* insisted that Reynolds, a man of magnetic personality with a large following, was a formidable candidate, and whatever one thought of his views, it was awfully hard to dislike him.[61] Dr. Louise Ingersall reminded Graham supporters that Reynolds was astute and "such a charmer that he would pull a large number of votes in the mountain area."[62] Even the *Asheville Citizen* warned that Reynolds had proved to be a "cagey politician with fingertips sensitive to the fickle wind. His return to the fray indicates that he knows something."[63]

Nor were conservatives pleased with Reynolds's declaration. In their view Reynolds could not defeat Graham. For all his liberalism and his reputation as an impractical reformer, Graham was loved like no other citizen of the state, was an incumbent senator, and would be a formidable candidate. Reynolds's bid for office, as conservatives read it, was a dangerous distraction, as it threatened to turn the race into a political carnival that would obscure the issues conservatives hoped to raise. Reynolds, as one observer noted, was simply an opportunist, filled with the "hollow ring of the phoney he is."[64]

Press reaction to the new entry in the race was immediate. "Candidate Reynolds," declared the *Greensboro Daily News*, "has never publicly subscribed to Barnum's dictum that a sucker is born every minute, but his platform indicates that he is working on the assumption that a lot of them have come of age in North Carolina since he left the Senate."[65] For the *Charlotte Observer* it was the "same Old Bob." His views had not changed, cautioned the *Observer*, but he should not be counted out of the campaign. Despite his penchant for buffoonery, he had proved himself a master of political psychology and had been an exceptional vote-getter in the past.[66] The *New York Times*, reporting on the race, referred to Reynolds as "Hope Diamond, Jr." and "the highest paid baby [Mamie] sitter in North Carolina."[67]

Privately, many citizens expressed their dismay over Reynolds's announcement. One observer wrote Governor Scott that Reynolds could not carry a single county in western North Carolina as his days of "demagogic backslapping" were over.[68] Louis Round Wilson, director of the libraries at the University of North Carolina, confided to Frank Graham that Reynolds was a "bad actor" whose campaign would stir up the unthinking and the prejudiced in the state.[69] Gerald Johnson, editor of the *Baltimore Sun*, cautioned Graham not to relax his efforts just because "Reynolds was a joke. After all, he is a very bad one."[70]

The *Washington (N.C.) Daily News* had the most perceptive analysis of the impact of Reynolds's entry into the race. His candidacy, wrote the paper, had created an opening for a third entrant in the field. The third candidate would make a much stronger bid than might be made alone, because Reynolds's loyal supporters would certainly cut into some of Graham's vote. Since many North Carolina voters could stomach neither Graham nor Reynolds, the paper surmised that a large mass of anti-Graham conservatives still had no candidate.[71]

The anti-Graham forces did not have long to wait. On February 24, 1950, the conservatives got the candidate they wanted when Raleigh attorney Willis Smith paid his filing fee for Graham's seat. Smith had been long removed from elective politics, having served three terms (one as Speaker of the House) in the state House of Representatives from 1927 through 1933. He did, however, have a distinguished record of professional accomplishment (past president of the American Bar Association) and a long career of private volunteer service (president of the Duke University Board of Trustees). Conservatives quickly rallied to his standard.[72]

Neither Graham nor Scott had any comment on Smith's announcement, but Reynolds warmly welcomed Smith into the race, believing it would make the contest more interesting and would provide the electorate with a greater variety of candidates and views. No matter how many candidates there were, Reynolds blustered, he was confident he would win the first primary.[73]

Few others shared Reynolds's optimism, but commentators agreed that Smith was the candidate around which the opposition to Graham would coalesce. For those who liked exciting campaigns, the Smith-Graham-Reynolds contest loomed as the greatest fight of the century.[74] Political pundit Wade Lucas of the *Charlotte Observer* understood immediately that Smith's entry assured a second primary between Smith and Graham. Lucas thought that Smith seemed certain to finish second—he would be the principal beneficiary of the hard-hitting attacks everyone expected Reynolds to aim at front-runner Graham.[75]

Senator Frank Graham, now faced with two serious rivals, formally opened his campaign on March 2, 1950. His platform was a mainstream New Deal–Fair Deal amalgam that called for world peace, better educational opportunities, improved health care, and other predictable Democratic objectives.[76] While Graham and Smith vigorously stumped the state, the unpredictable Bob Reynolds slowly eased into the contest.[77]

As he began his comeback, Reynolds had some significant assets. In addition to his exuberant personality and a sharp tongue, he presented a platform designed to appeal to a large voting bloc. C. A. McKnight of the *Charlotte News*, observing

Reynolds's campaign, marveled at his ability to work a crowd, speaking to each person, shaking hands, and occasionally throwing an arm intimately around a shoulder.[78]

The positive aspects of his personality would help his candidacy, but Reynolds's liabilities were crippling. He was thought of as a political "has-been" and had a highly vulnerable record as an isolationist. The pro-Nazi charges as well as his association with such radicals as Gerald L. K. Smith and Gerald Winrod hurt him. Finally, Reynolds had a reputation as a lightweight legislator who put personal publicity above statesmanship.

In the early part of the campaign Reynolds did little more than print some literature and mail out a form letter asking for contributions and support. Irving C. Crawford, chairman of the Reynolds for Senate Finance Committee, asked friends to organize Bob Reynolds Clubs in their counties.[79] Many friends, like Congressman Thurmond Chatham, refused to take part in Reynolds's campaign but predicted that Reynolds would make the race lively and interesting.[80]

As he had promised, Reynolds formally filed as a candidate on March 17, plunking down 125 one-dollar bills to cover the cost of filing. When asked to confirm the rumor that he intended to highlight the Communist issue by donning a red suit, a red hat, and riding the campaign trail in a red car while playing the "Communist Internationale" at every stop, Reynolds feigned outrage. He explained that he had never had the slightest notion of pulling a ridiculous stunt that would be beneath the dignity of the office. Breezy and jovial as usual, Reynolds managed to repeat the major points of his campaign platform and maintained that if Congress had passed his bill requiring aliens to be fingerprinted ten years earlier, "we would not have the 54,000 Russian communists we now have."[81]

From this point on, Reynolds did not engage in race-baiting and did not attack Graham's alleged socialist tendencies, although the nation in 1950 was caught up in the Joe McCarthy–inspired Red Scare. Throughout the campaign Willis Smith hammered away at Graham on the issue of Graham's affiliation with red-tinged organizations and his purported softness on Communism. Smith lambasted Graham for favoring "Truman socialism" and promised to stop the ultraliberals and traitors in Washington.[82] Reynolds either decided that Smith was doing such a fine job on the Communist issue that his voice was not needed, or he simply decided to omit attacks on Communism as counterproductive.

When he filed for the race, Reynolds told the press that he had decided to forgo a headquarters office in Raleigh because it was too expensive. "I need the money for postage."[83] Eager to get on the campaign trail, Our Bob planned to drive his cream-colored Studebaker over every dirt road in North Carolina while devoting his time to "some politicking, some handshaking, some requesting of votes."[84]

With the formal entry process concluded, Reynolds set out on his quest for votes. After two radio speeches in Raleigh, he stopped at numerous crossroads filling stations to talk with folks about the election and rail against excessive taxes and deficit spending.[85] On his first trip Reynolds was charged up about campaigning and admitted that he liked "to get out and plump the old handle." He was once spotted enthusiastically talking with a group of men from Georgia. When asked why he was spending so much time on Georgia citizens who could not vote in North Carolina, Reynolds replied that once he got to running for office, "I can't stop at state lines."[86]

Reynolds returned to Asheville on March 28 after his initial foray on the campaign circuit, claiming that he had logged over one thousand miles. Exhausted from his efforts, he planned to stay at home for a time, drafting campaign literature and answering correspondence.[87] Voters did not yet know it, but this initial campaign trip proved to be the high water mark of his effort to win office. He would remain in the race, but his future efforts would be sporadic and, with but one or two notable exceptions, ineffective.

At age sixty-five Bob Reynolds was simply too old and too tired for the rigors of intensive electioneering, and he could not sustain the enthusiasm he once exhibited. According to Irving C. Crawford, Reynolds wanted to go back to the Senate but was not willing to make the necessary effort. Reynolds knew that he had to start his political career all over again, persuading a new set of voters that he was the person for the job. His trip around the state convinced him he could not win, and the loss would not hurt as badly if he did not mount a real campaign.[88]

As a seasoned vote-getter, Reynolds understood his plight. His meandering down dirt roads had inspired only random clouds of red clay dust, and instead of generating voter enthusiasm, he had done little more than provide occasional comic relief at a score of country stores. Voters had reacted to his call with the most dismissive response in public life—indifference. Yet Reynolds would not withdraw. Committed to the race, he would see it through to the end rather than once again face the embarrassment of withdrawal. He would savor whatever public attention he could claim, reveling in the occasional opportunity to press the flesh.

Reynolds's opponents and their supporters were slow to realize that Reynolds's campaign was moribund. Fixated on his wondrous upset of Morrison in 1932, they held to the view that anything was possible in an election. Some of Graham's advocates feared that Bumptious Bob might get hot and claim another stunning triumph. To forestall such an outcome, Graham's friends decided to attack Reynolds's "obnoxious" record.[89]

Jonathan Daniels contributed a harsh editorial broadside denouncing Reynolds. Daniels wrote that Our Bob's request for Tar Heel money to finance his return to the Senate, "where he disgraced North Carolina before in order that he may disgrace it again[,] is unmitigated gall." Daniels reminded readers that Rey-

An affable Bob Reynolds has his arm around Senator Frank P. Graham as they and Willis Smith
attend a Young Democrats rally in Asheville during the 1950 Senate campaign. This was the only
occasion on which all three appeared together. (From *Time* magazine, May 15, 1950)

nolds had consorted with Nazi sympathizers during World War II when America's
security was at stake. He also pointed out that Reynolds did not need campaign
contributions, because he had married into one of the richest families in America
and received a big allowance as guardian for his daughter—an amount that would
buy a lot of caviar.[90]

Jeff Johnson, Graham's campaign manager, recognized that Senator Graham's
principal opponent was Willis Smith, not Bob Reynolds, and the Graham forces
focused their attention on the Raleigh attorney. As the campaign progressed,
Smith and Graham seldom mentioned Reynolds, and the press studiously ignored
him.

Reynolds did appear at a Young Democrats rally in Asheville. He mounted
the platform with Smith, Graham, and the keynoter, Sam Rayburn, Speaker of the
United States House of Representatives. Although he had been reduced to the
status of an also-ran, Reynolds exuded the confidence of a front-runner, telling
the crowd that he felt "as spry as a grasshopper."[91] Reynolds, of course, was under
no illusion regarding his chances. He knew that the race had narrowed to a contest
between Smith and Graham, but he also knew he now occupied a pivotal role. He
could not win, but he could determine who the eventual victor would be.

While Willis Smith launched a series of vigorous attacks on Frank Graham's alleged communist affiliations and his liberal position on race, Reynolds hunkered up at his mountain retreat, away from the infighting. He told the press that he would continue to work on campaign literature and would spend some of his time talking with "country folks" and "just visiting."[92] Reynolds's lack of activity astonished political observers. The *Elizabeth City Daily Advance* regretted that Reynolds had not come up with the colorful, energetic campaign expected of him and declared that Reynolds would not get enough votes to force a runoff between Smith and Graham.[93]

Reynolds, bored with his self-imposed exile and stung by some of the criticism, launched a flurry of campaigning in early April. On a two-day visit to Charlotte he revived his 1932 performances. The ebullient Reynolds predicted that he would win the election as he once again had the common people with him. He reverted to the ploy that had worked in 1932. In an astonishing non sequitur, he claimed that he was just a poor boy from the hills without the money to set up a proper campaign organization. "I'm my own campaign manager and publicity director and wherever my car happens to be parked is state headquarters. I won't have any paid workers—just don't have the money."[94]

Reynolds launched a brief offensive against the Graham forces. He called Jonathan Daniels, perhaps Graham's most important confidant, the "self-appointed commissar of North Carolina politics" and even made a halfhearted attack on Senator Graham, calling him a "well-meaning, dreamy-eyed reformer who wants to make over this nation and the whole world to suit his own ideals."[95] In a radio address Reynolds intensified his criticism of Graham, focusing on Graham's Wilsonian idealism and his commitment to world federalism. Dr. Graham, intoned Reynolds, would understand America better if he "would come down out of these fleecy clouds of idealism, take off those golden slippers, unfurl those angelic robes from around his shoulders and put on the brogans of the world of stark reality."[96]

Although Reynolds received mildly enthusiastic responses to his Charlotte speeches, he nonetheless returned to the seclusion of Reynolds Mountain. Some of his friends realized that his heart was not in the race—only the exhilaration of occasional stump oratory now beckoned.[97] J. B. Moore, an astute follower of state politics, expected that Reynolds's campaign effort would soon dwindle to nothing.[98] Whatever the case, the Reynolds campaign of 1950 was thin gruel for those who had feasted on the banquet spectacle of 1932.

One reason that Reynolds cut back his campaigning was the realization that Smith was the standard-bearer of the anti-Graham conservatives and had a better chance to defeat Graham. Reynolds told Hoover Adams, Smith's publicity director, that he had reduced his activity in order to avoid damaging Smith. "I can't win, but your man can."[99]

Buncombe Bob, despite his lack of effort, continued to report wonderful progress, explaining that seven out of ten people he talked to had made up their minds to vote for him.[100] Such bravado might have salved Reynolds's feelings of disappointment in his campaign, but the media were not impressed. Rumors persisted that Reynolds's withdrawal from the race was imminent. Wesley McDonald had to issue a public statement that Reynolds had no intention of quitting.[101] The Smith forces understandably wanted Reynolds to remain in the contest as he was certain to draw some votes from Graham. Without Reynolds, Smith might not be able to prevent Graham from achieving a majority in the first primary.

Throughout April and May, Smith hammered away at Graham in one of the most divisive and ugly contests in North Carolina political history. Smith continued to attack Graham on the issue of race, especially the Truman administration's establishment of the federal Fair Employment Practices Commission (FEPC). Smith's supporters stoked a firestorm of racial bigotry by passing out flyers entitled "White People Wake Up" and by falsely accusing Graham of having appointed a "nigger to West Point." Smith also denounced Graham's close ties to the liberal Truman administration and pounded away at his alleged socialistic tendencies. The Graham forces pictured Smith as a reactionary, uncaring, closet Republican who favored big business at the expense of the common man. Reynolds chose not to join in the vituperative attacks against either opponent, contenting himself with a restatement of his philosophy and a personal appeal for votes.[102] Columnist Tom Bost claimed that instead of succumbing to the low tenor of the race and making remarks against blacks, Jews, and labor, Reynolds had conducted an essentially decent campaign.[103]

Although a less than active campaigner, Reynolds decided to attend the North Carolina State Democratic convention in May. Governor Scott told reporters that Reynolds came up to him at the opening of the convention, tapped him on the shoulder, and said: "Governor, somebody told me that I ought to tell you that you are too active for Graham. So, I am telling you." Reynolds then added, "That's to be expected. After all, you appointed Graham to the Senate. But it's all right with me, I'm going to beat him anyway."[104]

Following the state convention, Our Bob returned to Charlotte, his favorite campaign stop. He addressed an enthusiastic crowd of about fifteen hundred supporters, who urged him on with cries of "Go ahead, boy," and "You tell 'em, Bob." After taking a strong stance against the Marshall Plan and immigration, Reynolds stirred up the crowd with an impassioned anticommunist harangue. The country, shouted Reynolds, was "honeycombed with spies and Russian agents and the idea of one world was ridiculous since the Communists had already enslaved half of the world." Fred Kirby, a guitar-strumming radio singer, enlivened the festivities with a song he wrote for the occasion: "God Made America for

Did YOU know ?

Over 28% of the population of North Carolina is COLORED

FEPC, if enacted, means more than that you might be working next to and sharing facilities with some one not of your choice ... and probably not of your employer's choice, either.

It means that if you are working in a plant that employs 1,000 people, 280 of them will be someone besides you or your friends.

If you work in a plant employing 375 people, 105 of them won't be you or your friends.

Or, if you just work where there are three people, one of them won't be you or your present associates.

This is not a pretty picture ... but these are the facts.

Do not be fooled ... most of all, do not be lulled by sweet words of high-flown idealists.

The SOUTHERN WORKING MAN *MUST NOT BE SACRIFICED* to vote-getting ambitions of political bosses!

A Vote for *Willis Smith*   SATURDAY JUNE 24th   is a Vote for *Your* Freedom

WORKING MEN FOR SMITH COMMITTEE

JOHN M. CULP

"Did *You* Know Over 28% of the Population of North Carolina Is *Colored*?" Race was the crucial issue of the 1950 Senate campaign, as illustrated by this pro–Willis Smith flyer denouncing the Fair Employment Practices Commission (FEPC).

Americans to Live In." Reynolds insisted that he would win the race because "I'm working while they are jawing. I'm getting the votes while they are making the noise."[105]

Four days later, Reynolds predicted that he would win by twenty-five thousand votes. The claim was spurious, of course, but Reynolds, in moments of fantasy, apparently envisioned Smith and Graham canceling each other out and opening a path for his victory. He was "pleased to see Smith at Graham's throat and Graham attacking Smith, it's pie for me."[106]

Seeking an advantage from the brutal battle between Smith and Graham, Reynolds presented himself as the plausible alternative to both his opponents. In a prototype advertisement in the *Jacksonville (N.C.) News and Views* ("The Only Newspaper in the World That Gives a Whoop about Onslow County"), Reynolds cleverly told voters: "If Frank Graham is what the Willis Smith supporters say he is, and if Willis Smith is what Frank Graham's supporters say he is, then vote for Robert R. Reynolds."[107]

The week before the first primary balloting, Reynolds had no set schedule of speeches, just a series of "spot talks." He ran newspaper advertisements statewide asking people to "Vote American," reminding them that he was against all things with a "red or a pink or a socialistic tinge." The ad portrayed Reynolds as a man of conviction who always voted in the interest of his country and "not with a view of continuing himself in office."[108]

In his final campaign appearance, a joyous Reynolds, face flushed and hands waving, again railed against U.S. aid to Europe. "Paris hotels," he trumpeted, "are filled with French tourists having a helluva good time on your hard-earned money. Those European gals, loaded down with jewelry, make the girls in our own Stork Club look like orphans."[109]

As the campaign neared its end, A. B. Upchurch, publicity director for Graham, tried to persuade Reynolds to quit the race. The Graham forces realized that the former senator would almost certainly get enough votes to prevent a clear victory by Graham in the first primary, and they wanted to avoid a runoff. Reynolds would have none of it and remained in the contest.[110]

During the last week, Reynolds claimed to be in the middle of a "whirlwind finish" and to have the masses behind him.[111] The old spellbinder proclaimed that he would be carried to Washington on the mounting swell of the "great silent vote."[112] In Winston-Salem he said that the nomination was "in the bag," and after returning to Asheville he told the press that "victory is ours. The bag is tied up. It merely remains for us to keep the bag tied."[113]

His braggadocio did not obscure the reality that Reynolds was never in the race. It was obvious to everyone, including Reynolds, that he had no chance to win, but he continued to make outlandish predictions. He had run a disorganized campaign with only an occasional glimpse of the desire and rhetoric that had characterized his previous efforts. The press had long predicted that he would finish third.[114] Marquis Childs, in the *Richmond Times-Dispatch*, put it best when he predicted that Reynolds would finish third because his demagoguery was dated, "its edges curled with a weary cynicism, lacking the gusto that Ouah Bob once put into it."[115]

Despite his inept effort, forecasters believed that Reynolds could summon the votes of at least fifty thousand diehards, enough to deny Graham a majority.[116] Senator Clyde Hoey, unopposed in his campaign, thought that there would be a runoff if Reynolds received a respectable number of votes.[117]

On May 27, 1950, Bob Reynolds garnered 58,752 (9.3 percent) votes and forced a runoff. Frank Graham led the first primary with 303,605 (48.9 percent), while Willis Smith received 250,222 (40.5 percent) and Olla Ray Boyd finished last with 5,600 votes (1.3 percent). In the largest turnout in North Carolina political history, Graham had come agonizingly close to victory, needing only 11,921 more votes to win outright.[118] Reynolds ran third in ninety-nine of the one hundred counties and came in second in his home county of Buncombe. His heaviest votes in 1950 were the same counties where he ran strong in 1932 and 1938, indicating that the bulk of his votes were the remnants of a once large personal following.

Racial slurs and attacks on Graham's left-wing associations were the crucial factors in denying Graham a first primary majority. Some political observers, however, including R. Mayne Albright, Raleigh attorney and gubernatorial candidate in 1948, along with William W. Staton and Frank Graham himself, thought that Bob Reynolds's candidacy was the most significant reason for Graham's failure to get over 50 percent of the votes. If Reynolds had not been in the contest, reasoned Albright, Graham certainly would have received the additional votes he needed for victory.[119]

Reynolds's presence in the contest and his refusal to abandon a hopeless effort fueled speculation that he had taken on the role of spoiler in collaboration with the Smith forces. No evidence sustains this speculation. Almost all contemporary observers—among them Irving C. Crawford and Paul Teal, Reynolds's law partners; his close friend Hubert H. Rand; William D. Snider; John L. Sanders; Terry Sanford; and William W. Staton—deny the theory. They agreed that Reynolds was too independent, too contrary, and too vain to be a stalking-horse for anyone.[120]

Reynolds, who spent only $9,335.87 on the race, primarily on postage and advertisements, had taken in only $3,503.00 in contributions.[121] He was "more than pleased" with the election results and pronounced the vote a victory for Americanism. He did not indicate what he might do in the event that Smith called for a runoff, but clearly Reynolds's supporters would be the key to the second primary.[122]

Although the *Philadelphia Bulletin* and other papers saw the election as a "merited rebuke" and a serious defeat for him,[123] Reynolds tried to put the best face possible on his loss. He told the press that he had not taken his campaign too seriously and had merely wanted to present to the electorate a platform representing his fundamental political beliefs.[124] This statement, of course, was typical for Reynolds and a far cry from his posturing and predictions during the campaign about the great victory he was about to achieve.

While Willis Smith pondered the possibility of calling for a runoff, a few of Reynolds's campaign workers announced that they would support Graham if a second primary materialized.[125] Most of the state press, however, expected Reynolds's votes to go to Smith. The *Fayetteville Observer* agreed that Smith would get Reynolds's votes since those who voted for Reynolds did so because of his stand against socialism and Communism, which corresponded to Smith's views on those subjects.[126] Tilford E. Dudley, assistant director of the Congress of Industrial Organizations (CIO) Political Action Committee, disagreed. He concluded that it was not certain that Reynolds's votes would go to Smith, because those voters were loyalists who supported Reynolds because of past favors, and Our Bob could not transfer those votes.[127]

On June 7, armed with promises of adequate funds and bolstered by three Supreme Court decisions that threatened to overturn segregation in the South, Smith called for a runoff.[128] Shortly thereafter, while on vacation in Hot Springs, Arkansas, Reynolds endorsed Smith's candidacy and promised to return to North Carolina to campaign for the challenger. Reynolds said that he was convinced that the Senate needed a man of the character, ability, and sound progressive ideas of Willis Smith. Campaign aide Wesley McDonald also declared for Smith and asked all those who voted for Reynolds to join him in voting for Smith.[129] Wesley McDonald, along with other Reynolds stalwarts, later joined Willis Smith's campaign staff.[130]

Not all Reynolds's workers were persuaded by his decision to back Smith. Ray Owen, campaign manager for Reynolds in Mecklenburg County, said that many of Reynolds's adherents felt let down by the former senator. Reynolds had asked for their support and then gave the impression that he did not care whether he won or not. Owen said that Reynolds's former supporters would no longer follow his lead and would work for Graham.[131]

Jeff Johnson, Graham's campaign manager, cautioned his county managers not to get too excited about the Reynolds endorsement as he would not be a significant force in the runoff.[132] The *Durham Sun* and the *High Point Enterprise* both agreed that Reynolds's endorsement was of questionable value given that the trend had already turned in Smith's favor.[133]

The Smith forces, however, were elated with Reynolds's backing. Willis Smith wrote many of Reynolds's supporters, reminding them of Our Bob's endorsement and asking for their aid and vote.[134] James K. Dorsett Jr., attorney and son-in-law of Willis Smith, judged that while most of Reynolds's advocates would have voted for Smith anyway, his endorsement might have helped people get to the polls and was thus important.[135]

Eventually Reynolds made one radio speech for Smith. He had endorsed Smith "wholeheartedly and unequivocally," Reynolds told the audience, because Smith was a true believer in states' rights and would not bend his knee to certain minority groups out of political expediency. Here Reynolds referred to the Smith charge that Graham had compromised himself through promises to blacks in return for their vote. Reynolds concluded his talk by declaring that he had chosen to endorse Smith free from any coercion or promise of political reward.[136]

On June 24, 1950, Willis Smith defeated Frank Graham by 18,675 votes in the most racially charged campaign in modern North Carolina history.[137] After the Smith victory, Reynolds wrote conservative author John T. Flynn, an anti–New

Deal and anti-Roosevelt writer, claiming to have done everything possible to help elect Willis Smith. Reynolds explained that he had contacted friends all over the state and believed that eight out of every ten Reynolds votes had gone to Smith in the runoff. Reynolds took comfort "in the fact we defeated Graham."[138]

Reynolds greatly exaggerated the importance of his assistance in defeating Graham in the second primary, partly because his entire political life had been an exercise in extended hyperbole. One is unable to determine if Reynolds transferred his votes to Smith. It seemed logical that since both Smith and Reynolds were conservative states' rights activists in a racist contest, most of Reynolds's voters would be drawn to Smith, with or without prompting from Reynolds.

In his desire to enjoy the glories of the campaign trail one more time, Reynolds had prevented Graham from winning a majority in the first primary. Bob Reynolds did not win his last hurrah, but he did help determine the winner, and he gained some satisfaction in that accomplishment.

[Epilogue]

After his final fling at politics, Reynolds devoted his waning years to his daughter Mamie. Reynolds told reporters: "I've got all I want on this mountain and all I can do. I don't entertain. The happiest job in the world I've got—making sure she grows in happiness, equipped for judgment and stability and a good life."[1] Harriet Louise "Mimi" Palmer, Mamie's companion, described Reynolds as "a kind, loving father who was able to get down to her age and level. They were good friends."[2] Bob Reynolds had given up his yearning for publicity and had found peace and contentment in the simple life on Reynolds Mountain.

The inveterate traveler, Reynolds wanted Mamie to enjoy the benefits of world exploration as much as he had. "Travel is the great educator," explained Reynolds, "and contact with many people broadens an individual's background." Together, Bob and Mamie visited all the state capitals and went around the world four times before Mamie was twelve.[3]

Reynolds dabbled in some business ventures. He owned Caribbean Ferries Inc., which consisted of a single ship ferrying passengers and autos between Key West and Havana, Cuba. He also advertised that he ran the Circle R Ranch, which sold and bred "Mexican burros, African Pigmy and Sicilian donkeys, Palomino horses, . . . and livestock in general."[4]

On October 17, 1950, Reynolds learned that his son, Robert R. Reynolds Jr., had been killed in an automobile accident. The grieving Reynolds buried his son in Riverside Cemetery.[5] After his son's death, Bob Reynolds lavished even more attention on Mamie. As his daughter approached eighteen, Reynolds decided to give her a lavish "coming out" party. Meyer Davis, the famed society orchestra leader, was flown in from New York and wrote a song for the occasion, appropriately called "Mamie." Mamie wore a white organza silk gown created for her by Christian Dior of Paris. The champagne flowed, and guests enjoyed a vast array of hors d'oeuvres, including caviar.[6] Bob Reynolds had come a long way since 1932. He started his career denouncing "Red Russian fish aigs" and ended up serving them to five hundred guests during an elaborate party that would have made Evalyn Walsh McLean proud.

According to one reporter, Reynolds at seventy still exhibited the same flamboyance, the same vigor, and the same garrulity. The aging politician kept up with world affairs and could not resist commenting on international events. If his physical appearance remained unchanged, so did his political philosophy. Reynolds cautioned the federal government against spending too much money abroad—he had learned over the years that "we can't buy friendship." He declared, to no one's surprise, that he was "as nationalist as ever."[7] In a 1962 interview for *The State* magazine, Reynolds commented that he continued to oppose membership in the United Nations because it was a sounding board for the Russians and "the sooner we withdraw our membership the better."[8]

Our Bob died on February 13, 1963, at the age of seventy-eight. He had cancer of the bladder and did not survive the removal of half his bladder during his last operation. Reynolds was ashamed of his illness and asked that "died of a heart attack" be given to the press as the cause of death.[9]

Governor Terry Sanford and Secretary of State Thad Eure led a group of 250 mourners who came to pay their respects at the All Souls Episcopal Church in Asheville. In accordance with his will, Senator Reynolds's body was cremated and his remains buried in the family plot at Riverside Cemetery. The Wachovia Bank and Trust Company was the executor of Reynolds's estate, valued at $57,792. His will left one-third of his estate to each of his two daughters, Mamie Spears Reynolds and Frances Reynolds Oertling. The final one-third went to his three grandchildren, the children of Bob Jr.[10]

"In traveling this state," Sanford said, "I have found friends of 'Our Bob' Reynolds from the peaks and coves of the mountains to the coastline along the Atlantic. Mrs. Sanford and I join other North Carolinians in sorrow over the death of Senator Reynolds." Other friends, such as state senator James Stikeleather, put Buncombe Bob's death in perspective: "His death represents the passing of an era in North Carolina politics. He was the last of the old timers in politics."[11]

Congressman Monroe Redden referred to Reynolds as "a vivacious politician and a lone wolf campaigner. He surprised friends and foes alike. His personal charm was perhaps his greatest attribute, but he never forgot his friends." Congressman Roy A. Taylor followed up on Redden's theme, saying that Reynolds's "rich personality, keen sense of humor, and loyalty to his friends endeared him to the people of North Carolina."

On a more substantive level, Senator Sam Ervin praised Senator Reynolds for the courage of his convictions. Reynolds, said Ervin, fought hard to keep the United States out of war even though he knew his course was unpopular. In the end, said Ervin, Reynolds stuck by his views rather than follow the popular course, and his courage led directly to the loss of his Senate seat.

The two Asheville papers remembered Reynolds fondly, and the bitterness of the 1940s vanished in a wave of nostalgia. His foremost opponent, the *Asheville Citizen*, asserted that Reynolds had his flaws, especially when he mistook America's dislike for war for a mass retreat into isolationism. His isolationist views, recalled the paper, broke him politically. The *Citizen*, however, focused on his exuberance for life. Reynolds "lived more of a life than a dozen men normally live and if he didn't enjoy most of the conscious moments he fooled a lot of people." Reynolds, continued the *Citizen*, had been a "migrant, cowboy, roustabout, adventurer, clown, bon vivant, U.S. Senator"—and "he played each of these roles with zest and seeming ease." The paper best remembered Buncombe Bob as a man who could bounce off a train in any hamlet in the state and begin calling people by their first names.[12]

The *Asheville Times* recalled Reynolds in the same fashion. The *Times* claimed that Reynolds "had a knack for making people feel they were important, that they were friends, and that he valued their friendship. He did." The paper concluded by noting that Reynolds "loved life and lived it with a verve, and an enthusiasm that showed. Somehow, folks like a man like that."[13]

On a more negative note, the *Durham Morning Herald* wrote that it was best to remember Reynolds as a campaigner because the ideas he espoused "never did become him or the state he represented." The paper summed up his career with a pithy analysis. "Although North Carolina long ago outgrew the naiveté that Bob Reynolds exploited in his climb to prominence, though it clearly repudiated the xenophobia he preached, it never lost a certain affection for the man. Whatever else 'Our Bob' was, he was always interesting."[14]

As one can discern by reading Reynolds's obituaries, a final assessment of his life is not an easy prospect. It would be simple to dismiss him as a clown, an entertainer, and a lightweight senator, but that would be a facile judgment.

Anyone who has studied Bob Reynolds's career would define him as a showman of the first order. Our Bob loved publicity and travel more than anything else. Clearly, he spent far too much time on foreign junkets and inconsequential activities when he should have been devoting more energy to his legislative responsibilities. Irving C. Crawford insisted that Reynolds was not lazy but energetic and the soul of integrity. But, Crawford added, Reynolds simply was not very interested in legislative matters and did not read, study, or think enough about the bills he considered. His major weaknesses, concluded Crawford, were a lack of information and the inability to judge or discriminate in his friendships.[15]

Bob Reynolds came to Washington in 1932 with a desire to help people, and he did an excellent job of attending to constituents' needs. At the height of the depression he took the time to meet personally with as many job seekers as possible. He could not find jobs for most, but he cared, and his fellow Tar Heels knew it.

Tar Heel voters appreciated his outgoing personality, his lone-wolf campaigns, and his sympathetic responses. They supported him in large numbers in 1932 and 1938, and he commanded over fifty-eight thousand votes with minimum effort in 1950. The press adored him because he was usually available for an interview and frequently provided them with a great story or a witty comment.

Bob Reynolds was easy to like. He was brash, warm, and outgoing. He charmed most people he met because he genuinely liked people. In the Senate he was courteous, open, and friendly when greeting his colleagues. Many fellow senators might have disapproved of his lack of preparation and his views on immigration or foreign affairs, but with few exceptions, they were fond of Bob Reynolds.

Affability, however, is not the sine qua non of legislative achievement. As a senator he did not propose much significant legislation, but he did have some impact on the registration of aliens (the Smith Act), immigration laws, and government control of labor unions. He voted for the relief, recovery, and reform of New Deal legislation during his first term and praised the New Deal programs for alleviating suffering and saving the free enterprise system. He did make excellent and thoughtful suggestions for highway safety, a national approach to crime, benefits for veterans, reforms to the Washington, D.C., government, and the expansion of the U.S. defense perimeter to Alaska. Most of these proposals were never transformed into legislation because of a dearth of legislative skill and the lack of interest in seeing the bills through to their conclusion. Some of his ideas, such as the vote for District of Columbia citizens in national elections, were later adopted. Overall, however, his legislative career lacked constructive thought and appeals to nobility of sentiment.

Senator Reynolds made an important contribution to his home state with his unremitting efforts to obtain federal funding for the Blue Ridge Parkway and the Great Smoky Mountains National Park. Largely due to his efforts, North Carolinians today enjoy a wonderfully preserved part of the state's natural beauty. Bob Reynolds also worked very hard to secure funds for federal work relief projects. He obtained money for the Civilian Conservation Corps and for the WPA, PWA, and other public works programs.

Reynolds the politician was a throwback to the old-time Populists—a "populist demagogue." He claimed to be for the little people and denounced the large corporations and the moneyed interests for their greed. Reynolds was the pure product of democracy and was twice elected to the Senate without the aid of a political machine because the voters believed that he effectively articulated their frustrations and fears.

Our Bob, however strong his stated commitment to the general welfare, had one main goal in mind throughout his career—the election of Bob Reynolds. He rode the success of the New Deal and Roosevelt's popularity into a second term and then, sensing a more conservative mood in the state, abandoned both Roosevelt and the New Deal. By 1950 he was a states' righter denouncing the excessive spending and the repressive influence of the federal government.

In foreign policy, Bob Reynolds sincerely believed that a noninterventionist (unilateralist) policy was best for America, and he remained convinced of the rightness of his beliefs throughout his career. Reynolds refused to accept the term "isolationist"—he simply saw himself as a nationalist who placed the interests of his country ahead of those of any other country. The only noninterventionist from the South, he refused to alter his views even when it meant political defeat in the long run.

His philosophy on foreign affairs was so out of temper with the times that he was vilified as a traitor and a Nazi sympathizer. Other prominent Americans, including Burton K. Wheeler and Charles A. Lindbergh, were also characterized as unpatriotic and in line with Hitler's propaganda. Any noninterventionist would, by virtue of his or her position, agree with some of Hitler's propaganda. Their isolationist positions did not make Lindbergh or Reynolds or America First members disloyal, but after Pearl Harbor, their views were anathema to Americans.

Once the United States had been attacked, Bob Reynolds abandoned his isolationist stance and voted for war against Germany, Japan, and Italy. He was a dedicated chairman of the Military Affairs Committee during World War II. Although frequently bypassed by the Roosevelt administration, Reynolds did all he could to expedite the war effort. However, in 1944, with the war almost won, he reverted to his noninterventionist views and voted against American entrance into the United Nations. While wrong on the coming of World War II, Reynolds was perceptive in his warnings about a Russian takeover of Eastern Europe and the evils of Communism.

Reynolds's greatest mistakes came in his choice of friends and associates and in his willingness to make erroneous statements without the necessary facts and without much thought for the consequences. In the mid-1940s he was guilty of intemperate comments, cynicism, and some hate-filled rhetoric. His friendships with Gerald L. K. Smith, George Deatherage, and others of their ilk demonstrated not only a lack of judgment but also support for their views. At the very least he could be characterized as xenophobic and a shrill nativist.

Bob Reynolds was neither a Nazi nor a fascist, but much of what he did and said was fascist, and some of the people he befriended were also fascist. These groups fostered religious hatred and nurtured anti-Semitic passions, but they were essentially rabble-rousers who failed to subvert democracy. Without question, Reynolds believed in capitalism, and his devotion was to a democratic United States, not to a totalitarian state. This did not mean that he disliked all aspects of fascism, for its nationalistic fervor and the anti-Semitism appealed to him. Reynolds flaunted his anti-Semitism in his Vindicators Association, and his Border Patrol smacked of the Nazi Youth. All his patriotic organizations, including the Nationalist Party, were characterized by excessive anticommunism and alien bashing. He blatantly appealed to such openly bigoted groups as the United Sons of America in his pursuit of membership for his third party. While trying to take advantage of the insecurities, anxieties, and unrest of Americans in the 1930s in the Vindicators and the Nationalist Party, Reynold lacked the ability, organizational skills, and charisma of Huey Long or Father Charles Coughlin. Thus he never created a large national following. Before World War II Reynolds admitted persecution and illegal aggression by Hitler, but to conform to his isolationist beliefs, he passed off these violations of human rights as not serious enough for war. Here Reynolds missed the mark badly, because those violations were the exact reasons the free world ultimately went to war—to preserve democracy and human freedoms.

During his second term Reynolds slid down into the abyss of bigotry. Reynolds held strong anti-Semitic and antialien views and worked with Gerald L. K. Smith and others because their views coincided with his own. More damaging were his sojourns with George Sylvester Viereck and Prescott Dennett, Nazi propagandists. Other senators were fooled by these clever men, but there was no excuse for not carefully checking out these individuals. His old friend J. Edgar Hoover could have supplied him with the necessary information, but Reynolds either did not care or did not want to know. He was very stubborn and inflexible in his beliefs and refused to listen to his friends or to criticism from the press. He never really understood the folly of his bad judgment until November 1943 when he realized that many people in his home state despised him. At that juncture he knew he would face a severe drubbing in 1944 and bowed out of politics. He had destroyed himself.

In a final judgment of Reynolds's senatorial career, perhaps it is relevant to recall the views of his closest observers—his colleague Senator Josiah Bailey and his hometown newspaper, the *Asheville Citizen*. Bailey, angered at Reynolds's inconsequential performance in the Senate, labored vigorously behind the scenes to deny him a third term. He denounced Reynolds's ignorance and thoughtlessness and was convinced that his colleague's isolationist views and harsh comments about Britain and France during wartime had undermined Allied unity. The *Asheville Citizen* rendered a harsh assessment when Bob Reynolds withdrew from the Senate race in 1943. The paper vilified him for his lack of constructive thought and for his obstruction, cynicism, and hate spieling. The *Citizen* also rebuked him for his narrowness of mind and for his years misrepresenting the state.

Bob Reynolds nonetheless succeeded as a politician because he was a marvelous storyteller and exuded magnetism with the personal, intimate appeal of the old-style politician. By blaming the Republicans and Wall Street for the depression, he gave the voters a focus for their anger and frustration. By presenting himself as their savior, he gave them a symbol of hope for the future. In the final analysis, Allen Drury understood Bob Reynolds's political personality. He was not a clown, but a shrewd, clever man who used his folksy, colorful persona to induce in the voters the sort of amused contempt he needed to foster his purposes.

In the end, no man, save Huey Long, provided a better show for the American people from 1933 to 1945. Buncombe Bob was a tireless politician who won support and affection from a large number of Tar Heels. Reynolds was not a great senator, but he did have an impact on his country with immigration legislation, as chairman of the Military Affairs Committee, and as a noninterventionist. He was one of a kind, sui generis, in the modern South—a New Deal populist and an isolationist. No other southern senator during the Roosevelt era demonstrated his colorful personality or matched his attitudes and attributes.

Bob Reynolds rattled out of the mountains of North Carolina in a rusty Tin Lizzie in 1932 to seek the approbation of his fellow Tar Heels. He managed to gain enough power to snub kings and infuriate presidents. And this was much more than anyone had expected. As one of his constituents recalled in 1944 as Buncombe Bob's political career was coming to an end, "Yeh. We've gotta get Bob home I guess. But boys, he was a caution while he was in there, hear?"[16]

Notes

INTRODUCTION

1. Key, *Southern Politics*, 206; Luthin, *American Demagogues*, 3; *Charlotte News*, n.d., quoted in the *Asheville Citizen*, July 6, 1932.

2. Key, *Southern Politics*, 206.

3. Drew Pearson and Robert S. Allen, "Merry Go-'Round," *Raleigh News and Observer*, January 18, 1939.

4. Ray Arsenault, "The Folklore of Southern Demagoguery," in Eagles, ed., *Is There a Southern Political Tradition?*, 79–132.

CHAPTER ONE

1. *Time*, June 3, 1944.

2. *Asheville Citizen*, February 14, 1963; University of North Carolina Alumni Association Files, Chapel Hill, N.C.

3. *Greensboro Daily News*, December 4, 1932.

4. *Raleigh News and Observer*, July 17, 1932.

5. *Greensboro Daily News*, December 4, 1932; author's interview with Frances Reynolds Oertling.

6. *Asheville Citizen-Times*, July 3, 1932.

7. *Winston-Salem Journal*, July 17, 1932.

8. *Biographical Dictionary of the American Congress*, 1731; *Raleigh News and Observer*, September 7, 1941.

9. Robert R. Reynolds, *Wanderlust*, 1–2.

10. Ibid., 2–11.

11. Ibid., 12–24.

12. *Yackety Yack*, 1903, 51.

13. *Asheville Citizen*, February 14, 1963.

14. Author's interview with Frank P. Graham; *Raleigh News and Observer*, July 17, 1932.

15. *Yackety Yack*, 1906, 42; Reynolds, *Wanderlust*, 25.

16. *Winston-Salem Journal*, July 17, 1932; Reynolds, *Wanderlust*, 26–36.

17. Morrison, *Governor O. Max Gardner*, 14–15.

18. Oliver Max Gardner to Robert Rice Reynolds, December 16, 1946, O. Max Gardner Papers, Southern Historical Collection, University of North Carolina, Chapel Hill.

19. Reynolds, *Wanderlust*, 44–64.

20. Author's interview with Fred W. Morrison.

21. *Daily Tar Heel*, October 26, 1905.

22. Ibid., November 9, December 7, 1905.

23. Author's interview with Fred W. Morrison; author's interview with Irving C. Crawford.

24. *Daily Tar Heel*, January 18, 1905.

25. *Yackety Yack*, 1905, 46; ibid., 1906, 144, 195, 254, 266.

26. Ibid., 1905, 223; *Daily Tar Heel*, February 8, 1905.

27. Transcript of Robert Rice Reynolds, 1902–5, Office of the Registrar, University of North Carolina, Chapel Hill, N.C.

28. *Yackety Yack*, 1906, 42.

29. *Asheville Citizen-Times*, December 3, 1933; *Raleigh News and Observer*, July 17, 1932.

30. *Asheville Magazine*, January 1907.

31. *Raleigh News and Observer*, August 24, 1941.

32. Reynolds, *Wanderlust*, 66–86.

33. Transcript of Robert Rice Reynolds, 1902–5.

34. *Raleigh News and Observer*, July 17, 1932; author's interview with Frances Reynolds Oertling; *Winston-Salem Journal*, July 17, 1932.

35. Reynolds, *Wanderlust*, 86–91.

36. *Winston-Salem Journal*, July 17, 1932.

37. Author's interview with James S. Howell; author's interview with Frances Reynolds Oertling.

38. *Washington Times-Herald*, August 17, 1941.

39. *New Orleans Bee*, January 20, 1910.

40. Author's interview with Frances Reynolds Oertling; *Raleigh News and Observer*, August 24, 1941.

41. *Raleigh News and Observer*, July 17, 1932.

42. Burke Davis, "Senator Bob Reynolds," 363.

43. *Greensboro Daily News*, February 14, 1963.

44. Author's interview with Paul Teal Jr.; with Margaret Reynolds; and with J. Gerald Cowan.

45. Michie and Ryhlick, *Dixie Demagogues*, 232.

46. Burke Davis, "Senator Bob Reynolds," 363.

47. *Raleigh News and Observer*, October 12, 1941. "Buncombe" means empty or meaningless talk, especially by a politician. The term was derived from Buncombe County after a speech made around 1820 by Felix Walker, a United States congressman, who made a fatuous speech and called it "a speech from Buncombe." Small wonder then that Bob Reynolds was known throughout his career as Buncombe Bob.

48. Puryear, *Democratic Party Dissension*, 131; Coughlan, "Our Bob Reynolds," 48; *Asheville Citizen*, February 4, 1963.

49. McCormick, "Buncombe Bob," 38; *Asheville Citizen*, February 14, 1963.

50. *Asheville Citizen*, February 14, 1963.

51. *Asheville Citizen-Times*, November 23, 1958.

52. Author's interview with Paul Teal Jr.

53. Author's interview with Frances Reynolds Oertling; author's interview with Margaret Reynolds; *Winston-Salem Journal*, July 17, 1932.

54. Author's interview with Frances Reynolds Oertling; author's interview with Margaret Reynolds; *Raleigh News and Observer*, September 7, 1941; *Washington Sunday Times*, August 17, 1941.

55. *Raleigh News and Observer*, July 17, 1932; Puryear, *Democratic Party Dissension*, 131.

56. *Washington Times-Herald*, August 17, 1941.

57. Author's interview with Frances Reynolds Oertling; Burke Davis, "Senator Bob Reynolds," 363; Michie and Ryhlick, *Dixie Demagogues*, 240. These two men eventually ended up as col-

leagues in the United States Senate in 1933, and no one could have imagined that the manager of a roller skating rink and a fledgling attorney would one day be powerful members of the Senate.

58. Author's interview with Frances Reynolds Oertling, *Raleigh News and Observer*, July 17, 1932; Robert Rice Reynolds, *Gypsy Trails*, 21–22.

59. Harry H. Vaughan to Jonathan Daniels, March 10, 1950, Jonathan Worth Daniels Papers, Southern Historical Collection, University of North Carolina, Chapel Hill; author's interview with Frances Reynolds Oertling; *Raleigh News and Observer*, July 17, 1932.

60. Author's interview with Frances Reynolds Oertling; *Washington Sunday Times*, August 7, 1941; *Raleigh News and Observer*, August 7, 1941.

61. *Raleigh News and Observer*, September 7, 1941.

62. *Washington Times-Herald*, August 17, 1941; *Raleigh News and Observer*, July 17, 1932.

63. Reynolds, *Gypsy Trails*, preface; *Raleigh News and Observer*, July 17, 1932.

64. Reynolds, *Gypsy Trails*, 9–12, 20–28.

65. Ibid., 36–55.

66. *Asheville Citizen-Times*, November 23, 1958; McCormick, "Buncombe Bob," 38.

67. *Greensboro Daily News*, February 14, 1963.

68. Robert Rice Reynolds to John Humphrey Small, October 12, 1923, John Humphrey Small Papers, Duke University Library, Durham.

69. *Raleigh News and Observer*, August 24, 1941.

70. *Durham Herald-Sun*, April 27, 1941.

71. Robert Rice Reynolds to John C. Sikes, July 15, 1925, Edwin Clarke Gregory Papers, Duke University Library; *Asheville Citizen*, February 14, 1925.

72. *Southern Tourist*, February 1925, 9.

73. Author's interview with Frances Reynolds Oertling.

74. Ibid.; author's interview with Irving C. Crawford.

75. Reynolds to Sikes, July 15, 1925; Robert R. Reynolds to Frank M. Wooten Sr., July 15, 1925, Frank M. Wooten, Sr. Papers, Manuscript Collection, East Carolina University, Greenville.

76. Robert R. Reynolds to "Fellow Alumnus," March 8, 1926, Charles O'Hagan Laughinghouse Papers, Manuscript Collection, East Carolina University, Greenville.

77. John C. Sikes to Lee S. Overman, July 23, 1925, and Frank M. Wooten to Lee S. Overman, July 23, 1925, Gregory Papers.

78. P. Cleveland Gardner to Robert R. Reynolds, March 9, 1926, and Robert R. Reynolds to P. Cleveland Gardner, March 12, 13, May 19, 1926, all in P. Cleveland Gardner Papers, Duke University Library.

79. B. I. Moore to "Dear Sir," May 20, 1926, Gardner Papers; *Raleigh News and Observer*, May 18, 1926; Harry H. Vaughan to Jonathan Daniels, March 10, 1950, Daniels Papers; author's interview with Frances Reynolds Oertling.

80. Heard and Strong, *Southern Primaries and Elections*, 97.

81. P. Cleveland Gardner to Robert R. Reynolds, June 19, 1926, Gardner Papers.

82. Author's interview with Frances Reynolds Oertling; author's interview with Margaret Reynolds; *Washington Sunday News*, August 17, 1941.

83. Robert Rice Reynolds to C. L. Shuping, April 7, 1930, and Reynolds to Josiah W. Bailey, April 1, 1930, Josiah W. Bailey Papers, Duke University Library.

84. Lefler and Newsome, *North Carolina*, 573.

85. Robert Rice Reynolds to Josiah W. Bailey, February 14, March 14, and March 21, 1930, Bailey Papers.

86. Josiah W. Bailey to Robert Rice Reynolds, January 16, April 1, 1930, Bailey Papers.

87. Lefler and Newsome, *North Carolina*, 573.

CHAPTER TWO

1. Lefler and Newsome, *North Carolina*, 571; Moore, *Senator Josiah William Bailey*, 58.

2. Key, *Southern Politics*, 227; Lefler and Newsome, *North Carolina*, 573.

3. Puryear, *Democratic Party Dissension*, 46.

4. Tindall, *Emergence of the New South*, 249–253; Key, *Southern Politics*, 207–228; Badger, *North Carolina and the New Deal*, 7.

5. *Charlotte Observer*, December 4, 1930.

6. Ibid., December 5, 1930.

7. Ibid.

8. Josiah Bailey to Mr. Warren, February 11, 1931, Josiah W. Bailey Papers, Duke University Library, Durham.

9. *Charlotte Observer*, December 5, 1930.

10. Ibid., December 6, 7, 1930; *Raleigh News and Observer*, December 13, 1930.

11. *Raleigh News and Observer*, August 30, 1931; Puryear, *Democratic Party Dissension*, 123; *Raleigh News and Observer*, December 14, 1930.

12. *Raleigh News and Observer*, December 14, 1930; *Charlotte Observer*, December 14, 1930.

13. *Raleigh News and Observer*, December 18, 1930; *Charlotte Observer*, December 18, 1930; Puryear, *Democratic Party Dissension*, 124.

14. *Raleigh News and Observer*, December 19, 1930; *Charlotte Observer*, December 19, 1930.

15. *Congressional Record*, 71st Cong., 3d sess., 1931, p. 1269.

16. *Raleigh News and Observer*, December 25, 1930.

17. *Scotland Neck Commonwealth*, January 9, 1931.

18. *Elizabeth City Independent*, January 23, 1931.

19. W. A. Brown to Josiah W. Bailey, February 2, 1931, Bailey Papers.

20. *Raleigh News and Observer*, December 22, 1930.

21. *Charlotte Observer*, March 25, 1931.

22. *Raleigh News and Observer*, June 14, July 15, 1931.

23. Robert Rice Reynolds to E. A. Hughes, June 19, 1930, Bailey Papers.

24. *Raleigh News and Observer*, July 26, 1931; *New York Times*, July 27, 1931.

25. *Raleigh News and Observer*, August 2, 1931.

26. Ibid., August 30, 1931; Puryear, *Democratic Party Dissension*, 128.

27. *Raleigh News and Observer*, July 14, 1931.

28. Cameron Morrison, *Public Papers and Letters of Cameron Morrison*, xviii–xvix, xx–xxiii; Lefler and Newsome, *North Carolina*, 565–66.

29. London, *North Carolina Manual, 1931*, 155.

30. Burke Davis, "Senator Bob Reynolds," 364.

31. Johnson, *Judge Tam C. Bowie*; *Raleigh News and Observer*, July 19, August 2, 1931, February 13, 1947.

32. Connor, *North Carolina*, 2:397.

33. *Raleigh News and Observer*, August 4, 6, 1931.

34. Ibid., July 26, 1931.

35. Ibid.

36. Cash, "Paladin of the Drys," 139.

37. *Raleigh News and Observer*, August 3, 1931.

38. *New York Times*, August 16, 1931.

39. *Raleigh News and Observer*, July 30, 1931.

40. Ibid., October 17, 1931.

41. Ibid., January 3, 1932.

42. Edwin Gill to Cameron Morrison, January 22, 1932, O. Max Gardner Papers, Southern Historical Collection, University of North Carolina, Chapel Hill.

43. O. Max Gardner to Cameron Morrison, February 5, 1932, Gardner Papers.

44. William Bailey Jones to Josiah W. Bailey, March 3 and 16, 1932, Bailey Papers.

45. James S. Manning to Josiah W. Bailey, March 15, 1932, Bailey Papers.

46. Josiah W. Bailey to James S. Manning, March 21, 1932, and to William Bailey Jones, March 21, 1932, Bailey Papers. See also Moore, *Senator Josiah W. Bailey*, 88.

47. Lindsay Warren to Carroll E. Kramer, June 22, 1932, Lindsay Carter Warren Papers, Southern Historical Collection, University of North Carolina, Chapel Hill.

48. *Durham Morning Herald*, June 12, 1932.

49. Moore, *Senator Josiah W. Bailey*, 88.

50. Shelton, "Buncombe Bob," 140.

51. *Greensboro Daily News*, May 17, 1932.

52. *Raleigh News and Observer*, January 17, 27, 1932; *Asheville Citizen*, January 17, 1932.

53. *Raleigh News and Observer*, January 22, 1932.

54. Ibid.

55. Ibid., February 12, 1932.

56. Ibid., May 3, 1932.

57. Shelton, "Buncombe Bob," 140.

58. *Durham Herald-Sun*, April 27, 1941.

59. *Houston Chronicle*, April 26, 1941; author's interview with Frances Reynolds Oertling; *Asheville Citizen*, July 3, 1932.

60. Shelton, "Buncombe Bob," 142.

61. *Durham Herald-Sun*, April 27, 1941.

62. Author's interview with Frances Reynolds Oertling.

63. *Raleigh News and Observer*, May 14, 1932.

64. *Raleigh Times*, February 20, 1932.

65. Davis, "Senator Bob Reynolds," 366.

66. Puryear, *Democratic Party Dissension*, 140.

67. *Asheville Citizen*, July 10, 1932.

68. *Durham Morning Herald*, April 27, 1941.

69. McCormick, "Buncombe Bob," 38.

70. *Raleigh News and Observer*, May 31, 1932.

71. *Asheville Citizen*, April 3, 1933, February 14, 1963. See also Michie and Ryhlick, *Dixie Demagogues*, 234; *Raleigh News and Observer*, September 7, 1941; and Piller, *Time Bomb*, 103.

72. Author's interview with Frances Reynolds Oertling.

73. *American Mercury*, May 1939, 306–7.

74. *Asheville Citizen*, February 14, 1963.

75. Badger, *North Carolina and the New Deal*, 1–7.

76. *Historical Statistics of the United States to 1970*, 1:164, 169–70, 213, 300–302, cited in Robert S. McElvaine, *Down and Out in the Great Depression* (Chapel Hill, 1983), 17.

77. McElvaine, *Down and Out*, 109–110, 85–86, 158.

78. *Asheville Citizen*, April 20, 23, March 22, 25, May 25, 1932; *Raleigh News and Observer*, February 20, March 22, 25, April 12, 26, 1932.

79. Shelton, "Buncombe Bob," 142–43.

80. *Raleigh News and Observer*, February 20, 1932.

81. *Asheville Citizen*, March 16, 20, 1932.

82. *Asheville Citizen*, March 22, 25, 1932; *Raleigh News and Observer*, March 25, 1932.

83. Robert R. Reynolds to Josiah W. Bailey, March 17, 1932, Bailey Papers.

84. *Asheville Citizen*, April 21, 1932.

85. *Raleigh News and Observer*, March 25, 1932; *Asheville Citizen*, March 25, 1932.

86. *Durham Morning Herald*, April 27, 1941; *Raleigh News and Observer*, April 24, 1932.

87. McCormick, "Buncombe Bob," 38.

88. *New York Times*, April 3, 1932.

89. Whitener, *Prohibition in North Carolina*, 193; *Raleigh News and Observer*, November 9, 1928.

90. Whitener, *Prohibition in North Carolina*, 197.

91. James S. Manning to Josiah W. Bailey, April 5, 16, 19, 1932, Bailey Papers.

92. N. Henry Moore to Lindsay Warren, May 3, 1932, Warren Papers.

93. William Bailey Jones to Josiah W. Bailey, April 22, 1932, Bailey Papers.

94. H. G. Gulley to Josiah W. Bailey, May 15, 1932, Bailey Papers.

95. *Asheville Citizen*, April 17, 22, 1932.

96. Robert R. Reynolds to Josiah W. Bailey, March 17, 1932, Bailey Papers.

97. *Asheville Citizen*, April 8, 1932.

98. *Raleigh News and Observer*, May 12, 1932.

99. Ibid., March 24, 1931, March 15, 1932.

100. *Asheville Citizen*, April 22, 1932; *Raleigh News and Observer*, April 22, 1932.

101. *Raleigh News and Observer*, April 22, May 14, 1932; *Asheville Citizen*, May 31, 1932.

102. *Asheville Citizen*, May 31, 1932.

103. Ibid., May 14, 1932; *Raleigh News and Observer*, May 13, 1932.

104. *Asheville Citizen*, May 31, 1932.

105. Ibid., May 3, 1932.

106. *Raleigh News and Observer*, March 16, 1932; *Asheville Citizen*, May 6, 1932.

107. Josiah W. Bailey to H. G. Gulley, May 27, 1932, Bailey Papers.

108. *Raleigh News and Observer*, May 27, 1932.

109. Ibid.

110. William E. Bragham to Lindsay Warren, June 1, 1932, Warren Papers.

111. *Raleigh News and Observer*, May 25, 27, 1932; *Asheville Citizen*, May 25, 26, 27, 28, 30, 31, 1932.

112. *Raleigh News and Observer*, June 3, 1932; undated flyer, Bailey Papers.

113. *Raleigh News and Observer*, June 4, 1932; *Asheville Citizen*, June 4, 1932.

114. *Asheville Citizen*, May 29, June 2, 3, 1932.

115. Angus W. McLean to O. Max Gardner, June 1, 1932, Gardner Papers.

116. *Asheville Citizen*, May 24, 28, June 4, 1932; *Raleigh News and Observer*, June 4, 1932.

117. *Asheville Citizen*, May 31, June 2, 1932.

118. London, *North Carolina Manual, 1933*, 101–2; *Raleigh News and Observer*, June 11, 1932; *Asheville Citizen*, June 11, 1932.

119. *Durham Morning Herald*, June 12, 1932.

120. E. R. Preston to Josiah W. Bailey, June 11, 1932, Bailey Papers.

121. Lindsay Warren to R. Bruce Etheridge, June 9, 1932, Warren Papers.

122. James S. Manning to Josiah W. Bailey, June 7, 1932, Bailey Papers.

123. Thurmond Chatham to Josiah W. Bailey, June 7, 1932, Bailey Papers.

124. William Bailey Jones to Josiah W. Bailey, June 6, 1932, Bailey Papers.

125. C. H. Robertson to Josiah W. Bailey, June 9, 1932, Bailey Papers.

126. Paul R. Ervin to Josiah W. Bailey, June 10, 1932, and Josiah W. Bailey to Paul R. Ervin, June 13, 1932, Bailey Papers.

127. E. G. Flanagan to Lindsay Warren, June 10, 1932, Warren Papers.

CHAPTER THREE

1. *Asheville Citizen*, June 9, 1932; *Raleigh News and Observer*, June 9, 1932.
2. *Raleigh Times*, June 6, 8, 1932.
3. *Raleigh News and Observer*, June 9, 12, 1932.
4. Ibid., June 9, 1932.
5. O. Max Gardner to John W. Hanes, June 21, 1932, O. Max Gardner Papers, Southern Historical Collection, University of North Carolina, Chapel Hill; *New York Times*, June 12, 1932.
6. *Asheville Citizen*, June 10, 1932.
7. *Raleigh News and Observer*, June 8, 1932; *Asheville Citizen*, June 8, 10, 1932.
8. *Charlotte Observer*, June 8, 1932.
9. *Raleigh News and Observer*, June 12, 1932.
10. Ibid., June 14, 1932; *Asheville Citizen*, June 14, 1932.
11. *Asheville Citizen*, June 14, 1932; *Raleigh News and Observer*, June 14, 1932.
12. *Asheville Citizen*, June 16, 1932; *Raleigh News and Observer*, June 16, 1932.
13. *North Carolina Democratic Handbook, 1936*, 8, 10, 11; *New York Times*, June 26, 1932; *Raleigh News and Observer*, June 17, 1932; *Asheville Citizen*, June 17, 1932.
14. *New York Times*, June 30, 1932.
15. *Asheville Citizen*, June 16, 1932.
16. O. Max Gardner to John W. Hanes, June 21, 1932, Gardner Papers.
17. *Asheville Citizen*, June 9, 10, 11, 1932.
18. Ibid., June 12, 1932.
19. Ibid., June 7, July 10, 1932.
20. *Raleigh News and Observer*, June 28, 1932; *Asheville Citizen*, June 21, 1932.
21. *Raleigh News and Observer*, June 26, 1932.
22. *Asheville Citizen*, June 22, 23, 1932.
23. Ibid., June 24, 25, 1932.
24. Ibid., June 22, 1932.
25. *Raleigh News and Observer*, June 28, 1932; *Asheville Citizen*, June 26, 1932.
26. *Asheville Citizen*, June 23, 1932.
27. William Bailey Jones to Thad Page, June 27, 1932, Josiah W. Bailey Papers, Duke University Library, Durham.
28. John Bright Hill to P. Cleveland Gardner, June 22, June 30, 1932, P. Cleveland Gardner Papers, Duke University Library, Durham; *Asheville Citizen*, June 28, 30, July 1, 1932.
29. *Asheville Citizen*, June 30, 1932.
30. Ibid., July 2, 1932; *Raleigh News and Observer*, July 2, 1932.
31. *Asheville Citizen*, July 1, 1932.
32. *Raleigh News and Observer*, July 1, 1932.
33. London, *North Carolina Manual, 1933*, 101–2; *Raleigh News and Observer*, July 3, 1932; *Asheville Citizen*, July 10, 1932.
34. *Asheville Citizen*, July 3, 4, 1932.
35. Josiah W. Bailey to Cameron Morrison, July 5, 1932, Bailey Papers.
36. *Asheville Citizen*, July 3, 1932.
37. *Raleigh Times*, n.d., and *Charlotte News*, n.d., quoted in the *Asheville Citizen*, July 6, 1932.
38. Josiah W. Bailey to Gerald W. Johnson, July 6, 1932, and Bailey to J. S. Manning, July 6, 1932, Bailey Papers.
39. William Bailey Jones to Thad Page, July 7, 1932, Bailey Papers.
40. *Raleigh News and Observer*, July 7, 1932.
41. *New York Times*, June 12, 1932.

42. *Raleigh News and Observer*, June 12, 1932.

43. *Baltimore Evening Sun*, n.d., quoted in the *Raleigh News and Observer*, July 17, 1932.

44. *Plain Talk*, September 1932, n.p., in possession of Frances Reynolds Oertling.

45. McLean, "Where Cam Made His Mistake," 16; *Raleigh Times*, July 4, 1932; *Asheville Citizen*, July 5, 1932.

46. *New York Times*, July 10, 1932.

47. William Bailey Jones to Thad Page, July 5, 1932, Bailey Papers.

48. Puryear, *Democratic Party Dissension*, 151.

49. *Dayton Daily News*, n.d., quoted in the *Asheville Citizen*, February 13, 1950.

50. *Raleigh News and Observer*, July 17, 1932.

51. *Wilmington Star-News*, n.d., quoted in the *Asheville Citizen*, July 6, 1932.

52. *New York Times*, June 12, 1932.

53. *Raleigh News and Observer*, July 5, 1932.

54. *Richmond News Leader*, July 5, 1932.

55. *Raleigh News and Observer*, July 2, 1932; *Asheville Citizen*, July 6, 1932.

56. Charles W. Tillett to Josiah W. Bailey, July 7, 1932, Bailey Papers.

57. Whitener, *Prohibition in North Carolina*, 197.

58. William Bailey Jones to Thad Page, July 7, 1932, Bailey Papers.

59. O. Max Gardner to Governor Franklin D. Roosevelt, July 22, 1932, Gardner Papers.

60. Key, *Southern Politics*, 3–4, 205–6, 213–20.

61. Gerald W. Johnson to Josiah W. Bailey, July 4, 1932, Bailey Papers.

62. Lerche, *Uncertain South*, 54.

63. Badger, *North Carolina and the New Deal*, 12.

64. *Raleigh News and Observer*, July 17, 1932.

65. *Asheville Citizen*, August 3, 1932; *Raleigh News and Observer*, August 3, 1932.

66. *Asheville Citizen*, July 8, 1932.

67. Ibid., July 16, 1932.

68. Interview with R. Grady Rankin by Joseph L. Morrison, November 26, 1968, Joseph L. Morrison Papers, Southern Historical Collection.

69. *Asheville Citizen*, August 3, 1932.

70. Puryear, *Democratic Party Dissension*, 152.

71. *Asheville Citizen*, August 6, 7, 8, 9, 10, 1932; *Raleigh News and Observer*, August 9, 1932.

72. *Raleigh News and Observer*, September 18, 1932; *Asheville Citizen*, September 18, 1932.

73. *Durham Morning Herald*, November 3, 1932.

74. Ibid., September 24, 1932.

75. *Raleigh News and Observer*, September 27, 1932.

76. Rupert S. Bagley to Josiah W. Bailey, October 17, 1932, Bailey Papers.

77. *Raleigh News and Observer*, September 23, 1932; *Asheville Citizen*, September 23, 1932, October 15, 1932.

78. *Raleigh News and Observer*, September 25, 1932; *Asheville Citizen*, September 25, 1932.

79. *Raleigh News and Observer*, September 30, 1932; *Asheville Citizen*, September 30, October 18, 1932.

80. *Asheville Citizen*, October 11, 1932; *Raleigh News and Observer*, October 18, 1932.

81. *Raleigh News and Observer*, October 27, 1932.

82. Ibid., October 16, 1932.

83. Ibid., October 1, 1932; *Asheville Citizen*, October 1, 1932.

84. Josiah W. Bailey to *Caswell Messenger*, October 31, 1932, Bailey Papers; *Asheville Citizen*, October 22, 23, 1932.

85. *Raleigh News and Observer*, October 22, 1932.

86. *Asheville Citizen*, July 6, 1932.

87. *Raleigh News and Observer*, October 22, 1932.

88. Ibid., November 1, 1932.

89. *Asheville Citizen*, November 6, 1932; *Raleigh News and Observer*, November 6, 1932.

90. *Asheville Citizen*, November 7, 1932.

91. Heard and Strong, *Southern Primaries and Elections*, 99; *Asheville Citizen*, November 20, 1932; *Raleigh News and Observer*, November 24, 1932.

92. Heard and Strong, *Southern Primaries and Elections*, 5.

93. Ibid., 111.

94. Robert R. Reynolds to Franklin D. Roosevelt, November 8, 1932, and Franklin D. Roosevelt to Robert R. Reynolds, November 19, 1932, Franklin Delano Roosevelt Papers, Franklin Delano Roosevelt Library, Hyde Park, New York.

95. *Raleigh News and Observer*, July 17, 1932.

96. Josiah W. Bailey to Robert R. Reynolds, July 4, 1932, Bailey Papers.

97. Robert R. Reynolds to Josiah W. Bailey, August 15, October 3, 1932, Bailey Papers.

98. Bailey to Reynolds, October 5, 1932, and Reynolds to Bailey, October 7, 1932, Bailey Papers.

99. *Raleigh News and Observer*, November 9, December 6, 1932. Cameron Morrison's appointment to the United States Senate in December 1931 was only until the next general election in November 1932.

100. *Congressional Record*, 72d Cong., 2d sess., December 5, 1932, p. 4; *Raleigh News and Observer*, December 6, 1932; *Charlotte Observer*, December 6, 1932.

CHAPTER FOUR

1. *Raleigh News and Observer*, December 19, 1932; *Asheville Citizen*, January 29, 1933.

2. *Congressional Record*, 72d Cong., 2d sess., 1932, p. 1619.

3. *Congressional Record*, 73d Cong., 1st sess., 1933, p. 4453; *Asheville Citizen*, May 30, 1933.

4. Author's interview with Hubert H. Rand Jr., September 24, 1991; author's interview with Wesley E. McDonald Sr.

5. *Raleigh News and Observer*, May 8, 1933; *Asheville Citizen*, November 10, 13, 1932, January 20, 27, March 24, 1933.

6. *Winston-Salem Journal*, December 18, 1932.

7. *Asheville Citizen*, January 20, 1933, quoting the *New York World Telegraph*, n.d.

8. *Asheville Citizen*, April 3, 1933.

9. *Raleigh News and Observer*, January 13, 1933, December 6, 1932; *Asheville Citizen*, January 20, 1933.

10. Wheeler, *Yankee from the West*, 279–80; author's interview with Burton K. Wheeler.

11. Author's interview with Wesley E. McDonald Sr.

12. *Asheville Citizen*, February 3, 1933.

13. Jeansonne, *Messiah of the Masses*, 2–4, 53–62, 104–15, 164–68.

14. *The State*, July 15, 1933, 8.

15. Robert R. Reynolds to Harriett [*sic*] M. Berry, February 2, 1933, Harriet M. Berry Papers, Southern Historical Collection, University of North Carolina, Chapel Hill.

16. *Raleigh News and Observer*, May 14, 1933.

17. Puryear, *Democratic Party Dissension*, 232; Moore, *Senator Josiah William Bailey*, 89.

18. Moore, *Senator Josiah William Bailey*, 99.

19. *Raleigh News and Observer*, December 20, 1932.

20. Josiah W. Bailey to Johnston Avery, November 21, 1933, Josiah W. Bailey Papers, Duke University Library, Durham.

21. *Asheville Citizen*, February 27, 1933.

22. Ibid., March 29, April 1, 1933; Moore, *Senator Josiah William Bailey*, 99–100.

23. *Charlotte Observer*, April 26, 1933; *Asheville Citizen*, April 27, June 6, 1933.

24. *Durham Sun*, June 29, 1933.

25. *Gastonia Gazette*, June 29, 1933.

26. *Raleigh News and Observer*, August 21, 1933.

27. *Durham Sun*, July 7, 1933.

28. O. Max Gardner to Robert R. Reynolds, July 18, 1933, O. Max Gardner Papers, Southern Historical Collection.

29. Robert R. Reynolds to O. Max Gardner, July 26, 1933, Gardner Papers; *Burlington Times*, October 19, 1933.

30. *Asheville Citizen*, February 23, April 1, 1933; *Raleigh News and Observer*, February 28, 1933.

31. Author's interview with Irving C. Crawford.

32. Robert R. Reynolds to Franklin D. Roosevelt, April 3, 24, 1933, and to Louis M. Howe, secretary to the president, April 9, 1933, Franklin Delano Roosevelt Papers, Franklin D. Roosevelt Library, Hyde Park.

33. *Asheville Citizen*, October 22, 23, 25, 1933.

34. *Raleigh News and Observer*, November 17, 1933; *Asheville Citizen*, November 17, 1933.

35. *Asheville Citizen*, November 21, 1933.

36. *Washington Post*, June 15, 1933; *New York Times*, June 14, 1933; *Raleigh News and Observer*, June 14, 1933; *Asheville Citizen*, June 14, 23, 1933.

37. *Asheville Citizen*, June 15, 1933; *Raleigh News and Observer*, June 15, 1933.

38. *Asheville Citizen*, June 17, 1933; *Raleigh News and Observer*, June 17, 1933.

39. *Asheville Citizen*, June 21, 1933; *Raleigh News and Observer*, June 21, 1933.

40. *Asheville Citizen*, April 19, June 7, 1933; *Raleigh News and Observer*, April 19, 1933; Robert R. Reynolds to C. F. Kirksey, April 10, 1934, Clarence Leroy Shuping Papers, Manuscript Collection, East Carolina University, Greenville.

41. *Asheville Citizen*, May 10, 1933.

42. Ibid., April 2, 14, 15, 19, 1933.

43. *Raleigh News and Observer*, June 30, 1933; *Asheville Citizen*, June 30, 1933.

44. *Asheville Citizen*, March 12, 14, 15, 16, 1933.

45. Ibid., March 24, 1933.

46. Ibid., April 23, 1933.

47. Salmone, *Civilian Conservation Corps*, preface, 3–25; Ellis, *Nation in Torment*, 296–307.

48. *Raleigh News and Observer*, September 6, 1933.

49. *Asheville Citizen*, September 6, 14, 1933.

50. *New York Times*, September 28, 29, 1933.

51. *Raleigh News and Observer*, October 14, 15, 1933; *Asheville Citizen*, October 15, 16, 1933.

52. *Raleigh News and Observer*, October 21, 1933; *Asheville Citizen*, October 21, 1933.

53. *Durham Morning Herald*, October 26, 1933.

54. Bennett, *Franklin D. Roosevelt and the Search for Security*, xiii–xvii, 1–24.

55. *Asheville Citizen*, November 18, 1933.

56. *Charlotte Observer*, October 15, 1933.

57. *Raleigh News and Observer*, December 24, 1932.

58. *Congressional Record*, 72d Cong., 2d sess., 1933, p. 4231; *Asheville Citizen*, February 17, 1933; *Raleigh News and Observer*, February 17, 1933.

59. *Asheville Citizen*, May 30, 1933; *Raleigh News and Observer*, June 20, 1933.

60. *Asheville Citizen*, June 18, July 7, 8, 1933; Robert R. Reynolds to John W. Hinsdale, June 27, 1933, Hinsdale Family Papers, Duke University Library.

61. Whitener, *Prohibition in North Carolina*, 202–4.

62. *Winston-Salem Journal*, November 3, 1933; *Asheville Citizen*, October 20, 1933.

63. *Raleigh News and Observer*, October 24, 1933; *Asheville Citizen*, October 24, 1933.

64. *Winston-Salem Journal*, October 25, 26, 1933.

65. Whitener, *Prohibition in North Carolina*, 203–4; *Asheville Citizen*, October 28, 1933.

66. *Raleigh News and Observer*, November 1, 1933; *Asheville Citizen*, November 1, 1933.

67. *Raleigh News and Observer*, November 2, 1933; *Asheville Citizen*, November 2, 3, 4, 1933.

68. *Raleigh News and Observer*, November 5, 1933.

69. Ibid., November 8, 1933; *Asheville Citizen*, November 7, 1933.

70. London, *North Carolina Manual, 1935*, 112–13; *Durham Morning Herald*, November 8, 1933; *Asheville Citizen*, November 8, 1933.

71. *Asheville Citizen*, November 8, 1933; *Raleigh News and Observer*, November 8, 1933.

72. *Durham Morning Herald*, November 9, 1933; *Raleigh News and Observer*, November 9, 1933; *Asheville Citizen*, November 9, 1933.

73. *Asheville Citizen*, January 4, 26, July 12, 1933.

74. Ibid., April 15, 1934.

75. Ibid., September 25, 1934.

76. Ibid., November 11, December 13, January 3, 15, 1933.

77. *Congressional Record*, 73d Cong., 2d sess., 1934, p. 6574; *Asheville Citizen*, April 7, 1934.

78. Author's interview with Wesley E. McDonald Sr.

79. *Congressional Record*, 73d Cong., 2d sess., 1934, pp. 5482, 5486–87, 5503.

80. Ibid., 73d Cong., 2d sess., 1934, pp. 8503–6; *Asheville Citizen*, January 20, 28, May 13, 14, 1934; *Raleigh News and Observer*, March 13, 1934.

81. *Congressional Record*, 73d Cong., 2d sess., 1934, pp. 3304, 3308; *Raleigh News and Observer*, February 28, 1934; *Asheville Citizen*, February 28, March 16, 28, 29, 30, 1934; Schlesinger, *Age of Roosevelt*, vol. 3, *Politics of Upheaval*, 504.

82. *Raleigh News and Observer*, June 22, 1934.

83. Ibid., June 30, 1934.

84. Ibid., November 2, 3, 1934.

85. *Asheville Citizen*, June 26, 1934; *Raleigh News and Observer*, November 3, 1934.

86. *Raleigh News and Observer*, October 10, 1934; *Asheville Citizen*, September 1, October 10, November 2, 1934.

87. *Raleigh News and Observer*, October 25, 1934; *Asheville Citizen*, November 2, 1934.

88. Josephus Daniels, *Shirt-Sleeve Diplomat*, 362–64.

89. *El Nacional*, February 9, 1935, in Josephus Daniels Papers, Library of Congress, Washington, D.C. *El Nacional* was the organ of the Mexican Revolutionary Party.

90. *Greensboro Daily News*, February 8, 1935; *Raleigh News and Observer*, February 7, 1935.

91. *Asheville Citizen*, February 17, 19, 22, June 2, December 14, 1934; *Raleigh News and Observer*, December 14, 1934.

92. Robert R. Reynolds to Josephus Daniels, November 24, 1934, Josephus Daniels Papers.

93. Author's interview with T. Lamar Caudle, Frances Reynolds Oertling, and Margaret Reynolds.

94. *Raleigh News and Observer*, May 10, 1934.

95. *Asheville Citizen*, June 22, 23, 1934.

96. *Raleigh News and Observer*, June 23, 1934.

97. Ibid., December 3, 1934.

98. *Asheville Citizen*, January 11, 1935.

99. *Raleigh News and Observer*, January 11, 1935; *Asheville Citizen*, January 11, 1935.

100. *Congressional Record*, 74th Cong., 1st sess., 1935, pp. 1242–43.

101. *Asheville Citizen*, January 31, 1935.

102. *Congressional Record*, 74th Cong., 1st sess., 1935, pp. 13660–62; *Raleigh News and Observer*, August 20, 1935.

103. Rauch, *History of the New Deal*, 156–160; Burns, *Roosevelt: The Lion and the Fox*, 205, 225.

104. Josephus Daniels to Robert R. Reynolds, January 14, 1935, Josephus Daniels Papers; *Asheville Citizen*, January 5, 1935.

105. *Raleigh News and Observer*, January 15, 1935; *Asheville Citizen*, January 15, 1935.

106. *Asheville Citizen*, June 20, 1935; *Raleigh News and Observer*, August 15, 1935.

107. *Raleigh News and Observer*, September 1, 1935.

108. *Congressional Record*, 74th Cong., 1st sess., 1935, p. 11526; *Raleigh News and Observer*, July 23, 1935.

109. *Congressional Record*, 74th Cong., 1st sess., 1935, p. 13254; *Raleigh News and Observer*, August 16, 1935; Rauch, *History of the New Deal*, 308.

110. *Raleigh News and Observer*, September 7, 1935.

111. *Asheville Citizen*, May 21, 1935; Rauch, *History of the New Deal*, 185–87.

112. *Congressional Record*, 74th Cong., 1st sess., 1935, p. 9065; *Asheville Citizen*, June 12, 1935.

113. Josephus Daniels to Jonathan Daniels, July 3, 1935, Josephus Daniels Papers.

114. *Asheville Citizen*, April 3, 1935; *Raleigh News and Observer*, May 16, 1935; Rauch, *History of the New Deal*, 180–81.

115. *Congressional Record*, 74th Cong., 1st sess., 1935, p. 8067; *New York Times*, May 24, 1935; *Asheville Citizen*, May 24, 1935.

116. *Asheville Citizen*, February 22, 28, 1935; *Raleigh News and Observer*, February 28, March 1, 1935; Badger, *The New Deal*, 200–203.

117. *Asheville Citizen*, March 1, 1935; *Raleigh News and Observer*, March 2, 1935.

118. *Asheville Citizen*, February 28, 1935.

119. *Congressional Record*, 74th Cong., 1st sess., 1935, p. 2711; see also ibid., pp. 3455, 3458, 3460, 3701–3, 3718; *Asheville Citizen*, March 2, 1935.

120. *Congressional Record*, 74th Cong., 1st sess., 1935, pp. 2724–29; *Asheville Citizen*, March 2, 1935.

121. *Asheville Citizen*, March 2, 4, 1935; R. L. Gwyn to George Stephens, February 23, 1935, George Stephens to R. L. Gwyn, February 27, 1935, and Mayne Albright to Robert R. Reynolds, March 12, 1935, George E. C. Stephens Papers, Southern Historical Collection.

122. *Congressional Record*, 74th Cong., 1st sess., 1935, p. 2728.

123. Ibid., 3704; *Asheville Citizen*, March 13, 14, 16, 1935.

124. *Congressional Record*, 74th Cong., 1st sess., 1935, p. 3724; see also ibid., pp. 2724–29; 3702–3, 3717; *Asheville Citizen*, March 16, 1935.

125. *Congressional Record*, 74th Cong., 1st sess., 1935, p. 5135; *Asheville Citizen*, March 20, 24, 1935.

126. Divine, *American Immigration Policy*, 86; *Interpreter Releases* (New York: Foreign Language Information Service, 1924–40); Common Council for American Unity, *The Alien and the Immigration Law*, 12.

127. Robert R. Reynolds, "Aliens and the Unemployment Problem," radio speech, 1935.

128. *Raleigh News and Observer*, January 15, 1935; *Asheville Citizen*, January 15, 1935.

129. Robert R. Reynolds to H. Patrick Taylor Sr., May 18, 1935, H. Patrick Taylor, Sr. Papers, Manuscript Collection, East Carolina University, Greenville; *New York Times*, April 20, 1935; *Raleigh News and Observer*, April 20, 1935; *Asheville Citizen*, March 3, April 18, 1935.

130. Pilat, *Drew Pearson*, 173.

131 Ralph W. Gardner to Joseph L. Morrison, December 18, 1968, Joseph L. Morrison Papers, Southern Historical Collection.

132. *Raleigh News and Observer*, May 10, 1935.

133. *New York Times*, May 11, 1935.

134. *Raleigh News and Observer*, May 12, 1935.

135. Diaries of Harold L. Ickes, May 17, 1935, 977–78, Harold L. Ickes Papers, Library of Congress; *Asheville Citizen*, May 13, 1935; *Raleigh News and Observer*, May 13, 1935.

136. *Raleigh News and Observer*, May 15, 1935.

137. Dairies of Harold L. Ickes, May 17, 1935, 978; *Asheville Citizen*, May 15, 1935.

138. H. Patrick Taylor Sr. to Robert R. Reynolds, May 28, 1935, H. Patrick Taylor, Sr. Papers.

139. *Raleigh News and Observer*, May 17, 1935; *Asheville Citizen*, May 17, 1935; *Congressional Record*, 74th Cong., 1st sess., 1935, p. 12966.

140. *Raleigh News and Observer*, May 24, 1935; *Asheville Citizen*, May 24, 1935.

141. *Raleigh News and Observer*, May 25, 1935.

142. *Asheville Citizen*, July 24, 1935; *Raleigh News and Observer*, July 24, 1935; Pilat, *Drew Pearson*, 174–77.

143. Divine, *Illusion of Neutrality*, 80.

144. Hull, *Memoirs*, 2:288–89.

145. *Congressional Record*, 74th Cong., 1st sess., 1935, pp. 771–77; *Asheville Citizen*, January 22, 1935.

146. *Asheville Citizen*, January 24, 1935.

147. *Congressional Record*, 74th Cong., 1st sess., 1935, pp. 886–90; *Asheville Citizen*, January 23, 24, 1935.

148. Radio speech reprinted in the *Congressional Record*, 74th Cong., 1st sess., 1935, pp. 1149–50; *Raleigh News and Observer*, January 28, 1935; *Asheville Citizen*, January 28, 1935.

149. *Raleigh News and Observer*, January 29, 1935.

150. Robert R. Reynolds to Frank P. Graham, January 31, 1935, Frank P. Graham Papers, Southern Historical Collection; *Congressional Record*, 74th Cong., 1st sess., 1935, p. 1147; *Asheville Citizen*, January 30, 1935; Cole, *Roosevelt and the Isolationists*, 120–25.

151. *Asheville Citizen*, January 30, 1935.

152. Ibid., January 18, 29, February 2, 1935.

153. *Greensboro Daily News*, January 24, 1935.

154. *Raleigh News and Observer*, February 24, 1935.

155. John W. Hinsdale to Robert R. Reynolds, January 29, 1935, Hinsdale Family Papers.

156. *Asheville Citizen*, October 6, 7, 1935; Divine, *Illusion of Neutrality*, 115.

157. Dallek, *Roosevelt and American Foreign Policy*, 106–14.

158. *Raleigh News and Observer*, August 30, 1935; *Asheville Citizen*, August 30, 1935.

159. *Raleigh News and Observer*, September 2, 1935; *Asheville Citizen*, August 30, 1935.

160. *Asheville Citizen*, August 22, 25, 1935.

161. Author's interview with Wesley E. McDonald Sr.

162. Robert R. Reynolds to Marvin McIntyre, February 28, May 5, June 12, August 31, 1934; Marvin McIntyre to Robert R. Reynolds, November 24, 1934, January 25, 1935; and Stephen Early to Robert R. Reynolds, October 9, 1934, all in Roosevelt Papers.

163. Robert R. Reynolds to J. Edgar Hoover, January 25, 1934; J. Edgar Hoover to Robert R. Reynolds, February 6, 1934; and J. Edgar Hoover, memorandum to Attorney General Homer S. Cummings, February 20, 1934, Federal Bureau of Investigation (hereafter FBI) file 94-1-12142, serials 18, 19.

164. Robert R. Reynolds to J. Edgar Hoover, July 16, November 16, 1934, FBI Ifile 94-1-12142.

165. Robert R. Reynolds to J. Edgar Hoover, January 18, 1935; Hoover to Reynolds, February 5, 1935; and *The Nationalist*, January 1935, 2, in FBI file 62-32211-8.

166. FBI memorandum to Clyde Tolson, January 28, 1935, and Robert R. Reynolds, "Demand It," *Master Detective*, January 1935, 5, 76, in FBI file 62-22444-1-241.

167. Powers, *Secrecy and Power*, 198–99.

168. *Asheville Citizen*, July 31, 1935.

169. *Raleigh News and Observer*, June 22, 1935.

170. Ibid., June 29, 1935.

171. *Raleigh News and Observer*, August 6, 1935.

172. White House memorandum to Missy LeHand, September 4, 1935, Roosevelt Papers.

173. Albert R. MacKusick to Franklin D. Roosevelt, September 7, 1935, and Robert R. Reynolds to Marvin McIntyre, April 12, 1935, Roosevelt Papers; *Boston Post*, September 6, 1935; *Boston Evening American*, September 6, 1935.

174. *Raleigh News and Observer*, September 9, 1935; *Asheville Citizen*, September 9, 1935.

175. *Asheville Citizen*, September 8, 1935.

176. *Charlotte Observer*, October 4, 1935; *Asheville Citizen*, October 4, 1935.

177. *Asheville Citizen*, November 15, 1935; Connally, *My Name Is Tom Connally*, 179–80.

178. *New York Times*, December 29, 1935; *Raleigh News and Observer*, December 3, 29, 1935; *Asheville Citizen*, December 3, 29, 1935.

179. Author's interview with Burton K. Wheeler.

CHAPTER FIVE

1. *Washington Evening Star*, January 17, 1936; *Asheville Citizen*, January 19, 1936.

2. Robert R. Reynolds to Franklin D. Roosevelt, December 22, 1935, and Roosevelt to Reynolds, January 17, 1936, Franklin Delano Roosevelt Papers, Franklin D. Roosevelt Library, Hyde Park; *Charlotte Observer*, October 4, 1935; *Wilmington Star-News*, September 7, 1935.

3. *Raleigh News and Observer*, May 19, 1936; *Greensboro Daily News*, May 19, 1936; *Asheville Citizen*, May 19, 1936.

4. Author's interview with Frances Reynolds Oertling; *New York Times*, August 2, 1936; *Asheville Citizen*, July 30, August 1, 1936; *Raleigh News and Observer*, August 4, 1936.

5. *Charlotte News*, July 30, 1936.

6. *Raleigh News and Observer*, January 16, 1936.

7. *Washington Evening Star*, January 17, 1936; *Asheville Citizen*, January 19, 1936.

8. *New York Times*, January 17, 1936; *Asheville Citizen*, January 17, 1936.

9. *Raleigh News and Observer*, February 22, 1936; *Asheville Citizen*, February 22, 1936.

10. *Congressional Record*, 74th Cong., 2d sess., 1936, pp. 1960–68; *Asheville Citizen*, February 14, March 1, 1936.

11. *Asheville Citizen*, February 15, 1936.

12. *Congressional Record*, 74th Cong., 2d sess., 1936, pp. 3744–48; *Asheville Citizen*, March 8, 1936; *Raleigh News and Observer*, March 13, 1936.

13. *Raleigh News and Observer*, March 18, 1936.

14. *Congressional Record*, 74th Cong., 2d sess., 1936, pp. 4908–20; *New York Times*, April 4, 1936.

15. *Congressional Record*, 74th Cong., 2d sess., 1936, pp. 4958–69; *New York Times*, April 5, 1936; *Asheville Citizen*, April 5, 1936.

16. *Congressional Record*, 74th Cong., 2d sess., 1936, pp. 5789–90, 5836; *New York Times*, April 22, 1936; Badger, *The New Deal*, 154–55.

17. *Congressional Record*, 74th Cong., 2d sess., 1936, pp. 5940–42; *Asheville Citizen*, April 24, 1936.

18. *Raleigh News and Observer*, April 25, 1936; *Asheville Citizen*, April 25, 1936.

19. *Congressional Record*, 74th Cong., 2d sess., 1936, pp. 5941–48; *Asheville Citizen*, April 24, 1936.

20. *Raleigh News and Observer*, May 3, 1936; *Asheville Citizen*, April 25, May 3, 7, 1936.

21. *Congressional Record*, 74th Cong., 2d sess., 1936, pp. 10501–5; *New York Times*, June 21, 1936.

22. *Raleigh News and Observer*, April 23, 1936.

23. *Washington News*, July 4, 1936.

24. *New York Times*, June 20, 1936.

25. *Asheville Citizen*, July 12, 1936.

26. Anson W. Betts to the editor, *Asheville Citizen*, July 12, 1936.

27. *Asheville Citizen*, June 13, 14, 1936.

28. Ibid., June 15, 23, 1936.

29. *Raleigh News and Observer*, June 25, 1936; *Asheville Citizen*, June 24, 25, 1936; Burns, *Roosevelt: The Lion and the Fox*, 272–75.

30. *Charlotte Observer*, October 22, 1936; *Asheville Citizen*, November 6, 1936; Robert R. Reynolds to Josephus Daniels, November 5, 1936, Josephus Daniels Papers, Library of Congress, Washington, D.C.

31. Robert R. Reynolds to Jonathan Daniels, August 25, 1936, Jonathan Worth Daniels Papers, Southern Historical Collection, University of North Carolina, Chapel Hill; R. R. Reynolds to H. Patrick Taylor Sr., August 27, 1936, H. Patrick Taylor Sr. Papers, Manuscript Collection, East Carolina University, Greenville; R. R. Reynolds to P. Cleveland Gardner, May 25, 1936, P. Cleveland Gardner Papers.

32. *Raleigh News and Observer*, March 26, April 1, 1936; *Asheville Citizen*, April 1, 1936; *Congressional Record*, 74th Cong., 2d sess., 1936, pp. 4694–96.

33. R. R. Reynolds to Josephus Daniels, April 2, 1936, Josephus Daniels Papers; *Asheville Citizen*, April 2, 1936.

34. *Raleigh News and Observer*, July 18, 1936.

35. *Asheville Citizen*, September 6, 1936.

36. *Raleigh News and Observer*, October 6, 14, 1936.

37. *Asheville Citizen*, September 6, 1936.

38. Ibid., September 9, 10, 11, 1936.

39. Burns, *Roosevelt: The Lion and the Fox*, 284.

40. Josiah W. Bailey to Robert R. Reynolds, November 10, 1936, Josiah W. Bailey Papers, Duke University Library, Durham.

41. *New York Times*, January 10, 1937.

42. *Congressional Record*, 75th Cong., 1st sess., 1937, p. 547.

43. *Raleigh News and Observer*, January 10, 1937.

44. Pamphlet of the American Coalition, February 12, 1937, n.p., H. Patrick Taylor Sr. Papers; pamphlet of the American Coalition, Washington, D.C., February 12, 1937, Gordon Gray Papers, Southern Historical Collection.

45. *Raleigh News and Observer*, May 1, 1939.

46. Ibid., June 10, 1937.

47. *New York Times*, August 9, 1937.

48. Gellerman, *Martin Dies*, 52; *Raleigh News and Observer*, April 8, 1938.

49. Announcement, January 6, 1938, American Immigration Conference Board Records, Manuscripts and Archives, Yale University, New Haven; *Congressional Record*, 75th Cong., 2d sess., 1937, p. 1170.

50. Ibid.; *Congressional Record*, 75th Cong., 2d sess., 1937, appendix, p. 1542.

51. *Raleigh News and Observer*, July 21, 1938.

52. *Congressional Record*, 74th Cong., 2d sess., 1936, p. 703; *Asheville Citizen*, January 21, 25, 26, 27, 1936.

53. Leuchtenburg, *Franklin D. Roosevelt and the New Deal*, 171.

54. *Raleigh News and Observer*, September 9, December 9, 1937; *Congressional Record*, 75th Cong., 2d sess., 1937, p. 6221.

55. FBI record of telephone call, June 14, 1937; T. D. Quinn to Clyde R. Tolson, June 14, 1937; Robert R. Reynolds to T. D. Quinn, June 22, 1937; and J. W. Vincent to J. Edgar Hoover, June 22, 1937, all in FBI file 94-1-195.

56. *Raleigh News and Observer*, May 13, 1937; *Asheville Citizen*, May 13, 1937.

57. *Raleigh News and Observer*, April 24, 1937.

58. Divine, *Illusion of Neutrality*, 165.

59. Dallek, *Roosevelt and American Foreign Policy*, 117–21.

60. Ibid., 120.

61. *Asheville Citizen*, January 4, 1937; *Raleigh News and Observer*, January 20, 1937.

62. Hull, *Memoirs*, 1:478–79.

63. Rosenman, *Papers and Addresses of Franklin D. Roosevelt*, 7:192–93.

64. Divine, *Illusion of Neutrality*, 165–73.

65. Ibid., 178–94; Rauch, *History of the New Deal*, 329–31.

66. *Asheville Citizen*, March 4, 1937; *Raleigh News and Observer*, March 4, 1937.

67. *Asheville Citizen*, October 18, December 28, 1937.

68. *Congressional Record*, 75th Cong., 2d sess., 1937, p. 1325; *Asheville Citizen*, December 12, 1937.

69. *Congressional Record*, 75th Cong., 2d sess., 1937, pp. 1356–58; *Asheville Citizen*, December 13, 14, 1937.

70. *Asheville Citizen*, December 15, 1937.

71. *New York Times*, December 14, 1937.

72. *Raleigh News and Observer*, January 10, 1938.

73. Rosenman, *Papers and Addresses of Franklin D. Roosevelt*, 7:410–11.

74. *Raleigh News and Observer*, March 18, 19, 1937.

75. Ibid., January 11, 1938; Cole, *Roosevelt and the Isolationists*, 253–62.

76. Speech by Robert R. Reynolds over the Mutual Broadcasting Company, April 3, 1938, p. 1, in Josephus Daniels Papers; *Congressional Record*, 75th Cong., 2d sess., 1937, p. 5824.

77. Josephus Daniels to Robert R. Reynolds, April 13, 1938, Josephus Daniels Papers.

78. *Raleigh News and Observer*, February 8, 1938.

79. *Army-Navy Journal*, October 8, 1938, 101, 114; see also *Congressional Record*, 75th Cong., 2d sess., 1937, pp. 219–22.

80. *New York Times*, September 3, 1938.

81. *Congressional Record*, 75th Cong., 1st sess., 1937, pp. 7863, 7877–88; *Asheville Citizen*, July 31, 1937.

82. *Congressional Record*, 75th Cong., 1st sess., 1937, p. 7863; *Asheville Citizen*, August 1, 1937.

83. Rauch, *History of the New Deal*, 305–6.

84. *Asheville Citizen*, December 5, 1937.

85. *Raleigh News and Observer*, December 8, 1937; *Asheville Citizen*, December 8, 1937.

86. Rauch, *History of the New Deal*, 293; *Asheville Citizen*, April 23, 1937.

87. *Raleigh News and Observer*, December 17, 1937.

88. *Asheville Citizen*, February 28, March 2, 1937.

89. *Congressional Record*, 75th Cong., 1st sess., 1937, pp. 3308–9; *Asheville Citizen*, March 3, April 10, 1937.

90. *Asheville Citizen*, May 16, 18, 20, 1937.

91. *Congressional Record*, 75th Cong., 1st sess., 1937, pp. 42, 8600; *Raleigh News and Observer*, April 11, 1937; *Asheville Citizen*, April 11, 1937.

92. *Congressional Record*, 75th Cong., 1st sess., 1937, p. 9130; *Raleigh News and Observer*, August 13, 1937; *Asheville Citizen*, August 18, 1937.

93. *Raleigh News and Observer*, September 17, 1937.

94. *Winston-Salem Journal*, September 19, 1937.

95. Burns, *Roosevelt: The Lion and the Fox*, 312–13; Freyer, *Hugo L. Black*, 66–71; Virginia Van der Veer, "Hugo Black and the KKK," *American Heritage*, April 1968, 61–64, 108–11; Leuchtenburg, *Supreme Court Reborn*, 180–212.

96. Leuchtenburg, *Franklin D. Roosevelt and the New Deal*, 231–38; Burns, *Roosevelt: The Lion and the Fox*, 293–315; Hall, *Magic Mirror*, 282.

97. *New York Times*, February 10, 1937; *Raleigh News and Observer*, February 7, 1937; *Asheville Citizen*, February 14, 20, 1937.

98. Josiah W. Bailey to D. Hiden Ramsey, February 26, 1937, Bailey Papers.

99. *Asheville Citizen*, March 2, April 14, 15, May 18, 1937.

100. *Congressional Record*, 75th Cong., 1st sess., 1937, p. 7163; *New York Times*, April 16, 1937; *Asheville Citizen*, April 16, 1937.

101. *Congressional Record*, 75th Cong., 1st sess., 1937, pp. 1042–45; *Asheville Citizen*, May 1, 1937.

102. *Congressional Record*, 75th Cong., 1st sess., 1937, p. 7381; *Asheville Citizen*, July 23, 1937; Link, *American Epoch*, 415–16; Burns, *Roosevelt: The Lion and the Fox*, 313–15; Leuchtenburg, *Franklin D. Roosevelt and the New Deal*, 236–38.

103. *Raleigh News and Observer*, January 31, 1937; *Asheville Citizen*, January 31, 1937.

104. *Life*, February 15, 1937, 20.

105. *Asheville Citizen*, January 31, 1937.

106. *Raleigh News and Observer*, September 4, 1941.

107. Walter Brown to John Santford Martin, January 30, 1937, John Santford Martin Papers, Duke University Library, Durham.

108. *Life*, June 14, 1937, 24.

109. *New York Times*, March 7, 1937.

110. *Raleigh News and Observer*, April 27, 1937; *Asheville Citizen*, April 27, 1937; Franklin D. Roosevelt to Robert R. Reynolds, April 23, 1937, and Franklin D. Roosevelt to the Pages of the U.S. Senate, April 1937, Roosevelt Papers.

111. Davis, "Senator Bob Reynolds," 367.

112. *Asheville Citizen*, June 3, 1937.

113. Robert R. Reynolds to Marvin H. McIntyre, September 4, 1937, and Marvin H. McIntyre to Robert R. Reynolds, September 7, 1937, Roosevelt Papers.

114. *New York Times*, February 2, 1937; *Raleigh News and Observer*, February 2, 1937; *Asheville Citizen*, February 2, March 2, 1937.

115. *Asheville Citizen*, February 25, 1937.

116. Ibid., February 26, 1937.

117. *Raleigh News and Observer*, February 26, 1937.

CHAPTER SIX

1. Leuchtenburg, *Franklin D. Roosevelt and the New Deal*, 186.

2. Rauch, *History of the New Deal*, 315–17; Schlesinger, *Politics of Upheaval*, 436–38; Badger, *The New Deal*, 252.

3. Robert R. Reynolds, "In Washington—What Is Taking Place," January 24, 1938, n.p., in possession of Frances Reynolds Oertling.

4. *Congressional Record*, 75th Cong., 3d sess., 1938, pp. 86–96, 217–24, 258, 312, 315–16, 368, 375–76, 429, 583–85; *Asheville Citizen*, January 7, 9, 10, 1938; *Raleigh News and Observer*, January 10, 13, 1938.

5. *Congressional Record*, 75th Cong., 3d sess., 1938, p. 1166; *Asheville Citizen*, January 28, 1938.

6. *Congressional Record*, 75th Cong., 3d sess., 1938, p. 2210; *Raleigh News and Observer*, February 22, 1938; *Asheville Citizen*, February 22, 1938; Schlesinger, *Politics of Upheaval*, 438.

7. *Asheville Citizen*, February 2, 1938.

8. *Raleigh News and Observer*, February 10, 1938.

9. Ibid., February 12, 1938; *Asheville Citizen*, February 12, 1938.

10. *Asheville Citizen*, February 13, 15, 1938.

11. *Congressional Record*, 75th Cong., 3d sess., 1938, pp. 2424, 2435, 4204; *Asheville Citizen*, March 29, 1938; *Raleigh News and Observer*, March 29, 1938; Leuchtenburg, *Franklin D. Roosevelt and the New Deal*, 277–80.

12. Elizabeth F. Clarke to Robert R. Reynolds, March 24, 1938; Reynolds to Clarke, March 27, 1938; and Clarke to Lindsay Warren, March 31, 1938, all in Lindsay Carter Warren Papers, Southern Historical Collection, University of North Carolina, Chapel Hill.

13. *Congressional Record*, 75th Cong., 3d sess., 1938, p. 6135; *Asheville Citizen*, February 12, 1938.

14. *Congressional Record*, 75th Cong., 3d sess., 1938, pp. 220, 258; *New York Times*, January 9, 1938.

15. *Asheville Citizen*, February 23, 1938.

16. Ibid., September 25, 1938.

17. Ibid., January 10, 1938.

18. Ibid., January 11, 1938.

19. *Congressional Record*, 75th Cong., 3d sess., 1938, p. 1489; *Asheville Citizen*, February 5, 1938.

20. Announcement, n.d., American Immigration Conference Board, FBI file 62-34356-10.

21. J. Edgar Hoover to Clyde R. Tolson, April 12, 1938, and J. Edgar Hoover to Robert R. Reynolds, April 16, 1938, FBI files 62-34356-9, -10.

22. *Asheville Citizen*, January 9, 1938.

23. Author's interview with Frances Reynolds Oertling.

24. McCormick, "Buncombe Bob," 38.

25. Robert R. Reynolds to Josiah W. Bailey, January 9, 1930, Josiah W. Bailey Papers, Duke University Library, Durham.

26. *Raleigh News and Observer*, April 14, 1937.

27. *Asheville Citizen*, May 7, 1937.

28. Ibid., May 13, 1937.

29. *Charlotte News*, December 30, 1936; *Raleigh News and Observer*, June 5, 1937.

30. Clyde R. Hoey to Josiah W. Bailey, April 30, 1935, Bailey Papers; newspaper clipping, September 18, 1937, n.p., Robert Rice Reynolds Papers, Asheville.

31. *Concord Tribune*, July 10, 1937.

32. R. Gregg Cherry to James L. McNair, November 6, 1937, Robert Gregg Cherry Papers, Department of Archives and History, Raleigh.

33. *Raleigh News and Observer*, June 5, 1937.

34. Ibid., December 21, 1937.

35. Ibid., May 17, 1937, quoting *Colliers*, n.d., n.p.

36. Josiah W. Bailey to Frank Hancock, October 13, 1937; Bailey to Clay Williams, October 18, 1937; and Bailey to Robert R. Reynolds, January 17, 1938, Bailey Papers.

37. *Asheville Citizen*, June 30, 1937.

38. *Asheville Citizen*, March 10, October 12, 1937; *Greensboro Daily News*, March 28, 1937.

39. Ernest M. Green to Robert L. Doughton, May 8, 1937, Robert L. Doughton Papers, Southern Historical Collection.

40. Robert L. Doughton to James H. Holloway, April 30, 1937; Doughton to Philip R. Whitley, May 13, 1937; and Doughton to Clyde R. Gooch, May 13, 1937, Doughton Papers.

41. *Raleigh News and Observer*, June 9, 1937.

42. Ibid., September 13, 1937.

43. Henry E. Fries to Robert L. Doughton, May 21, 1937; L. D. Robinson to Doughton, June 5, 1937; and U. B. Blalock to Doughton, June 7, 1937, Doughton Papers.

44. Robert L. Doughton to Cora A. Harris, June 1, 1937, and Doughton to L. D. Robinson, June 9, 1937, Doughton Papers.

45. *Raleigh News and Observer*, June 14, 1937.

46. Ibid.; *Asheville Citizen*, June 20, 1937.

47. *Raleigh News and Observer*, July 23, 1937.

48. Tyre Taylor to O. Max Gardner, August 5, 1937, O. Max Gardner Papers, Southern Historical Collection.

49. O. Max Gardner to Tyre Taylor, August 7, 1937, Gardner Papers.

50. *Raleigh News and Observer*, July 23, 1937.

51. *Asheville Citizen*, October 13, 1937.

52. Morrison, *O. Max Gardner*, 194–95.

53. Josiah W. Bailey to Frank Hancock, October 13, 1937, Bailey Papers.

54. *Asheville Citizen*, October 14, 1937; Robert L. Doughton to George P. Pell, October 16, 1937, and Doughton to W. E. Smith, October 21, 1937, Doughton Papers.

55. Frank Hancock to Robert L. Doughton, October 19, 1937, Doughton Papers.

56. *Asheville Citizen*, October 14, 15, 1937.

57. Josiah W. Bailey to E. C. Greene, October 18, 1937, and Frank P. Hobgood to Josiah W. Bailey, November 17, 1937, Bailey Papers.

58. *Raleigh News and Observer*, October 14, 15, 1937.

59. *Asheville Citizen*, October 26, 1937; *Raleigh News and Observer*, November 2, 1937.

60. *Raleigh News and Observer*, October 14, November 3, 1937, February 16, 1938; *Asheville Citizen*, November 16, 1937; Badger, *North Carolina and the New Deal*, 83.

61. *Asheville Citizen*, January 21, 1937.

62. Author's interview with Hubert H. Rand Jr.

63. *Raleigh News and Observer*, October 14, 15, November 11, 1937; *Asheville Citizen*, November 11, 1937.

64. Author's interview with Hubert H. Rand Jr.

65. William B. Bankhead to Lindsay Warren, October 16, 1937, Warren Papers.

66. *Asheville Citizen*, February 11, 1938; *Raleigh News and Observer*, February 11, 1938.

67. Robert R. Reynolds to Gordon Gray, September 20, 1937, Gordon Gray Papers, Southern Historical Collection.

68. Robert R. Reynolds to R. A. Dunn, April 14, 1938, Romulus A. Nunn Papers, Duke University Library.

69. Robert R. Reynolds to W. C. White, April 11, 1938, Nunn Papers.

70. Robert R. Reynolds to Romulus A. Nunn, May 5, 1938, Nunn Papers.

71. *Raleigh News and Observer*, May 1, 1938.

72. *Asheville Citizen*, April 12, 1938; *Raleigh News and Observer*, April 13, 1938.

73. *Asheville Citizen*, April 12, 1938; *Raleigh News and Observer*, April 12, 1938.

74. Charles A. Webb to Robert R. Reynolds, January 8, 1938, and Helen R. Wohl to Robert R. Reynolds, April 30, 1938, Nunn Papers; Couch, *These Are Our Lives*, 3–11.

75. *Charlotte Observer*, April 16, 1938.

76. *Raleigh News and Observer*, April 26, 29, 1938; *Asheville Citizen*, April 29, 1938.

77. *Raleigh News and Observer*, May 15, 1938; *Asheville Citizen*, May 15, 1938.

78. *Raleigh News and Observer*, May 5, 1938; Pepper, *Pepper*, 69–74.

79. *Raleigh News and Observer*, May 19, 1938.

80. Robert R. Reynolds to Chairmen, Reynolds Reelection Organization, May 6, 12, 16, 25, 27, 1938, Nunn Papers.

81. *St. Louis Star-Times*, May 8, 1938.

82. O. Max Gardner to Clyde R. Hoey, March 1, 1938, Gardner Papers; *Raleigh News and Observer*, May 19, 1938.

83. *Charlotte Observer*, May 18, 1938.

84. *Greensboro Daily News*, May 21, 1938; *Raleigh News and Observer*, May 20, 1938; *Asheville Citizen*, May 20, 1938.

85. *Raleigh News and Observer*, May 21, 1938.

86. Robert R. Reynolds to E. H. Evans, May 15, 1938, Bailey Papers; Robert R. Reynolds to R. A. Nunn, June 3, 1938, Nunn Papers.

87. *Asheville Citizen*, May 26, 1938; *Raleigh News and Observer*, May 27, 1938.

88. *Raleigh News and Observer*, May 29, 1938.

89. Ibid., June 1, 1938.

90. *Greensboro Daily News*, June 2, 1938; *Asheville Citizen*, June 2, 1938; *Raleigh News and Observer*, June 2, 1938.

91. *Asheville Citizen*, June 3, 1938; *Raleigh News and Observer*, June 3, 1938.

92. *Durham Morning Herald*, June 4, 1938; *Greensboro Daily News*, June 4, 1938; *Raleigh News and Observer*, June 4, 1938.

93. Robert R. Reynolds to "My dear friend," May 27, 1938, Nunn Papers.

94. *Asheville Citizen*, June 4, 1938.

95. London, *North Carolina Manual, 1939*, 98–99; Heard and Strong, *Southern Primaries and Elections*, 100.

96. London, *North Carolina Manual, 1939*, 98–99.

97. *New York Times*, June 6, 1938; *Raleigh News and Observer*, June 6, 1938; *Asheville Citizen*, June 6, 1938.

98. *Raleigh News and Observer*, June 7, 1938.

99. *Asheville Citizen*, June 5, 1938.

100. *Charlotte News*, June 6, 1938.

101. W. J. Armfield III to Josiah W. Bailey, June 6, 1938, Bailey Papers.

102. *Greensboro Daily News*, June 5, 1938.

103. *Asheville Citizen*, June 1, 1938; *Raleigh News and Observer*, June 1, 1938.

104. *Asheville News*, October 14, 1966.

105. Davis, "Senator Bob Reynolds," 367.

106. *Raleigh News and Observer*, June 8, 1938; *Asheville Citizen*, June 8, October 4, 9, 1938; Robert R. Reynolds to O. Max Gardner, October 17, 1938, Gardner Papers.

107. *Asheville Citizen*, March 17, 1938; *Charlotte News*, October 26, 1938; *Raleigh News and Observer*, September 13, 1938.

108. Charles A. Jonas to Willis G. Briggs, July 5, 1938, Willis G. Briggs Papers, Department of Archives and History, Raleigh.

109. *Asheville Citizen*, October 7, November 9, 1938.

110. O. Max Gardner to Robert R. Reynolds, October 13, 1938, and Gardner to Wiseman Kendall, November 7, 1938, Gardner Papers.

111. Morrison, *O. Max Gardner*, 194–95.

112. O. Max Gardner to Robert R. Reynolds, October 13, 24, 1938, Gardner Papers.

113. *Raleigh News and Observer*, October 23, 1938; *Asheville Citizen*, October 23, 1938.

114. *Raleigh News and Observer*, November 1, 1938; *Asheville Citizen*, November 2, 1938.

115. Robert R. Reynolds to Franklin D. Roosevelt, November 4, 1938, Roosevelt Papers.

116. Josiah W. Bailey to H. G. Gulley, November 3, 1938, Bailey Papers.

117. *Asheville Citizen*, November 9, 1938.

118. Heard and Strong, *Southern Primaries and Elections*, 100.

119. J. Edgar Hoover to Robert R. Reynolds, November 12, 1938, FBI file 62-34356-11.

120. Matthews, *North Carolina Votes*, 215.

121. Confidential memo to the State Department, Washington, D.C., December 6, 1938, Hugh Gladney Grant Papers, Duke University Library.

CHAPTER SEVEN

1. Badger, *North Carolina and the New Deal*, introduction, 37, 71–96; Lefler and Newsome, *North Carolina*, 586–88.

2. *New York Times*, September 22, 1938.

3. *Raleigh News and Observer*, August 31, 1938.

4. *New York Times*, September 22, 1938.

5. *Raleigh News and Observer*, September 25, 1938.

6. Ibid., October 4, 1938.

7. *Asheville Citizen*, December 23, 1938; *Raleigh News and Observer*, December 23, 1938.

8. *Raleigh News and Observer*, December 24, 1938.

9. *Asheville Citizen*, November 10, 1938; *Raleigh News and Observer*, November 10, 1938.

10. *New York Times*, December 24, 1938; *Raleigh News and Observer*, December 24, 1938.

11. *Charlotte News*, March 15, 1938.

12. *Asheville Citizen*, December 27, 1938, January 11, 28, 1939.

13. Pearson and Allen, "Merry-Go-'Round," *Raleigh News and Observer*, January 18, 1939.

14. Author's interview with Frances Reynolds Oertling.

15. When asked by the author to produce documentation from his files supporting his accusations against Reynolds, Pearson chose not to comply with the request. Author's interview with Drew Pearson.

16. Pearson and Allen, "Merry-Go-'Round," *Raleigh News and Observer*, February 24, 1939.

17. *Life*, March 6, 1939, 57–63; *Asheville Citizen*, March 4, 1939.

18. *Ken*, quoted in the *Asheville Citizen*, April 16, 1939.

19. *Asheville Citizen*, April 26, 1939.

20. Lerche, *Uncertain South*, 19–20.

21. Hero, *Southerner and World Affairs*, 78.

22. Lerche, *Uncertain South*, 40–41.

23. Hero, *Southerner and World Affairs*, 91; Rieselbach, *Roots of Isolationism*, 107.

24. Lerche, *Uncertain South*, 52–56.

25. Ibid., 53–55, 258–59.

26. Author's interview with Frances Reynolds Oertling and Hubert H. Rand Jr.

27. Author's interview with Wesley E. McDonald Sr.

28. Author's interview with Frances Reynolds Oertling.

29. Author's interview with Hubert H. Rand Jr.

30. Hero, *Southerner and World Affairs*, 1, 5, 96–97. When referring to Reynolds the terms "unilateralist" and "isolationist" will be used interchangeably, with the understanding that I

consider Reynolds to be a unilateralist rather than a true isolationist in the strictest sense. Contemporary reports always referred to Reynolds as an isolationist; thus, to avoid confusion and be consistent, Reynolds will be described as an isolationist.

31. Divine, *Illusion of Neutrality*, 229–31.

32. *Asheville Citizen*, January 1, 3, 1939; *Raleigh News and Observer*, January 7, 1939.

33. *Asheville Citizen*, January 10, 1939; *Raleigh News and Observer*, January 10, 1939.

34. *Voelkischer Beobachter*, February 2, 1939, 3.

35. *Winston-Salem Journal*, January 12, 1939.

36. *Asheville Citizen*, April 11, 1939; *Raleigh News and Observer*, April 11, 1939; Ketchum, *Borrowed Years*, 520–21; Kessler, *Sins of the Father*, 185–94.

37. *Congressional Record*, 76th Cong., 1st sess., 1939, appendix, pp. 263–64.

38. Ibid., pp. 745–65.

39. *Raleigh News and Observer*, January 27, 1939.

40. *New York Times*, January 28, February 2, 1939; *Asheville Citizen*, January 30, 1939; *Raleigh News and Observer*, January 30, 1939; Ketchum, *Borrowed Years*, 174–77; Cole, *Senator Gerald P. Nye*, 154–55; Cole, *Roosevelt and the Isolationists*, 302–4; *Congressional Record*, 76th Cong., 1st sess., pp. 1021–28, 2135–36.

41. Transcript of the Conference with the Military Affairs Committee, Executive Office of the White House, January 31, 1939, President's Personal File, 1-P, Franklin Delano Roosevelt Papers, Franklin D. Roosevelt Library, Hyde Park; author's interview with Gerald P. Nye; Ketchum, *Borrowed Years*, 175–77; Cole, *Senator Gerald P. Nye*, 155; Cole, *Roosevelt and the Isolationists*, 303–6; Kenneth S. Davis, *FDR: Into the Storm*, 406–8.

42. *New York Times*, February 2, 1939; *Asheville Citizen*, February 1, 1939; *Raleigh News and Observer*, February 1, 1939; author's interview with Gerald P. Nye.

43. *Raleigh News and Observer*, February 4, 1939.

44. Ibid., February 2, 4, 1939; *Asheville Citizen*, February 4, 1939; *Congressional Record*, 76th Cong., 1st sess., 1939, pp. 1023–27.

45. *Congressional Record*, 76th Cong., 1st sess., 1939, pp. 2717–27; *Asheville Citizen*, February 28, March 15, 1939.

46. Shepardson, *United States in World Affairs*, 51–52.

47. *Congressional Record*, 76th Cong., 1st sess., 1939, pp. 4219–29.

48. Ibid, 76th Cong., 1st sess., 1939, appendix, pp. 1958–59; *Raleigh News and Observer*, May 16, 1939; *Asheville Citizen*, May 16, 1939.

49. Author's interview with Hubert H. Rand Jr.

50. *Raleigh News and Observer*, February 22, 1939.

51. *New York Times*, April 24, 1939.

52. *Congressional Record*, 76th Cong., 1st sess., 1939, pp. 7445–55.

53. *New York Times*, January 17, 1939.

54. *Asheville Citizen*, June 6, 1939; *Raleigh News and Observer*, June 6, 1939.

55. *Raleigh News and Observer,* June 3, 1939.

56. Davis, *FDR: Into the Storm*, 447–49.

57. *Asheville Citizen*, June 6, 1939; *Raleigh News and Observer*, June 6, 1939; Ketchum, *Borrowed Years*, 152–55.

58. *Asheville Citizen*, June 11, 1939.

59. *Raleigh News and Observer*, June 18, 1939.

60. Ibid., June 27, 1939.

61. *Asheville Citizen*, July 2, 1939; *Raleigh News and Observer*, July 2, 1939.

62. *Raleigh News and Observer*, June 27, 1939.

63. *Asheville Citizen*, May 10, 1939; *Raleigh News and Observer*, May 11, 1939.

64. Author's interview with Irving C. Crawford.

65. Divine, *Illusion of Neutrality*, 235.

66. Ibid., 239–45.

67. *New York Times*, March 25, 1939.

68. *Asheville Citizen*, April 6, 1939; *Raleigh News and Observer*, April 6, 1939.

69. *Asheville Citizen*, April 14, 1939; *Congressional Record*, 76th Cong., 1st sess., 1939, appendix, p. 1362.

70. Divine, *Illusion of Neutrality*, 248–52.

71. Robert Dallek, *Franklin D. Roosevelt and American Foreign Policy*, 186–87; *Raleigh News and Observer*, May 28, 1939.

72. *New York Times*, July 5, 1939; *Asheville Citizen*, July 5, 1939.

73. *New York Times*, July 8, 9, 1939; "Thirty-four in a Lair," *Time*, July 17, 1939, 13.

74. *New York Times*, July 12, 1939; *Asheville Citizen*, July 12, 13, 1939; *Raleigh News and Observer*, July 12, 1939; Shepardson, *United States in World Affairs*, 86; Davis, *FDR: Into the Storm*, 453–55.

75. O. Max Gardner to Julian Miller, September 12, 1939, O. Max Gardner Papers, Southern Historical Collection, University of North Carolina, Chapel Hill.

76. *Charlotte Observer*, September 14, 1939.

77. *Asheville Citizen*, July 5, August 5, 1939.

78. Dallek, *Franklin D. Roosevelt and American Foreign Policy*, 199.

79. *New York Times*, September 19, 1939; *Asheville Citizen*, September 19, 1939; Ketchum, *Borrowed Years*, 199–200.

80. *Asheville Citizen*, September 6, 1939.

81. *Raleigh News and Observer*, September 20, 1939.

82. *New York Times*, September 21, 1939; *Asheville Citizen*, September 21, 1939.

83. *Raleigh News and Observer*, September 20, 1939; *Asheville Citizen*, September 20, 1939.

84. *New York Times*, September 22, 1939; *Asheville Citizen*, September 22, 1939; Ketchum, *Borrowed Years*, 220–24.

85. *Raleigh News and Observer*, September 23, 1939.

86. *Greensboro Daily News*, September 26, 1939; *Asheville Citizen*, September 24, October 4, 1939.

87. *New York Times*, September 29, 1939; *Asheville Citizen*, September 29, 1939.

88. *Greensboro Daily News*, September 26, 1939; *Raleigh News and Observer*, September 28, 1939; *Asheville Citizen*, September 28, 1939.

89. *Congressional Record*, 76th Cong., 2d sess., 1939, p. 237; *Asheville Citizen*, October 11, 1939; *Charlotte Observer*, October 11, 1939; *Raleigh News and Observer*, October 11, 1939.

90. *Asheville Citizen*, October 15, 1939; *Congressional Record*, 76th Cong., 2d sess., 1939, pp. 7449–50.

91. *Congressional Record*, 76th Cong., 2d sess., 1939, p. 1146.

92. Joe L. Lee to A. Hand James, October 17, 20, 1939, Josiah W. Bailey Papers, Duke University Library, Durham.

93. *Congressional Record*, 76th Cong., 2d sess., 1939, pp. 687–703.

94. *American Vindicator*, November 1939, 6.

95. *Congressional Record*, 76th Cong., 2d sess., 1939, pp. 687–703; *New York Times*, October 22, 1939; *Raleigh News and Observer*, October 22, 1939.

96. *Congressional Record*, 76th Cong., 2d sess., 1939, p. 1024; *Asheville Citizen*, October 27, 28, 1939; Ketchum, *Borrowed Years*, 228–29; Cole, *Roosevelt and the Isolationists*, 328–30.

97. *Asheville Citizen*, November 30, 1939.

CHAPTER EIGHT

1. *American Vindicator*, March 1939, 1–8; Robert R. Reynolds to H. Patrick Taylor Sr., January 18, 1940, H. Patrick Taylor, Sr. Papers, Manuscript Collection, East Carolina University, Greenville; *Asheville Citizen*, February 1, March 23, 1939; author's interview with Hubert H. Rand Jr. The dictionary definition of "vindicate" is to clear of blame or to provide justification for something. An alternative definition was to defend or insist on the recognition of one's rights. See *American Heritage Dictionary of the American Language* (New York: Houghton Mifflin, 1969), 1430.

2. Carlson, *Under Cover*, 228; author's interview with Wesley E. McDonald Sr.; Piller, *Time Bomb*, 103.

3. *American Vindicator*, March 1939, 1–8.

4. *Congressional Record*, 76th Cong., 1st sess., 1939, pp. 1822–23, 5422–23.

5. Drew Pearson and Robert S. Allen, "Merry-Go-'Round," *Raleigh News and Observer*, September 6, 1939.

6. Robert R. Reynolds to "My Dear Fellow North Carolinian," January 18, 1939, Taylor Papers.

7. Childs, *I Write from Washington*, 159.

8. *Asheville Citizen*, March 25, 1939.

9. Ibid., February 12, 1939.

10. *Raleigh News and Observer*, February 2, 1939.

11. *Newsweek*, May 1, 1939, 15–16.

12. *Asheville Citizen*, April 16, 1939, quoting *Ken* magazine.

13. *American Vindicator*, March 1939, 4.

14. Ibid., August 1939, 4. It should not be assumed that all letters and articles were as fanatic or as badly written as the above examples. There were several thoughtful, articulate missives, but the general attitude and tone of the newspaper and its subscribers are best illustrated by the two examples cited.

15. Ibid., June 1939, 3–4.

16. Ibid.

17. Ibid., July 1939, 1.

18. Ibid., November 1939, 3.

19. C. Wilson to Robert R. Reynolds, August 12, 1940, and C. Wilson to Morris Sheppard, J. Edgar Hoover, and Martin Dies, August 12, 1940, Thomas Terry Connally Papers, Library of Congress, Washington, D.C.; S. C. Brady to the Adjutant General of the Army, April 26, 1942, document no. 62-34350-34, Military Intelligence Service, War Department, Washington, D.C.

20. *American Vindicator*, September 1940, 1.

21. Stout, *Illustrious Dunderheads*, xiii–xiv, 14–15.

22. *New York Times*, March 19, 1939.

23. *Raleigh News and Observer*, February 8, 9, 1939.

24. Ibid., May 4, 1939.

25. *New York Times*, May 7, 1939.

26. *New York World Telegram*, May 8, 1939.

27. *New York Times*, June 8, 1940.

28. *Greensboro Daily News*, February 12, 1939.

29. *Raleigh News and Observer*, May 18, 1939.

30. Ibid., May 15, 1939.

31. Quotations here and in next four paragraphs from Ulric Bell, "Senator Reynolds Saves America," *American Mercury*, November 1939, 304–11.

32. *New York Times*, April 23, 1939.

33. G. Egerton Harriman to Frank P. Graham, May 12, 1939, Frank P. Graham Papers, Southern Historical Collection, University of North Carolina, Chapel Hill.

34. *Durham Morning Herald*, May 12, 1939.

35. *Asheville Citizen*, May 11, 1939.

36. *Congressional Record*, 76th Cong., 1st sess., 1939, pp. 745–47, 5412.

37. *Asheville Citizen*, May 12, 1939.

38. *Congressional Record*, 76th Cong., 1st sess., 1939, pp. 5412–32; see also ibid., pp. 1822, 1931; *Raleigh News and Observer*, May 12, 1939; *Asheville Citizen*, May 12, 1939.

39. *Raleigh News and Observer*, May 13, 1939.

40. *Asheville Citizen*, May 13, 1939.

41. *Asheville Citizen-Times*, May 14, 1939.

42. *Asheville Citizen*, May 17, 1939, and *Asheville Citizen-Times*, May 17, 1939.

43. *Asheville Citizen*, May 21, 1939.

44. *Life*, March 6, 1939, 61.

45. Frye, *Nazi Germany*, 22; Lavine, *Fifth Column in America*, 162.

46. Report on the German-American Bund, n.p., n.d., Graham Papers.

47. J. Wheeler-Hill, German-American Bund, to All Organizations of American Patriots, December 9, 1938, Connally Papers.

48. Frye, *Nazi Germany*, 80–81, 88; Sayers and Kahn, *Plot against the Peace*, 173–77; Dies, *Trojan Horse in America*, 310.

49. Frye, *Nazi Germany*, 95–97.

50. Johnson, *Viereck*, 3–4, 212.

51. Ibid., 195–202.

52. Frye, *Nazi Germany*, 140; Farago, *Game of the Foxes*, 377–89; Johnson, *Viereck*, 2, 212, 217–21.

53. Frye, *Nazi Germany*, 158–61; Rogge, *Official German Report*, 153; *Time*, March 2, 1942, 14; *Newsweek*, October 20, 1942, 21–22; Johnson, *Viereck*, 217–18.

54. *Congressional Record*, 76th Cong., 3d sess., 1940, pp. 2252, 2285–86; Rogge, *Official German Report*, 154; Sayers and Kahn, *Plot against the Peace*, 189–90.

55. Rogge, *Official German Report*, 370; Sayers and Kahn, *Plot against the Peace*, 190; Johnson, *Viereck*, 223, 233, 250.

56. Rogge, *Official German Report*, 171.

57. Ibid., 157; Frye, *Plot against the Peace*, 140.

58. Cole, *Senator Gerald P. Nye*, 211. See also Hull, *Memoirs*, 613–14, 641–42.

59. Warren, *Radio Priest*, 242.

60. *New Masses*, quoted in *American Vindicator*, October 1940, 6.

61. *Jewish Examiner*, June 21, 1940.

62. *American Vindicator*, September 1940, 6.

63. Frye, *Nazi Germany*, 92; Lavine, *Fifth Column in America*, 63–66.

64. Pearson and Allen, "Merry-Go-'Round," *Raleigh News and Observer*, June 12, 1939; *Asheville Citizen*, May 12, 1939; Carlson, *Under Cover*, 228.

65. *New York Times*, April 30, 1940; Alan Brinkley, *Voices of Protest*, 267.

66. *Social Justice*, February 27, 1939, March 20, 1939, May 8, 15, 1939, August 19, 1940.

67. Ibid., July 1, 1940.

68. Brinkley, *Voices of Protest*, 268.

69. *Liberation*, March 28, 1938.

70. Ibid., April 14, 1940.

71. *Asheville Citizen*, August 24, 1939.

72. *Liberation*, January 21, 1939.

73. *Congressional Record*, 76th Cong., 1st sess., 1939, pp. 749–50, 6207, 9636, 9671, and 76th Cong., 3d sess., 1940, pp. 10043–44; Sayers and Kahn, *Sabotage*, 226–29; Piller, *Time Bomb*, 104.

74. *Congressional Record*, 76th Cong., 1st sess., 1939, appendix, p. 4107.

75. *Defender*, August 1939.

76. Gerald B. Winrod to Gerald L. K. Smith, March 20, 1942, Gerald L. K. Smith Papers, Manuscript Collections, Bentley Library, University of Michigan, Ann Arbor.

77. Gerald B. Winrod to Robert R. Reynolds, March 20, 1942, Smith Papers.

78. *The Nation*, April 8, 1939, 403.

79. *Congressional Record*, 76th Cong., 1st sess., 1939, p. 4546; File no. 62-34350-37X2, November 23, 1942, Military Intelligence Service, War Department.

80. Jeansonne, *Gerald L. K. Smith*, 87.

81. *Congressional Record*, 76th Cong., 3d sess., 1939, p. 9607.

82. *American Vindicator*, April 1942, 1.

83. *The Cross and the Flag*, May 1942.

84. Robert R. Reynolds to Mrs. J. Wistar Evans, June 10, 1944, Smith Papers.

85. *The Cross and the Flag*, May 1942, July 1943.

86. Jeansonne, *Gerald L. K. Smith*, 69, 81–89.

CHAPTER NINE

1. *Asheville Citizen*, January 5, 1939; *Raleigh News and Observer*, January 24, 1939.

2. Robert R. Reynolds to May Thompson Evans, January 31, 1939, May Thompson Evans Papers, Department of Archives and History, Raleigh; *Congressional Record*, 76th Cong., 1st sess., 1939, pp. 887, 912–13, 3886; *Raleigh News and Observer*, January 28, 1939; *Asheville Citizen*, January 28, 1939.

3. *Congressional Record*, 76th Cong., 1st sess., 1939, pp. 9028–29; *New York Times*, July 14, 17, 1939.

4. *Congressional Record*, 76th Cong., 1st sess., 1939, pp. 8924–29, 9028–30.

5. *New York Times*, July 19, 1939.

6. *Congressional Record*, 76th Cong., 1st sess., 1939, pp. 11091, 11146.

7. Quotations here and in the previous two paragraphs from *Congressional Record*, 76th Cong., 1st sess., 1939, pp. 363–66.

8. Author's interview with Wesley E. McDonald Sr.

9. *New York Times*, May 26, 1940.

10. Joe Wiegers, "Senator Bob Reynolds: Athlete of Capitol Hill," *Health Review*, July 1939, 16.

11. *New York Times*, March 15, 1940.

12. *Washington Evening Star*, January 30, 1939; *Asheville Citizen*, February 1, 1939; *Raleigh News and Observer*, February 1, 1939.

13. *Asheville Citizen*, February 9, 1939; *Raleigh News and Observer*, February 9, 1939.

14. *Asheville Citizen*, July 18, 30, 1939; *Raleigh News and Observer*, July 29, 30, 1939; *Washington Star*, July 30, 1939.

15. Frank P. Graham to Robert R. Reynolds, August 12, 1939, Frank P. Graham Papers, Southern Historical Collection, University of North Carolina, Chapel Hill; Franklin D. Roosevelt to Robert R. Reynolds, July 31, 1939, Franklin Delano Roosevelt Papers, Franklin D. Roosevelt Library, Hyde Park; and J. Edgar Hoover to Robert R. Reynolds, August 1, 1939, FBI file 62-34356-14.

16. *Asheville Citizen*, August 3, 1939.

17. *Raleigh News and Observer*, August 6, 1939.

18. Lerche, *Uncertain South*, 59–64.

19. *Congressional Record*, 76th Cong., 1st sess., 1939, p. 90, 3395; *New York Times*, January 5, 6, 1939.

20. Transcript of radio address by Robert R. Reynolds over NBC, January 12, 1939, Graham Papers.

21. *New York Times*, June 19, 1939.

22. Ibid., March 26, 1939.

23. *Huntington Advertiser*, March 16, 1939.

24. *Raleigh News and Observer*, February 28, 1939; *Asheville Citizen*, March 10, 1939.

25. *Asheville Citizen*, June 25, 1939; *Raleigh News and Observer*, June 25, 1939.

26. *Raleigh News and Observer*, July 2, 1939; *Asheville Citizen*, June 25, 1939.

27. *American Vindicator*, July 1939, 1.

28. Ibid., July 1939, 4, and July 1940, 2.

29. Divine, *American Immigration Policy*, 99–100; Maney, *Roosevelt Presence*, 117–18.

30. *Asheville Citizen*, March 16, 1939; Robert R. Reynolds, "No-Keep the Bars Up," *Rotarian*, February 1940, 12–13.

31. *American Vindicator*, May 1939, 7.

32. Divine, *American Immigration Policy*, 102.

33. *Congressional Record*, 76th Cong., 3d sess., 1940, pp. 4141–45.

34. Ibid., 76th Cong., 3d sess., 1940, pp. 6378–89, 6889–99, 6900.

35. *New York Times*, May 29, 1940.

36. *Congressional Record*, 76th Cong., 3d sess., 1940, p. 6904; *New York Times*, May 29, 1940.

37. Morse, *Six Million Died*, 259.

38. Ickes, *Secret Diary*, May 26, 1940, 3:189, and June 2, 1949, 3:198.

39. Robert R. Reynolds to J. Edgar Hoover, January 30, 1940, FBI file 94-34-909-1. See also *Congressional Record*, 76th Cong., 3d sess., 1940, 6229–30, 6771–77.

40. Reynolds to Hoover, June 7, 1941, FBI file 94-34-218-1.

41. Hoover to Reynolds, February 1, 1940, FBI file 94-34-909-1.

42. *Raleigh News and Observer*, August 21, 1940.

43. *New York Times*, May 23, 1940; *Raleigh News and Observer*, May 23, 1940. See also *Congressional Record*, 76th Cong., 3d sess., 1940, pp. 6608, 9504, 9557, 9985–87, 10574, 10929–31.

44. *Congressional Record*, 76th Cong., 3d sess., 1940, p. 8048; *Raleigh News and Observer*, June 13, 1940; *Asheville Citizen*, June 13, 1940.

45. Marion Bennett, *American Immigration Policies*, 65–66.

46. *Raleigh News and Observer*, July 9, 15, 1940; *New York Times*, July 16, 1940.

47. *Raleigh News and Observer*, April 11, 1940; *Asheville Citizen*, April 11, 1940.

48. Robert R. Reynolds, *Threats to America become Realities*, pamphlet, Southern Historical Collection; *Daily Tar Heel*, January 19, 1940; *Raleigh News and Observer*, January 19, 1940; *Asheville Citizen*, January 19, 1940; *Congressional Record*, 76th Cong., 3d sess., 1940, appendix, p. 675.

49. *Daily Tar Heel*, January 20, 1940.

50. *Raleigh News and Observer*, January 18, 1940; *Asheville Citizen*, January 25, February 8, 1940; Leuchtenburg, *Franklin D. Roosevelt and the New Deal*, 396–97.

51. *Congressional Record*, 76th Cong., 3d sess., 1940, pp. 1273–74, 1396–1405; *New York Times*, February 14, 1940; *Greensboro Daily News*, February 14, 1940; *Asheville Citizen*, February 14, 1940.

52. *Asheville Citizen*, March 15, 16, and 17, 1940.

53. *Congressional Record*, 76th Cong., 3d sess., 1940, pp. 2153, 15130; *Raleigh News and Observer*, January 27, 1940; *Asheville Citizen*, January 27, 1940.

54. Leuchtenburg, *Franklin D. Roosevelt and the New Deal*, 289–91.

55. *Congressional Record*, 76th Cong., 3d sess., 1940, pp. 566, 1295–96; *Asheville Citizen*, February 18, 1940; *Raleigh News and Observer*, March 2, 1940.

56. *Congressional Record*, 76th Cong., 3d sess., 1940, pp. 1821, 3745–48, 3817–3820, 3923; *Asheville Citizen*, April 2, 3, 1940; Long, *War Diary*, 74; *Documents on German Foreign Policy*, vol. 9, nos. 24, 45; Lash, *Roosevelt and Churchill*, 118–19.

57. *New York Times*, April 3, 1940; *Asheville Citizen*, April 3, 1940; *Raleigh News and Observer*, April 3, 1940.

58. *Asheville Citizen*, April 4, 1940.

59. Ketchum, *Borrowed Years*, 299–304, 422–23, 539.

60. *Raleigh News and Observer*, June 21, 1940; *Congressional Record*, 76th Cong., 3d sess., 1940, pp. 9341, 9411.

61. *Congressional Record*, 76th Cong., 3d sess., 1940, pp. 4136–38, 4352–53; *Asheville Citizen*, April 10, 15, 1940.

62. *Asheville Citizen*, April 10, 1940.

63. *Raleigh News and Observer*, July 13, 1940; *Congressional Record*, 76th Cong., 3d sess., 1940, pp. 9605–6.

64. *Congressional Record*, 76th Cong., 3d sess., 1940, pp. 10111, 10482–84, 10652–69, 11142, 11755, 11996, 12156; *Raleigh News and Observer*, August 6, 29, 1940; Leuchtenburg, *Franklin D. Roosevelt and the New Deal*, 307–8.

65. Frank P. Graham to Robert R. Reynolds, August 5, 1940, Graham Papers.

66. Reynolds to Graham, August 6, 1940, Graham Papers.

67. *Raleigh News and Observer*, September 17, 1940.

68. Ramsey to Josiah W. Bailey, Darley Hiden Ramsey Papers, Southern Historical Collection.

69. *New York Times*, October 27, 1940; *Raleigh News and Observer*, October 27, November 20, 1940.

70. *New York Times*, September 20, 1940.

71. *Raleigh News and Observer*, January 7, 1940; *Asheville Citizen*, January 7, 1940.

72. *Raleigh News and Observer*, March 11, 1940.

73. Ibid., September 4, 1940.

74. *Asheville Citizen*, September 8, 1940; *Raleigh News and Observer*, September 8, 1940.

75. *Raleigh News and Observer*, September 13, 1940.

76. Ibid., October 31, 1940.

CHAPTER TEN

1. *Raleigh News and Observer*, January 3, 1941.

2. Ibid., January 8, 1941.

3. *Congressional Record*, 77th Cong., 1st sess., 1941, p. 195.

4. *Asheville Citizen*, January 22, 1941; *Raleigh News and Observer*, January 22, 1941.

5. *Raleigh News and Observer*, January 24, 1941; *Washington News*, January 22, 1941; newspaper clipping, n.p., n.d., possession of Frances Reynolds Oertling.

6. *Congressional Record*, 77th Cong., 1st sess., 1941, p. 2714.

7. *America First Bulletin*, August 2, 1941.

8. *Congressional Record*, 77th Cong., 1st sess., 1941, pp. 2715–16.

9. Cole, "America First and the South," 36–40.

10. Ruth Sarles to R. A. Moore, September 22, 1941, America First Manuscripts, Hoover Institution on Revolution, War, and Peace, Stanford University, Palo Alto; Cole, *America First*, 51–60.

11. William S. Foulis to Robert R. Reynolds, November 1, 1941; Foulis to Wesley E. McDonald Sr., November 10, 28, 1941; and McDonald to Foulis, November 3, 12, 1941, America First Manuscripts.

12. Robert R. Reynolds to William S. Foulis, November 27, 1941, and Foulis to Reynolds, December 5, 22, 1941, America First Manuscripts.

13. *Raleigh News and Observer*, September 11, 1941.

14. Ibid., October 10, 1941.

15. Cole, *America First*, 104–128.

16. Berg, *Lindbergh*, 402.

17. Ibid., 409.

18. Ibid., 424–25, 427.

19. Ibid., 420–21.

20. Ketchum, *Borrowed Years*, 571–78; Heinrichs, *Threshold of War*, 11, 16; *Raleigh News and Observer*, January 11, 1941; Cole, *Roosevelt and the Isolationists*, 480.

21. Robert R. Reynolds to Frances Reynolds Oertling, February 7, 1941, Robert Rice Reynolds Papers, Asheville; Berg, *Lindbergh*, 415.

22. *Raleigh News and Observer*, February 16, 1941.

23. *Congressional Record*, 77th Cong., 1st sess., 1941, pp. 1644–48, 1984.

24. *Raleigh News and Observer*, February 20, 1941.

25. *Congressional Record*, 77th Cong., 1st sess., 1941, pp. 1209–17, 1636–50.

26. Gerald L. K. Smith to Robert R. Reynolds, February 24, 1941, Smith Papers, Manuscript Collection, Bentley Library, University of Michigan, Ann Arbor.

27. E. Dana Malpass to Robert R. Reynolds, February 22, 1941, Josiah W. Bailey Papers, Duke University Library, Durham.

28. Jonathan Daniels, "Interlude for an Isolationist," 183.

29. *Greensboro Daily News*, February 23, 1941.

30. C. C. Duke to Robert R. Reynolds, February 21, 1941, Bailey Papers.

31. E. G. Flanagan to Josiah W. Bailey, February 21, 1941, Bailey Papers.

32. *Raleigh News and Observer*, February 26, 1941.

33. Ibid., March 7, 1941.

34. Ibid., March 1, 1941.

35. *Springfield (Mo.) Daily Events*, February 22, 1941, clipping in Reynolds Papers.

36. William J. Cocke to Robert R. Reynolds, February 14, 1941, and Reynolds to Cocke, February 26, 1941, William J. Cocke Papers, Southern Historical Collection, University of North Carolina, Chapel Hill; *Raleigh News and Observer*, February 27, 1941.

37. Robert R. Reynolds to "My dear Friend," March 27, 1941, Smith Papers.

38. Robert R. Reynolds to William J. Cocke, March 10, 1941, Cocke Papers.

39. *New York Times*, March 8, 1941.

40. *Congressional Record*, 77th Cong., 1st sess., 1941, p. 2097; Ketchum, *Borrowed Years*, 581; Heinrichs, *Threshold of War*, 11, 16.

41. *Raleigh News and Observer*, March 18, 1941.

42. Ketchum, *Borrowed Years*, 602–6.

43. *Raleigh News and Observer*, September 30, 1941.

44. Ibid., October 10, 21, 1941; *New York Times*, October 10, 1941.

45. *Congressional Record*, 77th Cong., 1st sess., 1941, p. 8680; Heinrichs, *Threshold of War*, 206.

46. *Greensboro Daily News*, April 10, 1941; *Raleigh News and Observer*, April 10, 1941.

47. Newspaper clipping, n.p., n.d., in possession of Frances Reynolds Oertling.

48. *Greensboro Daily News*, April 11, 1941.

49. *Raleigh News and Observer*, April 11, 1941.

50. *Charlotte News*, August 2, 1941.

51. *Charlotte Observer*, April 25, 1941.

52. *Cincinnati Enquirer*, April 24, 1941.

53. *Kansas City Journal*, May 9, 1939.

54. *Baltimore Evening Sun*, n.d., Frank P. Graham Papers, Southern Historical Collection, University of North Carolina, Chapel Hill.

55. *Time*, May 26, 1941, 16.

56. *New York Post*, July 18, 1941.

57. *Raleigh News and Observer*, April 17, 1941.

58. *Asheville Citizen*, April 19, 1941.

59. Tom Glasgow to Franklin D. Roosevelt, April 10, 1941, Franklin Delano Roosevelt Papers, Franklin D. Roosevelt Library, Hyde Park.

60. Isidor Shaffer to Franklin D. Roosevelt, April 17, 1941, Roosevelt Papers.

61. Louis Lober to Franklin D. Roosevelt, September 15, 1941, and Marvin H. McIntyre to Louis Lober, September 19, 1941, Roosevelt Papers.

62. Joseph J. Spengler to Josiah W. Bailey, April 17, 1941; W. A. Perlzweig to Bailey, April 22, 1941, Bailey Papers.

63. O. H. Johnson to Bailey, April 23, 1941, Bailey Papers.

64. W. J. Cash to Bailey, April 20, 1941, Bailey Papers.

65. Josiah W. Bailey to R. W. Winston, April 23, 1941; to J. B. Kuykendall Jr., May 7, 1941; and to Mary E. Parish, May 7, 1941, Bailey Papers.

66. *New York Times*, April 23, 1941.

67. Ibid., May 6, 1941.

68. Kefauver and Levin, *Twentieth Century Congress*, 135.

69. Burns, *Congress on Trial*, 60.

70. *Raleigh News and Observer*, April 23, 1941.

71. Ibid., April 22, 1941.

72. *Asheville Citizen*, April 18, 1941.

73. *Raleigh News and Observer*, April 22, 1941.

74. Ibid., April 26, 1941.

75. Author's interviews with Frances Reynolds Oertling and Hubert H. Rand Jr.

76. *New York Times*, May 4, 1941; *Charlotte Observer*, May 4, 1941.

77. *Raleigh News and Observer*, May 5, 1941.

78. Ibid., May 15, 1941.

79. *New York Times*, May 16, 1941; *Greensboro Daily News*, May 16, 1941.

80. *New York Times*, May 17, 1941.

81. Ibid., May 16, 1941; *Greensboro Daily News*, May 16, 1941.

82. *Raleigh News and Observer*, May 23, 1941.

83. Young, *This Is Congress*, 250–51.

84. Author's interview with Senators Gerald P. Nye and Burton K. Wheeler.

85. *Raleigh News and Observer*, June 6, 1941.

86. *Congressional Record*, 77th Cong., 1st sess., 1941, pp. 4083, 6451, 6849.

87. *New York Times*, July 12, 1941; *Raleigh News and Observer*, July 13, 1941.

88. *New York Times*, July 15, 1941.

89. *Washington Star*, quoted in the *Asheville Citizen*, August 3, 1941.

90. Ketchum, *Borrowed Years*, 643–45; *Congressional Record*, 77th Cong., 1st sess., 1941, p. 9969.

91. *Raleigh News and Observer*, July 28, 1941.

92. *Congressional Record*, 77th Cong., 1st sess., 1941, p. 6881; Ketchum, *Borrowed Years*, 645; Heinrichs, *Threshold of War*, 160; Dallek, *Roosevelt and American Foreign Policy*, 276–78.

93. *Raleigh News and Observer*, July 29, 1941.

94. Ibid., June 27, 1941.

95. *American Vindicator*, November 1941, 4; Gerald L. K. Smith to Reynolds, August 7, 1941, and Reynolds to Smith, August 14, 1941, Smith Papers.

96. Bailey and Samuel, *Congress at Work*, 295.

97. Oral interview with Harry H. Vaughan by Jerald L. Hill and William D. Stilley, March 20, 1976, and by Charles T. Morrissey, January 14, 16, 1963, Harry S Truman Library, Independence.

98. Author's interview with Frances Reynolds Oertling.

99. Burns, *Roosevelt: The Soldier of Freedom*, 505.

100. *Raleigh News and Observer*, July 19, 1941, quoting *New Republic*.

101. *Raleigh News and Observer*, April 2, 1941.

102. *Congressional Record*, 77th Cong., 1st sess., 1941, pp. 3055, 3068, 4753–54.

103. James Pitteau to Robert R. Reynolds, June 15, 1940; unsigned to Reynolds, February 10, 1941; Reynolds to J. Edgar Hoover, February 10, 1941; Hoover to Reynolds, August 21, 1941, all in FBI file 95-5083.

104. *Williamston Enterprise*, March 4, 1941.

105. Kenneth Colgrove to Frank P. Graham, August 15, 1941, and Graham to Colgrove, September 11, 1941, Graham Papers.

106. *Asheville Citizen-Times*, September 14, 1941.

107. *Washington Star*, April 27, 1947.

108. *Sunday News*, November 22, 1942, n.p., Reynolds Papers; *Raleigh News and Observer*, September 7, 1941.

109. *Raleigh News and Observer*, September 21, 1946.

110. *Washington Times-Herald*, August 17, 1941.

111. Ibid., August 12, 1941.

112. Author's interview with Hubert H. Rand Jr.

113. Author's interview with T. Lamar Caudle.

114. *Raleigh News and Observer*, August 12, 1941.

115. *Asheville Citizen*, August 16, 1941.

116. *New York Times*, October 5, 1941.

117. *Raleigh News and Observer*, September 7, 1941.

118. *New York Times*, October 10, 1941.

119. *Raleigh News and Observer*, October 10, 1941.

120. Robert R. Reynolds to Judge Robert E. Mattingly, December 4, 1941, Reynolds Papers.

121. *Raleigh News and Observer*, November 29, 1941; *Asheville Citizen*, November 29, 1941.

122. Ketchum, *Borrowed Years*, 782–88; *Raleigh News and Observer*, December 8, 1941; *Asheville Citizen*, December 8, 1941; author's interview with Hubert H. Rand.

123. *Asheville Citizen*, December 8, 1941.

124. Ibid.; *Raleigh News and Observer*, December 8, 1941.

125. Robert R. Reynolds to William S. Foulis, December 12, 1941, America First Papers.

126. *Congressional Record*, 77th Cong., 1st sess., 1941, pp. 9506, 9652–53.

127. *Asheville Citizen*, December 9, 1941.

128. *Raleigh News and Observer*, December 11, 1941.

CHAPTER ELEVEN

1. David Brinkley, *Washington Goes to War*, xxii.

2. *American Vindicator*, December 1941–January 1942, 1.

3. Ibid., April 1942, 1; *Raleigh News and Observer*, October 24, 1942.

4. Author's interviews with Gerald P. Nye and Burton K. Wheeler; *Raleigh News and Observer*, February 15, 1942.

5. *Raleigh News and Observer*, February 15, 1942.

6. Robert R. Reynolds to Henry C. Lodge, February 4, 25, 1942, Henry Cabot Lodge Jr. Papers, Massachusetts Historical Society, Boston.

7. *Raleigh News and Observer*, February 15, 1942; *Asheville Citizen*, December 19, 20, 1941.

8. *Raleigh News and Observer*, May 26, 1942.

9. *New York Times*, September 11, 1942.

10. Robert Patterson to Robert R. Reynolds, October 21, 1942, Robert M. Patterson Papers, Library of Congress, Washington, D.C.

11. *Congressional Record*, 77th Cong., 2d sess., 1942, p. 8531.

12. *Raleigh News and Observer*, October 14, November 2, 1942.

13. Ibid., October 17, 24, 1942.

14. Interview with Edward Greenbaum, October 25, 1942, p. 237, Columbia Oral History Collection, Columbia University Library, New York.

15. *Asheville Citizen*, February 17, 1942; Johnson, *Viereck*, 222–33.

16. *Asheville Citizen*, June 10, February 21, and May 7, 1942.

17. Ibid., May 23, 1942.

18. *Raleigh News and Observer*, February 15, 1942.

19. Jonathan Daniels, "Interlude for an Isolationist," 183.

20. Robert R. Reynolds to Gerald L. K. Smith, March 31, 1942, January 19, 1943, Gerald L. K. Smith Papers, Manuscript Collection, Bentley Library, University of Michigan, Ann Arbor.

21. Reynolds, "Weak Links in Our Defense," 14–15; *Raleigh News and Observer*, February 26, 1942; *Congressional Record*, 77th Cong., 2d sess., 1942, p. 1625.

22. *Time*, February 1, 1943, 14–16.

23. *Congressional Record*, 77th Cong., 2d sess., 1942, pp. 6887–93; *Raleigh News and Observer*, August 21, 22, 1942.

24. The senators were Styles Bridges, Walter F. George, George W. Norris, Tom Connally, Theodore F. Green, and Alben W. Barkley.

25. *Congressional Record*, 77th Cong., 2d sess., 1942, pp. 2889–95; *New York Times*, August 21, 1942; *Asheville Citizen*, August 21, 1942.

26. *New York Sun*, August 28, 1942.

27. *New York Times*, August 22, 1942.

28. *Asheville Citizen*, August 19, 21, 1942.

29. *New York Times*, August 24, 1942.

30. *Raleigh News and Observer*, August 23, 1942.

31. Kimball, *Juggler*, 134–40.

32. *Greensboro Daily News*, January 17, 1942; *Asheville Citizen*, January 17, 1942.

33. *Asheville Citizen*, January 17, 1942.

34. *Raleigh News and Observer*, January 21, 1942.

35. Berg, *Lindbergh*, 397, 406, 420–21.

36. *New York Times*, June 24, 1942; *Raleigh News and Observer*, June 24, 1942; *Asheville Citizen*, June 24, 1942.

37. *American Vindicator*, June 1942, 1.

38. *Raleigh News and Observer*, June 26, 1942.

39. *National Record*, March 1942, 1.

40. Robert R. Reynolds to "Fellow American," October 20, 1943, Smith Papers.

41. *New York Times*, October 16, 1942.

42. *Greensboro Daily News*, November 11, 1943.

43. *Raleigh News and Observer*, October 24, 1943.

44. Ibid., February 20, 1943; *Congressional Record*, 78th Cong., 1st sess., 1943, pp. 1090–92.

45. *Congressional Record*, 78th Cong., 1st sess., 1943, p. 37; *National Record*, March 1943, 1, and June 1943, 2.

46. *National Record*, March 1943, 2, and June 1943, 2.

47. "Resolution Adopted by Enka Rayon Workers," March 25, 1943, Josiah W. Bailey Papers, Duke University Library, Durham; *Raleigh News and Observer*, April 13, 1943.

48. *Raleigh News and Observer*, April 30, 1943.

49. *Congressional Record*, 78th Cong., 1st sess., 1943, p. 3993; *Raleigh News and Observer*, May 6, 1943; Robert R. Reynolds to Gerald L. K. Smith, March 4, 1944, Smith Papers.

50. *Congressional Record*, 78th Cong., 1st sess., 1943, p. 6489.

51. *Hot Springs (Ark.) Record*, July 25, 1943; *New York Times*, July 25, 1943.

52. *Raleigh News and Observer*, January 6, 1941.

53. Robert R. Reynolds to Harry S Truman, January 30, 1945, Harry S Truman Papers, Harry S Truman Library, Independence.

54. *Congressional Record*, 78th Cong., 1st sess., 1943, p. 1901.

55. Ibid., 77th Cong., 1st sess., 1941, p. 1626.

56. Ibid., 1941, appendix, pp. 919–920.

57. Robert R. Reynolds to Elbert D. Thomas, August 13, 20, 1943, and Thomas to Reynolds, November 11, 1943, Elbert D. Thomas Papers, Utah State Historical Society, Salt Lake City.

58. *New York Times*, January 16, 1943; *Raleigh News and Observer*, January 24, 1943; Roger Daniels, *Prisoners without Trial*, 65–71.

59. *Congressional Record*, 78th Cong., 1st sess., 1943, pp. 2722–26.

60. Irons, *Justice at War*, 58–68.

61. *Raleigh News and Observer*, March 28, April 19, 1943; *New York Journal-American*, June 5, 1943; Nicholas, *Washington Despatches*, 173.

62. *Congressional Record*, 78th Cong., 1st sess., 1943, pp. 5367–71; *New York Times*, June 5, 1943.

63. *Charlotte Observer*, June 4, 11, 1943.

64. *Greensboro Daily News*, June 26, 1943.

65. *Raleigh News and Observer*, October 22, 1943; Cole, *Senator Gerald P. Nye*, 207.

66. *Raleigh News and Observer*, October 24, 1943.

67. *Congressional Record*, 78th Cong., 1st sess., 1943, pp. 8929–30; *New York Times*, November 1, 2, 1943.

68. Arthur Vandenberg to A. Haapanen, June 20, 1943 and to Frank Januszewski, November 6, 1943, Arthur H. Vandenberg Papers, Manuscript Collections, Bentley Library, University of Michigan.

69. *New York Times*, November 6, 1943.

70. Ibid., November 2, 3, 4, 1943.

71. *Congressional Record*, 78th Cong., 1st sess., 1943, pp. 9221–22; author's interview with Burton K. Wheeler; Nicholas, *Washington Despatches*, 269.

72. Cole, *Roosevelt and the Isolationists*, 523–25.

73. Nicholas, *Washington Despatches*, 269.

74. Robert R. Reynolds to Mrs. Ernest Lundeen, March 9, 1944, Ernest Lundeen Papers, Hoover Institution on Revolution, War, and Peace, Stanford University, Palo Alto.

75. Long, *War Diary*, 332.

76. *Raleigh News and Observer*, January 3, 1943.

77. *Elizabeth City Daily Advance*, December 12, 1942.

78. *High Point Enterprise*, n.d., Robert Rice Reynolds Papers, Asheville.

79. O. Max Gardner to Senator Walter F. George, December 17, 1942, O. Max Gardner Papers, Southern Historical Collection, University of North Carolina, Chapel Hill.

80. Gardner to Mildred G. Barnwell, December 22, 1942, and Gardner to Frank Hancock, February 15, 1943, Gardner Papers.

81. Gardner to W. Thomas Bost, January 1, 1943, Gardner Papers.

82. *Charlotte News*, January 3, 1943; *Greensboro Daily News*, January 3, 1943; *High Point Enterprise*, January 4, 1943.

83. *Raleigh News and Observer*, January 19, 1943.

84. Interview with Wesley E. McDonald Sr., July 25, 1968, by Joseph L. Morrison, Joseph L. Morrison Papers, Southern Historical Collection.

85. O. Max Gardner to D. Hiden Ramsey, February 16, 17, 1943, and "Senator Reynolds Reminds Us," by Josiah W. Bailey, February 16, 1943, both in Darley Hiden Ramsey Papers, Southern Historical Collection.

86. D. Hiden Ramsey to O. Max Gardner, March 2, 1943, Ramsey Papers.

87. Document, 1943, n.p., in H. Patrick Taylor Sr. Papers, Manuscript Collection, East Carolina University, Greenville.

88. Josiah W. Bailey to O. Max Gardner, January 9, 1943, Josiah W. Bailey Papers, Duke University Library, Durham; *Raleigh News and Observer*, February 17, 1943.

89. O. Max Gardner to Josephus Daniels, February 17, 1943, Gardner Papers; O. Max Gardner to D. Hiden Ramsey, February 4, 1943, Ramsey Papers.

90. Robert R. Reynolds to William J. Cocke Jr., February 1, 1943, William J. Cocke Jr. Papers, Southern Historical Collection; *Raleigh News and Observer*, February 17, 1943.

91. *Greensboro Daily News*, February 20, 1943; *Raleigh News and Observer*, February 22, 1943.

92. *Charlotte Observer*, March 3, 1943.

93. O. Max Gardner to Frank Hancock, February 15, 1943, Gardner Papers.

94. O. Max Gardner to D. Hiden Ramsey, March 5, 1943, Ramsey Papers: O. Max Gardner to Charles M. Johnson, March 11, 1943, Gardner Papers.

95. O. Max Gardner to D. Hiden Ramsey, March 1, 1943, Ramsey Papers.

96. Santford Martin to O. Max Gardner, March 16, 21, 1943, John Santford Martin Papers, Duke University Library.

97. Lindsay Warren to Harry McMullen, April 2, 1943, Lindsay Carter Warren Papers, Southern Historical Collection; D. Hiden Ramsey to O. Max Gardner, April 14, 1943, Ramsey Papers.

98. O. Max Gardner to D. Hiden Ramsey, April 23, 1943, Ramsey Papers; Gardner to Josiah W. Bailey, April 23, 1943, Bailey Papers; *Sanford Herald*, April 24, 1943; *Raleigh News and Observer*, April 23, 1943; *Greensboro Daily News*, April 24, 1943.

99. *Raleigh News and Observer*, April 23, 1943.

100. W. Emmett McNeill to W. Kerr Scott, April 20, 1943, W. Kerr Scott Papers, Department of Archives and History, Raleigh.

101. *Raleigh News and Observer*, April 28, 1943.

102. O. Max Gardner to Lindsay Warren, April 21, 1943, Warren Papers.

103. O. Max Gardner to Robert W. Woodruff, June 1, 1943, Gardner Papers.

104. *Raleigh News and Observer*, May 2, 1943.

105. *Charlotte Observer*, April 29, 1943.

106. Josiah W. Bailey to O. Max Gardner, April 29, 1943, Bailey Papers.

107. *New York Journal-American*, May 15, 1943; *Pittsburgh Sun-Telegram*, May 15, 1943.

108. *Greensboro Daily News*, June 28, 1943.

109. *Raleigh News and Observer*, September 12, October 20, 1943.

110. Ibid., October 23, 1943.

111. Marvin McIntyre to Jonathan Daniels, August 3, 1943, Jonathan Worth Daniels Papers, Southern Historical Collection.

112. *High Point Enterprise*, October 17, 1943.

113. *Raleigh News and Observer*, November 2, 1943.

114. *New York Times*, November 9, 1943; *Greensboro Daily News*, November 9, 1943; *Raleigh News and Observer*, November 9, 1943.

115. *Raleigh News and Observer*, November 9, 19, 1943.

116. Ibid., November 13, 1943.

117. *Greensboro Daily News*, November 10, 1943.

118. Nicholas, *Washington Despatches*, 277, 450.

119. *Durham Morning Herald*, November 10, 1943.

120. *Asheville Citizen*, November 14, 1943.

121. Henry A. Grady to Lindsay Warren, November 14, 1943, Warren Papers.

122. *New York Times*, November 9, 1943.

123. *Chicago Sun*, quoted in the *Asheville Citizen*, November 22, 1943.

124. *Raleigh News and Observer*, November 14, 1943.

125. Author's interview with T. Lamar Caudle.

126. Author's interview with Frances Reynolds Oertling.

127. This group had no relationship with the America First organization that disbanded after Pearl Harbor.

128. *Raleigh News and Observer*, November 14, 16, 1943; FBI report on Gerald L. K. Smith, September 27, 1944, FBI file F62-43818-570; *Washington Times-Herald*, November 16, 1943.

129. *Raleigh News and Observer*, November 15, 16, 1943.

130. Robert R. Reynolds to Mrs. J. Wistar Evans, June 10, 1944, Smith Papers.

131. Robert R. Reynolds to C. L. Fleet, April 21, 1942, Smith Papers.

132. Robert R. Reynolds to Gerald L. K. Smith, July 30, August 3, 6, 8, 1943, Smith Papers.

133. Prescott Dennett to Robert R. Reynolds, October 4, 1943, and Reynolds to Dennett, October 7, 1943, Smith Papers.

134. *Daily Worker*, March 28, 29, 1942.

135. *The Cross and the Flag*, March 1943, 170.

136. Robert R. Reynolds to Gerald L. K. Smith, March 9, 1943, and Smith to Reynolds, March 16, 1943, Smith Papers.

137. *Raleigh News and Observer*, December 12, 1943.

138. Edward J. Smythe to Reynolds for President Club, December 9, 1943, Smith Papers.

139. *Raleigh News and Observer*, November 28, 1943.

140. *Asheville Citizen*, November 14, 1943.

141. *National Record*, November 1943, 2; *Raleigh News and Observer*, November 20, 1943.

142. *Raleigh News and Observer*, November 20, 1943.

CHAPTER TWELVE

1. *Raleigh News and Observer*, January 2, 1944.

2. Ibid., January 23, 1944.

3. Drury, *Senate Journal*, 46.

4. Quotations here and in next paragraph from ibid., 146, 194.

5. *Raleigh News and Observer*, March 8, 1944.

6. *New York Times*, February 10, 1944; Drury, *Senate Journal*, 73–74, 146.

7. *New York Times*, January 23, 1944.

8. Drury, *Senate Journal*, 239.

9. *Congressional Record*, 78th Cong., 2d sess., 1944, pp. 1797–1805, 1826, 1829; *New York Times*, February 18, 1944; *Raleigh News and Observer*, February 18, 1944.

10. Burns, *Roosevelt: The Soldier of Freedom*, 429, 515–18.

11. Long, *War Diary*, 378.

12. *New York Times*, October 14, 1944.

13. *National Record*, March 1944, 1.

14. *New York Times*, October 14, 1944; *National Record*, November 1944, 1.

15. *National Record*, March 1944, 3, and June 1944, 8.

16. *Raleigh News and Observer*, February 20, 1944.

17. Gerald L. K. Smith to Robert R. Reynolds, January 20, 1944, Gerald L. K. Smith Papers, Manuscript Collections, Bentley Library, University of Michigan, Ann Arbor; Jeansonne, *Gerald L. K. Smith*, 82–83; *Raleigh News and Observer*, March 6, 1944; Piller, *Time Bomb*, 102.

18. Robert R. Reynolds to Gerald L. K. Smith, January 22, May 15, July 28, 1944, Smith Papers.

19. *Raleigh News and Observer*, June 10, 1944.

20. Robert R. Reynolds to Mrs. Evans, June 10, 1944, Smith Papers.

21. Robert R. Reynolds to Gerald L. K. Smith, June 8, 1944, Smith Papers.

22. Robert R. Reynolds to John McCormack, July 15, 1944, Smith Papers.

23. Eulau, "False Prophets in the Bible Belt," 169–71.

24. Reynolds to Gerald L. K. Smith, August 11, 1944, Smith Papers.

25. Ibid., August 2, 1944.

26. *Raleigh News and Observer*, June 12, 1944; *New York Times*, June 12, 1944.

27. *National Record*, March 1944, 1–8.

28. Ibid., April 1944, 1.

29. Ibid., July 1944, 6.

30. "The Summary of Department of California, Veterans of Foreign Wars Hearing," August 9, 1944, 1–18, in FBI report, FBI file 62-34350-54x, June 11, 1945; *New York Times*, August 22, 1944; *Raleigh News and Observer*, August 2, 1944.

31. Robert R. Reynolds to M. C. Hermann, August 8, 1944, FBI report 62-34350-54x, June 11, 1945.

32. *New York Herald Tribune*, January 8, 1945.

33. *National Record*, January 1945, 1, and February 1945, 1–8; *Miami Herald*, January 16, 1945.

34. *Raleigh News and Observer*, June 20, 1945; *Cleveland Press*, June 12, 1945.

35. *Chicago Sun*, July 8, 1945.

36. *Worcester (Mass.) Daily Telegram*, June 29, 1945.

37. *Indianapolis Times*, June 28, 1945.

38. *Raleigh News and Observer*, August 5, 6, 7, 1945.

39. Ibid., August 9, 1945.

40. Quotations here and in the following paragraph are from the *National Record*, September 1945, 1.

41. *Washington Post*, October 29, 1945.

42. *Washington (N.C.) Daily News*, September 28, 1945; *New York World Telegram*, September 28, 1945.

43. Drury, *Senate Journal*, 278, 308.

44. Robert R. Reynolds to Clyde R. Hoey, June 8, 1944, and Hoey to Reynolds, July 24, 1944, Clyde Roark Hoey Papers, Duke University Library, Durham.

45. Drury, *Senate Journal*, 326.

46. *Congressional Record*, 78th Cong., 2d sess., 1944, pp. 9708–13.

47. *Raleigh News and Observer*, December 21, 1944.

48. *Winston-Salem Journal*, December 22, 1944.

49. *Asheville Citizen*, December 22, 1944.

CHAPTER THIRTEEN

1. Robert R. Reynolds to Gerald L. K. Smith, December 28, 1944, Smith Papers; *Asheville Citizen*, April 12, 1945. Much of this chapter appeared in the *North Carolina Historical Review* 65 (January 1988): 52–75.

2. *Charlotte Observer*, September 9, 1944; *Asheville Times*, December 18, 1944.

3. *Asheville Citizen*, April 14, 1945; *Raleigh News and Observer*, April 15, 1945.

4. *Asheville Citizen*, September 21, 1946; *Raleigh News and Observer*, September 21, 1946.

5. *Winston-Salem Journal*, October 4, 1946; *New York Times*, October 4, 1946.

6. Author's interview with A. Magruder McDonald.

7. Author's interview with Frances Reynolds Oertling.

8. Abe Fortas to Mrs. Evalyn Walsh McLean, July 6, 1946, Evalyn Walsh McLean Papers, Library of Congress, Washington, D.C.

9. Author's interview with Hubert H. Rand Jr.

10. Author's interview with T. Lamar Caudle.

11. Bill of sale for the Hope Diamond, Cartier, August 1, 1918, McLean Papers; McLean, *Father Struck It Rich*, 155–56; Patch, *Blue Mystery*, 1–64; *Christian Science Monitor*, November 12, 1958.

12. *Raleigh News and Observer*, October 10, 1946; *American Weekly*, February 9, 1947; *Greensboro Daily News*, May 11, 1947.

13. *Asheville Times*, April 10, 1951; *Raleigh News and Observer*, March 12, 1951; *US News and World Report*, March 12, 1950, 1.

14. *Asheville Citizen*, February 14, 1963; Robert R. Reynolds to Justice Frank Murphy, December 23, 1947, Robert Rice Reynolds Papers, Asheville.

15. *Asheville Citizen-Times*, December 1, 1946.

16. *Charlotte Observer*, August 30, 1947; *Raleigh News and Observer*, August 31, 1947; *West Asheville News*, June 6, 1947; newspaper clipping, February 27, 1948, n.p., Reynolds Papers.

17. *Washington Sunday-Star*, April 27, 1947; *Washington Post*, May 1, 1947.

18. *Washington Times-Herald*, May 18, 1947; *Raleigh News and Observer*, May 11, 1947; *Asheville Times*, May 1, 1947.

19. *Washington Times-Herald*, May 11, 1947; *Greensboro Daily News*, May 11, 1947; *Asheville Citizen-Times*, January 1, 1948.

20. *Asheville Citizen*, March 17, 1948.

21. *Washington Post*, March 19, 1949; *Charlotte Observer*, March 27, 1949.

22. Patch, *Blue Mystery*, 35.

23. *Washington Post*, May 27, 1947; *Durham Morning Herald*, June 28, 1947.

24. Author's interview with Irving C. Crawford.

25. Robert R. Reynolds to Harry S Truman, May 8, 1949; Truman to Reynolds, May 10, 1949; Reynolds to Truman, May 14, 1949, all in President's Personal File, Harry S Truman Papers, Harry S Truman Library, Independence.

26. *Raleigh News and Observer*, March 7, 1949; *Charlotte Observer*, March 7, 1949.

27. W. Kerr Scott, "Why I Appointed Frank Graham to the Senate," n.d., Oscar Jackson Coffin Papers.

28. General and Miscellaneous Files, PC 1175, W. Kerr Scott Papers, Department of Archives and History, Raleigh.

29. *Raleigh News and Observer*, March 23, 1949; *New York Times*, March 23, 1949.

30. Pleasants and Burns, *Frank Porter Graham*, 5–45.

31. Key, *Southern Politics*, 206; Cash, *Mind of the South*, 349.

32. Ashby, *Frank Porter Graham*, 99–317.

33. *Raleigh Times*, March 30, 1949; *Charlotte Observer*, March 30, 1949.

34. *Charlotte Observer*, April 3, 1949.

35. Ibid., March 30, 1949.

36. Author's interview with Paul Teal Jr.

37. *Charlotte Observer*, April 3, 10, 1949.

38. Ibid., July 20, 1949; *Durham Morning Herald*, July 26, 1949.

39. *Charlotte Observer*, September 15, 1949.

40. C. Sylvester Green to Jonathan Daniels, August 23, 1949, Jonathan Worth Daniels Papers, Southern Historical Collection, University of North Carolina, Chapel Hill.

41. Clyde R. Hoey to Clyde A. Erwin, July 30, 1949, Clyde Roark Hoey Papers, Duke University Library, Durham.

42. *New York Mirror*, December 8, 1949.

43. *Charlotte Observer*, October 29, 1949; *Durham Morning Herald*, December 14, 1949.

44. *Elizabeth City Daily Advance*, January 4, 1950; *Charlotte Observer*, January 16, 1950.

45. T. C. Johnson to Capus Waynick, December 8, 1949, Capus Miller Waynick Papers, Manuscript Collection, East Carolina University, Greenville.

46. *Washington Daily News* (North Carolina), January 11, February 23, 1950.

47. *Asheville Citizen-Times*, January 7, 1950.

48. "No Competition in the East," *The State*, January 21, 1950, 12.

49. *Charlotte Observer*, January 14, 1950.

50. Author's interview with Irving C. Crawford.

51. *Elizabeth City Daily Advance*, January 26, 1950.

52. *Raleigh News and Observer*, January 31, 1950; *New York Times*, January 31, 1950; *Charlotte Observer*, January 31, 1950; *New York Herald Tribune*, February 23, 1950.

53. *Charlotte Observer*, n.d., in Reynolds Papers.

54. Author's interview with Irving C. Crawford.

55. Author's interview with Hoover Adams.

56. Author's interview with Terry Sanford.

57. Author's interview with Richard E. Thigpen.

58. Campaign platform of Robert Rice Reynolds, candidate for the United States Senate, 1950, in Frank P. Graham Papers, Southern Historical Collection; in Robert Gregg Cherry Papers, Department of Archives and History, Raleigh; and in John A. Lang Jr. Papers, Manuscript Collection, East Carolina University; *Raleigh News and Observer*, January 31, 1950; *New York Times*, January 31, 1950.

59. *Raleigh News and Observer*, January 31, February 1, 1950; *Winston-Salem Journal*, January 31, 1950; Jonathan Daniels to Maurice Rosenblatt, February 20, 1950, Jonathan Daniels Papers; Charles Eagles's interview with Jonathan Daniels, Southern Oral History Collection.

60. *Elizabeth City Daily Advance*, February 2, 1950; *Raleigh News and Observer*, February 2, 1950.

61. *Dunn Dispatch*, February 13, 1950.

62. Dr. Louise M. Ingersall to Gladys T. Coddington, January 3, 1950, Gladys Tillett Papers.

63. *Asheville Citizen*, February 13, 1950.

64. Holt McPherson to Clyde R. Hoey, January 14, 1950, Hoey Papers.

65. *Greensboro Daily News*, February 3, 1950.

66. *Charlotte Observer*, January 8, 1950.

67. *New York Times*, March 30, 1950.

68. A. L. Brumlett to W. Kerr Scott, February 7, 1950, Scott Papers.

69. Louis Round Wilson to Frank P. Graham, February 1, 1950, Louis Round Wilson Papers, Southern Historical Collection.

70. Gerald Johnson to Frank P. Graham, February 16, 1950, Graham Papers.

71. *Washington (N.C.) Daily News*, February 1, 1950.

72. *Raleigh News and Observer*, February 25, 1950.

73. *Asheville Citizen*, February 25, 1950.

74. Ibid.

75. *Charlotte Observer*, February 27, 1950.

76. "Frank Porter Graham, Candidate for the United States Senate," n.d., pamphlet in Jefferson Deems Johnson Papers, Duke University Library; *Greensboro Daily News*, March 3, 1950.

77. *Charlotte Observer*, March 7, 1950; *Durham Morning Herald*, March 7, 1950.

78. *Charlotte News*, n.d., in Reynolds Papers; Tom Schlesinger, "Frank Graham's Primary Education," *The Nation*, April 22, 1950, 367–68.

79. Irving C. Crawford to Dear Friend, February 22, 1950, Cherry Papers; author's interview with Irving C. Crawford.

80. Thurmond Chatham to Robert R. Reynolds, March 22, 1950, Thurmond Chatham Papers.

81. *Asheville Citizen*, March 18, 1950; *Charlotte Observer*, March 18, 1950.

82. *Charlotte Observer*, May 7, 1950; *Asheville Citizen*, May 7, 1950.

83. *Durham Morning Herald*, March 12, 1950.

84. *Elizabeth City Daily Advance*, March 17, 1950.

85. *Asheville Citizen*, March 19, 1950; *Elizabeth City Daily Advance*, March 17, 20, 1950.

86. *Raleigh News and Observer*, March 18, 1950.

87. *Asheville Citizen*, March 28, 1950.

88. Author's interview with Irving C. Crawford.

89. C. W. Tillett to Allard Lowenstein, February 16, 1950, Allard Kenneth Lowenstein Papers, Southern Historical Collection.

90. *Raleigh News and Observer*, March 2, 1950.

91. *Asheville Citizen*, March 26, 1950.

92. Ibid., April 25, 1950.

93. *Elizabeth City Daily Advance*, May 13, 1950.

94. *Charlotte Observer*, April 4, 5, 9, 1950.

95. *Greensboro Daily News*, April 5, 1950.

96. Radio address by Robert Rice Reynolds, April 4, 1950, Lang Papers.

97. *Charlotte Observer*, April 13, 1950.

98. J. B. Moore to Capus Waynick, April 12, 1950, Waynick Papers.

99. Author's interview with Hoover Adams.

100. *Charlotte Observer*, April 9, 1950.

101. *Asheville Citizen*, April 15, 1950.

102. Pleasants and Burns, *Frank Porter Graham*, 145–87; "What's Going On in North Carolina," *The State*, May 13, 1950, 17.

103. *Greensboro Daily News*, May 18, 1950.

104. *Goldsboro New Argus*, May 12, 1950; *Charlotte Observer*, May 13, 1950; *Asheville Citizen*, May 13, 1950.

105. *Charlotte Observer*, May 6, 1950; *Asheville Citizen*, May 6, 1950.

106. *Asheville Citizen*, May 10, 1950.

107. *Jacksonville News and Views*, May 23, 1950.

108. *Asheville News*, May 12, 1950; *Asheville Citizen*, May 21, 1950; *Charlotte Observer*, May 25, 1950; *Elizabeth City Daily Advance*, May 25, 1950.

109. *Cleveland County Times* (Shelby, N.C.), May 23, 1950.

110. Author's interview with Roy Wilder Jr.

111. *Asheville Citizen*, May 25, 1950.

112. *Raleigh News and Observer*, May 12, 1950.

113. *Asheville Citizen*, May 26, 27, 1950.

114. *Greensboro Daily News*, February 14, 1950.

115. *Richmond Times-Dispatch*, May 25, 1950.

116. *Durham Sun*, May 26, 1950; *Raleigh News and Observer*, May 21, 1950; *New York Herald Tribune*, May 25, 1950.

117. Clyde R. Hoey to O. L. Moore, May 15, 1950, Hoey Papers.

118. London, *North Carolina Manual, 1951*, 236.

119. Author's interviews with R. Mayne Albright, William W. Staton, and Frank Porter Graham.

120. Author's interviews with Irving C. Crawford, Paul Teal Jr., Hubert H. Rand Jr., William D. Snider, John L. Sanders, William W. Staton, and Terry Sanford.

121. North Carolina Secretary of State, Candidates' Statement of Contribution and Expenses, Robert R. Reynolds, May 22, 1950; *Greensboro Daily News*, June 17, 1950.

122. *New York Times*, May 29, 1950; *Charlotte Observer*, May 29, 1950.

123. *Philadelphia Bulletin*, May 30, 1950; *Raleigh News and Observer*, May 28, 1950.

124. *Sentinel Record* (Hot Springs, Ark.), June 15, 1950.

125. *Raleigh News and Observer*, June 1, 1950.

126. *Charlotte News*, May 28, 1950; *Fayetteville Observer*, June 2, 1950.

127. Tilford E. Dudley to Daniel Powell, June 2, 1950, Daniel Augustus Powell Papers, Southern Historical Collection.

128. *Greensboro Daily News*, June 8, 1950.

129. *High Point Enterprise*, June 9, 1950; *Durham Morning Herald*, June 9, 1950; *Charlotte Observer*, June 9, 1950; *Greensboro Daily News*, June 9, 1950.

130. *Greensboro Daily News*, June 14, 1950; *Asheville Citizen*, June 15, 1950.

131. *Charlotte Observer*, June 9, 10, 1950.

132. Jeff Johnson to County Managers, June 10, 1950, Johnson Papers.

133. *Durham Sun*, June 16, 1950; *High Point Enterprise*, June 9, 1950.

134. Willis Smith to My Dear Friend, June 20, 1950, Scott Papers.

135. Author's interview with James K. Dorsett Jr.

136. *Raleigh News and Observer*, June 21, 1950; *Charlotte Observer*, June 21, 1950.

137. *Asheville Citizen*, July 1, 1950.

138. Robert R. Reynolds to John T. Flynn, July 2, 1950, John T. Flynn Papers, University of Oregon Library, Eugene.

EPILOGUE

1. *Charlotte Observer*, July 10, 1955.

2. Author's interview with Harriet Louise "Mimi" Palmer.

3. Robert R. Reynolds to Eleanor Baumgardner, August 9, 1952, Robert Rice Reynolds Papers, Asheville; *Asheville Citizen*, July 25, 1963.

4. Documents in Reynolds Papers.

5. *Washington Star*, October 17, 1950; *Raleigh News and Observer*, October 18, 1950; *Asheville Citizen*, October 18, 1950.

6. *Asheville Citizen-Times*, August 28, 1960; *Washington Star*, August 28, 1960.

7. *Detroit Free Press*, July 17, 1955; *Charlotte Observer*, July 10, 1955; *Asheville Citizen-Times*, November 23, 1958.

8. Bill Sharpe, "Bob Reynolds 1962 Version," *The State*, November 10, 1962, 11–12.

9. Author's interview with Mimi Palmer; undated newspaper clipping, n.p., Reynolds Papers.

10. Final will of Robert Rice Reynolds, dated February 1, 1957, Superior Court, Buncombe County, Asheville; *Asheville Citizen*, February 17, April 19, 1963.

11. Quotations here and in next two paragraphs are from *Asheville Citizen*, February 14, 1963; *Charlotte Observer*, February 14, 1963; *Greensboro Daily News*, February 14, 1963; *Raleigh News and Observer*, February 14, 1963.

12. *Asheville Citizen*, February 15, 1963.

13. *Asheville Times*, February 15, 1963.

14. *Durham Morning Herald*, February 15, 1963.

15. Author's interview with Irving C. Crawford.

16. Document, 1943, n.p., in H. Patrick Taylor Sr. Papers, Manuscript Collection, East Carolina University, Greenville.

Bibliography

Author's note: The best manuscript sources for Reynolds include the Josiah W. Bailey Papers, the O. Max Gardner Papers, the Darley Hiden Ramsey Papers, the Frank P. Graham Papers, the Gerald L. K. Smith Papers, and the Lindsay Carter Warren Papers. Other essential research materials include the *Congressional Record* and the complete collection of Reynolds's newspapers: the *American Vindicator* and the *National Record*. The Library of Congress also has copies of *Social Justice, Liberation,* and the *Cross and the Flag,* papers published by his cohorts in intolerance. The most important interviews were with Frances Reynolds Oertling, Hubert H. Rand Jr., Wesley E. McDonald Sr., Irving C. Crawford, and Paul Teal Jr. These five individuals were very close to Reynolds and were able to provide insight into Reynolds's motivation and to supply information unavailable elsewhere.

MANUSCRIPTS

Albuquerque, New Mexico
Manuscript Collections, University of New Mexico
  Dennis Chavez Papers

Ann Arbor, Michigan
Manuscript Collection, Bentley Library, University of Michigan
  Frank Murphy Papers
  Gerald L. K. Smith Papers
  Arthur H. Vandenberg Papers

Asheville, North Carolina
Robert Rice Reynolds Papers, in possession of his family
Superior Court, Buncombe County
  Probated will of Robert Rice Reynolds

Athens, Georgia
Richard B. Russell Library, University of Georgia
  Richard B. Russell Papers

Austin, Texas
Manuscript Collections, University of Texas
  Morris Sheppard Papers

Baton Rouge, Louisiana
Oral History Collection and Manuscript Collection, Louisiana State University
  Huey Pierce Long Papers

Boston, Massachusetts
Massachusetts Historical Society
  Henry Cabot Lodge Jr. Papers

Cambridge, England
Cambridge University Library
  Oswald Moseley Papers

Chapel Hill, North Carolina
Alumni Association Files, University of North Carolina
North Carolina Collection, University of North Carolina
Office of the Registrar, University of North Carolina
    Academic transcript of Robert Rice Reynolds
Southern Historical Collection, University of North Carolina
  Dudley Warren Bagley Papers
  Harriet M. Berry Papers
  Thurmond Chatham Papers
  William J. Cocke Jr. Papers
  Oscar Jackson Coffin Papers
  William Terry Couch Papers
  Jonathan Worth Daniels Papers
  Robert L. Doughton Papers
  O. Max Gardner Papers
  Frank P. Graham Papers
  Louis and Mildred Graves Papers
  Gordan Gray Papers
  William Thomas Joyner Sr. Papers
  Allard Kenneth Lowenstein Papers
  Holt McPherson Papers
  Joseph L. Morrison Papers
  Howard Washington Odum Papers
  Daniel Augustus Powell Papers
  Darley Hiden Ramsey Papers
  John Humphrey Small Papers
  George E. C. Stephens Papers
  Gladys Tillett Papers
  John Wesley Umstead Papers
  William B. Umstead Papers
  Lindsay Carter Warren Papers
  Louis Round Wilson Papers

Charlottesville, Virginia
Special Collections, Alderman Library, University of Virginia
  Harry Flood Byrd Papers
  Carter Glass Papers

Clemson, South Carolina
Special Collections, Clemson University
  James F. Byrnes Papers

Durham, North Carolina
Duke University Library
  American Socialist Party Papers
  Josiah W. Bailey Papers
  Charles A. Ellwood Papers
  P. Cleveland Gardner Papers
  Hugh Gladney Grant Papers
  Edwin Clarke Gregory Papers
  Hinsdale Family Papers
  Clyde Roark Hoey Papers
  Jefferson Deems Johnson Papers
  Allen Langston Papers
  John Santford Martin Papers
  Romulus A. Nunn Papers
  Lucy Randolph Papers
  John Humphrey Small Papers
  Willis Smith Papers

Eugene, Oregon
University of Oregon Library
  John T. Flynn Papers

Fayetteville, Arkansas
Department of Special Collections, University of Arkansas
  J. William Fulbright Papers

Gainesville, Florida
P. K. Yonge Library, University of Florida
  Spessard Lindsay Holland Papers

Greenville, North Carolina
Manuscript Collection, East Carolina University
  John A. Lang Jr. Papers
  Charles O'Hagan Laughinghouse Papers
  Clarence Leroy Shuping Papers
  Johnetta Webb Spilman Papers
  H. Patrick Taylor Sr. Papers
  Capus Miller Waynick Papers
  Frank M. Wooten Sr. Papers

Helena, Montana
Montana Historical Society
  Burton K. Wheeler Papers

Hyde Park, New York
Franklin D. Roosevelt Library
  Franklin Delano Roosevelt Papers

Independence, Missouri
Harry S Truman Library
  Harry S Truman Papers

Jackson, Mississippi
Mississippi Department of Archives and History
    Theodore G. Bilbo Papers

Laramie, Wyoming
Manuscript Collections, University of Wyoming
    Joseph O'Mahoney Papers

Lexington, Kentucky
Manuscript Collections, University of Kentucky
    Alben W. Barkley Papers
    Albert Benjamin Chandler Papers

Memphis, Tennessee
Memphis Public Library
    Kenneth D. McKellar Papers

Montgomery, Alabama
Alabama Department of Archives and History
    John Hollis Bankhead Jr. Papers

New Haven, Connecticut
Manuscripts and Archives, Yale University
    American Immigration Conference Board Records

Norman, Oklahoma
Western History Collection, University of Oklahoma
    Elmer Thomas Papers

Palo Alto, California
Hoover Institution on Revolution, War, and Peace, Stanford University
    America First Manuscripts
    Ernest Lundeen Papers

Raleigh, North Carolina
Department of Archives and History
    Lynton Yates Ballentine Papers
    Willis G. Briggs Papers
    Robert Gregg Cherry Papers
    David S. Coltrane Papers
    Ruth Current Papers
    May Thompson Evans Papers
    Nell Battle Lewis Papers
    Clarence H. Poe Papers
    W. Kerr Scott Papers

Reno, Nevada
Nevada Historical Society
    Patrick McCarran Papers

St. Paul, Minnesota
Minnesota Historical Society
    Henrik Shipstead Papers

Salt Lake City, Utah
Utah State Historical Society
   Elbert D. Thomas Papers

Tallahassee, Florida
Mildred and Claude Pepper Library, Florida State University
   Claude Pepper Papers

Tempe, Arizona
Carl Hayden Library, Arizona State University
   Carl Hayden Papers

Thibodaux, Louisiana
Manuscript Collections, Nicholls State University
   Allen J. Ellender Papers

Topeka, Kansas
Kansas State Historical Society
   Arthur Capper Papers

Tuscaloosa, Alabama
Manuscript Collections, University of Alabama
   Lister Hill Papers

Washington, D.C.
Library of Congress
   George David Aiken Papers
   Hugo L. Black Papers
   William E. Borah Papers
   Harold Hitz Burton Papers
   Raymond Clapper Papers
   Thomas Terry Connally Papers
   Thomas G. Corcoran Papers
   Bronson W. Cutting Papers
   Josephus Daniels Papers
   Norman H. Davis Papers
   Cordell Hull Papers
   Harold L. Ickes Papers
   Jack Kroll Papers
   Robert Marion La Follette Papers
   Evalyn Walsh McLean Papers
   Robert M. Patterson Papers
   Key Pittman Papers
   Robert A. Taft Papers
   Frederick Moore Vinson Papers
   Henry Agard Wallace Papers
   Thomas J. Walsh Papers
Manuscript Collection, Georgetown University
   Robert Wagner Papers
Registrar of Wills Office
   Probated wills of Evalyn Walsh McLean and Evalyn Washington McLean
War Department, Military Intelligence Service

Williamsburg, Virginia
Manuscript Collections, William and Mary College
    A. Willis Robertson Papers

Winston-Salem, North Carolina
Baptist Historical Collection, Wake Forest University
    C. B. Deane Papers, Personal Collections, Wake Forest University
    Odus McCoy Mull Papers

NEWSPAPERS

North Carolina Newspapers (1914–1963)

Asheville Citizen
Asheville Citizen-Times
Asheville News
Asheville Times
Burlington Times
Carolina Times (Durham), selected issues
Chapel Hill Weekly
Charlotte News
Charlotte Observer
Cleveland County Times, selected issues
Concord Tribune, selected issues
Daily Tar Heel
Dunn Dispatch
Durham Herald-Sun
Durham Morning Herald
Durham Sun
Elizabeth City Daily Advance
Elizabeth City Independent
Fayetteville Observer
Gastonia Gazette
Goldsboro News Argus
Greensboro Daily News
Greensboro Record
High Point Enterprise
Jacksonville News and Views, selected issues
Kinston Daily Free Press, selected issues
Lexington Dispatch, selected issues
Moore County News, selected issues
Onslow County News and Views, selected issues
The Pilot (Southern Pines)
Raleigh News and Observer
Raleigh Times
Sanford Herald
Scotland Neck Commonwealth
Shelby Daily Star, selected issues

Washington (N.C.) Daily News, selected issues
West Asheville News
Williamston Enterprise
Wilmington Star-News
Winston-Salem Journal

Out-of-State Newspapers

Atlanta Constitution, selected issues
Atlanta Journal
Baltimore Evening Sun
Boston Evening American
Boston Globe
Boston Post, selected issues
Chicago Sun
Christian Science Monitor
Cincinnati Enquirer
Cleveland Press
Daily Events (Springfield, Mo.)
The Daily Worker
Dayton (Ohio) Daily News
Detroit Free Press
Galveston Daily News
Hot Springs Record
Houston Chronicle
Huntington Advertiser
Indianapolis Times
Jewish Examiner
Kansas City Journal
Miami Herald
Mobile Press
El Nacional
Nashville Banner
New Orleans Bee
New York Herald Tribune
New York Journal-American
New York Mirror
New York Times
New York World Telegram
Norfolk Virginian-Pilot
Philadelphia Bulletin
Philadelphia Inquirer
Pittsburgh Sun-Telegraph
Richmond News Leader
Richmond Times-Dispatch
St. Louis Globe-Democrat
St. Louis Star-Times
Sentinel Record (Hot Springs, Ark.)
Voelkischer Beobachter

Washington Evening Star
Washington News
Washington Post
Washington Star and *Washington Sunday Star*
Washington Sunday Times
Washington Times-Herald
Worcester (Mass.) Daily Telegram

INTERVIEWS

By the Author

Hoover Adams, Dunn, N.C., May 26, 1983
R. Mayne Albright, Raleigh, N.C., November 30, 1984
T. Clyde Auman, West End, N.C., May 23, 1983
H. Clifton Blue, Aberdeen, N.C., May 23, 1983
J. Melville Broughton Jr., Raleigh, N.C., December 12, 1984
Theron Lamar Caudle, Wadesboro, N.C., August 12, 1968
J. Gerald Cowan, Asheville, N.C., August 8, 1969
Irving C. Crawford, Asheville, N.C., August 7, 1969
James K. Dorsett Jr., Raleigh, N.C., December 12, 1984
Carl W. Durham, Chapel Hill, N.C., May 23, 1968
John C. B. Ehringhaus, Annapolis, Md., November 10, 1984
Samuel J. Ervin Jr., telephone conversation, November 9, 1984
Thad Eure, Raleigh, N.C., December 11, 1984
Kathryn N. Folger, Dobson, N.C., December 6, 1984
William C. Friday, Chapel Hill, N.C., (with A. M. Burns), October 17, 1984
Frank Porter Graham, Chapel Hill, N.C., July 1, 1969
Jesse A. Helms, Raleigh, N.C., December 11, 1984
James H. Hensley Jr., Asheville, N.C., May 31, 1972
James S. Howell, Asheville, N.C., May 30, 1972
H. G. Jones, Chapel Hill, N.C., November 6, 1984
John Jordan Jr., Raleigh, N.C., December 12, 1984
William Joslin, Raleigh, N.C., December 12, 1984
William Thomas Joyner Jr., Raleigh, N.C., December 13, 1984
I. Beverly Lake, Wake Forest, N.C., December 10, 1984
David M. McConnell, Charlotte, N.C., September 13, 1984
Donald McCoy, Fayetteville, N.C., December 7, 1984
A. Magruder McDonald, Washington, D.C., June 19, 1969, by telephone
Wesley E. McDonald Sr., Washington, D.C., May 18, 1972
Duncan E. McIver, Sanford, N.C., December 14, 1967
Lennox Polk McLendon, Greensboro, N.C., November 2, 1984
Joseph P. Marley, Southern Pines, N.C., December 15, 1970
Joseph L. Morrison, Chapel Hill, N.C., June 1, 1969
Gerald P. Nye, Washington, D.C., June 17, 1969
Frances Reynolds Oertling, Florence, Italy, August 16, 1971

Harriet Louise "Mimi" Palmer, Asheville, N.C., August 24, 1969
Drew Pearson, Washington, D.C., July 21, 1968, by telephone
Claude M. Pepper, Washington, D.C., October 31, 1969
Sam Ragan, Southern Pines, N.C., October 25, 1984
Hubert H. Rand Jr., Durham, N.C., August 25, 1969, September 24, 1991
Margaret Reynolds, Asheville, N.C., August 8, 1969
John L. Sanders, Chapel Hill, N.C., October 17, 1984
Terry Sanford, Durham, N.C., December 3, 1984
Ralph W. Scott, Haw River, N.C., October 31, 1984
William D. Snider, Greensboro, N.C., October 30, 1984
William W. Staton, Sanford, N.C., October 21, 1984
Paul Teal Jr., Asheville, N.C., August 7, 1969
Richard E. Thigpen, Charlotte, N.C., December 5, 1984
Roy Thompson, Fayetteville, N.C., November 1, 1984
Burton K. Wheeler, Washington, D.C., June 18, 1969
James B. Whittington, Charlotte, N.C., December 5, 1984
Tom Wicker, Chapel Hill, N.C., October 30, 1984
Roy Wilder Jr., Spring Hope, N.C., December 13, 1984

Other Interviews

Columbia Oral History Collection, Columbia University Library, New York, New York
    Roger Nash Baldwin, by Harlan B. Phillips, New York, N.Y., 1954
    Chester A. Bowles, by Neil Gold, Washington, D.C., 1963
    Jonathan Worth Daniels, by Dan Singal, Chapel Hill, N.C., 1972
    Robert H. Jackson, by Harlan Phillips, Durham, N.C., 1952
    Henry Agard Wallace, by Dean Albertson, South Salem, N.Y., 1953

East Carolina University Library, Greenville, North Carolina
    Capus Miller Waynick, August 1, 1979, September 19, 1979, January 30, 1980

Richard B. Russell Library, University of Georgia, Athens, Georgia
    Robert Troutman Jr., by Hugh Cates, n.d.

Southern Historical Collection, University of North Carolina, Chapel Hill, N.C
    Wesley E. McDonald Sr., by Joseph E. Morrison, n.d., Joseph E. Morrison Papers

Southern Oral History Collection, University of North Carolina, Chapel Hill, N.C
    David Burgess, by Jacquelyn Hall and Bill Finger, Upper Montclair, N.J., September 25, 1974;
        by D. Blanchard, August 12, 1983
    Jonathan Worth Daniels, by Daniel Singal, Chapel Hill, N.C., March 22, 1973; by Charles
        Eagles, Hilton Head, S.C., March 9–11, 1977
    Thad Eure, by Jack Bass and Walter DeVries, Raleigh, N.C., December 12, 1973
    Frank Porter Graham, by Charles Jones, Ann Queen, Stuart Willis, Jonathan Daniels, Hank
        Patterson, James Wallace, Joel Fleishman, Terry Sanford, William Friday, Warren Ashby,
        Chapel Hill, N.C., June 9–12, 1962
    Jesse A. Helms, by Jack Bass, Raleigh, N.C., March 8, 1974
    Holt McPherson, by Jack Bass, High Point, N.C., April 9, 1975
    Terry Sanford, by Joe Frantz, Austin, Tex., May 15, 1971; by Brent Glass, Durham, N.C., March
        1, 1972, May 14, 1976, August 20, 1976, December 16–18, 1986

Ralph W. Scott, by Jack Bass, Burlington, N.C., December 20, 1973; by Jacquelyn Hall and Bill
     Finger, Haw River, N.C., April 22, 1974
Gladys Avery Tillett, by Jacquelyn Hall, Charlotte, N.C., March 20, 1974

CONTEMPORARY PERIODICALS CONSULTED

America First Bulletin
American Magazine
American Mercury
American Vindicator
American Weekly
Army-Navy Journal
Asheville Magazine
Atlantic Monthly
Colliers
Congressional Digest
Cross and the Flag
Defender
Fortune
Harper's Magazine
Health Review
Interpreter Releases
Journal of Southern History
Ken
Liberation
Life
Literary Digest
Look
The Nation
National Record
New Republic
Newsweek
North Carolina Historical Review
Plain Talk
Political Science Journal
Popular Mechanic
Progressive
Rotarian
Saturday Evening Post
Scribner's Commentator
Social Forces
Social Justice
South Atlantic Quarterly
Southern Tourist
The State
Time
US News and World Report
Western Political Quarterly

PAMPHLETS

Johnston, Ira T. *Judge Tam C. Bowie Worthy of Your Support.* N.d. North Carolina Collection, University of North Carolina, Chapel Hill.

Reynolds, Robert R., *Radio Address by Robert R. Reynolds over the National Broadcasting Company.* January 12, 1939. North Carolina Collection, University of North Carolina, Chapel Hill.

———. *Radio Speech on Aliens and the Unemployment Problem.* N.p., n.d. North Carolina Collection, University of North Carolina, Chapel Hill.

———. *The Test of Prohibition in the South.* Raleigh, N.C.: Democratic Executive Committee, 1932. North Carolina Collection, University of North Carolina, Chapel Hill.

———. *Threats to America Become Realities.* N.p., n.d. North Carolina Collection, University of North Carolina, Chapel Hill.

MEMOIRS AND DIARIES

Connally, Thomas T. *My Name Is Tom Connally.* New York: Thomas Y. Crowell, 1954.

Dies, Martin. *The Trojan Horse in America.* New York: Dodd, Mead, 1940.

Dodd, William E., Jr., and Dodd, Martha. *Ambassador Dodd's Diary, 1933–1938.* New York: Harcourt, Brace, 1941.

Hull, Cordell, *The Memoirs of Cordell Hull.* 2 vols. New York: Macmillan, 1948.

Ickes, Harold L. *The Autobiography of a Curmudgeon.* New York: Reynal and Hitchcock, 1943.

———. *The Secret Diary of Harold L. Ickes.* 3 vols. New York: Simon and Schuster, 1954.

Lindbergh, Charles A. *The Wartime Journals of Charles A. Lindbergh.* New York: Harcourt, Brace, Jovanovich, 1970.

Long, Breckinridge. *The War Diary of Breckinridge Long.* Edited by Fred L. Israel. Lincoln: University of Nebraska Press, 1966.

Pepper, Claude. Diary. Tallahassee, Fla.

Perkins, Frances. *The Roosevelt I Knew.* New York: Harper and Row, 1964.

Reynolds, Robert R. *Gypsy Trails.* Asheville: Advocate Publishing, n.d.

———. *Wanderlust.* New York: Broadway Publishing Company, 1913.

Vandenberg, Arthur H. *The Private Papers of Senator Vandenberg.* Boston: Houghton Mifflin, 1952.

Wheeler, Burton K., with Paul F. Healy. *Yankee from the West: The Candid Turbulent Life Story of the Yankee-Born U.S. Senator from Montana.* New York: Doubleday, 1962.

GOVERNMENT DOCUMENTS AND OTHER OFFICIAL RECORDS

Federal Government

Congressional Record. Washington, D.C., 1933–45.

Documents on German Foreign Policy, 1918–1945. Ser. D. Washington, D.C., 1949–62.

Federal Bureau of Investigation, Washington, D.C. Raw files relating to Robert R. Reynolds, including 62-34356, serials 9, 10, 11; 94-1-195; 94-1-12142, serials 18, 19; 62-32211, serials 5, 7, 8; 62-22444-1-241; 94-34-909-1; 94-34-218-1; 95-5083.

Hildebrand, William H. *A Guide to Research Collections of U.S. Senators, 1789–1982.* Washington, D.C.: Office of the U.S. Senate, 1983.

U.S. Congress. *Congressional Quarterly Almanac*. Washington, D.C., 1941–1944, 1950.
——. Committee on the District of Columbia. Records of U.S. Senate, National Archives, Washington, D.C.
——. Committee on Military Affairs, 1847–1946. Records of the U.S. Senate, National Archives.
——. Special Committee of the Senate to Investigate the National Defense Program, 1941–1948. Records of the U.S. Senate, National Archives.

State Government

London, Henry M., ed. *North Carolina Manual, 1931*. Raleigh: N.C. Historical Commission, 1931.
——. *North Carolina Manual, 1933*. Raleigh: N.C. Historical Commission, 1933.
——. *North Carolina Manual, 1935*. Raleigh: N.C. Historical Commission, 1935.
——. *North Carolina Manual, 1937*. Raleigh: N.C. Historical Commission, 1937.
——. *North Carolina Manual, 1939*. Raleigh: N.C. Historical Commission, 1939.
——. *North Carolina Manual, 1951*. Raleigh: N.C. Historical Commission, 1951.
Morrison, Cameron. *Public Papers and Letters of Cameron Morrison, Governor of North Carolina, 1921–1925*. Compiled by William H. Richardson, edited by D. L. Corbitt. Raleigh: Edwards and Broughton, 1927.
The North Carolina Democratic Handbook, 1932. Raleigh: State Democratic Executive Committee, 1932.
The North Carolina Democratic Handbook, 1936. Raleigh: State Democratic Executive Committee, 1936.
The North Carolina Democratic Handbook, 1938. Raleigh: State Democratic Executive Committee, 1938.
The North Carolina Democratic Handbook, 1940. Raleigh: State Democratic Executive Committee, 1940.
The North Carolina Democratic Handbook, 1944. Raleigh: State Democratic Executive Committee, 1944.
North Carolina Secretary of State. Candidates' Statements of Contributions and Expenses, Office of the Secretary of State, Raleigh, 1932, 1938, 1950.

MISCELLANEOUS

Biographical Dictionary of the American Congress, 1774–1949. Washington, D.C., 1952.
Summary of Department of California, Veterans of Foreign Wars, Hearing, August 9, 1944, in FBI report, 62-343554X, June 11, 1945.
Yackety Yack, yearbook of the University of North Carolina. 1902–6.

SECONDARY SOURCES

Articles

Cash, Wilbur J. "Paladin of the Drys." *American Mercury* 24 (October 1931): 139–47.
Cole, Wayne S. "America First and the South, 1940–1941." *Journal of Southern History* (February 1956): 36–47.

Coughlan, Robert. "Our Bob Reynolds." *Life*, September 8, 1941, 47–53.

Daniels, Jonathan. "Interlude for an Isolationist." *The Nation*, August 30, 1941, 183.

Davis, Burke. "Senator Bob Reynolds. Retrospective View." *Harper's Magazine*, March 1944, 362–69.

Eulau, Heinz H. F. "False Prophets in the Bible Belt." *New Republic*, February 7, 1944, 169–71.

Ferkiss, Victor C. "Populism—Myth, Reality, Current Danger." *Western Political Quarterly* 14 (September 1961): 737–40.

———. "Populist Influences on American Fascism." *Western Political Quarterly* 10 (June 1957): 350–73.

Fredette, Robert L. "Men behind the Headlines—Senator Bob Reynolds." *Affairs*, February 7, 1941, 67.

Holbo, Paul S. "Wheat of What? Populism and American Fascism." *Western Political Quarterly* 14 (September 1961): 727–36.

Lubell, Samuel. "Who Votes Isolationist and Why." *Harper's Magazine*, April 1951, 29–36.

McCormick, Robert. "Buncombe Bob." *Colliers*, May 21, 1938, 36–38.

McLean, P. O. "Where Cam Made His Mistake." *The State*, September 1933, 16–24.

Miller, Julian S. "The South Is Still Solid—North Carolina." *Review of Reviews*, January 1936, 37–40.

Reynolds, Robert R. "The Weak Links in Our Defense." *American Magazine*, September 1941, 14–15.

Schlesinger, Tom. "Frank Graham's Primary Education." *The Nation*, April 22, 1950, 367–68.

Sharpe, Bill. "Bob Reynolds, 1962 Version." *The State*, November 10, 1962, 11–12.

Shelton, Arthur L. "Buncombe Bob." *American Mercury*, October 1932, 140–47.

Wiegers, Joe. "Senator Bob Reynolds: Athlete of Capitol Hill." *Health Review*, July 1937, 17–20.

Books

Adler, Selig. *The Isolationist Impulse: Its Twentieth-Century Reaction*. New York: Collier Books, 1961.

Allswang, John M. *The New Deal and American Politics*. New York: John Wiley and Sons, 1978.

Anderson, Kristi. *The Creation of a Democratic Majority, 1928–1936*. Chicago: University of Chicago Press, 1979.

Anderson, William. *The Wild Man from Sugar Creek: The Political Career of Eugene Talmadge*. Baton Rouge: Louisiana State University Press, 1975.

Ashby, Warren. *Frank Porter Graham: A Southern Liberal*. Winston-Salem, N.C.: John F. Blair, 1980.

Ashmore, Harry S. *Hearts and Minds: The Anatomy of Racism from Roosevelt to Reagan*. New York: McGraw-Hill, 1982.

Ayers, Edward L. *The Promise of the New South: Life After Reconstruction*. New York: Oxford University Press, 1992.

Badger, Anthony J. *The New Deal: The Depression Years, 1933–1940*. New York: Farrar, Straus and Giroux, 1989.

———. *North Carolina and the New Deal*. Raleigh: North Carolina Department of Cultural Resources, 1981.

Bailey, Stephen K., and Howard D. Samuel. *Congress at Work*. New York: Henry Holt, 1952.

Baker, Ross K. *Friend and Foe in the U.S. Senate*. New York: Free Press, 1980.

Bartley, Numan V., and Hugh Davis Graham. *Southern Politics and the Second Reconstruction*. Baltimore: Johns Hopkins University Press, 1975.

Bass, Jack, and Walter DeVries. *The Transformation of Southern Politics*. New York: Basic, 1976.

Bass, Jack, and Thomas E. Terrill, eds. *The American South Comes of Age*. New York: Alfred A. Knopf, 1986.

Beard, Charles A. *President Roosevelt and the Coming of War, 1941*. New Haven: Yale University Press, 1949.

Becnel, Thomas. *Senator Allen Ellender of Louisiana*. Baton Rouge: Louisiana State University Press, 1995.

Bennett, David H. *Demagogues in the Depression: American Radicals and the Union Party, 1932–1936*. New Brunswick: Rutgers University Press, 1969.

Bennett, Edward M. *Franklin D. Roosevelt and the Search for Security: American-Soviet Relations, 1933–1939*. Wilmington, Del.: SR Books, 1985.

Bennett, Marion. *American Immigration Policies*. Washington: Public Affairs Press, 1963.

Berg, A. Scott. *Lindbergh*. New York: G. P. Putnam's Sons, 1998.

Bernard, William S., ed. *American Immigration Policy: A Reappraisal*. New York: Harper and Brothers, 1950.

Beschloss, Michael R. *Kennedy and Roosevelt: The Uneasy Alliance*. New York: W. W. Norton, 1980.

Beyle, Thad, and Merle Black. *Politics and Policy in North Carolina*. New York: MSS Information, 1975.

Billington, Monroe Lee. *The Political South in the Twentieth Century*. New York: Charles Scribner's Sons, 1975.

Black, Earle, and Merle Black. *Politics and Society in the South*. Cambridge: Harvard University Press, 1987.

Blum, John Morton. *V Was for Victory*. New York: Harcourt Brace Jovanovich, 1977.

Brinkley, Alan. *Voices of Protest: Huey Long, Father Coughlin, and the Great Depression*. New York: Vintage, 1983.

Brinkley, David. *Washington Goes to War*. New York: Ballantine, 1988.

Buell, Raymond. *Isolated America*. New York: Alfred A. Knopf, 1940.

Bunche, Ralph. *The Political Status of the Negro in the Age of FDR*. Edited by Dewey W. Grantham. Chicago: University of Chicago Press, 1973.

Burdette, Franklin L. *Filibustering in the Senate*. New York: Russell and Russell, 1965.

Burns, James M. *Congress on Trial*. New York: Harper and Brothers, 1949.

——. *Roosevelt: The Lion and the Fox*. New York: Harcourt, Brace and World, 1956.

——. *Roosevelt: The Soldier of Freedom*. New York: Harcourt Brace Jovanovich, 1970.

Byrnes, James F. *Speaking Frankly*. New York: Harper and Brothers, 1947.

Carlson, John Roy [Arthur Derounian]. *The Plotters*. New York: E. P. Dutton, 1946.

——. *Under Cover*. New York: E. P. Dutton, 1943.

Carr, Robert K. *The House Committee on Un-American Activities*. Ithaca: Cornell University Press, 1952.

Cash, W. J. *The Mind of the South*. New York: Alfred A. Knopf, 1941.

Childs, Marquis. *I Write from Washington*. New York: Harper and Brothers, 1942.

Clancy, Paul R. *Just a Country Lawyer: A Biography of Senator Sam Ervin*. Bloomington: Indiana University Press, 1974.

Clarke, Jeanne Nienaber. *Roosevelt's Warrior: Harold Ickes and the New Deal*. Baltimore: Johns Hopkins University Press, 1996.

Coffin, Tristam. *Senator Fulbright: Portrait of a Public Philosopher*. New York: E. P. Dutton, 1966.

Cole, Wayne S. *America First: The Battle against Intervention, 1940–1941*. Madison: University of Wisconsin Press, 1953.

——. *Charles A. Lindbergh and the Battle against American Intervention in World War II*. New York: Harcourt Brace Jovanovich, 1974.

——. *Roosevelt and the Isolationists, 1932–1945*. Lincoln: University of Nebraska Press, 1983.

——. *Senator Gerald P. Nye and American Foreign Relations*. Minneapolis: University of Minnesota Press, 1962.

Colgrove, Kenneth. *The American Senate and World Peace*. New York: Vanguard, 1944.

Common Council for American Unity. *The Alien and the Immigration Law: A Study of 1,446 Cases Arising under the Immigration and Naturalization Laws of the United States, under the Direction of Edith Lowenstein*. New York: Oceana Publishers, 1957.

Connor, R. D. W. *North Carolina: Rebuilding an Ancient Commonwealth, 1584–1925*. 2 vols. New York: American Historical Society, 1929.

Cook, Blanche Wiesen. *Eleanor Roosevelt*. Vol. 2, *1933–1938*. New York: Viking Penguin, 1999.

Couch, W. T., and the Federal Writers' Project. *These Are Our Lives*. Chapel Hill: University of North Carolina Press, 1967.

Culver, John C., and John Hyde. *American Dreamer: A Life of Henry A. Wallace*. New York: W. W. Norton, 2000.

Dabney, Dick. *A Good Man: The Life of Sam J. Ervin*. Boston: Houghton Mifflin, 1976.

Dallek, Robert. *Democrat and Diplomat: The Life of William E. Dodd*. New York: Oxford University Press, 1968.

——. *Franklin D. Roosevelt and American Foreign Policy, 1932–1945*. New York: Oxford University Press, 1981.

Daniel, Pete. *Standing at the Crossroads: Southern Life in the Twentieth Century*. New York: Hill and Wang, 1986.

Daniels, Jonathan Worth. *A Southerner Discovers the South*. New York: Macmillan, 1938.

——. *Tar Heels: A Portrait of North Carolina*. New York: Dodd, Mead, 1941.

Daniels, Josephus. *Editor in Politics*. Chapel Hill: University of North Carolina Press, 1941.

——. *Shirt-Sleeve Diplomat*. Chapel Hill: University of North Carolina Press, 1947.

Daniels, Roger. *Prisoners without Trial*. New York: Hill and Wang, 1993.

Davis, Kenneth S. *FDR: Into the Storm, 1937–1940*. New York: Random House, 1993.

——. *The New Deal Years: 1933–1937*. New York: Random House, 1986.

Davis, Polly A. *Alben W. Barkley: Senate Majority Leader and Vice President*. New York: Garland, 1979.

Degler, Carl N. *Out of Our Past: The Forces That Shaped America*. New York: Harper and Row, 1959.

DeLoach, Cartha D. *Hoover's FBI: The Inside Story by Hoover's Trusted Lieutenant*. Washington: Regnery Publishing, 1995.

Dennis, Lawrence. *The Coming American Fascism*. New York: Harper and Brothers, 1936.

Dennis, Lawrence, and Maximilian St. George. *A Trial on Trial: The Great Sedition Trial of 1944*. N.p.: National Civil Rights Committee, 1946.

Dennison, Eleanor. *The Senate Foreign Relations Committee*. Stanford: Stanford University Press, 1942.

Dies, Martin. *The Trojan Horse in America*. New York: Dodd, Mead, 1940.

Divine, Robert A. *American Immigration Policy*. New Haven: Yale University Press, 1957.

——. *The Illusion of Neutrality*. Chicago: University of Chicago Press, 1962.

——. *The Reluctant Belligerent*. New York: Wiley, 1965.

——. *Roosevelt and World War II*. New York: Penguin, 1970.

——. *Second Chance: The Triumph of Internationalism in America during World War II*. New York: Atheneum, 1967.

Doak, Frances Renfrow. *Why North Carolina Voted Dry*. Raleigh: Capitol Printing, 1963.

Drury, Allen. *A Senate Journal, 1943–1945*. New York: McGraw-Hill, 1963.

Dykeman, Wilma, and James Stokely. *Seeds of Southern Change: The Life of Will W. Alexander*. Chicago: University of Chicago Press, 1962.

Eagles, Charles W. *Jonathan Daniels and Race Relations: The Evolution of a Southern Liberal*. Knoxville: University of Tennessee Press, 1982.

——. ed. *Is There a Southern Political Tradition?* Jackson: University Press of Mississippi, 1996.

Ellis, Edward Robb. *A Nation in Torment: The Great American Depression, 1929–1939*. New York: Capricorn, 1971.

Ervin, Sam J., Jr. *Preserving the Constitution: The Autobiography of Senator Sam Ervin*. Charlottesville: Michie, 1984.

Farago, Ladislas. *The Game of the Foxes*. New York: D. McKay, 1971.

Feinman, Ronald L. *Twilight of Progressivism: The Western Republican Senators and the New Deal*. Baltimore: Johns Hopkins University Press, 1981.

Feis, Herbert. *The Road to Pearl Harbor*. Princeton: Princeton University Press, 1950.

Ferrell, Robert H., ed. *Off the Record: The Private Papers of Harry S. Truman*. New York: Penguin, 1980.

Fite, Gilbert C. *Richard B. Russell, Jr.: Senator from Georgia*. Chapel Hill: University of North Carolina Press, 1991.

Fleer, Jack D. *North Carolina Politics*. Chapel Hill: University of North Carolina Press, 1968.

Flynn, John T. *The Road Ahead*. New York: Devin-Adair, 1949.

Fraser, Steve, and Gary Gerstle, eds. *The Rise and Fall of the New Deal Order, 1930–1980*. Princeton: Princeton University Press, 1989.

Freyer, Tony. *Hugo L. Black and the Dilemma of American Liberalism*. Glenview, Ill.: Scott, Foresman, 1990.

Frye, Alton. *Nazi Germany and the American Hemisphere*. New Haven: Yale University Press, 1967.

Gabler, Neal. *Winchell: Gossip, Power, and the Culture of Celebrity*. New York: Vintage, 1994.

Garson, Robert A. *The Democratic Party and the Politics of Sectionalism, 1941–1948*. Baton Rouge: Louisiana State University Press, 1974.

Gellerman, William. *Martin Dies*. New York: John Day, 1944.

Gellman, Irwin F. *Secret Affairs: Franklin Roosevelt, Cordell Hull, and Sumner Welles*. Baltimore: Johns Hopkins University Press, 1995.

Gentry, Curt. *J. Edgar Hoover: The Man and the Secrets*. New York: W. W. Norton, 1991.

Glad, Betty. *Key Pittman: The Tragedy of a Senate Insider*. New York: Columbia University Press, 1986.

Goodman, Walter. *The Committee*. New York: Farrar, Straus and Giroux, 1964.

Grantham, Dewey. *The Democratic South*. New York: W. W. Norton, 1963.

Green, Adwin Wigfall. *The Man Bilbo*. Baton Rouge: Louisiana State University Press, 1963.

Hall, Kermit L. *The Magic Mirror: Law in American History*. New York: Oxford University Press, 1989.

Hamilton, Virginia Van der Veer. *Lister Hill: Statesman from the South*. Chapel Hill: University of North Carolina Press, 1987.

Havard, William C., ed. *The Changing Politics of the South*. Baton Rouge: Louisiana State University Press, 1972.

Heard, Alexander. *A Two-Party South?* Chapel Hill: University of North Carolina Press, 1952.

Heard, Alexander, and Donald S. Strong. *Southern Primaries and Elections, 1920–1949*. University: University of Alabama Press, 1950.

Heinrichs, Waldo. *Threshold of War: Franklin D. Roosevelt and American Entrance into World War II*. New York: Oxford University Press, 1988.

Hero, Alfred O., Jr. *The Southerner and World Affairs*. Baton Rouge: Louisiana State University Press, 1965.

Holmes, William F. *The White Chief: James Kimble Vardaman*. Baton Rouge: Louisiana State University Press, 1970.

Huthmacher, J. Joseph. *Senator Robert F. Wagner and the Rise of Urban Liberalism*. New York: Atheneum, 1968.

Irons, Peter. *Justice at War*. New York: Oxford University Press, 1983.

Jeansonne, Glen. *Gerald L. K. Smith: Minister of Hate*. New Haven: Yale University Press, 1988.

———. *Messiah of the Masses: Huey P. Long and the Great Depression*. New York: Harper Collins, 1993.

Johnson, Niel M. *George Sylvester Viereck: German-American Propagandist*. Urbana: University of Illinois Press, 1972.

Jonas, Manfred. *Isolationism in America, 1935–1941*. Ithaca: Cornell University Press, 1966.

Kefauver, Estes, and Jack Levin. *A Twentieth Century Congress*. New York: Duell, Sloan and Pearce, 1947.

Kessler, Ronald. *The Sins of the Father*. New York: Warner Books, 1996.

Ketchum, Richard. *The Borrowed Years, 1938–1941: America on the Way to War*. New York: Doubleday, 1989.

Key, V. O., Jr. *Southern Politics*. New York: Vintage, 1949.

Kimball, Warren F. *The Juggler: Franklin Roosevelt as Wartime Statesman*. Princeton: Princeton University Press, 1991.

Kirby, John B. *Black Americans in the Roosevelt Era: Liberalism and Race*. Knoxville: University of Tennessee Press, 1980.

Kirby, John Temple. *Darkness at the Dawning: Race and Reform in the Progressive South*. New York: J. B. Lippincott, 1972.

Krueger, Thomas. *And Promises to Keep: The Southern Conference for Human Welfare, 1938–1948*. Nashville: Vanderbilt University Press, 1967.

Langer, William L., and S. E. Gleason. *The Challenge to Isolationism, 1937–1940*. New York: Harper and Row, 1952.

———. *The Undeclared War, 1940–1941*. New York: Harper and Row, 1953.

Larrabee, Eric. *Commander-in-Chief*. New York: Simon and Schuster, 1987.

Lash, Joseph P. *Eleanor and Franklin*. New York: W. W. Norton, 1971.

———. *Roosevelt and Churchill, 1939–1941*. New York: W. W. Norton, 1976.

Lavine, Harold. *Fifth Column in America*. New York: Doubleday, Doran and Company, 1940.

Lawson, Steven. *Black Ballots: Voting Rights in the South, 1944–1969*. New York: Columbia University Press, 1976.

Lefler, Hugh T., and Albert R. Newsome. *North Carolina: The History of a Southern State*. Chapel Hill: University of North Carolina Press, 1963.

Lerche, Charles O., Jr. *The Uncertain South: Its Changing Pattern of Politics in Foreign Policy*. Chicago: Quadrangle, 1964.

Leuchtenburg, William E. *Franklin D. Roosevelt and the New Deal, 1932–1940*. New York: Harper and Row, 1963.

———. *The Supreme Court Reborn: The Constitutional Revolution in the Age of Roosevelt*. New York: Oxford University Press, 1995.

Link, Arthur S. *American Epoch: A History of the United States since the 1890s*. New York: Alfred A. Knopf, 1958.

Link, Arthur S., and William A. Link. *American Epoch: A History of the United States since 1900.* New York: Alfred A. Knopf, 1987.

Louchheim, Katie. *The Making of the New Deal: The Insiders Speak.* Cambridge: Harvard University Press, 1983.

Lower, Richard Cole. *A Bloc of One: The Political Career of Hiram W. Johnson.* Stanford: Stanford University Press, 1993.

Lowitt, Richard. *Bronson Cutting: Progressive Politician.* Albuquerque: University of New Mexico Press, 1992.

——. *George W. Norris: The Triumph of a Progressive.* Urbana: University of Illinois Press, 1978.

Luthin, Reinhard H. *American Demagogues.* Boston: Beacon, 1954.

McElvaine, Robert S. *Down and Out in the Great Depression.* Chapel Hill: University of North Carolina Press, 1983.

——. *The Great Depression: America, 1929–1941.* New York: Times Books, 1984.

McLean, Evalyn Walsh, with Boyden Sparks. *Father Struck It Rich.* Boston: Little, Brown, 1936.

Maney, Patrick J. *The Roosevelt Presence.* New York: Twayne Publishers, 1992.

——. *"Young Bob" La Follette: A Biography of Robert M. La Follette, Jr., 1895–1953.* Columbia: University of Missouri Press, 1978.

Martin, George. *Madam Secretary: Frances Perkins.* Boston: Houghton Mifflin, 1976.

Matthews, Donald. *North Carolina Votes.* Chapel Hill: University of North Carolina Press, 1962.

Maverick, Maury. *Maverick American.* New York: Covici, Friede, 1937.

Michie, Allan A., and Frank Ryhlick. *Dixie Demagogues.* New York: Vanguard, 1939.

Miller, William J. *Henry Cabot Lodge.* New York: James H. Heineman, 1967.

Mitchell, Broadus. *Depression Decade: From New Era through New Deal, 1929–1941.* New York: Harper and Row, 1947.

Moore, John Robert. *Senator Josiah William Bailey of North Carolina.* Durham: Duke University Press, 1968.

Morgan, Chester. *Redneck Liberal: Theodore G. Bilbo and the New Deal.* Baton Rouge: Louisiana University Press, 1985.

Morrison, Joseph L. *Governor O. Max Gardner: A Power in North Carolina and New Deal Washington.* Chapel Hill: University of North Carolina Press, 1971.

——. *Josephus Daniels, the Small-D Democrat.* Chapel Hill: University of North Carolina Press, 1966.

Morse, Arthur D. *Six Million Died.* New York: Random House, 1968.

Moseley, Nicholas. *Beyond the Pale: Sir Oswald Moseley and Family.* London: Secher and Warburg, 1983.

Mulder, Ronald A. *The Insurgent Progressives in the United States Senate and the New Deal.* New York: Garland, 1979.

Murphy, Raymond E., et al. *National Socialism: Basic Principles, Their Application by the Nazi Party's Foreign Organization, and the Use of Germans Abroad for Nazi Aims.* Washington: Government Printing Office, 1943.

Nicholas, H. G., ed. *Washington Despatches: 1941–1945.* Chicago: University of Chicago Press, 1981.

Ofner, Arnold A. *American Appeasement: United States Foreign Policy and Germany, 1933–1938.* Cambridge: Harvard University Press, 1969.

Ogden, August Raymond. *The Dies Committee.* Washington: Catholic University of America Press, 1959.

Ohl, John Kennedy. *Hugh S. Johnson and the New Deal.* DeKalb: Northern Illinois Press, 1985.

O'Neill, William L. *A Democracy at War: America's Fight at Home and Abroad in World War II.* Cambridge: Harvard University Press, 1993.

Parmet, Herbert, and Marie B. Hecht. *Never Again: A President Runs for a Third Term*. New York: Macmillan, 1968.

Patch, Susanne Steinem. *Blue Mystery: The Story of the Hope Diamond*. Washington, D.C.: Smithsonian Institution Press, 1976.

Patterson, James T. *Congressional Conservatism and the New Deal: The Growth of the Conservative Coalition in Congress, 1933–1939*. Lexington: University Press of Kentucky, 1967.

Pepper, Claude D., with Hays Gorey. *Pepper: Eyewitness to a Century*. New York: Harcourt Brace Jovanovich, 1987.

Perkins, Frances. *The Roosevelt I Knew*. New York: Harper and Row, 1946.

Perrett, Goeffrey. *Days of Sadness, Years of Triumph*. New York: Coward, McCann, and Geoghegan, 1973.

Pilat, Oliver. *Drew Pearson: An Unauthorized Biography*. New York: Harper's Magazine Press, 1973.

Piller, E. A. *Time Bomb*. New York: Arco Publishing, 1945.

Pleasants, Julian M., and Augustus M. Burns III. *Frank Porter Graham and the 1950 Senate Race in North Carolina*. Chapel Hill: University of North Carolina Press, 1990.

Pogue, Forrest C. *George C. Marshall: Ordeal and Hope, 1939–1942*. New York: Viking, 1966.

——. *George C. Marshall: Organizer of Victory*. New York: Viking, 1973.

Powers, R. Gid. *Secrecy and Power: The Life of J. Edgar Hoover*. New York: Free Press, 1987.

Prange, Gordon W. *At Dawn We Slept*. New York: Penguin, 1981.

Puryear, Elmer L. *Democratic Party Dissension in North Carolina, 1928–1936*. Chapel Hill: University of North Carolina Press, 1962.

Rauch, Basil. *The History of the New Deal*. New York: Capricorn, 1963.

——. *Roosevelt from Munich to Pearl Harbor*. New York: Creative Age Press, 1950.

Reed, John Shelton. *The Enduring South*. Chapel Hill: University of North Carolina Press, 1974.

Reynolds, David. *The Creation of the Anglo-American Alliance, 1937–1941*. Chapel Hill: University of North Carolina Press, 1982.

Ribuffo, Leo P. *The Old Christian Right: The Protestant Far Right from the Great Depression to the Cold War*. Philadelphia: Temple University Press, 1983.

Rice, Ross R. *Carl Hayden: Builder of the American West*. Lanham, Md.: University Press of America, 1994.

Rieselbach, Leroy N. *The Roots of Isolationism*. New York: Bobbs-Merrill, 1966.

Rogge, O. John. *The Official German Report*. New York: Thomas Yoseloff, 1961.

Roosevelt, Eleanor. *This I Remember*. New York: Harper and Brothers, 1949.

Roosevelt, Elliott, and James Brough. *A Rendezvous with Destiny: The Roosevelts of the White House*. New York: G. P. Putnam's Sons, 1975.

Rosenman, Samuel I., comp. *The Public Papers and Addresses of Franklin D. Roosevelt*. 13 vols. New York: Random House, 1938–50.

Salmone, John A. *The Civilian Conservation Corps, 1933–1942: A New Deal Case Study*. Durham: Duke University Press, 1967.

Sayers, Michael, and Albert E. Kahn. *The Plot against the Peace: A Warning to the Nation*. New York: Dial Press, 1945.

——. *Sabotage: The Secret War against America*. New York: Harper and Brothers, 1942.

Schlesinger, Arthur M., Jr. *The Age of Roosevelt*. 3 vols. Boston: Houghton Mifflin, 1957–60.

Seldes, George. *Facts and Fascism*. New York: In Fact, 1943.

Shepardson, Whitney H. *The United States in World Affairs: An Account of American Foreign Relations, 1939*. New York: Harper and Brothers, 1940.

Sherwood, Robert. *Roosevelt and Hopkins*. New York: Harper and Row, 1940.

Sitkoff, Harvard, ed. *Fifty Years Later: The New Deal Evaluated*. New York: Alfred A. Knopf, 1985.

Smith, Gaddis. *American Diplomacy during the Second World War, 1941–1945*. New York: John Wiley and Sons, 1965.

Smith, Richard Norton. *Thomas E. Dewey and His Times*. New York: Simon and Schuster, 1982.

Stimson, Henry L., and McGeorge Bundy. *On Active Service in Peace and War*. New York: Harper and Brothers, 1948.

Stout, Rex, ed. *The Illustrious Dunderheads*. New York: Alfred A. Knopf, 1942.

Sullivan, Patricia. *Day of Hope: Race and Democracy in the New Deal Era*. Chapel Hill: University of North Carolina Press, 1996.

Swain, Martha. *Pat Harrison: The New Deal Years*. Jackson: University Press of Mississippi, 1978.

Tindall, George B. *The Emergence of the New South, 1913–1945*. Baton Rouge: Louisiana State University Press, 1967.

Utley, Freda. *The Dream We Lost: Soviet Russia Then and Now*. New York: John Day, 1940.

Warren, Donald. *Radio Priest: Charles Coughlin, the Father of Hate Radio*. New York: Simon and Schuster, 1996.

Watkins, T. H. *Righteous Pilgrim: The Life and Times of Harold Ickes, 1874–1952*. New York: Henry Holt, 1990.

Welles, Sumner. *The Time for Decision*. New York: Harper and Brothers, 1944.

Wheeler, Burton K. *Yankee from the West*. Garden City: Doubleday, 1962.

White, Graham, and John Maze. *Harold Ickes of the New Deal*. Cambridge: Harvard University Press, 1985.

Whitener, Daniel Jay. *Prohibition in North Carolina, 1715–1945*. Chapel Hill: University of North Carolina Press, 1945.

Williams, T. Harry. *Huey Long*. New York: Alfred A. Knopf, 1969.

Williams, William Appleman. *The Tragedy of American Diplomacy*. Cleveland: World Publishing, 1959.

Wittke, Carl. *The German-Language Press in America*. Lexington: University Press of Kentucky, 1957.

Woodward, C. Vann. *Origins of the New South*. Baton Rouge: Louisiana State University Press, 1951.

Young, Roland. *This Is Congress*. New York: Alfred A. Knopf, 1943.

Youngs, J. William T. *Eleanor Roosevelt: A Personal and Public Life*. 2d ed. New York: Longman, 2000.

Theses and Dissertations

Brogden, Hope Marshall. "The Electoral Bases of Representation in North Carolina, 1916–1972." Ph.D. diss., University of North Carolina, 1976.

Parham, J. Covington. "The Democratic Senatorial Primary of North Carolina—1950." Senior thesis, Princeton University, 1952.

Pleasants, Julian M. "The Senatorial Career of Robert Rice Reynolds." Ph.D. diss., University of North Carolina, 1971.

Sewall, Arthur Freeman. "Key Pittman: The Senate Foreign Relations Committee and American Foreign Policy, 1933–1940." Ph.D. diss., University of Delaware, 1974.

Index